PACIFIC NOI
AMERICANA
1949-1974

A SUPPLEMENT TO CHARLES W. SMITH'S

THIRD EDITION 1950

EDITED BY
RICHARD E. MOORE
AND
NADINE H. PURCELL

Binford & Mort

Thomas Binford, Publisher

2536 S.E. Eleventh • Portland, Oregon 97202

Compiled by the Pacific Northwest Library Association
Committee on the Smith Bibliography Supplement:

Richard E. Moore, Chairman
Marvin W. Falk (Alaska)
Linda Webster (British Columbia)
Charles A. Webbert (Idaho)
Minnie Paugh (Montana)
Nadine H. Purcell (Oregon)
Nancy Pryor (Washington)

International Standard Book Number: 0-8323-0389-5
Library of Congress Catalog Card Number: 81-65510
Binford & Mort, Publishers, Portland, Oregon 97202
Printed in the United States of America
First Edition 1981

PREFACE TO THE THIRD EDITION SUPPLEMENT

This supplement to the Charles W. Smith _Pacific Northwest Americana_ edition revised and extended by Isabel Mayhew (Portland, Binford & Mort, 1950), is an effort to carry on the tradition of sharing resources in the PNLA region. While there are several changes from practices established by Smith and continued by Mayhew, the basic intent and purpose of the checklist has been retained.

The third edition contained publications issued through 1948, this supplement begins in 1949 and extends through 1974, a twenty-five year update. The supplement, unlike the basic volume, is arranged by geographic area: Alaska, British Columbia, Idaho, Montana, Oregon, and Washington, and a separate general section for items covering two or more areas. A second modification, the designators for holding libraries, is no longer used because of the presence of many union catalogs and bibliographic utilities that are developed for that purpose.

Other than the changes and limitations above, the general criteria used for selection pretty much follows that of Smith and Mayhew. Smith (and we) included all history (broadly) with certain limitations or exceptions, as follows: (not included) documents unless unusually important; Chamber of Commerce publications; magazine articles, clippings and book excerpts; city directories; manuscripts; scrapbooks; maps; and general works with an insignificant part on the Northwest. We have included new reprints and editions and have tried to include all items from standard commercial presses as well as significant items from the more fugitive type printery.

Work began on the supplement in 1973 with the appointment of a study committee. The present committee was appointed in mid-1978. One person from each region as listed with the appropriate section was appointed. That person was responsible for the basic make-up of their area list. From Alberta, Aileen Wright was appointed. After some discussion, and since Alberta was not in the original list, the Alberta section was dropped. A separate project will need to be undertaken requiring a large amount of time and effort.

Nadine Purcell took the PNLA Quarterly "Checklists," had them copied, cut and individually mounted on catalog cards, then interfiled by region along with lists issued prior to the checklists (1956) and the ending of the Smith coverage (1948). Each file was sent to the appropriate committee person who edited out items beyond the scope of this work and added cards for items lacking or compiled the list for any years no list was yet completed. The total effort was reviewed and put together with a general index of persons (authors and personal subjects) made up from the basic Smith volume as well as this supplement. You will note the gaps in item numbering throughout the list. After numbers were assigned, duplicated entries were found during the indexing, in such cases one item was removed or both removed and a single entry added to the general section.

It is the purpose of this supplement to provide libraries and interested individuals with a checklist of historical items from the several geographical areas in PNLA. The list, while not exhaustive, is extensive and includes items judged to be of some historical value. There are, no doubt, favorite items that are not included, some perhaps of questionable nature do appear in this list, but it is our best effort; it is intended as a quick guide to common items on the area as a whole. This list does not supplant an exhaustive geographical effort nor does it attempt to cover the material found in collections of the magnitude of the University of Washington Special Collection on Northwest history.

Resource accessibility was Charles Smith's primary goal in 1909; it is the committee's only goal today and it is recognized that a more local effort is necessary today. Hopefully, this list will stimulate every library in the region to keep a separate card file or listing of regional history items as the library acquires the material. Local lists can promote and facilitate the compilation of local history and current lists of available material. With the advent of large bibliographic utilities, it has become the responsibility of the local library to develop resource guides through locally generated bibliographies and checklists. Such guides are the only tools available to research persons to help locate and use local history materials. Local use of local history is the only way of ensuring that the material will be preserved. It is one way the local library can become important to local history and ensure visibility as well as additional support.

The effort here was an effort of PNLA, the decision and much of the funding for the compilation; however, the home institutions of the committee members provided much of the in-kind assistance. This makes up resource sharing at the basic level and is what PNLA is all about. The cost of this initial printing of the Supplement was subsidized by PNLA as an effort on their part to keep the list price at a minimum.

Richard E. Moore
Southern Oregon State College
Ashland, Oregon

CONTENTS

Abdill, George B
Pacific slope railroads. Seattle, Superior Publishing Co., 1959.
182 p. illus. S1

Abdill, George B
This was railroading. Seattle, Superior Publishing Co., 1958.
192 p. illus. S2

Adams, Kramer A
Covered bridges of the West. Berkeley, Calif., Howell-North, 1963.
146 p. maps. S3

Adams, Kramer
Logging railroads of the West. Seattle, Superior Publishing Co., 1961.
144 p. illus. S4

Adams, W. Claude
History of papermaking in the Pacific Northwest. Portland, Or. Binfords & Mort, n.d.
67 p. map S5

Allen, Alice Benson
Simon Benson: Northwest lumber king. Portland, Ore., Binfords & Mort, 1971.
144 p. illus. S6

Allen, Edward Weber
The vanishing Frenchman: the mysterious disappearance of La-Perouse. Rutland, Vt., Charles E. Tuttle Co., 1959.
321 p. illus. S7

Allen, Harold
Father Ravalli's missions. Chicago, Ill., The Good Lion, 1972.
104 p. illus. S8

Allen, James B
The company town in the American west. Norman, University of Oklahoma Press, 1966.
205 p. S9

Allen, John Logan
Passage through the garden: Lewis and Clark and the image of the American Northwest. Urbana, Ill., University of Illinois Press, 1975.
428 p. maps. S10

Allen, Opal (Sweazea)
Narcissa Whitman: an historic biography. Portland, Or., Binfords & Mort, 1959.
325 p. illus. S11

Alt, D.D. and D.W. Hyndman
Roadside geology of the Northern Rockies. Missoula, The Mountain Press, 1972. S12

American Heritage
Trappers and mountain men, by the editors of American Heritage. Narrative by Evan Jones, in consultation with Dale L. Morgan. N.Y., 1961.
155 p. illus. S13

American Heritage
Westward on the Oregon Trail, by the editors of American Heritage, the magazine of history. Narrative by Marian T. Place; consultant: Earl Pomeroy. 1st ed. New York, American Heritage Pub. Co., c1962.
153 p. S14

American West
The great Northwest; the story of a land and its people, by the editors of American West. Palo Alto, Calif,. American West Publishing Co., 1973
285 p. illus. S15

Anderson, Sylvia Finlay, ed.
Westward to Oregon. Edited by Sylvia F. Anderson and Jacob Korg. Boston, Heath, 1958.
112 p. illus. S16

Anderson, William Marshall, 1807-1881
The Rocky Mountain journals of William Marshall Anderson: the West in 1834. Edited by Dale L. Morgan and Eleanor Towles Harris. San Marino, Calif., Huntington Library, 1967.
430 p. illus. S17

Andrews, Ralph Warren, 1897-
Fish and Ships, by Ralph W. Andrews and A.K. Larssen. Seattle, Superior Publishing Co., 1959.
173 p. illus. S18

Andrews, Ralph Warren,
Glory days of logging. Superior Publishing Co., c1956.
176 p. illus. S19

Andrews, Ralph Warren
Heroes of the Western woods. N.Y., Dutton, 1960.
192 p. illus. S20

Andrews, Ralph Warren
Historic fires of the West. Seattle, Superior Publishing Co., 1966.
191 p. illus. S21

Andrews, Ralph Warren
Indian primitive: Northwest coast Indians of the former days. Seattle, Superior Publishing Co., 1960.
175 p. illus. S22

Andrews, Ralph Warren
Photographers of the frontier West; their lives and works, 1875-1915. Seattle Superior Publishing Co., 1965.
182 p. S23

Andrews, Ralph Warren
Picture gallery pioneers, 1850-1875. Seattle, Superior Publishing Co., 1964.
192 p. illus. S24

Andrews, Ralph Warren,
This was logging! Selected photos of Darius Kinsey. Text by Ralph W. Andrews. 1st ed. Seattle, Superior Publishing Co., 1954.
157 p. illus. S25

Andrews, Ralph Warren,
This was sawmilling. Seattle, Superior Publishing Co., c1957
175 p. illus. S26

Andrews, Ralph Warren
Timber; toil and trouble in the big woods. Seattle, Superior Publishing Co., 1968. S27

Angell, Tony
Birds of prey of the Pacific slope. Seattle, Pacific Search Books, 1972.
32 p. illus. S28

Ankeny, Nesmith, 1877-1954
The West as I knew it. Walla Walla, Wash., 1953.
148 p. illus. S29

Anness, Milford E
Song of metamoris; a story that remains of a people who passed this way. Caldwell, Idaho, Caxton Printers, 1964.
509 p. illus. S30

Antles, Leo C
A man's footprints; a guide to orchard pollination and management. New York, Carlton Press, 1965.
277 p. illus. S31

Appleton, Marion Brymner, ed.
Index of Pacific Northwest portraits. Seattle, Wash., University of Washington Press, 1972.
210 p. S32

Aquatic Environments Limited
Fisheries research associated with proposed gas pipeline routes in Alaska, Yukon and Northwest territories. Edited by Peter J. McCart. 2nd ed. Calgary: Canadian Arctic Gas Study; s.l.: Alaska Arctic Gas Study Co., 1974.
183 (255) p. illus. S33

Arighi, Scott and Margaret S. Arighi
Wildwater touring: techniques and tours. New York, Macmillan, 1974.
334 p. illus. S34

Arrington, Leonard J
Beet sugar in the West: a history of the Utah-Idaho Sugar Co., 1891-1966. Seattle, University of Washington Press, 1966.
234 p. S35

Atkeson, Ray
Northwest heritage: the Cascade Range. Portland, Or., Charles Belding, 1969.
181 p. illus. S36

Atkeson, Ray
The Pacific coast. New York, Rand McNally, 1971.
136 p. S37

Atkin, Ronald
Maintain the right. New York, John Day, 1973.
400 p. illus. S38

Attwell, Jim
Columbia River Gorge history. Skamania, Wash., Tahlkie Books, 1974-75.
illus. S39

Audubon, John James, 1785-1851
Audubon in the West. Norman, University of Oklahoma, 1966, c1965.
131 p. illus. S40

Automobile Club of Southern California
Pacific coast highways: a visual and factual guide to the major north-south routes of the Pacific states and western Canada. Los Angeles, Calif., 1973.
158 p. illus.
Also: 1975 ed., 143 p. S41

Babcock, Chester D. and Clare A Babcock
Our Pacific Northwest, yesterday and today. St. Louis, Webster Publishing Division, McGraw-Hill, 1963.
444 p. illus. S42

Bach, Orville E., Jr.
Hiking the Yellowstone backcountry: a Sierra Club totebook. San Francisco, Calif., Sierra Club, 1973.
228 p. illus. S43

Bakeless, John Edwin
Lewis and Clark: partners in discovery. New York, Apollo Eds., 1962, c1947.
498 p. S44

Baker, Paul Earnest, 1893-
The forgotten Kutenai: a study of the Kutenai Indians. Bonners Ferry, Idaho. Creston, British Columbia, Canada, and other areas ... Boise, Idaho, Mountain States Press, 1955.
64 p. illus. S45

Baker, William Hudson
Wildlife of the northern Rocky Mountains: including common wild animals and plants. By William H. Baker and others. Ed. by Vinson Brown. Healdsburg, Claif., Naturegraph Co., c1961. American Wildlife region series, v. 6.
112 p. illus. S46

Ballantine, Bill, 1911-
High West. Photos by the author. Chicago, Rand McNally, 1969.
303 p. illus. S47

Banks, Sir Joseph
The endeavour journal of Joseph Banks, 1768-1771. Edited by J.C. Beaglehold. Sydney Trustees of the Public Library of New South Wales in association with Angus and Robertson, 1962.
2 vols. maps. S48

Barbeau, Charles Marius, 1883-
Indian days on the Western prairies. Ottawa, Canada, Department of Northern Affairs and Natural Resources, 1960.
234 p. illus. S49

Barbeau, Charles Marius
Pathfinders in the North Pacific. Drawings by Arthur Price. Caldwell, Idaho, Caxton Printers, 1958.
235 p. illus. S50

Barker, Burt Brown
The McLoughlin empire and its rulers: Doctor John McLoughlin, Doctor David McLoughlin, Marie Louise ... Glendale, Calif., Clark Co., 1959.
370 p. illus. S51

Barker, M.A.R.
Klamath grammar. Berkeley, University of California Press, 1964.
364 p. S52

Barnett, Homer Garner, 1906-
Indian Shakers: a messianic cult of the Pacific Northwest. Carbondale, Southern Illinois University Press, 1957.
378 p. illus. S53

Beal, Marril D., 1898-
The story of man in Yellowstone. Caldwell, Idaho, Caxton Printers, 1949.
320 p. illus.
Also: Rev. ed., Yellowstone Park, Wyo., 1956, 320 p. S54

Beaulieu, John D
Geologic field trips in northern Oregon and southern Washington. Portland, Or., Oregon Dept. of Geology and Mineral Industries, 1973.
206 p. illus., S55

The Beautiful Northwest, by the editors of Sunset. Book editor: Dorothy Drell. Menlo Park, Calif., Lane Magazine & Book Co., 1970.
255 p. illus. S56

Beaver, Herbert
Reports and letters, 1836-1838, of Herbert Beaver, chaplain to the Hudson's Bay Company and missionary to the Indians at Fort Vancouver. Edited by Thurman E. Jessett. Portland, Or., Champoeg Press, 1959.
xxiv, 148 p. illus. S57

Beavers, Helen Mary
From Point Barrow to Chemewa. New York, Carlton Press, 1970. S58

Beitz, Lester V
Treasury of frontier relics: a collectors guide. N.Y., Crown, 1966.
246 p. S59

Bellas, Carl J
Industrial democracy and the worker-owned firm: a study of twenty-one plywood companies in the Pacific Northwest. N.Y., Praeger Publishers, 1972.
xv, 117 p. illus. S60

Bennett, John W
Hutterian brethren: the agricultural economy and social organization of a communal people. Stanford University Press, 1967.
298 p. S61

Benoliel, Doug
Northwest foraging: a guide to edible plants of the Pacific Northwest. Lynwood, Wash., Signpost, 1974.
171 p. illus. S62

Berg, W.A.
Mysterious horses of Western North America. N.Y., Pageant Press, 1960.
298 p. S63

Bingham, Edwin R
The fur trade in the West, 1815-1846: selected source materials for college research papers. Boston, Heath 1960.
116 p. S64

Binns, Archie
Peter Skene Ogden - fur trader. Portland, Or., Binfords & Mort, 1964.
340 p. illus. Also: 2nd ed., 1967
363 p. S65

Bishop, Charles
The journals and letters of Captain Charles Bishop on the North-West coast of America, in the Pacific and in New South Wales, 1794-1799, ed. by Michael Roe. Cambridge, Eng., published for the Hakluyt Society at the University Press, 1967.
342 p. S65A

Bjork, Kenneth O
West of the Great Divide: Norwegian migration to the Pacific coast, 1847-1893. Northfield, Minn., Norwegian-American Historical Association, 1958
viii, 671 p. illus. S66

Blacklock, Les
The High West. New York, Viking Press; Toronto, Macmillan of Canada, 1974.
141 p. illus. S67

Blevins, Winfred
Give your heart to the hawks; a tribute to the mountain men. Los Angeles, Calif., Nash Publishing, 1973.
349 p. illus. S68

Bloomfield, Louis Mortimer, 1908-
Boundary waters problems of Canada and the United States (The International Joint Commission 1921-1958) by L.M. Bloomfield and Gerald F. Fitzgerald. Toronto, The Carswell Company, Limited, 1958.
x, 264 p. map. S69

The Blue Book of the Pacific Northwest Industry. Seattle, Century Publishing Corporation, 1960.
280 p. illus. S70

Boas, Franz
Kwakiutl ethnography. Edited by Helen Cordere. Chicago, University of Chicago Press, 1966.
439 p. illus. S71

Bodsworth, Fred
The Pacific coast. Toronto, Natural Science of Canada Ltd., 1970.
160 p. illus. S72

Bond, Rowland
Early birds in the Northwest: 100 years of western history from Jacques Raphael Finlay to Dutch Jake Goetz. Nine Mile Falls, Wash., Spokane House Enterprises, 1972.
248 p. illus. S73

Bond, Rowland
The original Northwester: David Thompson and the native tribes of North America. Nine Mile Falls, Wash., Spokane House Enterprises, 1972.
203 p. illus. S74

Bonney, Orrin H
Battle drums and geysers: the life and journals of Lt. Gustavus Cheyney Doane, soldier and explorer of the Yellowstone and Snake River regions, by Orrin H. and Lorraine Bonney. Chicago, Sage Books, 1970.
xxv, 622 p. illus. S75

Booth, Charles W
The northwestern United States. New York, Van Nostrand Reinhold, 1971.
115 p. maps S76

Bourke, Robert H. and Bard Glenne.
The nearshore physical oceanographic environment of the Pacific Northwest coast. Corvallis, Or., Oregon State University Dept. of Oceanography, 1972.
127 p. S77

Bressie, Wes and Ruby Bressie
Ghost town bottle guide. Salem, Or., Old Time Bottle Publishing Co., 1972.
100 p. illus. S78

Brewster, David, ed.
The best places: the gourmet notebook guide to the Pacific Northwest. Seattle, Wash., Madrona Publishers, 1975.
322 p. illus. S79

Brier, Howard Maxwell
Sawdust empire: the Pacific Northwest. New York, Knopf, 1958.
269 p. illus. S80

Britt, Albert.
Toward the western ocean - the story of the men who bridged the continent, 1803-1869. Barre, Mass., Barre Publishing Co., 1963.
164 p. illus. S81

Brown, Aaron Venable, 1798-1856
Oregon Territory. Fairfield, Wash., Ye Galleon Press, 1968.
24 p. Facsimile. S82

Brown, Giles T
Ships that sail no more: marine transportation from San Diego to Puget Sound, 1910-1940. University of Kentucky Press, Lexington, Kentucky, 1966.
287 p. illus. S83

Brown, Mark H
The flight of the Nez Perce: a history of the Nez Perce War. New York, Putnam's, 1967.
480 p. maps S84

Brown, William Compton, 1869-
The Indian side of the story: being a concourse of presentations historical ... in Washington Territory east of the Cascade Mountains during the period from 1853 to 1889 ... Spokane, C.W. Hill Printing Co., 1961.
469 p. illus. S85

Browning, Robert J
Fisheries of the north Pacific: history, species, gear and processes. Anchorage, Alaska, Northwest Publishing Co., 1974.
408 p. illus. S86

Brumfield, Kirby
This was wheat farming: a pictorial history of the farms and farmers of the Northwest who grow the nation's bread. Seattle, Superior Publishing Co., 1968.
191 p. illus. S87

Budlong, Caroline (Gale) 1856-1939
Memories: pioneer days in Oregon and Washington Territory. Eugene, Or., Printed by the Picture Press Printers, c1949.
45 p. illus. S88

Bullard, Oral
Crisis on the Columbia. Portland, The Touchstone Press, 1968?
S89

Bullard, Oral and Don Lowe
Short trips and trails: the Columbia Gorge. Beaverton, Or., The Touchstone Press, 1974.
128 p. illus. S90

Bunge, William
The economic base of Puget Sound region present and future. Olympia, Washington State Dept. of Commerce, 1960.
49 p. S91

Burgess, Fred E
Memoirs of eighty years of farming. Philadelphia, Pa., Dorrance, 1974.
131 p. S92

Burns, Robert Ignatius, S.J.
The Jesuits and the Indian wars of the Northwest. Yale University Press, 1966.
528 p. illus. S93

Byrne, Peter
The search for Big Foot: monster, myth or man? Washington, D.C., Acropolis Books, 1975.
263 p. illus. S94

Caesar, Gene
King of the mountain men: the life of Jim Bridger. N.Y., Dutton, 1961.
317 p. illus. S95

Calhoun, Bruce
Northwest Passages. San Francisco, Calif., Miller Freeman Publications, 1969-72.
2 v. illus. S96

California. University, San Diego. Library.
The Hill collection of Pacific Voyages, ed. by Ronald Louis Silveira de Braganza and Charlotte Oakes. San Diego, Calif., 1974.
333 p. illus. S97

Camp, Charles L. ed.
James Clyman, frontiersman: the adventures of a trapper and covered wagon emigrant as told in his own reminiscences and diaries. Portland, Or., Champoeg Press, 1960.
352 p. illus. S98

Campa Cos, Miguel de la
A journal of explorations northward along the coast from Monterey in the year 1775, by Fra Miguel de la Campa Cos, with illustrations in original colors by Luis Choris; edited by John Galvin. San Francisco, John Howell-Books, 1964.
67 p. maps S99

Campbell, Ernest Howard
The state legislatures of Alaska, Oregon and Washington: background papers for Northwest Regional American Assembly ... Seattle, University of Washington, c 1966.
62 p. S100

Campbell, Marjorie Elliott (Wilkins), 1901-
The North West Company. Toronto, The Macmillan Company of Canada, Limited, 1957.
xiv, 295 p. maps. S101

Campbell, Marjorie Elliott (Wilkins)
The Nor'Westers: the fight for the fur trade. Toronto, Macmillan, 1954.
vii, 2, 176 p. illus. S102

Cannon, Raymond
How to fish the Pacific coast; a manual for salt water fishermen. 2nd ed. Menlo Park, Calif., Lane Book Co., 1964
337 p. illus. S103

Cantwell, Robert
The hidden Northwest. Philadelphia, Pa., Lippincott, 1972.
335 p. maps S104

Caras, Roger A
Sockeye: the life of a Pacific Salmon. New York, Dial Press, 1975.
135 p. S105

Carhart, Arthur Hawthorne
The national forests. New York, Knopf, 1959.
225 p. S106

Carlson, Gordon
Seventy-five years history of Columbia Baptist Conference, 1889-1964. Seattle, Columbia Baptist Conference, 1964.
288 p. photos S107

Carlson, Sherrill
The Northwest coast Indians ABC book. Pullman, Wash., State Street Press, 1972.
32 p. illus. S108

Castor, Henry
Fifty-four forty or fight; a showdown between America and England settles the Oregon question. New York, Watts, 1970.
54 p. illus. S109

Caterpillar Tractor Company
Men of timber: the presidents of the Pacific Logging Congress. Peoria, Ill., The Author, c1954-1959.
3 v. ports. V. 2 and 3 called 2nd and 3rd eds. S110

Catholic Church Records of The Pacific Northwest: Vancouver, Vols. 1 and 2, and Stellamaris Mission, tr. by Mikell Delores Wormell Warner. St. Paul, Or., French Prairies Press, 1972.
1 v. illus. S111

Chalmers, Harvey, II.
The last stand of the Nez Perce: destruction of a people. New York, Twayne Publishers, Inc., 1962.
288 p. S112

Chalmers, J.W.
Fur trade governor. Edmonton. Institute of Applied Arts, 1960.
illus. S113

Chamberlain, Willard Joseph
The scolytoidea of the Northwest: Oregon, Washington, Idaho and British Columbia. Corvallis, Oregon State University, 1958.
208 p. illus. S114

Chaney, Ralph Works
Miocene floras of the Columbia plateaus, by Ralph W. Chaney and Daniel I. Axelrod. Washington, D.C., Carnegie Institution, 1959.
viii, 237 p. maps S115

Chicago Art Institute
Yakutat south Indian art of the northwest coast. Catalogue by Allen Wardwell (exhibition) the Art Institute of Chicago, 13 March-April 26,1964. Chicago, The Institute, 1964.
82 p. illus. S116

Chipman, Art
Wildflower trails of the Pacific Northwest. Medford, Or., Pine Cone Publishers, 1970. S117

Clark, Ella Elizabeth
Guardian spirit quest. Illustrated by Alex Bull Tail. Billings, Mont., Montana Indian Publications Fund, c1974.
36 p. S118

Clark, Ella E
Indian legends from the northern Rockies. Norman, University of Oklahoma Press, 1966.
350 p. illus. S119

Clark, Ella E
Indian legends of the Pacific Northwest: illustrated by Robert Bruce Inverarity. Berkeley, University of California Press, 1958.
225 p. illus. S120

Cline, Gloria Griffen
Peter Skene Ogden and the Hudson's Bay Company. Norman, Okla., University of Oklahoma Press, 1973.
300 p. illus. S121

Clinkinbeard, Philura (Vanderburgh)
Across the plains in '64, by prairie schooner to Oregon. From the stories of her mother, Philura V. Clinkinbeard, compiled and arr. by Anna Dell Clinkinbeard. New York, Exposition Press, 1953.
97 p. S122

Cochran, George M
Indian portraits of the Pacific Northwest. Portland, Or., Binfords & Mort, 1959.
64 p. illus. S123

Columbia Basin Inter-Agency Committee. Economics sub-committee.
Inventory of economic studies and data sources for the Pacific Northwest. Portland, Or., 1963.
226 p. S124

Columbia Basin Inter-Agency Committee.
Review of power planning in the Pacific Northwest, calendar year 1964. Olympia, Washington, 1965.
73 p. illus. S125

Conference in the matter of Pollution of the Interstate Waters of the Lower Columbia River and the Tributaries, Bonneville Dam to Cathlamet, 1965. Proceedings ... U.S. Dept. of Health, Education and Welfare, 1966?
2 v. illus. S126

Contemporary Indian Artists: Montana, Wyoming, Idaho. Browning, Mont. Museum of the Plains Indians, 1973.
80 p. illus. S127

Conway, Jim
Jim Conway's "fishin' holes". Portland, Or., Graphic Arts Center, 1969.
174 p. illus. S128

Conway, Steve.
Timber cutting practices: a manual on felling and bucking. San Francisco, Calif., M. Freeman, 1968.
65 p. illus. S129

Cook, James
The explorations of Captain James Cook in the Pacific as told by selections from his own journals, 1768-1779. Ed. by A. Grenfell Price. Illus. by Geoffrey C. Ingleton. New York, The Heritage Press, 1958.
xii, 296 p. illus. S130

Cook, James
The voyage of the Resolution and Discovery, 1776-1780. Edited by J.G. Beaglehole. Cambridge University Press, Hakluyt Society, 1967.
2 vols. illus. maps. S131

Cook, Warren L
Flood tide of empire: Spain and the Pacific Northwest, 1543-1819. New Haven, Conn., Yale University Press, 1973.
620 p. illus. S132

Coons, Frederica B
The trail to Oregon. Portland, Or., Binfords & Mort, 1954.
183 p. illus. S133

Cooper, William Skinner
Coastal sand dunes of Oregon and Washington. New York, Geological Society of America.
xii, 169 p. illus. S134

Corney, Peter
Early voyages in the north Pacific, 1813-1818. Introduction by Glen Cameron Adams. Fairfield, Wash., Ye Galleon Press, 1965.
238 p. illus. S135

Cornplanter, Jesse J
Legends of the longhouse: told to Sah-Nee-Weh, the white sister: with an introduction by Carl Carmer; illus. by the author. Port Washington, N.Y., Ira J. Friedman, 1963.
216 p. illus. S136

Cortesi, Lawrence
Jim Beckwourth, explorer-patriot of the Rockies. New York, Abelard-Schuman, 1971.
224 p. S137

Coutant, Charles Griffin
History of Wyoming and the far West. Argonaut Press, published for University Microfilms, 1966. 1 v. in 2, Reprint of 1899 ed.
736 p. S138

Cowan, Charles S
The enemy is fire. Seattle, Superior Publishing Co., 1961.
123 p. illus. S139

Cox, Ross
Adventures on the Columbia River. Condensed and edited by Alfred Powers. Portland, Or., Binfords & Mort, 1958.
124 p. illus. S140

Cox, Ross
The Columbia River: or, scenes and adventures during a residence of six years on the western side of the Rocky Mountains among various tribes of Indians ... with an introduction by Edgar I. Stewart and Jane R. Stewart. Norman, University of Oklahoma Press, 1957.
398 p. illus. S141

Cox, Thomas R
Mills and markets: a history of the Pacific coast lumber industry to 1900. Seattle, Wash., University of Washington Press, 1974.
332 p. illus. S142

Crawford, Medorem
Journal of Medorem Crawford. Fairfield, Wash., Ye Galleon Press, 1967. (Published in 1897 by the University of Oregon, Eugene).
26 p. S143

Crompton, Arnold
Unitarianism on the Pacific coast: the first sixty years. Boston, Beacon Press, 1957.
182 p. S144

Cross, Osborne
March of the regiment of mounted riflemen to Oregon in 1849; a report in the form of a journal. Fairfield, Wash., Ye Galleon Press, 1967. (Facsimile reprints of 1851 edition).
218 p. ports. S145

Crutchfield, James Arthur, ed.
The fisheries: problems in resource management. Foreword by Brewster C. Denny. Seattle, University of Washington Press, c1965.
136 p. illus. S146

Crutchfield, James A. and Giulio Pontecorvo.
The Pacific salmon fisheries: a study of irrational conservation. Baltimore, Md., Johns Hopkins Press, 1969.
200 p. S147

Cummins, Sarah J. (Lemmon)
Autobiography and reminiscences. Fairfield, Wash., Ye Galleon Press, 1968. (Reprint of 1914 edition). S148

Current Issues Conference, 1st, Portland, 1972. Timber supply and the environment: proceedings. Edited by Stuart U. Rich. Eugene, Or., University of Oregon Forest Industries Management Center, 1972.
109 p. illus. S149

Cushman, Dan.
The great north trail: America's route of the ages. New York, McGraw-Hill, 1966.
383 p. maps. S150

Cutright, Paul Russell, 1897-
A history of the Lewis and Clark journals by Paul Russell Cutright. 1st ed. Norman, University of Oklahoma Press, 1975.
xxi, 311 p. illus. ports. S151

Dake, Henry Carl
Northwest gem trails, a field guide for the gem hunter, mineral collector and tourist, covering both popular and little known areas of Oregon, Washington, Idaho, British Columbia. With additional material by Don MacLachlan. 3rd ed. completely rev. Mentone, Calif., Gembooks, c1962.
95 p. illus. S152

Davidson, Gordon Charles
The North West Company. New York, Russell and Russell, 1967. (Reprint of 1918 edition).
349 p. maps S153

Davis, Andrew
The journey of Moncacht-Ape. Fairfield, Wash., Ye Galleon Press, 1966. (Reprint from 1883). S154

Davis, Harold Lenoir
Kettle of fire. New York, Morrow, 1959.
189 p. S155

Davis, Lenwood G.
Blacks in the Pacific Northwest, 1788-1974: a bibliography of published works and of unpublished source materials on the life and contributions of black people in the Pacific Northwest. 2nd ed. Monticello, Ill., Council of Planning Librarians, 1975.
93 p. S156

Dawson, Will, 1909-
Coastal cruising: an authoritative guide to British Columbian and Puget Sound-San Juan Islands waters. Vancouver, B.C., Mitchell Press, c1959. illus. maps.
175 p. illus. maps.
Also: new enlarged ed., 1965. 243 p.
Also: rev. 3rd ed., 1973. 243 p.
S157

Dempsey, Hugh A
A Blackfoot winter count. Glenbow Foundation, Calgary, Alta, Canada. 1965.
20 p. S158

Dicken, Samuel Newton
Pacific Northwest. Garden City, New York, Doubleday, 1958.
64 p. illus. S159

Dierdorff, John
How Edison's lamp helped light the West. Portland, Or., Pacific Power and Light Co., 1971.
313 p. illus. S160

Dillon, Richard H
Siskiyou Trail: the Hudson's Bay Company route to California. New York, McGraw-Hill, 1975.
381 p. illus. S161

Dodge, Ernest Stanley
Northwest by sea. N.Y., Oxford University Press, 1961.
348 p. illus. S162

Doerksen, Harvey R
Columbia River Interstate Compact: politics of negotiation, by Harvey R. Doerksen. Pullman, Washington State University, 1972.
xiii, 196 p. S163

Donaldson, Ivan J. and Frederick K. Cramer.
Fishwheels of the Columbia. Portland, Or., Binfords & Mort, 1971.
124 p. illus. S164

Dorn, Edward and L. MacLucas.
The Shoshoneans: the people of the basin-plateau. Morrow, 1967.
96 p. S165

Douglas, James
James Douglas in California, 1841; being the journal of a voyage from the Columbia to California on behalf of the Hudson's Bay Company. Vancouver, B.C., The Library's Press, Vancouver Public Library, 1965.
90 p. illus. S166

Douglas, David, 1798-1834
The Oregon journals of David Douglas, of his travels and adventures among the traders and Indians in the Columbia, Willamette and Snake River regions during the years 1825, 1826 and 1827. Ed. with an introduction by David Lavender. Ashland, Or., 1972
2 v. illus. S166A

Douglas, William
My wilderness: the Pacific West. Garden City, N.Y., Doubleday, 1960.
206 p. illus. S167

Dow, Edson
Adventure in the Northwest. Wenatchee, Wash., Outdoor Publishing Co., 1964.
253 p. illus. S168

Dow, Edson
Passes to the north: history of Wenatchee Mountains (rev. ed). Wenatchee, Wash., Outdoor Publishing Co., 1964.
255 p. illus. S169

Down, Mary Margaret
A century of service, 1858-1958: a history of the Sisters of Saint Anne and their contribution to education in British Columbia, the Yukon and Alaska, Victoria, B.C., Sisters of Saint Anne, 1966.
195 p. illus. S170

Drucker, Phillip, 1911-
Cultures of the north Pacific coast. With an introduction by Harry B. Hawthorn. San Francisco, Calif., Chandler Publishing Co., 1965.
xvi, 243 p. illus. S171

Drucker, Phillip
Indians of the Northwest coast. New York, American Museum of Natural History (by) McGraw-Hill, c1955.
xii, 208 p. illus. map. S172

Drucker, Phillip
The native brotherhoods: modern intertribal organizations of the Northwest coast. Washington, U.S. Govt. Printing Office, 1958.
iv, 194 p. S173

Drury, Clifford Merrill, ed.
The diaries and letters of Henry H. Spalding and Asa Bowen Smith relating to the Nez Perce Mission 1838-1842. Glendale, Calif., Arthur Clark Co., 1958.
379 p. illus. S174

Drury, Clifford Merrill, ed.
First white women over the Rockies: diaries, letters and biographical sketches of the six women of the Oregon mission who made the overland journey in 1836 and 1838. Glendale, Calif., Arthur Clark Co., 1962-66.
3 vols. illus. map. S175

Drury, Clifford Merrill.
Marcus and Narcissa Whitman and the opening of old Oregon. Glendale, Calif., Arthur Clark Co., 1973.
2 v. illus. S176

Dryden, Cecil Pearl, 1887-
Give all to Oregon! Missionary pioneers of the far West. New York, Hastings House, 1968.
256 p. illus. S177

Dryden, Cecil Pearl
Mr. Hunt and the fabulous plan. Illus. by Beatrice Driessen. Caldwell, Idaho, Caxton Printers, 1958.
343 p. illus. S178

Dryden, Cecil Pearl
Up the Columbia for furs; illus. by E. Joseph Dreany. Caldwell, Idaho, Caxton Printers, 1949.
309 p. illus. S179

Duff, Wilson, ed.
Images: Stone: B.C. - thirty centuries of Northwest coast Indian sculpture. Saanichton, Hancock House, 1975.
191 p. illus. S180

Duncan, Janice K
Minority without a champion: Kanakas on the Pacific coast, 1788-1850. Portland, Or., Oregon Historical Society, 1972.
24 p. ports. S181

Dunlop, Richard
Trails of the West. Nashville, Tenn., Abingden, 1971.
320 p. illus. S182

Dunn, Jacob Piatt.
Massacres of the mountains: a history of the Indian wars of the far West, 1815-1875. New York, Archer House: distributed by Herman & Stephens, 1958. (reprint of 1886 edition).
669 p. illus. S183

Durham, Bill
Canoes and kayaks of western America. Seattle, Copper Canoe Press, 1960.
104 p. illus. S184

D'Wolf, John
A voyage to the north Pacific. Fairfield, Wash., Ye Galleon Press, 1968. (Reprint of 1861 edition). S185

Dye, Eva Emery
McLoughlin and old Oregon: a chronicle. Portland, Or., Binfords & Mort, 1957. (c1900)
386 p. S186

Eide, Ingvard Henry, comp.
American odyssey: the journey of Lewis and Clark. Chicago, Rand McNally, 1969.
xxii, 245 p. illus. S187

Eide, Ingvard H
The Oregon Trail. New York, Rand, 1972. S188

Ekman, Leonard C
Scenic geology of the Pacific Northwest. Edited by L.K. Phillips. Portland, Or., Binfords & Mort, 1962.
310 p. illus. S189

Elimov, Aleksei Vladimirovich, ed.
Atlas of geographical discoveries in Siberia and northwestern America: XVII-XVIII centuries. Moscow. Publishing House "Nauka", 1964.
135 p. maps S190

Eliot, Willard Ayres
Forest trees of the Pacific coast. Revised ed. Portland, Or., Binfords & Mort, 1963.
566 p. illus. S191

Elliott, Thompson Coit
Earliest travelers on the Oregon Trail. Fairfield, Wash., Ye Galleon, 1975.
18 p. illus. S192

Ellison, Ellis and Gayle Ellison
Wild flowers of the Pacific Northwest. Edmonds, Wash., Ellison Industries, 1971.
illus. S193

Enari, Leonid
Plants of the Pacific Northwest: 663 selected Northwest wild flowers, shrubs, trees and weeds. Portland, Or., Binfords & Mort, 1956.
315 p. illus S194

Ernst, Alice (Henson)
Trouping in the Oregon country: a history of frontier theatre. Portland, Oregon Historical Society, 1961.
197 p. illus. S195

Ernst, Alice (Henson)
The wolf ritual of the Northwest coast. Eugene, Or., University of Oregon, 1952.
ix, 107 p. illus. S196

Essig, Edward Oliver
Insects and mites of the western North America: a manual and text book for county, state and federal entomologists and agriculturists. 2nd ed. New York, Macmillan, 1958.
1050 p. illus. S197

Ewers, John Canfield
Artists of the old West. Garden City, New York, Doubleday and Co., 1965.
240 p. illus. S198

Fahey, Edmund
Rum road to Spokane. Missoula, University of Montana, 1972.
126 p. illus. S199

Fahey, John
The Flathead Indians. Norman, Oklahoma, University of Oklahoma Press, 1974.
366 p. illus. S200

Falter, Conrad Michael
Aquatic macrophytes of the Columbia and Snake River drainages (United States). Moscow, Idaho, University of Idaho, 1974.
xiv, 275 p. illus. S201

Farb, Peter
Man's rise to civilization as shown by the Indians of North America from primeval times to the coming of the industrial state. N.Y., Dutton, 1968.
332 p. illus. S202

Farmer, Judith A. and others
An historical atlas of early Oregon. Text by Kenneth L. Holmes. Portland Historical Cartographic Publications, 1973.
53 p. maps S202A

Favour, Alpheus Hoyt
Old Bill Williams, mountain man. With an introduction by William Brandon. (New ed.) Norman, Oklahoma, University of Oklahoma Press, 1962.
234 p. S203

Fejes, Claire, 1920-
People of the Noatak. Illustrated by the author. New York, Knopf, 1966.
xii, 368 p. illus. S204

Felt, Margaret Elley
Gyppo logger. Caldwell, Idaho, Caxton Printers, 1964.
315 p. illus. S205

Fisher, Anne M. (Reeploeg)
Exile of a race: a history of the forcible removal and imprisonment by the army of the 115,000 citizens and alien Japanese who were living on the West coast in the spring of 1942. Seattle, F. & T. Pubs., 1965.
245 p. illus. S206

Fisher, Vardis
Gold rushes and mining camps of the early American West. Caldwell, Idaho, Caxton Printers, 1968.
466 p. S207

Fitzgerald, Emily (McCorkle)
An Army doctor's wife on the frontier, letters from Alaska and the far West, 1874-1878. Edited by Abe Laufe. Pittsburgh, University of Pittsburgh Press, 1962.
352 p. illus. S208

Flora, Charles J
The sound and the sea: a guide to northwestern neritic invertebrate zoology, by Charles J. Flora and Eugene Fairbanks. 2nd ed. Bellingham, Wash., Pioneer Printing Co., 1966.
455 p. illus. S209

Florin, Lambert
Alaska, the Yukon and British Columbia ghost towns. Seattle, Wash., Superior Publishing Co., 1971.
72 p. illus S210

Florin, Lambert William, 1905-
Ghost town album. Seattle, Superior Publishing Co., 1962.
184 p. illus. S211

Florin, Lambert
Ghost town Eldorado. Seattle, Superior Publishing Co., 1968. S212

Florin, Lambert
Ghost town trails. Maps and drawings by David C. Mason. Seattle, Superior Publishing Co., c1963.
192 p. illus. S213

Florin, Lambert
Ghost town treasures. Seattle, Superior Publishing Co., 1965
192 p. S214

Florin, Lambert
A guide to western ghost towns. Seattle, Superior Publishing Co., 1967.
96 p. S215

Florin, Lambert
Historic western churches. Seattle, Superior Publishing Co., 1969.
192 p. illus. S216

Florin, Lambert
Montana, Idaho, Wyoming ghost towns. Seattle, Superior Publishing Co., 1971.
112 p. illus. S217

Florin, Lambert
Tales the western tombstones tell. Seattle, Superior Publishing Co., 1967.
192 p. illus. S218

Florin, Lambert
Western ghost towns. Seattle, Superior Publishing Co., 1961.
176 p. illus. S219

Florin, Lambert
Western ghost town shadows. Seattle, Superior Publishing Co., c1964.
189 p. illus. S220

Fodor, Eugene
Pacific states: southern California, northern California, Nevada, Idaho, Oregon, Washington, Alaska ... 2nd rev. ed., Litchfield, Conn., Fodor's Modern Guides; distributor: D. McKay Co., New York, 1967. (Fodor Shell travel guides, U.S.A., v. 8) S221

Foote, Mary (Hallock)
A Victorian gentlewoman in the far West: the reminiscences of Mary Hallock Foote. San Marino, Calif., Huntington Library, 1972.
416 p. illus. S222

Forestry Centennial Conference
The next one hundred years in forestry: proceedings at the conference, Oregon State College, Corvallis, Ore., Oregon State College, 1959.
67 p. S223

Foster, John W.
Four Northwest fundamentalists. Portland, Ore., The author, 1975.
128 p. illus. S224

Franchere, Gabriel
Adventure at Astoria, 1810-1814. Translated and edited by Hoyt C. Franchere. Norman, University of Oklahoma Press, 1967.
190 p. illus. S225

Franchere, Gabriel
Voyage to the northwest coast of America. Ed. by Milo Milton Quaife. Original publication 1854. New York, Citadel, 1968.
320 p. S226

Franklin, Dorothy Wilkins, ed.
West coast disaster, Columbus Day, 1962. Portland, Ore., Gann Publishing Co., 1963.
180 p. illus. S227

Franklin, George E
From Cotswolds to high Sierras. Caldwell, Caxton Printers, 1966.
167 p. S228

Franzwa, Gregory M
The Oregon Trail revisited. St. Louis Mo., Patrice Press, 1972.
417 p. illus. S229

Frazer, Robert Walter
Forts of the West: military forts and presidios, and posts commonly called forts, west of the Mississippi River to 1898. Norman, University of Oklahoma Press. c1965.
246 p. illus. S230

Frazier, Neta Lohnes
Five roads to the Pacific. New York, David McKay Co., 1964.
184 p. illus. S231

Frazier, Neta Lohnes.
Sacajawea: the girl nobody knows. New York, David McKay, 1967.
182 p. S232

Frazier, Neta Lohnes
Stout-hearted seven. New York, Harcourt Brace Jovanovich, 1973.
174 p. S233

Freeman, Otis Willard, 1889- , ed.
The Pacific Northwest, an overall appreciation. Editors: Otis W. Freeman, Howard H. Martin. 2nd ed. New York, Wiley, 1954.
xvi, 540 p. illus. S234

Freer, Blaine
The sportsman's guide to the Pacific Northwest. Garden City, N. Y., Doubleday, 1975.
290 p. illus. S235

Friedman, Ralph
Northwest passages: a book of travel. Portland, Ore., Pars Publishing Co., 1968
234 p. illus. S236

Fuller, Emaline
Left by the Indians. Fairfield, Wash., Ye Galleon Press, 1969.
S237

Fulton, Arabella (Clemens), 1844-1934
Tales of the trail. (Compiled by B.C. Payette). Montreal, Printed privately for Payette Radio, Ltd., 1965.
viii, 378 p. illus. S238

Fultz, Hollis B
Famous Northwest manhunts and murder mysteries. Elma, Wash., Fulco Publications, 1955.
229 p. illus. S239

Furlong, Marjorie and Virginia Pill
Wild edible fruits and berries. Healdsburg, Calif., Naturegraph, 1974.
64 p. illus. S240

Gabrielson, Ira Noel, 1889-
Birds of the Pacific Northwest: with special reference to Oregon, by Ira N. Gabrielson and Stanley G. Jewett. New York, Dover Publications, 1970.
xxx, 650 p. illus. S241

Galbraith, John S
The Hudson's Bay Company as an imperial factor, 1821-1869. Berkeley, University of California Press, 1957.
viii, 500 p. maps. S242

Garcia, Andrew
Tough trip through paradise, 1878-1879. Edited by Bennett H. Stein. Boston, Houghton Mifflin, 1967.
xciii, 446 p. illus. S243

Garfield, Viola (Edmundson), 1899-
The Tsimshian: their arts and music. New York, J.J. Augustin Publisher, 1951.
xii, 290 p. illus.
Parts 1 and 2 later published (1966) by the University of Washington, Seattle, under the title, "The Tsimshian Indians and their arts."
94 p. illus. S243A

Gartner, John.
Outdoor guide to the Pacific Northwest. Princeton, N.J., Van Nostrand, 1968.
300 p. S244

Gass, Patrick
A journal of the voyages and travels of a corps of discovery under the command of Capt. Lewis and Capt. Clarke of the Army of the United States, from the mouth of the river Missouri through the interior parts of North America to the Pacific Ocean, during the years 1804, 1805 and 1806. Minneapolis, Minn., Ross & Hanies, 1958 (c1807).
317 p. illus. S245

Gershevsky, Ruth Hale
PNLA 1909-1959: a chronological summary of fifty eventful years. Seattle, Pacific Northwest Library Assn., 1959.
43 p. S246

Gibbs, George, 1815-1873
Indian tribes of Washington Territory. Fairfield, Wash., Ye Galleon Press, 1967.
55 p. S247

Gibbs, George
Pacific Northwest letters of George Gibbs. Ed. by Vernon Carstensen. Portland, Ore., Oregon Historical Society, 1954.
52 p. S248

Gibbs, James Atwood
Disaster log of ships. Seattle, Superior Publishing Co., 1971.
176 p. illus. S249

Gibbs, James Atwood
Pacific graveyard. 3rd ed. Portland, Ore., Binfords & Mort, 1964.
375 p. illus. S250

Gibbs, James Atwood
Pacific square-riggers: pictorial history of the great windships of yesteryear. Seattle, Superior Publishing Co., 1969.
192 p. illus. S251

Gibbs, James Atwood
Shipwrecks of the Pacific coast. Portland, Ore., Binfords & Mort. 1957.
312 p. illus. S252

Gibbs, James Atwood
Shipwrecks of the Pacific coast. 2nd ed. Portland, Ore., Binfords & Mort, 1962.
352 p. illus. S253

Gibbs, James Atwood
Steamships and motor ships of the West coast. Seattle, Superior Publishing Co., 1968. S254

Gilbert, Edmund William
The exploration of western America, 1800-1850: an historical geography. New York, Cooper Square Publ., 1966. (First published in 1933).
233 p. S255

Gilbert, James Henry, 1876-
Trade and currency in early Oregon: a study in the commercial and monetary history of the Pacific Northwest. New York, AMS Press, 1967.
126 p. S256

Gilkey, Helen M
Weeds of the Pacific Northwest. Corvallis, Ore., Oregon State College, 1957.
xxix, 441 p. illus. S257

Gilkey, Helen M
Winter twigs: a wintertime key to deciduous trees and shrubs of northwestern Oregon and western Washington, by Helen M. Gilkey and Patricia L. Packard. Corvallis, Ore., Oregon State University Press, 1962.
109 p. illus. S258

Gill's dictionary of the Chinook jargon, with examples of use in conversation and notes upon tribes and tongues. English-Chinook and Chinook-English. 18th ed. compiled by John Gill. Portland, J.K. Gill Company, 1960.
80 p. S259

Glassley, Ray Hoard, 1887-
Pacific Northwest Indian wars: the Cayuse War of 1848, the Rogue River Wars of the '50s, the Yakima War, 1853-1856, the Coeur d'Alene War, 1857, the Modoc War, 1873, the Nez Perce War, 1877, the Bannock War, 1878, the Sheepeater's War of 1879. Portland, Or., Binfords & Mort, 1953.
266 p. illus.
Also: 2nd ed., 1971. S260

Glubok, Shirley
The art of the Northwest coast Indians. New York, Macmillan, 1975.
48 p. illus. S261

Gohs, Carl
Ed Quigley, western artist. Portland, Or., Geneva Hall Quigley, 1971.
168 p. illus. S262

Gough, Barry Morton
The Royal Navy and the Northwest coast of North America, 1810-1914: a study of British maritime ascendancy. Vancouver, University of British Columbia Press, 1971.
294 p. illus. S263

Grande, Walter R
Rails to the Pacific Northwest, comp. by Walter R. Grande and Richard F. Lind. Boulder, Colo., R.F. Lind, c1964.
130 p. illus. S264

Gray, William R
The Pacific Crest Trail. Washington, D.C., National Geographic Society. 1975.
199 p. illus. S265

Green, John Willison, 1927-
On the track of the sasquatch. Agassiz, Cheam Publishing, 1968.
78 p. S266

Green, John Willison
On the track of the sasquatch. New York, Ballantine Books, 1974, c1973.
211 p. illus. S267

Green, John Willison
The sasquatch file. Agassiz, B.C., Cheam Pub., Ltd., c1973.
80 p. illus. S268

Green, John Willison
Year of the sasquatch. 2nd ed. Agassiz, B.C., Cheam Pub., Ltd., 1970.
80 p. illus. S269

Gregg, Jacob Ray
A history of the Oregon Trail, Santa Fe Trail and other trails. Portland, Or., Binfords & Mort, 1955.
313 p. illus. S270

Gressley, Gene M
Bankers and cattlemen. New York, Knopf, 1966.
320 p. S271

Gross, Paul S
The Hutterite way: the inside story of the life, customs, religion and traditions of the Hutterites. Saskatoon, Sask., Freeman Publishing Co., 1965.
219 p. S272

Guberlet, Muriel Lewin
Animals of the seashore: descriptive guide to seashore invertebrates of the Pacific coast. 3rd ed. Portland, Or., Binfords & Mort, 1962.
472 p. illus S273

Gulick, Grover C
The land beyond (by) Bill Gulick. Boston, Houghton Mifflin, 1958.
234 p. S274

Gunther, Erna, 1896-
Art in the life of the Northwest Indian. With a catalog of the Rasmussen Collection of Northwest Indian Art at the Portland Art Museum. Portland, Or., Portland Art Museum, 1966.
275 p. illus. S275

Gunther, Erna
Indian life on the Northwest coast of North America, as seen by the early explorers and fur traders during the last decades of the eighteenth century. Chicago, University of Chicago Press, 1972.
xiv, 277 p. illus. S276

Guthrie, John Alexander
Western forest industry: an economic outlook by John A. Guthrie and George R. Armstrong. Baltimore, Johns Hopkins Press, 1961.
324 p. illus. S277

Hafen, LeRoy Reuben, 1893-
The mountain men and the fur trade of the far West: biographical sketches of the participants by scholars of the subject and with introductions by the editor. Glendale, Calif., Arthur H. Clark Co., 1965. 2 vols. S278

Hafen, LeRoy Reuben, ed.
To the Rockies and Oregon, 1839-1842: with diaries and accounts by Sidney Smith, Amos Cook, Joseph Holman, E. Willard Smith, Francis Fletcher, Joseph Williams, Obadiah Oakley, Robert Shortess and T.J. Farnham. Edited, and with analytical notes, by LeRoy R. Hafen and Ann W. Hafen. Glendale, Calif., A.H. Clark, Co., 1955.
315 p. illus. S279

Hagan, William Thomas
Indian police and judges. New Haven, Yale University Press, 1966.
194 p. S280

Haines, Aubrey L
Historic sites along the Oregon Trail, prepared by Aubrey L. Haines. Denver, Historic Preservation Team, Denver Service Center, National Park Service, 1973.
xi, 442, 27 p. illus. S281

Haines, Francis
Oregon in the U.S.A., by Francis Haines and E. Bernice Tucker. Portland, Ore., Cascade Pacific Books, 1955.
215 p. illus. S282

Hakola, John W., ed.
Frontier omnibus. Foreward by H.G. Merriam. Missoula, Montana State University Press: Helena Historical Society of Montana, c1962.
436 p. illus. S283

Hall, William Henry Harrison
The private letters and diaries of Captain Hall: an epic of an argonaut in the California gold rush. Oregon Territories, Civil War and Oil City. Glendale, Calif., London Book Co., 1974.
270 p. illus. S284

Halliday, William Reginald
Adventure is underground. New York, Harper, 1959.
206 p. illus. S285

Hanft, Marshall
The cape forts: guardians of the Columbia. Rev. ed. Portland, Or., Oregon Historical Society, 1973.
55 p. illus. S286

Hanley, Mike and Ellis Lucia
Owyhee trails: the West's forgotten corner. Caldwell, Idaho, Caxton Printers, 1973.
314 p. illus. S287

Hansen, Sofus E, comp.
Captain Farwell's Hansen handbook for piloting in the inland waters of the Puget Sound area, British Columbia, southeastern Alaska, southwestern Alaska, western Alaska, with some sketches from the original Hansen handbook. New and rev. ed. by R.F. Farwell. Seattle, Lowman & Hanford Co., 1951.
599 p. illus. S288

Hanson, Charles E, 1917-
The Northwest gun. Lincoln, Nebraska, Nebraska State Historical Society, 1955.
xii, 85 p. illus. S289

Harder, Annine Frederika (Hennings), 1880-
Opportunities of the golden West. Spokane, Wash., Ross Printing Co., 1960.
75 p. illus. S290

Harmon, Daniel Williams, 1778-1845
Sixteen years in the Indian country: the journal of Daniel Williams Harmon, 1800-1816: edited with an introduction by W. Kaye Lamb ... maps by C.C.J. Bond ... Toronto, The Macmillan Co., of Canada, Ltd., 1957.
xxviii, 277 p. maps. S291

Harris, Christie
Once upon a totem. Woodcuts by John Frazier Mills. New York, Atheneum, 1963.
148 p. illus. S292

Harris, Christie
Sky man on the totem pole? Toronto, McClelland and Stewart, 1975.
167 p. illus. S293

Harris, Edward, 1799-1863
Up the Missouri with Audubon: the journal of Edward Harris, edited and annotated by John Francis McDermott. Norman, University of Oklahoma Press, 1951.
xv, 222 p. illus. S294

Harris, John
Chant of the hawk, by John and Margaret Harris. New York, Random House, 1959.
308 p. S295

Harrison, A.E.
Exploring glaciers -- with a camera. San Francisco, Sierra Club, 1960.
71 p. illus. S296

Harrison, Fred, 1917-
Hell holes and hangings. Clarendon, Texas, Clarendon Press, 1968.
170 p. S297

Hart, Herbert M.
Old forts of the Northwest; illustrated by Paul J. Hartle, Seattle, Superior Publishing Co., 1963.
192 p. S298

Hart, Herbert M
Pioneer forts of the West. Seattle, Superior Publishing Co., 1967.
192 p. S299

Hassrick, Royal B
Western painting today: contemporary painters of the American West. New York, Watson-Guptil, 1975.
175 p. illus. S300

Hatch, Melville H., 1898-
The beetles of the Pacific Northwest. Part 5: Rhipiceroidea, Sternoxi, Phytaphaga, Rhynchophora and Lamellicornia. Seattle, Wash., University of Washington Press, 1971.
662 p. illus. S301

Hatch Melville H
A century of entomology in the Pacific Northwest. Seattle, University of Washington Press, 1949.
v, 42 p. ports. S302

Havighurst, Walter
The first book of the Oregon Trail. N.Y., Franklin Watts, Inc., 1960.
60 p. illus. S303

Hawgood, John A
America's Western frontiers. Knopf, 1967.
xxiii, 440 p. S304

Hawthorn, Audrey E
Art of the Kwakiutl Indians and other Northwest coast tribes. Vancouver, University of British Columbia: Seattle, Wash., University of Washington Press, 1967.
xxx, 410 p. S305

Haydon, John M
The off-beat guide to the waterfronts, Seattle and the Pacific Northwest including British Columbia. Seattle, Marine Digest, 1962.
96 p. illus. S306

Hayes, Doris W
Key to important woody plants of eastern Oregon and Washington, by Doris W. Hayes and George A. Garrison. Washington, U.S. Dept. of Agriculture, 1960.
227 p. illus. S307

Haynes, Bessie Doak
The grizzly bear: portraits from life. Norman, University of Oklahoma Press, 1966.
256 p. S308

Hays, Hoffman Reynolds
Children of the raven: the seven Indian nations of the Northwest coast. New York, McGraw-Hill, 1975.
314 p. illus. S309

Haywood, William D
Bill Haywood's book: the autobiography of William D. Haywood. New York, International Publications, 1958, (c1929).
368 p. S310

Hazlit, William Carew
British Columbia and Vancouver Island: comprising a historical sketch of the British settlements in the Northwest coast of America and a survey of the physical characteristics of that region. London, G. Routledge, 1858. (Reprint, New York, Johnson Reprint, 1967). S311

Hebard, Grace R
Sacajawea, a guide and interpreter of the Lewis and Clark expedition, with an account of the travels of Toussaint Charbonneau, and of Jean Baptiste, the expedition papoose. Glendale, Calif., Arthur H. Clark, 1957. (c1932). (Facsimile reprint).
340 p. illus. S312

Helm, Myra Sager
Lorinda Bewley and the Whitman massacre. Portland, Or., Metropolitan Press, c1951.
95 p. illus. S313

Helstrom, Henning
Henning's fishing, hunting, vacation guide to the Pacific Northwest. Portland Or., The author, 1969. S314

Henderson, Paul Clifton, 1894-
Landmarks on the Oregon Trail. New York, Published by Peter Decker for the Westerners, 1953.
61 p. illus. (part col.) fold. map. S315

Henry, Alexander
New light on the early history of the greater Northwest. The manuscript journals of Alexander Henry, fur trader of the Northwest Company, and of David Thompson, official geographer and explorer of the same company, 1799-1814. Edited with copious critical commentary by Elliott Coues. Minneapolis, Ross & Haines, 1965. (Reprint of 1897 ed.)
3 vols. in 2. maps. port. S316

Henry, Ralph Chester, 1912-
The majestic land: peaks, parks and prevaricators of the Rockies and highlands of the Northwest, by Eric Thane (pseud.). Indianapolis, Bobbs-Merrill, 1950.
347 p. illus. S317

Hewitt, James, comp.
Eye-witness to wagon trains West. Reading, Osprey Publishing, 1973.
178 (16) p. illus. S318

Hewitt, Randall Henry
Across the plains and over the divide: a mule train journey from East to West in 1862, and incidents connected therewith. New York, Argosy-Antiquarian, Ltd., 1964. (Reprint of 1906 ed.)
521 p. S319

Hewlett, Gilbey
Sealife of the Pacific Northwest. Toronto, McGraw-Hill-Ryerson, 1975. S320

Hidy, Ralph W., Frank E. Hill and Allen Nevins.
Timber and men: the Weyerhaeuser story. New York, Macmillan, 1963.
704 p. illus. S321

Highsmith, Richard Morgan, 1920-
Atlas of the Pacific Northwest resources and development. Corvallis, Or., Oregon State College, 1953.
vii, 118 p. illus. S322

Highsmith, Richard M., ed.
Atlas of the Pacific Northwest resources and development. 2nd ed. rev. and enl. Corvallis, Or., Oregon State College, 1957.
vii, 140 p. maps. S323

Highsmith, Richard M., ed.
Atlas of the Pacific Northwest: resources and development. 3rd ed. Corvallis, Or., Oregon State University Press, 1962.
168 p. illus. S324

Highsmith, Richard M.
Atlas of the Pacific Northwest. 4th ed. Oregon State University Press, 1968. S325

Highsmith, Richard and Robert Bard
Atlas of the Pacific Northwest. 5th ed. Corvallis, Or., Oregon State University Press, 1973.
128 p. illus. S326

Hill, Beth
Guide to Indian rock carvings of the Pacific Northwest coast. Saanichton, B.C., Hancock House, 1975.
49 p. illus. S327

Hill, Beth and Ray Hill
Indian petroglyphs of the Pacific Northwest. Seattle, Wash., University of Washington Press, 1975.
320 p. illus. S328

Hill, Beth and Ray Hill
Stone petroglyphs of the Northwest coast Indians. Saanichton, B.C., Hancock House, 1974.
256 p. illus. S329

Hill, Clara Chapman
Spring flowers of the lower Columbia valley. Illustrated by Mary Comber Miles. Seattle, University of Washington Press, 1958.
xi, 164 p. illus. S330

Hillary, Louise
Keep calm if you can: drawings by Paul Galdone. New York, Doubleday and Co., 1964.
184 p. S331

Hilson, Stephen E
Exploring Puget Sound and British Columbia. Holland, Mich., Van Winkle Publishing Co., 1975.
107 p. illus. S332

Hinckley, Theodore C., ed.
The westward movement and historical involvement of the Americas in the Pacific Basin. San Jose, The Historical Dept., San Jose State College, 1966.
74 p. S333

Hiscock, Barbara A
Wawona, the heritage of sailing in the north Pacific. Seattle, Save Our Ships, Inc., 1966.
24 p. illus. S334

Hitchcock, Charles Leo, 1902-
Flora of the Pacific Northwest: an illustrated manual, by C. Leo Hitchcock and Arthur Cronquist. Illus. by Jeanne R. Janish. Seattle, University of Washington Press, 1973.
xix, 730 p. illus. S335

Hitchcock, Charles Leo
Vascular plants of the Pacific Northwest. Seattle, University of Washington Press, 1964-69.
2 vols. illus. S336

Hitchcock, Sharon Yeltatzie
Illustrated legends of the Northwest coast Indians. Vancouver, B.C., University of British Columbia Indian Education Resource Center, 1973.
1 vol. illus. S337

Hoard, James Ellsworth, 1939- , ed.
Studies in Northwest Indian languages, edited by James E. Hoard and Thomas M. Hess. Sacramento, Calif., Sacramento Anthropological Society, Sacramento State College, 1971.
137 p. S338

Hodges, Lawrence K., ed.
Mining in the Pacific Northwest: a complete review of the mineral resources of Washington and British Columbia. Seattle, Shorey Book Store, 1967. (Facsimile reproduction of 1897 ed.)
244 p. maps. S339

Holbrook, Stewart Hall, 1893-1964
The Columbia. Illustrated by Ernest Richardson. New York, Rinehart and Co., 1956.
393 p. illus. S340

Holbrook, Stewart Hall
The Columbia River. Illustrated by Paul Laune. New York, Holt, Rinehart and Winston, 1965.
89 p. illus. S341

Holbrook, Stewart Hall
Far corner, a personal view of the Pacific Northwest. New York, Macmillan, 1952.
270 p. map. S342

Holbrook, Stewart Hall
The wonderful West. Garden City, N.Y., Doubleday and Co., 1963.
154 p. illus. S343

Holbrook, Stewart Hall
Yankee loggers: a recollection of woodsmen, cooks and river drivers. N.Y., International Paper Co., 1961.
123 p. illus. S344

Holloway, David
Lewis and Clark and the crossing of north America. New York, Saturday Review Press, 1974.
224 p. S345

Holm, Don
Pacific north! Sea trails for the sportsman of the north Pacific rim. Caldwell, Idaho, Caxton Printers, 1969.
283 p. illus. S346

Holm, Oscar William
Crooked beak of heaven: masks and other ceremonial art of the Northwest coast. Seattle, Wash., University of Washington Press, 1972.
96 p. illus. S347

Holm, Oscar William
Northwest coast Indian art: an analysis of form. Seattle, University of Washington Press, 1965.
115 p. illus. S348

Holmes, Kenneth L
Ewing Young, master trapper. Portland, Or., Binfords & Mort, 1967.
180 p. illus. S349

Horn, Elizabeth L
Wildflowers I: the Cascades. Beaverton, Or., Touchstone Press, 1972.
160 p. S350

Hostetler, John Andrew
The Hutterites in North America. Case studies in cultural anthropology. Holt, Rinehart and Winston, 1967.
viii, 119 p. S351

Howard, Harold P
Sacajawea. Norman, University of Oklahoma Press, 1971.
218 p. illus. S352

Howard, Harold P
Mystery of Sacajawea: Indian girl with Lewis and Clark. Stickney, S.D., c1967.
159 p. illus. S353

Howard, Helen Addison
Northwest trail blazers. Caldwell, Idaho, Caxton Printers, 1963.
418 p. illus. S354

Howard, Helen Addison
Saga of Chief Joseph. Maps and illustrations by George D. McGrath. Caldwell, Idaho, Caxton Printers, 1965. (Published in 1941 under title, "War Chief Joseph".)
395 p. S355

Howard, Helen Addison and Dan L. McGrath
War Chief Joseph: maps and illustrations by George D. McGrath. Lincoln, Nebraska, University of Nebraska Press, 1964.
368 p. S356

Howell, Erle
Methodism in the Northwest. Edited by Chapin D. Foster. Nashville, Tenn., Parthenon Press, 1966.
468 p. illus. S357

Hoyt, Edward Jonathan.
Buckskin Joe, being the unique and vivid memoirs of Edward Jonathan Hoyt, hunter-trapper, scout, soldier, showman, frontiersman, and friend of the Indians, 1840-1918. Lincoln, University of Nebraska Press, 1966.
194 p. S358

Hult, Ruby El
Guns of the Lewis and Clark Expedition. Tacoma, Washington State Historical Society, 1960.
unp. illus. S359

Hult, Ruby El
Lost mines and treasures of the Pacific Northwest. Portland, Or., Binfords & Mort, 1957.
257 p. illus. S360

Hult, Ruby El
Northwest disaster: avalanche and fire. Portland, Or., Binfords & Mort, 1960.
228 p. illus. S361

Hult, Ruby El
Treasure hunting Northwest. Portland, Or., Binfords & Mort, 1971.
216 p. illus. S362

Hunt, Garrett B
Indian wars of the inland empire. Spokane, Spokane Community College Library, 1966.
127 p. illus. ports. S363

Hunt, Wilson Price, 1783?-1842
The overland diary of Wilson Price Hunt. Translated from the French and edited by Hoyt C. Franchere. Ashland, Or., The Oregon Book Society, 1973.
67 p. illus. S364

Hunter, Don and Rene Dakinden
Sasquatch. Toronto, McClelland and Stewart, 1973.
192 p. S365

Hurd, Edith (Thacher)
Sailors, whalers and steamers: ships that opened the West. Menlo Park, Calif., Lane Book Co., 1964.
64 p. S366

Hurst, Randle M
The smokejumpers. Caldwell, Idaho, Caxton Printers, 1966.
284 p. S367

Hyman, Harold H
Soldiers and spruce: origins of the loyal legion of loggers and lumbermen. Los Angeles, Institute of Industrial Relations, University of California, 1963.
341 p. S368

Hynding, Alan, 1936-
The public life of Eugene Semple, promoter and politician of the Pacific Northwest. Seattle, University of Washington Press, 1973.
195 p. illus. S369

Ingraham, Joseph, 1762-1800
Journal of the brigantine Hope on a voyage to the northwest coast of North America, 1790-92. Illustrated with charts and drawings by the author. Edited, with notes and an introduction by Mark D. Kaplanoff. Barre, Mass., Imprint Society, 1971.
xxvii, 248 p. illus. S370

Inverarity, Robert Bruce, 1909-
Art of the Northwest coast Indians. Berkeley and Los Angeles, University of California Press, 1950.
xiv, 243 p. illus. S371

Irving, Washington
Adventures of Captain Bonneville, U.S.A., in the Rocky Mountains and the far West. Edited with an introduction by Edgely W. Todd. Norman, Oklahoma. University of Oklahoma Press, 1961.
421 p. illus. S372

Irwin, Leonard Bertram
Pacific railways and nationalism in the Canadian-American Northwest, 1845-1873. Philadelphia, 1939: New York, Greenwood Press, 1968.
246 p. S373

Ito, Kazuo
Issei: A history of Japanese immigrants in North America. Translated by Sinichiro Nakamura and Jean S. Gerard. Seattle, Executive Committee for Publication of Issei, 1973.
1016 p. illus. ports. S374

Jackson, Helen Maria (Fiske) Hunt
A century of dishonor: the early crusade for Indian reform. Edited by Andrew F. Bolle. Harper, 1965.
342 p. S375

Jackson, William Turrentine
Wagon roads west: a study of federal road surveys and construction in the trans-Mississippi West, 1846-1869. Foreword by William H. Goetzmann. New Haven, Conn., Yale University Press, 1965.
422 p. maps. S376

Jacobs, Melville
The people are coming soon: analyses of Clackamas Chinook myths and tales. Seattle, University of Washington Press, 1960.
359 p. front. S377

Jacobson, Daniel, 1923-
The fishermen. Illustrated by Richard Cuffari. New York, F. Watts, 1975.
87 p. illus. S378

January thaw: People at Blue Mt. Ranch write about living together in the mountains. New York, Times Change Press, distributed by Monthly Review Press, 1974.
156 p. illus. S379

Jaques, Florence (Page), 1890-
As far as the Yukon, by Florence Page Jaques. Illustrations by Francis Lee Jaques. New York, Harper & Brothers, Publishers, c1951.
x, 243 p. illus. S380

Jarrard, Leonard D
Uranium in the Northwest, mineralized areas and prospecting suggestions by Leonard D. Jarrard and Wayne S. Moen. Butte, Mont., The authors, 1955.
93 p. illus. S381

Jenkins, Mildred
Before the white man came: Pacific Northwest Indian culture: illustrated by Will D. Jenkins. Portland, Or., Binfords & Mort, 1951.
169 p. S382

Jessett, Thomas Edwin, 1902-
Chief Spokan Garry, 1811-1892, Christian, statesman and friend of the white man. Minneapolis, T.S. Denison, 1960.
232 p. illus. S383

Jessett, Thomas E
John McCarty and the Pacific Northwest. New York, The National Council, 1958.
17 p. S384

Jewett, Stanley Gordon.
Stoneflies (Plecoptera) of the Pacific Northwest. Corvallis, Oregon State College, 1959.
95 p. illus. S385

Jilek, Wolfgang George
Salish Indian mental health and cultural change: psychohygienic and therapeutic aspects of the guardian spirit ceremonial. Toronto, Holt, Rinehart and Winston of Canada, 1974.
131 p. illus. S386

Johannsen, Robert W
Frontier politics on the eve of the Civil War. Seattle, University of Washington Press, 1967. S387

Johansen, Dorothy O., 1904-
Empire of the Columbia, a history of the Pacific Northwest by Dorothy Johansen and Charles M. Gates. New York, Harper & Brothers Publishers, 1957.
xv, 685 p. illus. maps
--Empire of the Columbia. 2nd ed. by Dorothy O. Johansen. New York, Evanston, and London, Harper & Row, 1967.
xiii, (5) 654 p. illus. maps. S388

Johansen, Dorothy O., ed.
Voyage of the Columbia around the world with John Boit, 1790-1793. Portland, Or., Champoeg Press, 1960.
92 p. illus. S389

Johnson, Ebenezer
A short account of a northwest voyage performed in the years 1796, 1797 and 1798. Edited by M.S. Batts. Vancouver, The Alcuin Society, 1974.
22p. illus. S390

Johnson, Jalmar
Builders of the Northwest. With an introduction by Stewart H. Holbrook. New York, Dodd, Mead, 1963.
242 p. illus. S391

Johnson, Robert C
John McLoughlin: "Father of Oregon." Portland, Or., Binfords & Mort, 1958 (c1935).
302 p. illus. S392

Johnson, Virginia Weisel
The unregimented general: a biography of Nelson A. Miles. Illustrated with photographs and with maps prepared by Brigadier General W.M. Johnson. Boston, Houghton Mifflin, 1962.
401 p. illus. S393

Jonas, Frank H., ed.
Politics in the American West. Salt Lake City, Utah, University of Utah Press, 1969.
544 p. Suppl. 200 p. illus. S394

Jonas, Frank H
Western Politics. Salt Lake City, Utah. University of Utah Press, 1961.
401 p. tables. maps. S395

Jones, Nard
The great command: the story of Marcus and Narcissa Whitman and the Oregon country pioneers. Boston, Mass., Little, Brown & Co., 1959.
389 p. pl. S396

Jones, Nard
Marcus Whitman: the great command. 2nd ed. Portland, Or., Binfords & Mort, 1968.
322 p. illus. S397

Jones, Roy Franklin
Wappato Indians of the lower Columbia River valley. Compiled by Roy F. Jones. Edited by Anthony Netboy. Maps and illustrations by Herbert K. Beals. Vancouver, Wash., 1972.
ix, 237 p. illus. S398

Josephy, Alvin M., Jr.
The Nez Perce Indians and the opening of the Northwest. New Haven, Conn., Yale University Press, 1965.
705 p. illus. S399

Judson, Phoebe Newton (Goodell), 1832-1926
A pioneer's search for an ideal home: a book of personal memoirs. Edited and with a foreword by John M. McClelland, Jr. Tacoma, Washington State Historical Society, 1966.
xiii, 207 p. illus. S400

Kane, Paul
Paul Kane, the Columbia wanderer, 1846-47: sketches and paintings of the Indians and his lecture, "The Chinooks." Edited with an introduction by Thomas Vaughan. Portland, Or., Oregon Historical Society, 1971.
54 p. illus. S401

Karolevitz, Robert F
Doctors of the old West. Seattle, Superior Publishing Co., 1967.
192 p. S402

Karolevitz, Robert F
Newspapering in the old West: a pictorial history of journalism and printing on the frontier. Seattle, Superior Publishing Co., c1965.
191 p. illus. S403

Keith, Elmer, 1899-
Keith: an autobiography. New York, Winchester Press, c1974.
381 p. S404

Keithahn, Edward Linnaeus, 1900-
Monuments in cedar. Seattle, Superior Publishing Co., 1963.
160 p. illus. S405

Kelley, Donald Greame, 1913-
Edge of a continent: the Pacific coast from Alaska to Baja. With a foreword by Robert C. Miller. Palo Alto, Calif., American West Publishing Co., 1971.
288 p. illus. S406

Kew, Della and P.E. Goddard
Indian art and culture of the Northwest coast. Saanichton, B.C., Hancock House, 1974.
93 p. illus. S407

Kingsbury, Martha
Art of the thirties: the Pacific Northwest. Seattle, Wash., University of Washington Press, 1972.
95 p. illus. S408

Kirk, Ruth
The oldest man in America: an adventure in archaeology. Foreword by Roald Fryxell and Richard Daugherty. N.Y., Harcourt, Brace, Jovanovich, 1970.
95 p. illus. S409

Knight, Oliver
Following the Indian wars: the story of the newspaper correspondents among the Indian campaigners. Norman, University of Oklahoma Press, 1960.
348 p. S410

Krutilla, John V.
The Columbia River Treaty: the economics of an international river basin development. Baltimore, Md., Johns Hopkins Press, 1967.
xv, 211 p. S411

Krutilla, John V
Sequence and timing in river basin development with special application to Canadian-United States Columbia River Basin planning. Washington, D.C., Resources for the Future, 1961.
34 p. illus. S412

Kushner, Howard I
Conflict on the Northwest coast: American-Russian rivalry in the Pacific Northwest, 1790-1867. Westport, Conn., Greenwood Press, 1975.
227 p. map. S413

Kuykendall, E.V.
Eighty years in the changing West. Memoirs of E.V. Kuykendall. (n.p.), 1954.
ii, 164 p. S414

Kyner, James Henry
End of track. Gloucester, Mass., Peter Smith, 1964.
280 p. S415

Labbe, John T. and Vernon Goe
Railroads in the woods. Berkeley, Calif., Howell-North Press, 1961.
269 p. photographs. S416

Lage, Laura Tice
Sagebrush homesteads. Yakima, Wash., Franklin Press, 1967.
viii, 265 p. illus. S417

Lancaster, Richard.
Piegan: a look from within at the life, times and legacy of an American Indian tribe. Illustrated by Nancy McLaughlin. Garden City, N.Y., Doubleday, 1966.
359 p. illus. S418

Landis, Robert L
Post offices of Oregon, Washington and Idaho. Portland, Or., Patrick Press, 1969.
illus. S419

Langford, Nathaniel Pitt
Vigilante days and ways; the pioneers of the Rockies, the makers and making of Montana, Idaho, Oregon, Washington and Wyoming. With a new introduction by Dorothy M. Johnson. Missoula, Montana State University Press, 1957.
456 p. illus. S420

Larrison, Earl J. and others
Washington wildflowers. Including 1134 species of wildflowers most commonly found in the state of Washington and adjacent areas of Oregon, Idaho and British Columbia. Seattle, Wash., Seattle Audubon Society, 1974.
376 p. illus. S421

Lavender, David Stewart
Land of giants: the drive to the Pacific Northwest, 1750-1950. Garden City, N.Y., Doubleday, 1958.
468 p. illus. S422

Lavender, David
The Rockies. Harper, 1968.
414 p. S423

Lavender, David S.
Westward vision: the story of the Oregon Trail. New York, McGraw-Hill, 1963.
424 p. maps. S424

League of Women Voters of Idaho, Montana, Oregon and Washington. The great river of the West. Seattle, League of Women Voters, 1959.
32 p. S425

Ledyard, John
A journal of Captain Cook's last voyage: ed. by James Kenneth Munford: and with notes on plants by Helen M. Gilkey: and notes on animals by Robert M. Storm. Corvallis, Or., Oregon State University Press, 1964.
264 p. plates. maps. S426

Leonard, Zenas
Adventures of Zenas Leonard, fur trader. Edited by John C. Ewers. Norman, University of Oklahoma Press, 1959. (First published under the title, "Narrative of the adventures of Zenas Leonard," 1839.)
xxxv, 172 p. illus. S428

LeRoy, Bruce
Northwest forts and trading posts. Washington State Historical Society, 1968. S429

LeRoy, Bruce
Northwest history in art, 1778-1963. Olympia, Wash., Washington State Historical Society, 1963. S430

Leslie, Robert Franklin
High trails west. New York, Crown Publishers, 1967.
278 p. maps. ports. S431

Lesure, Thomas B
Harian's Pacific U.S.A. Greenlawn, N.Y., Harian Publications, 1960.
97 p. S432

Lewis & Dryden's marine history of the Pacific Northwest. E.W. Wright, ed. Seattle, Superior Publishing Co., 1967. (Reprint of 1895 ed.)
494 p. illus. S434

Lewis, Claudia Louise, 1907-
Indian families of the Northwest coast: the impact of change. Chicago, University of Chicago Press, 1970.
xi, 224 p. S435

Lewis, Meriwether and William Clark
History of the expedition under the command of Lewis and Clark. Edited by Elliott Coues. New York, Dover Publications, 1964.
3 vols. S436

Lewis, Meriwether
The journals of Lewis and Clark. New selection, introduction by John Bakeless. New York, New American Library of World Literature, 1964.
384 p. S437

Lewis, Meriwether
The journals of the expedition under the command of Capts. Lewis and Clark, to the sources of the Missouri, thence across the Rocky Mountains and down the river Columbia to the Pacific Ocean, performed during the years 1804-5-6 by order of the Government of the United States. Edited by Nicholas Biddle. With an introduction by John Bakeless, and illustrated with water colors and drawings by Carl Bodmer and other contemporary artists. New York, Heritage Press, 1962.
2 vols. xlv, 547 p. illus. S438

Lewis, Meriwether
The Lewis and Clark expedition. The 1814 ed. unabridged. Introduction by Archibald Hanna. Lippincott, 1961.
3 vols. S439

Lewis, Oscar, comp.
The autobiography of the West: personal narratives of the discovery and settlement of the American West, compiled and annotated by Oscar Lewis. New York, Holt, 1958.
310 p. S440

Lewis, Oscar
The war in the far West: 1861-1865. Garden City, N.Y., Doubleday, 1961.
263 p. S441

Little, (Arthur D.), Inc.
A regional analysis: economic and fiscal impacts of the aluminum industry in the Pacific Northwest: a report to the Western Aluminum Producers. Cambridge, Mass., 1974.
vii, 154 p. tables. S442

Long, Margaret, 1873-
The Oregon Trail: following the old historic pioneer trails on the modern highways. Denver, 1954.
xxii, 278, 32 p. illus. S443

Look Magazine
The Pacific Northwest. Des Moines, Iowa, Look Publishing Co., 1962.
114 p. illus. S444

Luce, Edward Smith
Keough, Comanche and Custer. Foreword by Robert M. Utley. 2nd ed. Ashland, Or., L. Osborne, 1974.
148 p. illus. S445

Lucia, Ellis
The big blow: the story of the Pacific Northwest's Columbus Day storm. Forest Grove, Or., News-Times Publishing Co., 1963.
64 p. illus. S446

Lucia, Ellis
The big woods: logging and lumbering, from bull teams to helicopters, in the Pacific Northwest. Garden City, N.Y., Doubleday, 1975.
222 p. illus. S447

Lucia, Ellis
Head rig: story of the west coast lumber industry. Introduction by Arthur Priaulx, Portland, Or., Overland West Press, 1965.
246 p. illus. S448

Lucia, Ellis
The saga of Ben Holladay: giant of the old West. New York, Hastings House, 1959.
374 p. illus. S449

Lucia, Ellis, ed.
This land around us: a treasury of Pacific Northwest writing. Garden City, N.Y., Doubleday, 1969.
981 p. illus. S450

Lucia, Ellis
Tough men, tough country. Englewood Cliffs, New Jersey, Prentice-Hall, 1963.
336 p. illus. S451

Lucia, Ellis
Wild water: the story of the far West's great Christmas week floods. Portland, Or., Overland West Press, 1965.
72 p. illus. S452

Lyman, William Denison
The Columbia River: its history, myths and commerce. Portland, Or., Binfords & Mort, 1959. (New ed.).
492 p. illus.
Also: 4th ed., 1963. 416 p.
S453

McCabe, James O
The San Juan water boundary question. Toronto, University of Toronto Press, c1964.
163 p. map S454

McConkey, Lois
Sea and cedar: how the Northwest coast Indians lived. Seattle, Wash., Madrona Press, 1973.
30 p. illus. S455

McCulloch, Walter F
Woods words: a comprehensive dictionary of loggers terms. Portland, Or., Oregon Historical Society, 1958.
vi, 219 p. front. S456

McDonald, Lucile Saunders, 1898-
Search for the Northwest passage. Illustrations by Parker McAllister. Portland, Or., Binfords & Mort, 1958.
137 p. illus. S457

McDonald, Lucile Saunders
Swan among the Indians: life of James G. Swan, 1818-1900: based upon Swan's hitherto unpublished diaries and journals, by Lucile McDonald. 1st ed. Portland, Or., Binfords & Mort, c1972.
233 p. illus. S458

McFeat, Tom Farrar Scott
Indians of the north Pacific coast: studies in selected topics. Toronto, Canada, McClelland & Stewart, 1966.
268 p.
Also: Seattle, University of Washington Press, 1967. S459

McKechnie, Robert Edward, 1906-
Strong medicine: a history of healing on the Northwest coast. West Vancouver, J.J. Douglas, 1972.
192 p. illus.
Also: 1975 ed. 208 p. S460

McKee, Bates
Cascadia: the geologic evolution of the Pacific Northwest. New York, McGraw-Hill, 1972.
394 p. illus. S461

McKelvey, Susan (Delano)
Botanical exploration of the trans-Mississippi west, 1790-1850. Jamaica Plain, Mass., Published by the Arnold Arboretum of Harvard University, 1955.
xi, 144 p. maps. S462

McKenny, Margaret and D.E. Stuntz
The savory wild mushroom. Seattle, Wash., University of Washington Press, 1962.
133 p. illus. S463

McKenny, Margaret
Wildlife of the Pacific Northwest. Portland, Or., Binfords & Mort, c1954
299 p. illus. S464

McKeown, Martha (Ferguson)
Come to our salmon feast. Portland, Or., Binfords & Mort, 1959
78 p. illus. S465

McKinley, Charles
Uncle Sam in the Pacific Northwest: federal management of natural resources in the Columbia River valley. Berkeley, University of California Press, 1952.
xx, 673 p. maps. S466

McLaughlin, Daniel
Sketch of a trip from Omaha to Salmon River by Daniel McLaughlin. Chicago, Printed for E.D. Graff by G. Martin, 1954.
20 p. S467

McLaughlin, Willard.
Notes on the cultivation of western wildflowers. Spokane, The author, 1959.
19 p. S468

McLoughlin, John, 1784-1857
The financial papers of Dr. John McLoughlin, being the record of his estate and of his proprietory accounts with the North West Company (1811-1821) and the Hudson's Bay Company (1821-1868), edited by Burt Brown Barker. Portland, Historical Society, 1949.
87 p. facsims. S469

McLoughlin, John
Letters of Dr. John McLoughlin, written at Fort Vancouver, 1829-1832. Edited by Burt Brown Barker. Portland, Binfords & Mort, 1948.
376 p. map. S470

McLoughlin, John
John McLoughlin's business correspondence, 1847-48. Edited by William R. Sampson. Seattle, Wash., University of Washington Press, 1973.
179 p. illus. S471

Marshall, David B
Familiar birds of the Northwest forests, fields and gardens. Portland, Or., Portland Audubon Society, 1973.
84 p. illus. S472

Martel, Donald J. and George N. Fredeen
Plant materials for landscaping: a list of plants for the Pacific Northwest classified by plant height, manner of growth, common name, botanical name, flowering habits, hardiness zones. Rev. Corvallis, Or., Oregon State University, Cooperative Extension Service, 1974.
30 p. illus. S473

Martin, Frances Gardiner McEntee
Raven-who-sets-things-right: Indian tales of the Northwest coast. Rev. ed. New York, Harper & Row, 1975.
90 p. illus. S474

Mathers, Michael
Sheepherders: men alone. Boston, Mass., Houghton Mifflin, 1975.
118 p. illus. S475

Mattila, Walter
The boarding house Finns. Portland, Or., Finnish-American Historical Society of the West, 1972.
24 p. illus. S476

Maxey, Chester Collins, 1890-
Marcus Whitman, 1802-1847: his courage, his deeds and his college. New York, Newcomen Society in North America, 1950.
40 p. illus. S477

Meade, Edward F
Indian rock carvings of the Pacific Northwest, by Edward Meade. Sidney, B.C., Gray's Publishing, c1971.
96 p. illus. S478

Meany, Edmond Stephen
Vancouver's discovery of Puget Sound: portraits and biographies of the men honored in the naming of geographic features in northwestern America. 2nd ed. with suppl. Portland, Or., Binfords & Mort, 1957 (c1935)
xvii, 344 p. illus. S479

Meining, D.W.
The great Columbia plain: a historical geography, 1805-1910. Seattle, University of Washington, 1968.
xxi, 576 p.illus. S480

Merk, Frederick, 1887-
Albert Gallatin and the Oregon problem: a study in Anglo-American diplomacy. Cambridge, Harvard University Press, 1950.
xi, 97 p. S481

Merk, Frederick
The Oregon question: essays in Anglo-American diplomacy and politics. Cambridge, The Belknap Press of Harvard University Press, 1967.
427 p. map. S482

Merriam, Willis B
A history of the Northwest Scientific Association. Pullman, Washington State University, 1960.
61 p. S483

Methodist Church, Pacific Northwest Conference. Historical Society.
Letters and papers of Rev. David E. Blaine and his wife, Catherine. Seattle, 1965? S484

Middleton, Lynn
Place names of the Pacific Northwest coast. Victoria, B.C., Elldee, 1969.
226 p. illus. S485

Miller, Helen Markley.
Lens on the West: the story of William Henry Jackson. Illustrated with photos and drawings by William Henry Jackson. Garden City, N.Y., Doubleday, 1966.
192 p. S486

Miller, Helen Markley
Thunder rolling: the story of Chief Joseph. New York, Putnam, 1959.
190 p. S487

Miller, Thomas Wayne
The north Cascades. Photographs by T. Miller, text by Harvey Manning. San Francisco, Sierra Club, 1964.
95 p. illus. S488

Mills, Randall Vause, 1907-
Stern-wheelers up Columbia: a century of steam-boating in the Oregon country. Palo Alto, Calif., Pacific Books, c1947.
212 p. illus. S489

Montgomery, Elizabeth Rider
When pioneers pushed west to Oregon. Champaign, Ill., Garrard, 1970.
95 p. illus. S490

Montgomery, Elizabeth R
World explorers Lewis and Clark. Champaign, Ill., Garrard, 1966.
96 p. S491

Montgomery, James W
The men of the crescent. Spokane, Published by the Eastern Washington State Historical Society, 1975.
23 p. illus. ports. S492

Mooney, James
The ghost dance religion and the Sioux outbreak of 1890. Abridged with an introduction by Anthony F.C. Wallace. Chicago, University of Chicago Press, 1965.
359 p. Paper. S493

Morgan, Dale Lowell, 1914-
Jedediah Smith and his maps of the American West, by Dale L. Morgan and Carl I. Wheat. With an introduction by Carl I. Wheat. San Francisco, California Historical Society, 1954.
86 p. maps. S494

Morgan, Dale Lowell
Jedediah Smith and the opening of the West. Lincoln, Nebraska, University of Nebraska Press, c1953.
illus. S495

Morgan, Dale Lowell, ed.
Overland in 1846: diaries and letters of the Oregon-California Trail. Georgetown, Calif., Talisman Press, 1963. ltd. ed.
2 vols. illus. S496

Morgan, Dale Lowell, ed.
The West of William H. Ashley: the international struggle for the fur trade of the Missouri, the Rocky Mountains and the Columbia, with explorations beyond the Continental Divide, recorded in the diaries and letters of William H. Ashley and his contemporaries, 1822-1838. Denver, The Old West Publishing Co., 1964.
341 p. S497

Morgan, Lewis Henry.
The Indian journals, 1859-62. Edited, and with an introduction by Leslie A. White. Selected and edited by Clyde Walton. Ann Arbor, Mich., University of Michigan Press, 1959.
318 p. S498

Morgan, Murray Cromwell, 1916-
The Columbia, powerhouse of the West. Seattle, Superior Publishing Co., 1949.
ix, 295 p. S499

Morgan, Murray Cromwell
The dam. New York, Viking Press, 1954.
162 p. illus. S500

Morgan, Murray Cromwell
The last wilderness. New York, Viking Press, 1955.
275 p. illus. S501

Morgan, Murray Cromwell
The northwest corner: the Pacific Northwest, its past and present. New York, Viking Press, 1962.
168 p. illus. S502

Morgan, Neil Bowen
The Pacific states: California, Oregon, Washington, by Neil Morgan and the editors of Time-Life Books. New York, Time, Inc., 1967. S503

Morgan, Thomas, 1870-
My story of the last Indian war in the Northwest: the Bannock, Piute, Yakima and Sheep Eater tribes, 1878-1879. Forest Grove, Or., 1954.
29 p. illus. S504

Morwood, William
Traveler in a vanished landscape. New York, Potter, 1972.
352 p. illus. S505

Moser, Don
The Snake River country. New York, Time-Life Books, 1974.
184 p. illus. S506

Mossman, Isaac Van Dorsey, 1830-1912.
A pony expressman's recollections. With an introduction and notes by J. Heine Christ. Portland, Or., Champoeg Press, 1955.
55 p. illus. S507

Mueller, Ted
Northwest ski trails. Seattle, Wash., Mountaineers/Craftsman Press, 1969.
224 p. illus. S508

Murray, Keith A
The pig war, by Keith A Murray. Tacoma, Washington State Historical Society, 1968.
84 p. illus. S509

Napier, John Russell
Bigfoot: the yeti and sasquatch in myth and reality. New York, Dutton, 1973.
240 (12) p. illus. S510

Nehls, Harry B
Familiar birds of Northwest shores and waters, covering birds found west of the Cascade Mountains ... Portland, Portland Audubon Society, 1975.
96 p. illus. S511

Netboy, Anthony, 1906- , ed.
The Pacific Northwest by Stewart Holbrook, Nard Jones and Roderick Haig-Brown. Illustrated with photographs. Garden City, N.Y., Doubleday, 1963.
191 p. illus. S512

Netboy, Anthony.
Salmon of the Pacific Northwest: fish vs. dams. Foreword by Richard L. Neuberger. Portland, Or., Binfords & Mort, 1958.
xii, 122 p. illus. S513

Netboy, Anthony
The Salmon: their fight for survival. Boston, Mass., Houghton Mifflin Co., 1974.
613 p. illus. S514

Neuberger, Richard Lewis, 1912-
The Lewis and Clark Expedition: illustrated by Winold Reiss. New York, Random House, 1951.
180 p. illus. S515

Newell, Gordon, ed.
The H.W. McCurdy marine history of the Pacific Northwest. An illustrated review of the growth and development of the maritime industry from 1895, the date of publication of the last such comprehensive history, Lewis and Dryden's marine history of the Pacific Northwest, to the present time, with sketches and portraits of a number of well known marine men. Seattle, Superior Publishing Co., under auspices of the Seattle Historical Society, 1966.
xvi, 706 (56) p. illus. S516

Newell, Gordon R
Pacific coastal liners, by Gordon Newell and Joe Williamson. Seattle, Superior Publishing Co., c1959. 1st ed.
192 p. illus. S517

Newell, Gordon and Joe Williamson
Pacific lumber ships. Seattle, Superior Publishing Co., 1960.
192 p. illus. S518

Newell, Gordon R
Pacific steamboats. Photos from the Joe Williamson Marine Collection. Seattle, Superior Publishing Co., 1958.
196 p. illus. S519

Newell, Gordon R
Pacific tugboats. Photos from the Joe Williamson Marine Collection. Seattle, Superior Publishing Co., 1957.
191 p. illus. S520

Newell, Gordon R
Rogues, buffoons and statesmen. Seattle, Hangman Press, 1975.
506 p. illus. S521

Newell, Gordon R
Sea rogue's gallery. Seattle, Superior Publishing Co., 1971.
143 p. illus. S522

Newell, Gordon R
SOS north Pacific: tales of shipwrecks off the Washington, British Columbia, and Alaska coasts. Portland, Or., Binfords & Mort, 1955.
216 p. illus. S523

Newell, Robert
Memoranda: travles in the teritory of Misourie: travle to the Kayuse war: together with a report on the Indians south of the Columbia River. Edited with notes and introduction by Dorothy O. Johansen. Portland, Or., Champoeg Press, 1959.
159 p. illus. S524

Newsom, David, 1805-1882
David Newsom: the western observer, 1805-1822. Introduction by E. Earl Newsom. Portland, Oregon Historical Society, 1972.
xii, 299 p. illus. S525

Nielson, Lyman J., comp.
Inventory of research in water pollution and related fields: Columbia basin and Pacific coast states. Corvallis, Or., U.S. Interior Dept. Federal Water Pollution Control Administration, Pacific Northwest Water Laboratory, 1966.
135 p. S526

Nordhoff, Charles
Northern California, Oregon and the Sandwich Islands. Centennial ed., Berkeley, Calif., Ten Speed Press, 1974.
256 p. illus. S527

Northwest regional American assembly on state legislatures in American politics. Final report. Seattle, University of Washington, 1967.
13 p. S528

Northwestern camping and trailering: including location maps. Washington, D.C., American Automobile Association. (no. 1) 1973/74. S529

Norton, Boyd
Rivers of the Rockies. Chicago, Rand McNally, 1975.
160 p. illus. S530

Notices & voyages of the famed Quebec mission to the Pacific Northwest, being the correspondence, notices, etc., of Fathers Blanchet and Demers, together with those of Fathers Bolduc and Langlois. Englished out of French by Carl Landerholm. Portland, Or., Oregon Historical Society, 1956.
iv, 243 p. map. plates. S531

Nunis, Doyce B., Jr.
The golden frontier: the recollections of Herman Francis Reinhart, 1851-1869. Austin, Texas, University of Texas Press, 1962.
353 p. illus. S532

Oceanography Study Committee
Oceanographic resources of the Pacific Northwest: inventory of capabilities for oceanographic and marine activities. Seattle, University of Washington Press, 1967.
256 p. illus. S533

Ogden, Peter Skene
Snake country journals, 1826-27, edited by K.G. Davies. London, Hudson's Bay Record Society, 1961.
xi, 225, xv p. maps. S534

Oliphant, James Orin
On the cattle ranges of the Oregon country. Seattle, Wash., University of Washington Press, 1968.
372 p. maps. S535

Olsen, Michael L., comp.
A preliminary list of references for the history of agriculture in the Pacific Northwest and Alaska. Davis, Agricultural History Center, University of California, 1968.
iv, 58 p. S536

O'Meara, Walter Andrew
The first northwest passage. Boston, Houghton Mifflin, 1960.
183 p. illus. S537

O'Meara, Walter Andrew
The savage country. Boston, Houghton Mifflin, 1960.
308 p. illus. S538

Oregon Historical Society
A bibliography of Pacific Northwest history. Edited by Thomas Vaughan and Priscilla Knuth. Portland, Oregon Historical Society, 1958.
45 l. S539

Oregon Historical Society, Portland
Steamboat days on the rivers. Portland, Or., 1969.
117 p. illus. S540

Oregon. State Highway Department
Route of the Oregon Trail: Fort Boise, Idaho to The Dalles, Oregon. Salem, Or., Highway Dept. 1959.
14 p. illus. sectional maps. S541

Oregon. State Water Resources Board
Snake River study. John D. Davis, Chairman. Salem, Or., State Water Resources Board, August, 1958.
205 p. graphs. S542

Oregon. University, Eugene. Museum of Natural History
Historical background on the flora of the Pacific Northwest by LeRoy E. Detling. Eugene, University of Oregon Museum of Natural History, 1968.
57 p. illus. S543

Oregon. University, Eugene. Museum of Natural History
Pliocene mammals of southeast Oregon and adjacent Idaho. Eugene, 1970.
103 p. S544

Oregon College of Education
Art and culture of the American Indian, a guide for adult education leaders. Independence, Or., 1971.
153 p. S545

Osborne, H. Douglas
Excavations in McNary reservoir basin near Umatilla, Oregon with appendices by Marshall T. Newman and others. Washington, Government Printing Office, 1957.
lx. 250 p. 40 pl. diagr. S546

Osborne, Kelsie Ramey
Peaceful conquest: story of the Lewis and Clark Expedition. Illustrated by Colista Dowling. Portland, Or., Beattie & Co., c1955.
iv, 123 p. illus. S547

Otto Seligman Gallery, Seattle.
Northwest artists of the Otto Seligman Gallery. Seattle, Wash., Otto Seligman Gallery, 1962.
illus. S548

Out West on the overland train.
Across the continent excursion with Leslie's Magazine in 1877, and the overland trip in 1967, by Richard Reinhardt. Palo Alto, American West Publishing Co., 1967.
207 p. S549

Pacific Northwest Library Association
Library development project reports. Edited by Morton Kroll. v. 1, Public libraries of the Pacific Northwest; v. 2, Elementary and secondary school libraries of the Pacific Northwest. Seattle, University of Washington Press, 1960.
461 p. 330 p. tables. S550

Pacific Northwest Library Association
Reference section. Who's who among Pacific Northwest authors. Edited with a preface by Hazel E. Mills. Eugene, Or., 1957.
114 p. S551

Paine, Lauren
Conquest of the great Northwest. N.Y., Robert M. McBride, 1959.
194 p. illus. S552

Parish, H.S.
Cancer in the Rocky Mountain Region. Boise, Idaho, Mountain States Regional Medical Program, 1972.
93 p. charts S553

Parker, Driscol G. and Beatrice Parker, comp.
Coast guide book. The authors, 1962. S554

Paterson, T.W.
Murder: brutal, bizarre and unsolved mysteries of the Northwest. Victoria, B.C., Solitaire Publications, 1973.
72 p. illus. S555

Paterson, T.W.
Shipwreck, piracy and terror in the Northwest. Victoria, B.C., 1972.
64 p. illus. S556

Paul, Virginia
This was cattle ranching, yesterday and today. Seattle, Wash., Superior Publishing Co., 1973.
192 p. illus. S558

Payette, B.C., comp.
Captain John Mullan: his life. Building the Mullan Road; as it is today, and interesting tales of occurrences along the road, by Louis C. Coleman and Leo Rieman. Montreal, Privately printed for Payette Radio Ltd., 1968.
490 p. illus. S559

Payette, B.C.
The Northwest. Montreal, Printed privately for Payette Radio Ltd., 1964.
732 p. illus. S560

Payette, B.C.
The Oregon country under the Union Jack, a reference book of historical documents for scholars and historians. Montreal, Printed privately for Payette Radio Ltd., 1962.
682 p. illus. S561

Pearse, Theed, 1871-
Birds of the early explorers in the northern Pacific. Comox, B.C., Theed Pearse, "The Close," 1968.
275 p. illus. S562

Peattie, Roderick, 1891- , ed.
The Cascades, mountains of the Pacific Northwest. New York, Vanguard Press, 1949.
417 p. illus. S563

Peery, Wilson Kimsey
And there was salmon; illustrated by Grace Livinia Pollock. Portland, Or., Binfords & Mort, 1949.
100 p. illus. S564

Peirce, Neal R
The Pacific states of America: people, politics and power in the five Pacific basin states by Neal R. Peirce. 1st ed. New York, W.W. Norton, 1972.
387 p. maps. S565

Penlington, Norman
The Alaska boundary dispute: a critical reappraisal. Toronto, New York, McGraw-Hill Ryerson, 1972.
141 p. illus. S565A

Peters, Lloyd
Lionhead lodge. How the movies came to Spokane, Washington and to beautiful Priest Lake, Idaho. An autobiography. Fairfield, Wash., Fairfield Press, 1967.
179 p. illus. S566

Philbrick, Francis Samuel
The rise of the West, 1754-1830. New York, Harper and Row, Publishers, c1965.
393 p. illus. S567

Phillips, Paul Chrisler
The fur trade. With concluding chapters by V.W. Smurr. Norman, University of Oklahoma Press, 1961.
2 vols. illus. S568

Pietroforte, Alfred
Songs of the Yokuts and Paiutes, edited by Vinson Brown. Healdsburg, Calif., Naturegraph Co., 1965.
64 p. illus. ports. S569

Place, Marian Templeton
On the track of bigfoot. New York, Dodd, Mead, 1974.
156 p. illus. S570

Place, Marian Templeton
Retreat to the bear paw: the story of the Nez Perce. New York, Four Winds Press, 1969.
190 p. illus. S571

Point, Nicolas
Wilderness kingdom, Indian life in the Rocky Mountains: 1840-1847: the journals and paintings of Nicolas Point. New York, Holt, Rinehart and Winston, 1967.
274 p. S572

Pomeroy, Earl Spencer
The Pacific slope: a history of California, Oregon, Washington, Idaho, Utah and Nevada. New York, Alfred A. Knopf, Inc., 1965.
408 p. illus. S573

Portland Art Museum
Paintings and sculptures of the Pacific Northwest, Oregon, Washington, British Columbia. Portland, Or., Portland Art Museum, 1959.
71 p. illus. S574

Possit, Edward A
Northwest mountaineering. Caldwell, Idaho. Caxton Printers, 1965.
206 p. illus. S575

Prater, Gene
Snowshoe hikes: in the Cascades and Olympics. Seattle, Wash., The Mountaineers, 1969.
95 p. illus. S576

Pratt, Shannon P. and Lawrence R. Ross
Investing in the great Northwest: a layman's guide to Northwest stocks and bonds. Portland, Willamette Management Associates, 1975.
320 p. S577

Preston, Ralph, N., comp.
Historical atlas of Oregon. Spokane, Wash., Christensen, 1969. S578

Preston, Ralph N
Historical Oregon. Corvallis, Or., Treasure Chest Maps, 1970.
34 p. illus. S579

Preston, Ralph N
Historical Oregon atlas rev. ed. Corvallis, Chandler Printing, 1971. S580

Preston, Ralph, ed.
Historical Oregon: old forts, old military roads, Indian battlegrounds, overland stage routes. Rev. ed. Corvallis, Western Guide Publishers, 1972.
58 p. maps. S581

Preuss, Charles
Exploring with Fremont: the private diaries of Charles Preuss, cartographer for John C. Fremont on his first, second and fourth expeditions to the far West. Translated and edited by Erwin G. and Elizabeth K. Gudde. Norman, University of Oklahoma Press, 1958.
xxix, 162 p. illus. S582

Prucha, Francis Paul
Broadax and bayonet: the role of the U.S. Army in the development of the Northwest, 1815-1860. Lincoln, University of Nebraska Press, 1967. (Reprint of 1953 ed.)
263 p. S583

Prucha, Francis Paul, ed.
Documents of United States Indian policy. Lincoln, University of Nebraska Press, 1975.
278 p. S584

Pugh, Ellen
The adventures of Yoo-Lah-Teen: a legend of the Salish coastal Indians. New York, Dial Press, 1975.
83 p. illus. S585

Pyle, Robert Michael
Watching Washington butterflies: an interpretive guide to the state's 134 species, including most of the butterflies of Oregon, Idaho and British Columbia. Seattle, Wash., Seattle Audubon Society, 1974.
109 p. illus. S586

Ranger, Ralph Daniel, Jr.
Pacific Coast Shay, strong man of the woods. San Marino, Calif., Golden West Books, 1964.
103 p. illus. S587

Raufer, Sister Maria Ilma
Black robes and Indians on the last frontier: a story of heroism. Milwaukee, Wis., Bruce Publishing Co., 1966.
489 p. illus. S588

Raymond, Steve
The year of the angler. Illustrated by Dave Whitlock. New York, Winchester Press, 1973.
205 p. illus. S589

Reed College, Portland, Oregon
Citizens' conference on Pacific Northwest forest resources. Salem, Or., Oregon State Library, 1959.
63 p. S590

Reid, William
Out of the silence. New York, Published for Amon Carter Museum, Fort Worth, Outerbridge and Dienstfrey, 1971.
120 p. illus. S591

Reimers, Henry L
Indian country: cultural views of the Spokanes. Minneapolis, Minn., T.S. Denison, 1973.
128 p. illus. S592

Reimers, Henry L
The secret saga of Five-Sack. Fairfield, Wash., Ye Galleon Press, 1975.
27 p. illus. S593

Relander, Click
Drummers and dreamers: the story of Smowhala the prophet and his nephew Puck Hyah Toot, the last prophet of the nearly extinct River People, the last Wanapums. By Click Relander (Now-Tow-Look). Caldwell, Idaho, Caxton Printers, 1956.
345 p. illus. S594

Relander, Click
Strangers on the land: a historiette of a longer story of the Yakima Indian Nation's efforts to survive against great odds, by Click Relander (Now-Tow-Look). Yakima, Wash., Franklin Press, c1962.
100 p. illus. S595

Relander, Click, ed.
Treaty centennial, 1855-1955, the Yakimas. Yakima, Wash., Republic Press, 1955.
64 p. illus. S596

Renz, Louis T
The construction of the Northern Pacific Railroad main line during the years 1870 to 1888. Walla Walla, Wash., The author, 1973.
64 p. S597

Reynolds, Helen (Baker)
Gold, rawhide and iron: the biography of Dorsey Syng Baker. Palo Alto, Calif., Pacific Books, 1955.
191 p. illus. S598

Rice, Gini.
Relics of the road: GMC gems, 1900-1950. Lake Grove, Or., Truck Tracks Inc., 1971.
illus. S599

Rice, Tom
Marine shells of the Pacific Northwest. Edmonds, Wash., Ellison Industries, 1971.
102 p. illus. S600

Rich, Edwin Ernest
The fur trade and the Northwest to 1857. Toronto, McClelland and Stewart, 1967.
336 p. maps. ports. S601

Rich, Edwin Ernest, ed.
The history of the Hudson's Bay Company, 1670-1870. Volume I: 1670-1673. With a foreword by the Right Honorable Sir Winston Churchill. London, The Hudson's Bay Record Society, 1958.
687 p. ports. maps. S602

Richardson, Bill and Dona Richardson
The appaloosa. South Brunswick, N.J., A.S. Barnes, 1969.
195 p. illus. S603

Ricketts, Edward Flanders, 1896-1948
Between Pacific tides: an account of the habits and habitats of some five hundred of the common, conspicuous seashore invertebrates of the Pacific coast between Sitka, Alaska and northern Mexico. 3rd ed. Revised by Joel W. Hedgpath. Stanford, Calif., Stanford University Press, 1962.
516 p. illus.
Also: 4th ed., 1968. S604

Riegel, Robert Edgar
The story of the western railroads from 1852 through the reign of the giants. Gloucester, Mass., Peter Smith, 1964.
345 p. S605

Rieger, Erwin
Up is the mountain and other views. Portland, Or., Published by Binfords & Mort for the Columbians, 1973.
184 p. illus. S606

Ripley, Thomas Emerson
Green timber: on the flood tide to fortune in the great Northwest. Palo Alto, Calif., American West Publishing Co., 1968.
126 p. illus. ports. S607

Rivers of the west. Edited by Elizabeth Hogan: illus. and maps, Steven Jacobs Design. Menlo Park, Calif., Lane Publishing Co., 1974.
223 p. illus. S608

Roberge, Earl
Timber country. Caldwell, Idaho, Caxton Printers, 1973.
182 p. illus. S609

Robertson, Frank Chester
Boom towns of the great basin. Denver, Colorado, Sage Books, 1962.
331 p. S610

Rodgers, John E
Shorebirds and predators Vol. I: Birds of the Pacific Northwest. Vancouver, B.C., J.J. Douglas, 1974. S612

Rosman, Abraham
Feasting with mine enemy: rank and exchange among Northwest coast societies, by Abraham Rosman and Paula G. Rubel. New York, Columbia University Press, 1971.
221 p. illus. S613

Rossit, Edward A
Northwest mountaineering. Caldwell, Idaho, Caxton Printers, 1965.
206 p. illus. S614

Ruby, Robert H and John A Brown
Ferryboats on the Columbia River. Including the bridges and dams. Seattle, Wash., Superior Publishing Co., 1974.
176 p. illus. S615

Ruby, Robert H
Half-Sun on the Columbia: a biography of Chief Moses, by Robert H. Ruby and John A Brown. Norman, University of Oklahoma Press, 1965.
xix, 377 p. illus. S616

Russell, Bert
Calked boots, and other Northwest writings. Harrison, Idaho, Lacon Publishers, 1967.
217 p. illus. S617

Rutan, Gerard F
Canadian-American relations in the West. The environmental problems, Seattle, Wash., Northwest Scientific Association, 1974.
70 p. S618

Ruxton, George Frederick Augustus, 1820-1848
Ruxton of the Rockies, collected by Clyde and Mae Reed Porter: edited by LeRoy R. Hafen. Norman, University of Oklahoma Press, 1950.
xxii, 325 p. plates S619

Sandoz, Mari Suzette, 1907-1966
The beaver men, spearheads of empire. New York, Hastings House, 1964.
xv, 335 p. maps. S620

Satterfield, Archie
Moods of the Columbia. Seattle, Superior Publishing Co., 1968.
64 p. photos. S621

Saum, Lewis O
The furtrader and the Indian. Seattle, University of Washington Press, c1965.
324 p. front. S622

Savannah Oregon Emigrating Society
The organizational journal of an emigrant train of 1845, captained by Solomon Tetherow. With an account of the wagon train mastered by Solomon Tetherow, by Fidelia March Bowers. Eugene, Or., Lane County Pioneer Historical Society, 1960.
29 p. front. S623

Scaylea, Josef
My Northwest. Seattle, Superior Publishing Co., c1970.
56 p. plates. S624

Schaeffer, Claude E
Bear ceremonialism of the Kutenai Indians. Browning, Mont., 1966.
54 p. S625

Schmitt, Martin F
General George Crook: his autobiography. Norman, University of Oklahoma Press, 1960. New ed.
326 p. illus. S626

Schoenberg, Wilfred P
A chronicle of the Catholic history of the Pacific Northwest, 1743-1960. Arr. after the manner of certain medieval chronicles and annotated with copious notes for further reference. Spokane, Gonzaga Preparatory School, 1962.
570 p. S627

Schoenberg, Wilfred P.-S.J.
Jesuit mission presses in the Pacific Northwest. A history and bibliography of imprints, 1876-1899. Portland, Or., Champoeg Press, 1957.
76 p. illus. facsim. S628

Schussler, Edith May, 1874-
Doctors, dynamite and dogs. Caldwell, Idaho, Caxton Printers, 1956.
189 p. illus. S629

Seaman, Norma Gilm, 1873-
Indian relics of the Pacific Northwest. 2nd ed. Portland, Or., Binfords & Mort, 1967.
255 p. illus. S630

Sears, Marian V
Mining stock exchanges, 1860-1930 An historical survey. Missoula, Mont., University of Montana Press, 1974.
228 p. S631

Seattle. Century 21 Exposition, 1962.
Northwest coast Indian art; an exhibit at the Seattle World's Fair fine arts pavilion, 1962. Catalogue by Erna Gunther. Seattle, 1962.
101 p. illus. S632

Seibert, Jerry
Sacajawea: guide to Lewis and Clark. Boston, Houghton Mifflin, 1960.
192 p. illus. S633

Sengstacken, Agnes Ruth (Lockhart), 1859-
Destination, West! A pioneer woman on the Oregon Trail. 2nd ed. Portland, Or., Binfords & Mort, c1972.
219 p. maps. S634

Sheller, Roscoe
Ben Snipes: Northwest cattle king. Portland, Or., Binfords & Mort, 1957.
205 p. illus.
Also: 3rd ed., 1959, 264 p. S635

Sheller, Roscoe
Blowsand. Portland, Or., Metropolitan Press, 1963.
230 p. illus. ports. S636

Sherfey, Florence E
This was their time. Fairfield, Wash., Ye Galleon Press, 1975.
188 p. illus. S637

Shirk, David Lawson, 1844-1928
The cattle drives of David Shirk from Texas to the Idaho mines, 1871 and 1873. Edited by Martin F. Schmitt. Portland, Or., Champoeg Press, 1956.
ix, 148 p. port. S638

Shrader, Grahame F
The Phantom war in the Northwest and an account of Japanese submarine operations on the west coast, 1941-42. Edmonds, Wash., 1970. (c1969).
60 p. illus. S639

Siebert, Erna
North American Indian art: masks, amulets, wood carvings and ceremonial dress from the Northwest coast, by Erna Siebert and Werner Forman, translation by Philippa Hentges. London, Hamlyn, 1967.
43 p. illus. col. plates. S640

Silber, Irwin and Earl Robinson
Songs of the great American West. New York, Macmillan, 1967.
334 p. S641

Silverberg, Robert
Ghost towns of the American West. New York, Thomas Y. Crowell Co., 1968.
309 p. S642

Simonin, Louis Laurent
The Rocky Mountain West in 1867. Translated and annotated by Wilson O. Clough from his Le Grand-Ouest des Etas-Unis. Lincoln, University of Nebraska, 1966.
177 p. S643

Simpson, Charles D. and E.R. Jackman
Blazing forest trails. Caldwell, Idaho, Caxton Printers, 1967.
xiv, 384 p. S644

Simpson, Sir George, 1792-1860
Fur trade and empire: George Simpson's journal. Edited with a new introduction by Frederick Merk. Rev. ed. Cambridge, Mass., Belknap Press of Harvard University, 1968.
370 p. S645

Simpson, Paul B
Regional aspects of business cycles and special studies of the Pacific Northwest. A study prepared for the Bonneville Administration. Eugene, Or., 1953.
i, 105 p. tables. S646

Skarsten, M.O.
George Drouillard: hunter and interpreter for Lewis and Clark and fur trader. 1807-1810. Glendale, Calif., Arthur H. Clark Co., 1964.
365 p. S647

Sloane, Howard N
The Goodyear guide to state parks: California, Washington, Oregon and Alaska, by Howard and Lucille Sloane. New York, Crown, 1968. S648

Smet, Pierre Jean de, 1801-1873
Life, letters and travels of Father de Smet. Edited by Hiram Martin Chittenden and Alfred Talbot Richardson. New York, Arno Press, 1969.
4 vols. illus. S649

Smith, Charles Wesley, 1877-
The early years of the PNLA: organization, the first decade, years of growth. n.p., 1949.
21 p. S650

Smith, Duane
Rocky Mountain mining camps. Bloomington, University of Indiana Press, 1967.
304 p. S651

Smith, Lynwood
Common seashore life of the Pacific Northwest. Healdsburg, Calif., Naturegraph Co., 1962.
66 p. illus. S652

Smith, Marian Wesley, 1907- , ed.
Indians of the urban Northwest. New York, Columbia University Press, 1949.
xix, 370 p. illus. S653

Smith, Olson J
Men against the mountains: Jedediah Smith and the great southwest expedition of 1826-29. New York, The John Day Co., 1965.
320 p. illus. S654

Smith, Ronald O. and Lynda Falkenstein
Rendezvous in the Pacific Northwest. Portland, Or., Great Western Publishing Co., 1974
192 p. illus. S655

Smithsonian Institution
National collection of fine arts. Art of the Pacific Northwest: from the 1930's to the present. Washington, D.C., Smithsonian Institution Press, 1974.
141 p. illus. S656

Snyder, Gerald S
In the footsteps of Lewis and Clark. Washington D.C., National Geographic Society, 1970.
215 p. illus. S657

Spalding, Henry Harmon, 1803-1874.
The diaries and letters of Henry H. Spalding and Asa Bowen Smith relating to the Nez Perce Mission, 1838-1842. Glendale, Calif., The Arthur H. Clark Co., 1958.
379 p. illus. S658

Speck, Gordon
Breeds and half breeds. New York, N. Potter, 1969.
361 p. illus. S659

Speck, Gordon
Northwest explorations. Edited by L.K. Phillips. Portland, Or., Binfords & Mort, 1954.
394 p. illus. S660

Spring, Ira and Harvey Manning
Wilderness trails Northwest: a hiker's and climber's overview guide to national parks and wilderness areas in Wyoming, Montana, Idaho, Northern California, Oregon, Washington, British Columbia and Canadian Rockies. Beaverton, Or., Touchstone Press, 1974.
192 p. illus. S661

Spring, Robert
60 unbeaten paths: an unusual guide to the unusual in the Northwest. Seattle, Wash., Superior Publishing Co., 1972.
143 p. illus. S662

Spring, Robert and Ira Spring
Wildlife encounters. Seattle, Wash., Superior Publishing Co., Wild Life Century, 1975.
112 p. S663

Stanford Research Institute
The impact of the aluminum industry on the economy of the Pacific Northwest: a digest, by Carleton Green, senior economist. Stanford, 1954.
38 p. illus. S664

Stenzel, Franz
An art perspective of the historic Pacific Northwest: from the collection of Dr. and Mrs. Franz R. Stenzel. Exhibited at Montana Historical Society, August, 1963. and at Eastern Washington State Historical Society, Sept. 1963. Portland, Or., 1963.
32 p. illus. S665

Stenzel, Franz.
Early days in the Northwest. Portland, Or., Portland Art Museum, 1959.
38 p. illus. S666

Stenzel, Franz
James Madison Alden: Yankee artist of the Pacific coast, 1845-1860. Fort Worth, Texas, Amon Carter Museum, 1975.
209 p. illus. S667

Stevens, James
Green power: the story of public law 273. Seattle, Superior Publishing Co., 1958.
xiii, 95 p. illus. S668

Steward, Albert N. and others
Aquatic etative keys. 2nd ed. Corvallis, Or., Oregon State University, 1963.
261 p. illus. S669

Stewart, Edgar I
Penny an acre empire in the West. University of Oklahoma, 1968.
304 p. S670

Stine, Thomas Ostenson
Scandinavians on the Pacific, by Thomas Ostenson Stine. San Francisco, R & E Associates, 1968 (c1900).
208 p. illus. S671

Stork, B.C.
Told around the campfire. Spokane, Wash., C.W. Hill Printing Co., 1962. S672

Stoutenburg, Adrien
Wild treasure: the story of David Douglas, by Adrien Stoutenburg and Laura Nelson Baker. New York, Scribner, 1958.
216 p. S673

Strayer, George D
Teaching in the Northwest: Idaho, Montana, Oregon, Washington. Los Altos, Calif., Howard Chandler, 1958.
31 p. illus. S674

Strong, Emory M
Stone age on the Columbia River. Portland, Binfords & Mort, 1959.
254 p. illus.
Also: 2nd ed., 1967, 254 p. S675

Stuart, Robert, 1785-1848
On the Oregon Trail: Robert Stuart's journey of discovery, edited by Kenneth A. Spaulding. Norman, University of Oklahoma Press, 1953.
xiii, 192 p. illus. S676

Stuckey, Martha and Ethel Hoffman-Biskar
Green plants for gray days: house plants for the Pacific Northwest. Portland, Or., Far West Book Service, 1975.
102 p. illus. S677

Sunset
Official guide to the Pacific Northwest century 21 exposition. Menlo Park, Calif., Lane Publishing Co., 1962.
176 p. illus. S678

Sunset
Pacific Northwest and British Columbia. 2nd ed. Menlo Park, Calif., Lane Publishing Co., 1963.
173 p. illus. S679

Sunset
Western campsite directory, 1964. Menlo Park, Calif., Lane Publishing Co., 1964.
112 p. illus. S680

Suphan, Robert J
Ethnological report on the Wasco and Tenino Indians. Ethnological report on the Umatilla, Walla Walla, and Cayuse Indians. New York, Garland Publishing, 1974.
534 p. maps. S681

Sutton, Ann and Myron Sutton.
The Pacific Crest Trail: escape to the wilderness. Philadelphia, Pa., Lippincott, 1975.
240 p. S682

Swan, Kenneth Dupee, 1887-
Splendid was the trail, by Kenneth D. Swan. Vignettes by Joseph S. Swan. Missoula, Mont., Mountain Press, 1968.
170 p. illus. S683

Talbot, Theodore, d. 1862.
Soldier in the West: letters of Theodore Talbot during his services in California, Mexico and Oregon, 1845-53. Edited by Robert V. Hine and Savoie Lottinville. Norman, University of Oklahoma Press, 1972.
xxv, 210 p. illus. S684

Tarrant, Robert F
Forest soils research in Oregon and Washington. Portland, Or., Pacific Northwest Forest and Range Experiment Station, 1964.
34 p. S685

Tatsey, John
The black moccasin. Comp. and ed. by Paul T. Devore. Spokane, The Curtis Art Gallery, 1971.
79 p. illus. S686

Taylor, Ronald J and George W. Douglas
Mountain wild flowers of the Pacific Northwest. Portland, Or., Binfords & Mort, 1975.
176 p. illus. S687

Taylor, Ronald J and Rolf W. Valum
Sagebrush country. Beaverton, Or., Touchstone Press, 1974.
143 p. illus. S688

Taylor, Samuel Wooley.
Line haul: the story of Pacific inter-mountain express. San Francisco, Filmer Publishing Co., 1959.
310 p. illus. S689

Taylor, Thomas Mayne Cunninghame
Pacific Northwest ferns and their allies. Toronto, University of Toronto Press, 1970.
247 p. illus. S690

Tebbel, John
The compact history of the Indian wars. New York, Hawthorn, 1966.
324 p. S691

Thomas, Edward Harper
Chinook: a history and a dictionary, new ed. Portland, Binfords & Mort, 1967.
186 p. S692

Thompson, David
David Thompson and the Lewis and Clark Expedition. Vancouver, B.C., The Library's Press, 1959.
14 p. S693

Thompson, David
Narrative 1784-1812. A new ed. with added material, edited with an introduction and notes by Richard Glover. Toronto, Champlain Society, 1962.
410 p. map. S694

Thompson, David
Travels in western North America, 1784-1812. Toronto, Macmillan of Canada, 1971.
342 p. maps. S695

Thompson, Erwin N
Shallow grave at Waiilatpu: the Sagers' West. Rev. ed. Portland, Or., Oregon Historical Society, 1973.
178 p. illus. S696

Thorp, Raymond W
Crow killer: the saga of Liver-Eating Johnson, by Raymond W. Thorp and Robert Bunker. Bloomington, Indiana University Press, 1958.
190 p. illus. S697

Tilden, Freeman
Following the frontier with F. Jay Haynes, pioneer photographer of the old West. New York, Alfred Knopf, Inc., 1964.
406 p. illus. S698

Tilghman, Zoe Agnes (Stratton)
Sacajawea: the Shoshoni. Oklahoma City, Harlow Publishing Co., 1958. S698A

Timmen, Fritz
Blow for the landing: a hundred years of steam navigation on the waters of the West. Caldwell, Idaho, Caxton Printers, 1973.
235 p. illus. S699

Tobie, Harvey Elmer, 1892-
No man like Joe: the life and times of Joseph L. Meek. Portland, Or., Published by Binfords & Mort for the Oregon Historical Society, 1949.
320 p. illus. ports. S700

Todd, Anne, comp.
Architectural craftsmen of the Northwest. Seattle, Architectural Craftsmen, 1961.
unpaged. illus. S701

Tollefson, Roger
A summary of fishery statistics of the Pacific coast. Tacoma, Northwest Pulp and Paper Association, 1955.
181 p. statistics. charts. S702

Tolmie, William Fraser, 1812-1886
The journals of William Fraser Tolmie, physician and fur trader. Vancouver, B.C., Mitchell Press, Ltd., 1963.
xv, 413 p. illus. ports. S703

Tomkins, Calvin, 1925-
The Lewis and Clark Trail. Introduction by Stewart L. Udall. New York, Harper & Row, 1965. viii, 117 p. illus. S704

Toponce, Alexander
Reminiscences of Alexander Toponce. Introduction by Robert A. Griffen. 2nd ed. Norman, University of Oklahoma Press, 1971. 272 p. illus. S705

Travis, Helga Anderson
Golden bonanza. Prosser, Wash., 1963. 38 p. illus. S706

Travis, Helga
The Nez Perce Trail. Yakima, Wash., Franklin Press, 1968. S707

Tyler, Robert Lawrence
Rebels of the woods: the I.W.W. in the Pacific Northwest. Eugene, Or., University of Oregon Books, 1967. 230 p. S708

Underhill, J.E.
Wild berries of the Pacific Northwest. Saanichton, B.C., Hancock House, 1974. 128 p. illus. S709

Union Pacific Railroad Company
Pacific Northwest and Alaska. Omaha, Nebraska, 1952. 42 p. illus. S710

U.S. Alaska International Rail and Highway Commission.
Transport requirements for the growth of Northwest North America. Washington, D.C., U.S. Govt. Printing Office, 1961. 3 vols. S711

U.S. Army Corps of Engineers
Water resources development of the Columbia River basin. A report by the Division Engineer, U.S. Army Engineer Division, North Pacific, to the Chief of Engineers. U.S. Army, June, 1958. (Portland: 1958). 5 vols. illus. S712

U.S. Bureau of Land Management
The BLM at work in Oregon and Washington. Washington, D.C., U.S. Govt Printing Office, 1964. 24 p. S713

U.S. Bureau of the Census
Statistics for states, standard metropolitan statistical areas and large industrial counties: pt. 9, Pacific: Washington, Oregon, California, Alaska, Hawaii. Washington, D.C., U.S. Govt Printing Office, Feb., 1964. 23 + A-3 p. S714

U.S. Congress, Senate Committee on Interior and Insular Affairs.
Indian land transactions. Memorandum of the chairman to the Committee on Interior, an analysis of the problems and the effects of our diminishing Indian land base, 1948-57. Washington, D.C., 1958. 838 p. charts. S715

U.S. Congress, Senate Committee on Interior and Insular Affairs
Review of national forest timber sales in three western regions. Memorandum of chairman to members of the Committee on Interior. Washington, U.S. Govt Printing Office, 1959. 151 p. illus. S716

U.S. Dept. of Agriculture, Soil Conservation Service
Federal-state-private cooperation snow surveys, 1921-1964, summary of snow survey measurements for Idaho and pertinent measurements in Montana, Wyoming, Utah and Nevada: prepared by Morlan W. Nelson and J. Alden Wilson. Washington D.C., Govt Printing Office, 1965.
192 p. S717

U.S. Dept. of the Interior
Biographical and historical index of American Indians and persons involved in Indian affairs. Boston, G.K. Hall and Co., 1966.
8 vols. S718

U.S. Dept. of the Interior
Depredations and massacre by the Snake River Indians. Washington, D.C., Govt Printing Office, 1861. (U.S. 36th Congress, 2nd session, House, Ex. Doc., No. 46) Reprinted Tacoma, Wash., Ye Galleon Press, 1966. S719

U.S. Office of Labor-Management and Welfare Pension Reports
Register of reporting labor organizations. Jan. 1, 1964, v. 5: western states, American Samoa, Guam, and Wake Island, Alaska, Arizona, California, Hawaii, Idaho, Montana, Nevada, Oregon, Utah, Washington. Washington, D.C., U.S. Govt Printing Office, 1964.
45 p. S720

U.S. President
Collection of official documents on San Juan Imbroglio, 1859-1872. Camp Murray, the National Guard, State of Washington, 1964.
64 p. S720A

U.S. Public Health Service
Indians on federal reservations in the United States: a digest. Portland area: Idaho, Oregon, Washington. June, 1958.
ix, 41 p. illus. S721

Utley, Robert M
Frontiersmen in blue: the United States Army and the Indian: 1848-1865. New York, Macmillan, 1967.
384 p. illus. S722

Van Every, Dale
The frontier people. New York, Wm. Morrow, 1965.
4 vols. S723

Van Orman, Richard A
A room for the night: hotels of the old West. Bloomington, Indiana University Press, 1966.
162 p. S724

Vaughan, Thomas, 1924-
Space, style and structure: building in northwest America. Portland, Or., Oregon Historical Society, 1974.
2 vols. illus. S725

Vaughn, Jesse Wendell
Indian fights: new facts on seven encounters. Norman, University of Oklahoma Press, 1966.
250 p. S726

Vestal, Stanley, 1887-
Joe Meek: the merry mountain man, a biography. Caldwell, Idaho, Caxton Printers, 1952.
336 p. illus. S727

Von Richthofen, Walter Baron
The Spanish toponyms of the British Columbia coast with side glances at those in the states of Washington, Oregon and Alaska. Winnipeg, Manitoba, Ukrainian Free Academy of Sciences, 1963.
24 p. S728

The voyage of the Racoon: a 'secret' journal of a visit to Oregon, California and Hawaii, 1813-1814. Edited with introduction and notes by John A. Hussey, drawings by Henry Rusk. San Francisco, The Book Club of California, 1958.
xxvii, 36 p. illus. S729

Wagner, Henry Raup
Spanish voyages to the northwest coast of America in the sixteenth century. Amsterdam, N. Israel, 1966. Reprint of the California Historical Society, 1929.
571 p. maps. S730

Walker, Deward E., Jr.
Conflict and schism in Nez Perce acculturation, a study in religion and politics. Pullman, Wash., Washington State University, 1968. S731

Walkington, Frances Ethlyn (Lindley)
Journey through a century. Twin Falls, Standard, c1966.
119 p. illus. S732

Wall, Brian R
Log production in Washington and Oregon: an historical perspective. Portland, Or., Pacific Northwest Forest and Range Experiment Station, 1972.
89 p. illus. S733

Wardwell, Allen and Lois Lebov
Annotated bibliography of Northwest coast Indian art. New York Museum of Primitive Art, 1970
25 p. S734

Warren, Sidney, 1916-
Farthest frontier: the Pacific Northwest. New York, Macmillan Co., 1949.
ix, 375 p. S735

Washington (State) Department of Commerce and Economic Development
Water transportation in the Pacific Northwest. Olympia, Wash., Department of Commerce and Economic Development, 1959.
67 p. tables. S736

Washington State Historical Society, Tacoma
Northwest forts and trading posts. With introduction and notes by Bruce LeRoy. Tacoma, 1968.
36 p. illus. S737

Washington State Historical Society, Tacoma
Northwest history in art, 1778-1963. Tacoma, 1963.
38 p. illus. S738

Washington State University, Music Department
Nez Perce songs of historical significance, as sung by "Sol" Webb. Pullman, Wash., 1971. S739

Washington State University, Library
The dictionary catalog of the Pacific Northwest collection. Boston, Mass., G.K. Hall, 1972.
6 vols. S740

Water Resources Scientific Information Center
A selected annotated bibliography on Columbia and Snake Rivers. Olympia, Wash., Washington Dept. of Ecology, 1973.
357 p. S741

Waterfield, Donald C
Continental waterboy: the Columbia River controversy. Toronto, Clarke, Irwin, 1970.
maps. S742

Weatherford, Mark Vern, 1886-
Bannack - Piute war, the campaign and battles. Corvallis, Or., Lehnert Printing Co., 1957.
93 p. S743

Weatherford, Mark V
Chief Joseph: his battles, his retreat. 2nd ed. Corvallis, Lehnert Printing Co., 1958.
127 p. S744

Webb, Todd
The gold rush trail and the road to Oregon. Garden City, N.Y., Doubleday, 1963.
224 p. illus. S745

Webber, Ebbert T
Beachcombing for driftwood, for glass floats, for agates, for fun. Fairfield, Wash., Ye Galleon Press, 1973.
35 p. illus. S746

Webber, Ebbert T
Retaliation: Japanese attacks and Allied counter-measures on the Pacific coast in World War II. Corvallis, Or., Oregon State University Press, 1975.
178 p. illus. S747

Weis, G
Stock raising in the Northwest, 1884. "Notes recueillies sur les elevages d'animaux dans les etats de l'Ouest de l'Amerique du Nord," translated by Herbert O. Brayer. Evanston, Ill., Branding Iron Press, 1951.
xii, 24 p. illus. S748

Weis, Norman D
Ghost towns of the Northwest. Caldwell, Idaho, Caxton Printers, 1971.
319 p. illus. S749

Weisel, George F., ed.
Men and trade on the Northwest frontier as shown by the Fort Owen ledger. Edited with an introduction by George F. Weisel. Missoula, Mont., Montana State University Press, 1955.
xxxix, 291 p. illus. S750

West, Leoti L., 1851-
The wide Northwest historic narrative of America's wonderland as seen by a pioneer teacher. Spokane, Wash., Shaw and Borden Co., 1927.
viii, 9-286 p. plates. S751

The Western shore: Oregon country essays honoring the American Revolution. Edited by Thomas Baughan. Portland, Or., Oregon Historical Society, 1975?
367 p. illus. S752

Weyerhaeuser Company
Weyerhaeuser company history. Tacoma, Wash., 1974.
51 p. illus. S753

Wheat, Carl I
Mapping the trans-Mississippi West: 1540-1861. San Francisco, Institute of Historical Cartography. 1957-63.
5 vols in 6 maps. S754

Wherry, Joseph H
Indian masks and myths of the West. New York, Funk and Wagnalls, 1969.
273 p. illus. S755

Wherry, Joseph H
The totem pole Indians. New York, Wilfred Funk, Inc., 1964.
152 p. S756

White, Helen (McCann), ed.
Ho! for the gold fields: northern overland wagon trains of the 1860's. St. Paul, Minnesota Historical Society, 1966.
viii, 289 p. illus. S757

White, Thomas, 1796-1869
To Oregon in 1853: letter of Dr. Thomas White. Edited by Oscar O. Winther and Gayle Thornbrough. Indianapolis, Indiana Historical Society, 1964.
37 p. S758

Who's who among Pacific Northwest authors. 2nd ed. Edited with a preface by Francis Wright. Missoula, Mont., PNLA Reference Division, 1970.
105 p. S759

Wight, E.L.
Indian reservations of Idaho, Oregon and Washington. Compiled by E.L. Wight (et al.) Portland, Or., U.S. Dept of the Interior, Bureau of Indian Affairs, 1960.
97 p. S760

Wiley, Leonard
The granite boulder: a biography of Frederic Homer Balch, author of The bridge of the gods. Portland, Or., 1970.
146 p. illus. ports. S761

Wilkes, Charles, 1798-1877
Life in Oregon country before the emigration. Edited by Richard E. Moore. Ashland, Or., Oregon Book Society, 1974-75.
2 vols. illus. S762

Williams, Richard Lippincott
The Cascades. New York, Time-Life Books, 1974.
184 p. illus. S763

Williams, Richard Lippincott
The Northwest coast. New York, Time-Life Books, 1973.
184 p. illus. S764

Wilson, Sir Charles William, 1836-1905
Mapping the frontier: Charles Wilson's diary of the survey of the 49th parallel, 1858-1862. Edited and with an introduction by George F.G. Stanley. Seattle, University of Washington Press, c1970.
182 p. maps. port. S765

Wilson, Elinor, 1914-
Jim Beckwourth: black mountain man and war chief of the Crows. Norman, University of Oklahoma Press, 1972.
248 p. illus. S766

Wilson, Eugene Tallmadge
Hawks and doves in the Nez Perce War of 1877: personal recollections of Eugene Tallmadge Wilson. Helena, Mont., Montana Historical Society, 1966.
20 p. S767

Wilson, James Wood
People in the way: the human aspects of the Columbia River project. Toronto, Buffalo, University of Toronto Press, 1973.
xiv, 200 p. illus. S768

Wiltsey, Norman B
Brave warriors. Caldwell, Idaho, Caxton Printers, 1964.
379 p. illus. S769

Winnett, Thomas and others
The Pacific Crest Trail. Vol. 2: Oregon and Washington, by Jeff Schaffer and others. Berkeley, Calif., Wilderness Press, 1974.
346 p. illus. S770

Winther, Oscar Osburn, 1903-
A classified bibliography of the periodical literature of the trans-Mississippi West, 1811-1957. Bloomington, Indiana University Press, 1961.
626 p. S771

Winther, Oscar Osburn
The great Northwest: a history. 2nd ed., rev. and enl. New York, Knopf, 1950.
xviii, 491 p. illus. maps. S772

Winther, Oscar Osburn,
The old Oregon country: a history of frontier trade, transportation and travel. Bloomington, Indiana University Press, 1950.
xvi, 348 p. plates. maps. S773

Wister, Owen
Owen Wister out West: his journals and letters. Edited by Fanny Kemble Wister. Chicago, University of Chicago Press, 1958.
269 p. illus. pl. S774

Wong, Karen C
Chinese history in the Pacific Northwest. 1st ed. n.p., c1972.
137 p. S775

Wood, Amos L
Beachcombing for Japanese glass-floats. Portland, Or., Binfords & Mort, 1965.
221 p.
Also: 2nd ed., 1971, 228 p. S776

Woods, Charles Raymond
Lines West: a pictorial history of the Great Northern Railway operations and motive power from 1887 to 1967. Seattle, Superior Publishing Co., 1967.
192 p. illus. S777

Wood, Charles Raymond
Northern Pacific, main street of the West. Seattle, Wash., Superior Publishing Co., 1968.
208 p. S778

Wood, Charles Raymond and Dorothy Wood
Spokane, Portland and Seattle Railway: the Northwest's own railway. Seattle, Wash., Superior Publishing Co., 1974.
159 p. illus. S779

Wood, Erskine
Days with Chief Joseph. Portland, Or., Oregon Historical Society, 1970 S780

Woodcock, George, 1912-
Ravens and prophets: an account of journeys in British Columbia, Alberta and southern Alaska. London, A Wingate, 1952.
244 p. illus. S781

Worcester, Donald Emmett, 1915-
Forked tongues and broken treaties, edited by Donald E. Worcester. Caldwell, Idaho, Caxton Printers, 1975.
xxi, 470 p. illus. S782

Work, John
The Snake country expedition of 1830-31: John Work's field journal. Edited by Francis D. Haines, Jr., Norman, Oklahoma, University of Oklahoma Press, 1971.
172 p. illus. S783

Wyeth, Nathaniel Jarvis
The journals of Captain Nathaniel J. Wyeth, with the Wyeth monograph on Pacific Northwest Indians appended. Fairfield, Wash., Ye Galleon Press, 1969.
131 p. S784

Yale University, Library
Yale collection of western Americana. A catalogue of the Frederick W. and Carrie S. Beinecke collection of western Americana. Boston, G.K. Hall, 1962.
4 vols. S785

Yarber, Esther
Land of the yankee fork by Esther Yarber, with the assistance of Edna and Arthur "Tuff" McGown. Denver, Sage Books, 1963.
207 p. illus. S786

Yocum, Charles Frederick
Pacific coastal wildlife region by Charles Yocum and Raymond Dasman. San Martin, Calif., Naturegraph Co., 1957.
112 p. illus. S787

Young, Bob, 1916-
"54-40 or fight": the story of the Oregon territory by Bob and Jan Young. Maps and drawings by Barry Martin. New York, Messmer Books, 1967.
190 p. illus. S788

Young, Nellie May
An Oregon idyl: a tale of a transcontinental journey, and life in Oregon in 1883-84, based on the diary of Janete Lewis Young. Glendale, Calif., A.H. Clark Co., 1961.
111 p. illus. S789

Zim, Herbert Spencer
The Pacific Northwest: a guide to the evergreen playground by Herbert S. Zim and Natt N. Dodge. New York, Golden Press, 1959.
159 p. illus.
Also: 1962 ed., 160 p. S790

ALASKA

Compiled by Marvin W. Falk,
University of Alaska

Ackerman, Maria
Tlingit stories. Anchorage, Alaska Methodist University Press, 1975.
94 p. illus. S791

Ackerman, Robert E
Prehistory in the Kushokwim-Bristol bay region, southwestern Alaska: a final report to the Arctic Institute of North America. Pullman, Wash., Laboratory of Anthropology, Washington State University, 1964.
iv, 48 p. illus. tables. S792

Adams, Andy
Alaska ghost glacier mystery. New York, Grosset & Dunlap, 1961.
175 p. illus. S793

Adams, Ben
Alaska: the big land. New York, Hill and Wang, 1959.
213 p. illus. S794

Adams, Ben.
The last frontier, a short history of Alaska. New York, Hill and Wang, 1961.
181 p. illus. S795

Adelman, Morris Albert and others
Alaskan oil: costs and supply. New York, Praeger Publishers, 1971.
127 p. S796

Alaska. Industrial Development Division
Alaska statistical review, 1970. Prepared by John R. Snodgrass, Jr. for Industrial Development Division, 1970. Juneau, 1970.
vi, 246 p. tables. maps. S797

Alaska, Ed. by Dorothy Krell
Menlo Park, Calif., Lane Magazine and Book Co., 1974.
207 p. illus. S798

The Alaska book: the story of our northern treasureland. Chicago, Ill., J.G. Ferguson Co., 1960.
320 p. illus. S799

Alaska hunting guide, by the editors of Alaska Magazine. Anchorage, Alaska Northwest Publishing Co., 1973.
170 p. illus. S800

Alaska Library Association
Songs and legends. Juneau, 1974.
1 vol. (Alaska Library Network Cassette Catalog). S801

Alaska Magazine
A boater's guide to the upper Yukon River: Carcross, Yukon to Fort Yukon, Alaska. Anchorage, Alaska Northwest Publishing Co., 1975.
66 p illus. S802

Alaska Native Foundation
Higher and adult education needs in rural Alaska. Anchorage, 1974.
76 p. S803

The Alaska sportsman
Blood on the arctic snow and seventeen other true tales of far north adventure from the Alaska sportsman: illustrated with photos and original drawings. Compiled and edited by B.G. Olson and Mike Miller. (Adventurers 1st ed.) Seattle, Superior Publishing Co., 1956.
279 p. illus. S804

Alaska Travel Publications.
Exploring Katmai National Monument and the Valley of Ten Thousand Smokes. Anchorage, 1974.
276 p. illus. S805

Alaska. Vast land on the edge of the Arctic, by Heinrich Gohl and others. Translated by Ewald Osers. Berne, Kummerly & Frey Geographic Publishers; Chicago, McNally, 1970.
140 p. illus S806

Alaska-Yukon favorites: three by Service, three by Beck. Seattle, Wash., Golden Nugget, 1970.
32 p. illus. S807

The Alaska-Yukon wild flowers guide from the editorial staff of Alaska Magazine. Anchorage, Alaska Northwest Publishing Co., 1974.
218 p. illus. S808

Alaskan Arctic tundra: proceedings of the 25th anniversary celebration of the Naval Arctic Research Laboratory. Edited by Max E. Britton. Technical editor, Wade W. Gunn. Washington, Arctic Institute of North America, 1973.
224 p. illus. S809

Alaskan science conference
Science in Alaska, proceedings of the 20th conference, College, August 24-27, 1969. New York, American Association for the Advancement of Science, 1970.
425 p. S810

Aldridge, James
A captive in the land. 1st ed. in the U.S.A. Garden City, N.Y., Doubleday, 1963.
381 p. S811

Allen, Lawrence J
The trans-Alaska pipeline: the beginning. Vol. 1. Seattle, Wash., Scribe Publishing Co., 1975.
151 p. illus. S812

Alliance in Eskimo society
Edited by Lee Guemple. Seattle, American Ethnological Society: distributed by the University of Washington Press, 1972.(Proceedings of the American Ethnological Society, 1971. Suppl.)
131 p. illus. S813

Ameigh, George C
Alaska's Kodiak Island: a camera report of life at Kodiak, Alaska by George C. Ameigh, Jr., and Yule M. Chaffin and others. Anchorage, 1962.
163 p. illus. S814

American Association of University Women
Alaskana study group. Anchorage branch. Native peoples of Alaska. Anchorage, 1973.
16 p. illus. S815

Anchorage Historical and Fine Arts Museum
An introduction to the native art of Alaska. Anchorage, 1972.
84 p. illus. S816

Andersen, Doris
Ways harsh and wild. Vancouver, J.J. Douglas, 1973.
239 p. illus. S817

Anderson, J.W., 1893-
Fur trader's story. 1961. S818

Anderson, Jacob Peter
Anderson's flora of Alaska and adjacent parts of Canada. Provo, Utah, Brigham Young University Press, 1974.
724 p. illus. S819

Andreev, Aleksandr Ignat'evich, 1887- ed.
Russian discoveries in the Pacific and in North America in the eighteenth and nineteenth centuries; a collection of materials. Translated from the Russian by Carl Ginsburg. Ann Arbor, Mich., published for American Council of Learned Societies by J.W. Edwards, 1952.(Russian translation Project series, 13).
214 p. S820

Andrews, Clarence Leroy, 1862-
The story of Alaska. Caldwell, Idaho, Caxton Printers, 1953.
303 p. ports. maps. S821

Annabel, Russell
Alaska tales. New York, A.S. Barnes, 1953.
137 p. S822

Anzer, Richard C
Klondike gold rush. N.Y., Pageant Press, Inc., 1959.
236 p. S823

Appel, Benjamin, 1907-
We were there in the Klondike gold rush. Historical consultant, Henry W. Clark. Illustrated by Irv Docktor. New York, Grosset & Dunlap, 1956. (We were there books, 6).
175 p. illus. S824

Appleton, Richard
The outlook: Alaska natives and their careers. Photos by Bob Koweluk, text by Richard Appleton. Anchorage, AMU Press, 1975.
76 p. illus. S825

Arnold, Winton C
Native land claims in Alaska. Anchorage, Alaska, 1967.
xviii, 78, 42 p. S826

Attla, George
Everything I know about training and racing sled dogs, by George Attla with Bella Levorsen. Novato, Calif., B. Levorsen, c1972.
181 p. illus. S827

Atwood, Evangeline
Anchorage: all-American city. Portland, Or., Binfords & Mort, 1957.
118 p. illus. S828

Atwood, Evangeline
We shall be remembered. 1st ed. Anchorage, Alaska Methodist University Press, 1966.
viii, 191 p. illus. S829

Atwood, George H
Along the Alcan. New York, Pageant Press, 1960.
212 p. S830

Bailey, Alfred Marshall, 1894-
Field work of a museum naturalist, 1919-1922, by Alfred M. Bailey. Denver, Denver Museum of Natural History, 1971. (Museum pictorial no. 22).
192 p. illus. S831

Balcom, Mary Gilmore
The Catholic church in Alaska. Chicago, Ill., Adams Press, 1970.
150 p. S832

Balcom, Mary Gilmore
Creek street. Chicago, Ill., Adams Press, 1963.
116 p. illus. port. S833

Balcom, Mary Gilmore
Ghost towns of Alaska. Centennial ed. Chicago, Ill., Adams Press, 1966.
vii, 80 p. illus. S834

Balcom, Mary Gilmore
Ketchikan, Alaska's totemland. 3rd. ed. Chicago, Adams Press, 1974, c1961
139 p. illus. S835

Ball, John Dudley, 1911-
Arctic showdown: an Alaskan adventure. New York, Duell, Sloan and Pearce, 1966.
147 p. illus. S836

Bandi, Han Georg
Eskimo prehistory. College, University of Alaska Press, 1969.
S837

Bank, Ted
Birthplace of the winds. New York, Crowell, 1956.
274 p. illus. S838

Bank, Ted
People of the Bering Sea. New York, MSS Educational Publishing Co., 1971.
101 p. illus. S839

Bank, Ted
Readings in anthropology: people of the Bering Sea, by Ted Bank, II. New York, MSS Educational Publishing Co., c1971.
101 p. illus. S840

Barber, Olive
Meet me in Juneau. 1st ed. Portland, Or., Binfords & Mort, 1960.
175 p. illus. S841

Barlow, Roger
Secret mission to Alaska. New York, Grosset & Dunlap, 1966, c1959.
158 p. S842

Barrow, Henry D
Paradise north: an Alaskan year. With drawings by Susan Barrow. New York, Dial Press, 1956.
242 p. illus. S843

Barry, Mary Jane
A history of mining on the Kenai Peninsula. Anchorage, Alaska Northwest Publishing Co., 1973.
ix, 214 p. illus. S844

Barry, Mary Jane
The Samovar, its history and use. Anchorage, 1971. S845

Beattie, William Gilbert
Marsden of Alaska, a modern Indian, minister, missionary, musician, engineer, pilot, boat builder, and church builder. New York, Vantage Press, 1955.
246 p. illus. S846

Beaver, C. Masten
Fort Yukon trader: three years in an Alaskan wilderness. 1st ed. New York, Exposition Press, 1955.
185 p. illus. S847

Becker, Ethel Anderson
Klondike '98: Hegg's album of the 1898 Alaska gold rush. Portland, Or., Binfords & Mort, 1949.
127 p. illus. ports. S848

Becker, Ethel Anderson
A treasury of Alaskana. Seattle, Wash., Superior Publishing Co., 1969.
183 p. S849

Bell, Margaret E
Touched with fire: Alaska's George William Steller. New York, William Morrow and Co., 1960.
189 p. S850

Bensin, Basil M
Russian Orthodox church in Alaska 1794-1967: special publication for the centennial celebration of the purchase of Alaska by the United States from the Russian Empire in 1867. Sitka, Russian Orthodox Greek Catholic Church of North America, Diocese of Alaska.
80 p. illus. S851

Berkh, Vasilii Nikolaevich
A chronological history of the discovery of the Aleutian Islands, or the exploits of Russian merchants: with a supplement of historical data on the fur trade. Kingston, Ontario, The Limestone Press, 1974. (Materials for the study of Alaska history, 5).
127 p. illus. S852

Berrier, Jean Claude
Alaska: splendeur sauvage. Texte de Jean-Claude Berrier. Photos de Jean-Claude Berrier assiste de Chantal Berrier et Jean-Michel Perche. Paris, F. Nathan, 1970.
156 p. illus. S853

Berrill, Jacquelyn
Wonders of the Arctic. Illustrated by the author. New York, Dodd, Mead, 1959.
94 p. illus. S854

Berry, Mary Clay.
The Alaska pipeline: the politics of oil and native land claims. Bloomington, Ind., Indiana University Press, 1975.
302 p. illus. S855

Berto, Hazel Dunaway
North to Alaska's shining river. 1st ed. Indianapolis, Bobbs-Merrill, 1959.
224 p. S856

Berton, Pierre, 1920-
A Klondike bibliography. Kleinsburg, Ont., 1958.
23 p. S857

Berton, Pierre,
Klondike fever: the life and death of the last great gold rush. Knopf, 1958.
457 p. maps. S858

Berton, Pierre
Klondike: the last great gold rush, 1896-1899. Rev. ed. Toronto, McClelland and Stewart, 1972.
xxiii, 472 p. illus. S859

Bleeker, Sonia
The Eskimo: Arctic hunters and trappers. Illustrated by Patricia Boodell. New York, Morrow, 1959.
160 p. illus. S860

Bloedel, Richard Henry
The Alaska statehood movement. Ann Arbor, Mich., Xerox University Microfilms, 1975. (A doctoral dissertation at the University of Washington, Seattle.)
723 p. S861

A boater's guide to the upper Yukon River: Carcross, Yukon to Fort Yukon, Alaska, from the editors of Alaska magazine, with special editorial assistance from Iris Warner, (et al.). Anchorage, Alaska Northwest Publishing Co., 1975.
ix, 66 p. illus. S862

Boehm, William D
Glacier Bay. Anchorage, Alaska Northwest Publishing Co., 1975.
134 p. illus. S863

Bohn, Dave
Glacier Bay, the land and the silence. Photos and text by Dave Bohn. Edited by David Brower. San Francisco, Sierra Club, 1967.
165 p. illus. ports. S864

Borigo, Edna
Sourdough schoolma'am. Chicago, Adams Press, 1969.
149 p. S865

Bosco, Antoinette
Charles John Seghers, pioneer in Alaska. New York, P.J. Kenedy, 1960. (American background books, 16).
190 p. illus. S866

Bowers, Shirley
The Petersburg velkommen book: Alaska's little Norway. Designed and illustrated by A.W. Higgins. Juneau, Alaska Litho, 1972.
21 p. S867

Breakthrough to tomorrow: Anchorage 1969-1989. Anchorage, 1969-1970.
S868

Brean, Alice
Athabascan stories. Anchorage, AMU Press, 1975.
79 p. illus. S868A

Breynat, Gabriel Joseph Elie, 1867-1954.
Bishop of the winds: fifty years in the Arctic regions. Translated from the French by Alan Gordon Smith. New York, Kenedy, 1955.
266 p. illus. S689

Briggs, Jean L
Never in anger: a portrait of an Eskimo family. Cambridge, Harvard University Press, 1970.
379 p. S870

Bright, Elizabeth (Parks)
Alaska, treasure trove of tomorrow: the story of the discovery, exploration, settlement, geography, people and towns, wildlife, industry and future of America's frozen asset. 1st ed. New York, Exposition Press, 1956.
203 p. S871

Brindze, Ruth, 1903-
The story of the totem pole. Illustrated by Yeffe Kinball. New York, Vanguard Press, 1951.
62 p. illus. S872

Brink, Frank
Cry of the wild ram. Kodiak, Kodiak Baranof Productions, 1973.
20 p. illus. S873

Brinsmade, Ellen M
Books on Alaska for young people: annotated bibliography. Fairbanks, Alder's Bookshop, 1962.
23 p. S874

Brooks, Alfred Hulse
Blazing Alaska's trails. Fairbanks, University of Alaska Press, 1973. (Originally issued in 1953).
567 p. illus. S875

Brooks, Paul
Roadless area. Drawings by the author. 1st ed. New York, Knopf, 1964.
xiii, 259 p. illus. S876

Brosted, Jens
Ulgunik: a report on integration and village organization in Alaska by Jens Brosted. Translated and typed by James Heimann. Copenhagen, c1975.
201 p. illus. S877

Brower, Kenneth
Earth and the great weather: the Brooks range. San Francisco, Calif., Friends of the Earth, 1971.
188 p. illus. S878

Brown, Angeline M
Alaska's fur home sewing guide Anchorage, Golden Mammoth Enterprises, 1971. Rev. ed.
79 p. illus. S879

Brown, C.M.
Aids to navigation in Alaska history. Anchorage, Alaska Division of Parks, 1974. (History and archaeology series, 7).
57 p. illus. S880

Brown, Dale
Wild Alaska. New York, Time-Life Books, 1972.
184 p. illus. S881

Brown, Emily Ivanoff
Eskimo legend of Kotzebue: ongilug' nylok, n.p., 1959.
18 p. illus. ports. S882

Brown, Emily Ivanoff
Grandfather of Unalakleet: the lineage of Alluyagnak, by Ticasuk (Emily Ivanoff Brown). 2nd ed. Fairbanks, Eskimo Indian Aleut Printing Co., 1974.
220 p. illus. tables. S883

Brown, Tom
Oil on ice: Alaskan wilderness at the crossroads. San Francisco, Calif., Sierra Club, 1971.
159 p. S884

Browne, Belmore, 1880-
The conquest of Mt. McKinley. Illustrated by Belmore Browne and Bradford Washburn. New ed. Boston, Houghton Mifflin, 1956.
381 p. illus. S885

Bruemmer, Fred
The Arctic. Photography and text by Fred Bruemmer. New York, Quadrangle New York Times Book Co., 1974.
208 p. illus. S886

Burch, Ernest S., 1938-
Eskimo kinsmen: changing family relationships in northwest Alaska. St. Paul, West Publishing Co., 1975.
xiii, 352 p. illus. S887

Burdick, Loraine
Alaskettes, Alaskan lore and crafts for children. Boulder, Colo., Johnson Publishing Co., 1967.
176 p. illus. S888

Burford, Virgil
North to danger, by Virgil Burford as told to Walt Morey. New York, J. Day Co., 1954.
254 p. illus. S889

Burke, Clara
Doctor Hap. New York, Coward-McCann, 1961.
319 p. S890

Burke, Joseph A
Picture Alaska: an index. 2nd ed. Fairbanks, Elmer E. Rasmuson Library, University of Alaska, 1974.
206 p. S891

Burnett, William Riley
The goldseekers. New York, Doubleday, 1962.
282 p. S892

Burroughs, Polly
The great ice ship Bear. New York, Van Nostrand Reinhold Co., 1970.
104 p. S893

Bush, Hal
Alaska travel handbook. Algonac, Mich.?, 1974.
155 p. map. S894

Butler, Evelyn I
Alaska, the land and the people, by Evelyn I. Butler and George A. Dale. Illustrated with photos. New York, Viking Press, 1957.
159 p. illus. S895

Campbell, John Martin, 1927-
Archaeological studies along the proposed trans-Alaska oil pipeline route. Washington, Arctic Institute of North America, 1973.
24 p. illus. S896

Campbell, Nola H
Talkeetna cronies. Anchorage, Color Art Printing Co., 1974.
72 p. illus. S897

Canonization of Saint Herman of Alaska. Kodiak, Alaska, 9 August, 1970 A.D. Sitka, Bishop Innocent Diocesan Press, 1972.
84 p. illus. S898

Cantin, Eugene, 1944-
Yukon summer. 1st ed. San Francisco, Chronicle Books, 1973.
ix, 198 p. illus. S899

Caras, Roger A
Monarch of Deadman Bay: the life and death of a Kodiak bear. Boston, Mass., Little, Brown and Co., 1969.
185 p. S900

Carey, Mary Latch
Alaska, not for a woman. Boston, Branden Press, c1975.
259 p. illus. S901

Carlson, Gerald F
Two on the rocks. New York, McKay, 1966.
xii, 193 p. illus. ports. S902

Carlson, William Samuel, 1905-
Lifelines through the Arctic. 1st ed. New York, Duell, Sloan and Pearce, 1962.
271 p. illus. S903

Carpenter, John Allan, 1917-
Alaska, from its glorious past to the present. Illustrated by Roger Herrington. Chicago, Childrens Press, 1965.
95 p. illus. S904

Carrighar, Sally
Icebound summer. Illustrated by Henry B. Kane. 1st ed. New York, Knopf, 1953.
262 p. illus. S905

Carrighar, Sally
Moonlight at midday. 1st ed. New York, Knopf, 1958.
392 p. illus. S906

Carrighar, Sally
Wild voice of the north. Garden City, N.Y., Doubleday, 1959.
191 p. illus. S907

Carroll, James A
The first ten years in Alaska: memoirs of a Fort Yukon trapper, 1911-1922. 1st ed. New York, Exposition Press, 1957.
120 p. illus. S908

Cashen, William R
Farthest north college president: Charles E. Bunnell and the early history of the University of Alaska. Fairbanks, University of Alaska Press, 1972.
387 p. S909

Caswell, John Edwards
Arctic frontiers: United States explorations in the far north. 1st ed. Norman, University of Oklahoma Press, 1956.
232 p. illus. S910

Cavagnol, Joseph J
Postmarked Alaska: a saga of the early Alaska mails. Holton, Kan., Gossio Printery, 1957.
105 p. illus. S911

Cease, Ronald C., comp.
The metropolitan experiment in Alaska: a study of borough government. Edited by Ronald Cease and Jerome R. Saroff. New York, Praeger, 1968.
xx, 449 p. map. S912

Chaffin, Yule M
Koniag to king crab: Alaska's southwest. Kodiak from sea otter settlement to king crab capitol: history of hunting and fishing industries, island villages and scenic beauty. Illustrated by Donald R. Pfrimmer. Anchorage, Chaffin, 1967
vii, 247 p. illus. S913

Chambers, John R
Arctic bush mission: the experiences of a missionary bush pilot in the far north. Seattle, Superior Publishing Co., 1970.
174 p. illus. ports. S914

Champness, W
To Cariboo and back in 1862. Fairfield, Wash., Ye Galleon Press, 1972.
106 p. illus. S915

Chance, Norman Allee, 1927-
The Eskimo of north Alaska. New York, Holt, Rinehart and Winston, 1966.
xii, 107 p. illus. S916

Chandler, Edna Walker
Pioneer of Alaska skies: the story of Ben Eielson by Edna Walker Chandler and Barrett Willoughby. Illustrated by Ray Quigley. Boston, Ginn, 1959.
179 p. illus. S917

Chasan, Daniel Jack
Klondike seventy: the Alaskan oil boom. New York, Praeger Publishers, 1971.
184 p. illus. S918

Chase, William Henry, 1874-
Pioneers of Alaska, the trail blazers of bygone days. Kansas City, Mo., Burton Publishing Co., 1951.
203 p. illus. S919

Cheney, T.A.
Land of the hibernating rivers: life in the Arctic. Illustrated with photos. New York, Harcourt, Brace and World, 1968.
121 p. illus. S920

Chevigny, Hector, 1904-
Lord of Alaska: Baranov and the Russian adventure. Portland, Or., Binfords & Mort, 1951. S921

Chevigny, Hector,
Russian America: the great Alaskan venture, 1741-1867. New York, Viking Press, 1965.
x, 274 p. maps. S921A

Chronology and documentary handbook of the State of Alaska. Dobbs Ferry, N.Y., Oceana Pub., 1972.
112 p. S922

Chugach Gem and Mineral Society, Inc.
Guide book for rockhounds. 2nd ed. Anchorage, 1970.
35 p. S923

Clark, Donald W. and Frederick A. Milan.
Contributions to the later prehistory of Kodiak Island, Alaska. Ottawa, Ont., National Museums of Canada, 1974. (Archaeological Survey of Canada papers, 20).
181 p. illus. S924

Clarke, Tom E
Alaska challenge. New York, Lothrop, Lee & Shepard Co., 1959.
222 p. S925

Clarke, Tom E
Back to Anchorage. New York, Lothrop, Lee & Shepard, 1961.
224 p. S926

Clarke, Tom E
The puddle jumper: the adventures of a young flyer in Alaska. N.Y., Lothrop, Lee & Shepard, 1960.
191 p. S927

Clifford, Howard
The Skagway story: a history of Alaska's most famous gold rush town and some of the people who made that history. Anchorage, Alaska Northwest Publishing Co., 1975.
vii, 167 p. illus. S928

Cline, Michael S
Tannik school: the impact of education on the Eskimos of Anaktuvuk Pass. Anchorage, Alaska Methodist University Press, 1975.
210 p. illus. S929

Cloutier, David
Spirit, spirit: shaman songs, incantations. Versions by David Cloutier. Providence, R.I., Copper Beech Press, 1973.
89 p. S930

Clymer, Theodore
The travels of Atunga. Illustrated by John Schoenherr. Boston, Little, Brown Co., 1973.
31 p. illus. S931

Coalson, Glo
Three stone woman. New York, Atheneum, 1971.
unp. col. illus. S932

Coffey, Leora (Stephenson)
Wilds of Alaska big-game hunting. With line drawings and photos by the author. Pref. by Carl Ristvedt. New York, Vantage Press, 1963.
172 p. illus. S933

Collier, John
Alaskan Eskimo education: a film analysis of cultural confrontation in the schools. New York, Holt, Rinehart and Winston, 1973.
130 p. illus. S934

Comins, Jeremy
Eskimo crafts and their cultural backgrounds. New York, Lothrop, Lee & Shepard Co., 1975.
125 p. illus. S935

Conference on Alaskan history, Alaska Methodist University, 1967. Proceedings of the conference on Alaskan history. Sponsored by the National Endowment for the Humanities. Anchorage, Alaska Methodist University Press, 1968.
172 p. illus. S936

The Cook Inlet collection: two hundred years of selected Alaskan history. Edited by Morgan Sherwood. Illustrated by Diana Tillion. Anchorage: Alaska Northwest Publishing Co., c1974.
xii, 222 p. map. S937

Cook Inlet Native Association historic sites project. Cook Inlet region inventory of native historic sites and cemeteries. Anchorage, 1975.
174 p. illus. S938

Cooley, Richard A
Land policy and the future of Alaska. Juneau, Alaska Research Center, 1965.
iii, 164 leaves. map S939

Cooley, Richard A
Alaska: a challenge in conservation. Madison, University of Wisconsin Press, 1966.
xv, 170 p. illus. S940

Cooley, Richard A
Politics and conservation: the decline of the Alaska salmon. New York, Harper & Row, 1963.
xxi, 230 p. illus. S941

Coombs, Charles Ira, 1914-
Alaska bush pilot. Illustrated by Raymon Naylor. Maps by Paul Hazelrigg. Evanston, Ill., Harper & Row, 1963.
256 p. illus. S942

Coombs, Charles Ira
Bush flying in Alaska. Illustrated by Morgan Henninger. New York, Morrow, 1961.
93 p. illus. S943

Cooney, Edith
Alaskamo. Yakima, Wash., Franklin Press, 1966.
iv, 149 p. port. S944

Cooper, Bryan
Alaska: the last frontier. New York, Morrow, 1973.
248 p. illus. S945

Copland, Dudley, 1901-
Livingstone of the Arctic. With a foreword by A.Y. Jackson. Ottawa, The author, 1967.
183 p. illus. S946

Corey, Audrey Leona
White angel of the trails. New York, Carlton Press, 1968.
99 p. S947

Cosgrove, Stephen
The gnome from Nome. Bothel, Wash., Serendipity Press, 1974.
unp. illus. S948

Couch, James S
Philately below zero: a postal history of Alaska. State College, Pa., American Philatelic Society, 1957.
81 p. illus. S949

Crisler, Lois
Arctic wild. New York, Harper & Row, 1973.
301 p. illus. S950

Crisp, William George
Trial by ice. Illustrated by Angus Macdonald. 1st ed. Toronto, Longmans, Green, 1961.
140 p. illus. S951

Croft, Toni and Phyllice Bradner
Touring Juneau: a collection of old time and modern photos, maps and bits and pieces of Juneau history. n.p., 1973.
32 p. illus. S952

Cross, Cliff
Alaska. Photos and most maps by the author. 1969-70 ed. North Palm Springs, Calif., 1969.
170 p. illus. S953

Crowe, George R
Plan-a-flight to Alaska: a complete flight guide to the famous Alaska highway, by George R. Crowe and Deloris Dee Crowe. Anchorage, Plan-A-Flight Publications, 1968.
113 p. illus. S954

Curtis, Jack
The kloochman: a novel. New York, Simon and Schuster, 1966.
286 p. S955

Curwood, James Oliver, 1878-1927
Nomads of the north: a story of romance and adventure under the open stars. Front: Charles Livingston Bull. New York, published by Doubleday, Page for P.F. Collier, 1925. (St. Clair Shores, Mich., Scholarly Press, 1972.)
318 p. S956

Damjan, Mischa, (pseud.)
Atuk. Pictures by Gian Casty. New York, Pantheon Books, 1966, c1964.
1 vol. unpaged illus. S957

Davidson, Art
Minus 148°. New York, Norton, 1969.
218 p. S958

Day, Beth (Feagles), 1924-
Glacier pilot: the story of Bob Reeve and the flyers who pushed back Alaska's air frontiers. New York, Holt, Rinehart & Winston, c1957.
348 p. illus. S959

Day, Stacey B
Tuluak and amaulik: dialogues on death and mourning with the Inuit Eskimo of Point Barrow and Wainwright, Alaska. Minneapolis, University of Minnesota Medical School, c1973.
xv, 176 p. illus. S960

DeArmond, Dale Burlison
Juneau: a book of woodcuts. Anchorage, Alaska Northwest Publishing Co., 1973.
53 p. illus. S961

DeArmond, Dale Burlison
Raven: a book of woodcuts. Anchorage, Alaska Northwest Publishing Co., 1975.
1 vol. illus. S962

De Armond, Robert Neil
The founding of Juneau. Juneau, Alaska, Gastineau Channel Centennial Association, 1967.
xvi, 214 p. illus. ports. S963

De Armond, Robert Neil, ed.
Stroller White: tales of a Klondike newsman. Vancouver, B.C., Mitchell Press, 1969.
182 p. S964

De Hart, Don
All about bears. Boulder, Colo., Johnson Publishing Co., 1971.
93 p. illus. S965

DeHart, Don and Vangie DeHart
A guide to the Yukon River. Cheyenne, Cheyenne Litho Inc., 1971.
47 p. illus. S966

DeHart, Don
Oh for the life of a guide. Boulder, Colo., Johnson Publishing Co., 1971.
116 p. illus. S967

De Laguna, Frederica, 1906-
Chugach prehistory: the archaeology of Prince William Sound, Alaska. Seattle, University of Washington Press, 1956.
xix, 289 p. illus. S968

De Laguna, Frederica
Under Mount Saint Elias: the history and culture of the Yakutat Tlingit. Washington, D.C., Smithsonian Institution, 1972.
3 vols. illus. S969

Denison, Webster
Alaska today, by B.W. Denison and associates. Rev. ed. Caldwell, Idaho, Caxton Printers, 1950.
xiv, 374 p. illus. ports. S970

Destination Juneau: a pictorial presentation of Alaska's capital city. Juneau, Alaskans United, 1964.
45 p. illus. S971

Dillingham High School, Alaskan history class.
The last of yesterday: the history of Dillingham and Nushagak Bay. n.p., 1974.
57 p. illus. S972

Dillingham High School, history and folktales class.
The story knife. Dillingham, 1975.
101 p. illus. S973

Dolch, Edward William, 1889-
Stories from Alaska by Edward W. Dolch and Marguerite P. Dolch. Illustrated by Carl Heldt. Champaign, Ill., Garrard Press, 1961.
168 p. illus. S974

Downes, Anne Miller
Natalia: a novel of old Alaska. Philadelphia, Lippincott, 1960.
286 p. S975

Dragon, Antonio, 1882-
Enseveli dans les neiges, le Pere Jules Jette. Montreal, Editions Bellarmin, 1951.
229 p. illus. S976

Drazan, Joseph.
Picture Alaska: an index. Fairbanks, Elmer E. Rasmuson Library, University of Alaska, 1973.
173 p. S977

Dudley, Bronson
The story of Alaska. Pictures by Charles Waterhouse. New York, Grosset & Dunlap, 1968.
61 p. illus. S978

Dufresne, Frank
My way was north: an Alaskan autobiography. Drawings by Rachel S. Horne. New York, Holt, Rinehart and Winston, 1966.
xiv, 274 p. illus. S979

Dufresne, Frank
No room for bears. With drawings by Rachel S. Horne. New York, Holt Rinehart and Winston, 1965.
252 p. illus. S980

Dumond, D.E.
A summary of archaeology in the Katmai region, southwestern Alaska. Eugene, Or., University of Oregon, Dept. of Anthropology, 1971.
viii, 61 p. illus. S981

Duncan, Tom and others
Alaska place names pronunciation guide. Fairbanks, University of Alaska, Elmer Rasmuson Library, 1975.
29 p. S982

Dunne, Mary Collins
Alaskan summer, illustrated by Elisabeth Grant. London, New York, Abelard - Schuman, 1968.
160 p. illus. S983

Eberhart, Beth
A crew of two. Illustrated by the author. 1st ed. Garden City, N.Y., Doubleday, 1961.
286 p. S984

Ederer, Bernard Francis
Through Alaska's back door. New York, Vantage Press, 1954.
162 p. illus. S985

Educational Research Council of America, Social Science staff.
Communities at home and abroad, Alaska and the Eskimos. Boston, Allyn and Bacon, 1974.
170 p. illus. S986

Eide, Arthur Hansin
Drums of Diomede: the transformation of the Alaska Eskimo. Hollywood, Calif., House-Warven, 1952.
241 p. illus. S987

Eide, Harold
The Alaska adventures of a Norwegian Cheechako: a greenhorn with a gold pan. Anchorage, Alaska Northwest Publishing Co., 1975.
128 p. illus. S988

Ellis, R.E.
What ... no landing field? Haines, Alaska, Chilkat Press, c1969.
50 p. illus. S989

Ellsworth, Lyman R
Guys on ice. New York, D.McKay Co., 1952.
277 p. S990

Ellsworth, Lyman R
Halibut schooner. New York, McKay Co., 1953.
241 p. S991

Elting, Mary, 1909-
The first book of Eskimos, by Benjamin Brewster (pseud.). Pictures by Ursula Koering. New York, F. Watts, 1952.
44 p. illus. S992

Emerson, William Canfield, 1893-
The land of the midnight sun: the story in words and pictures of the Alaska highway, Alaska, the Alaska Indians, and the Alaska Eskimos. Philadelphia, Dorrance, 1956.
179 p. illus. S993

Engle, Eloise Katherine
Earthquake! The story of Alaska's Good Friday disaster. New York, John Day Co., 1966.
217 p. illus. S994

Engstrom, Emil, 1879-
John Engstrom, the last frontiersman. New York, Vantage Press, 1957.
156 p. S995

Epstein, Samuel
The real book about Alaska by Samuel Epstein and Beryl Williams. Rev. ed. New York, Doubleday, 1961.
192 p. illus. S996

Erskine, Wilson Fiske
White water: an Alaskan adventure. New York, Abelard-Schuman, 1960.
256 p. illus. S997

Euller, John
Arctic world. Illustrated with photos and maps. London, New York, Abelard-Schuman, 1958.
142 p. illus. S998

The far north: 2,000 years of American Eskimo and Indian art by Henry B. Collins and others. Washington, National Gallery of Art, 1973.
xxx, 289 p. illus. S999

Fedorova, Svetlana J
The Russian population in Alaska and California, late 18th century - 1867. Translated and edited by Richard A. Pierce and Alton S. Donnelly. Kingston, Ont., Limestone Press, 1973.
376 p. S1000

Fish, Byron, 1909-
Alaska. Photography by Bob and Ira Spring. Text by Byron Fish. 1st ed. Seattle, Superior Publishing Co., 1965.
157 p. illus. S1001

Fish, Byron
Eskimo boy today. Anchorage, Alaska Northwest Publishing Co., 1971.
61 p. illus. S1002

Fitch, Edwin M
The Alaska railroad. Foreword by E.L. Bartlett. New York, Praeger, 1967.
x, 326 p. illus S1003

Foote, Don Charles
Man environment interactions in an Eskimo hunting system by Don Charles Foote and Bryn Greer-Wootten. Montreal, McGill University, 1966.
58 p. S1004

Ford, James Alfred, 1911-
Eskimo prehistory in the vicinity of Point Barrow, Alaska. With an appendix, skeletal remains from the vicinity of Point Barrow, by T.D. Stewart. New York, 1959.
272 p. illus. S1005

Franchere, Ruth
Stampede north. New York, Macmillan, 1969.
218 p. S1006

Frederick, Robert A., ed.
Writing Alaska's history: a guide to research. Vol. 1. Anchorage, Alaska Historical Commission, 1974.
162 p. S1007

Freuchen, Peter
Adventures in the Arctic. New York, J. Messner, 1960.
393 p. illus. S1008

Freuchen, Peter
Book of the Eskimos. Cleveland, World Publishing Co., 1961.
441 p. illus. S1009

Fullerton, Arthur Grey, 1878-1968
Sunset at midnight: autobiography. 1st ed. Portland, Or., Professional Pub. Print., Inc., 1969.
111 p. illus. ports. S1010

Gabrielson, Ira Noel, 1889-
The birds of Alaska, by Ira N. Gabrielson and Frederick C. Lincoln. Full color illustration by Olaus J. Murie and Edwin R. Kalmbach. Harrisburg, Pa., Stackpole Co., 1959.
922 p. illus. S1011

Gallagher, Hugh Gregory
Etok: a story of Eskimo power. New York, Putnam, c1974.
269 p. illus. S1012

Garfield, Brian
The thousand mile war. Garden City, N.Y., Doubleday, 1969.
351 p. S1013

Garfield, Viola Edmundson, 1899-
Meet the totem. Drawings by George Federoff. Sitka, Alaska, Sitka Print. Co., 1951.
54 p. illus. S1014

Gazaway, H.P.
Needed: an economic development program for rural Alaska. n.p., 1966.
iii, 41 p. map. S1015

Giddings, James Louis, 1909-1964
Ancient men of the Arctic. New York, Knopf, 1967.
xxxi, 391 p. illus. S1016

Giddings, James Louis
The archaeology of Cape Denbigh. Providence, Brown University Press, 1964.
xv, 331 p. illus. S1017

Giddings, James Louis
The Arctic woodland culture of the Kobuk River. Philadelphia, University Museum, University of Pennsylvania, 1952.
143, (96) p. illus. S1018

Gideon, Kenneth
Wandering boy: Alaska, 1913-18. Washington, Printed by Merkle Press, 1967.
73 p. ports. S1019

Gillham, Charles Edward
Medicine men of Hooper Bay: or, the Eskimo's arabian nights. London, Batchworth Press, 1955.
142 p. illus. S1020

Glanz, Rudolf
The Jews in American Alaska, 1867-1880. New York, H.H. Glanz, 1953.
46 p. S1021

Glenz, Marian
The BS counter: life in Alaska. New York, Exposition Press, 1971.
271 p. S1022

Glubok, Shirley
The art of the Eskimo. Designed by Oscar Krauss. Special photography by Alfred H. Tamarin. New York, Harper & Row, 1964.
48 p. illus. S1023

Godson, John
Runway. New York, Scribner, 1974.
192 p. illus. S1024

Gould, Maurice M
Alaska's coinage through the years. Racine, Wisc., Whitman Publishing Co., 1960.
46 p. illus. S1025

Gould, Peter Gordon
Methodism at work in Alaska. Philadelphia, 1949.
30 p. illus. S1026

Goulet, Emil Oliver, 1900-
Rugged years on the Alaska frontier. Philadelphia, Dorrance, 1949.
304 p. illus. ports. S1027

Grant, Norman B., ed.
Records of Alaska big game. Anchorage, Alaska Big Game Trophy Club, Inc., 1971.
111 p. illus. S1028

Gravel, Mike, 1930-
Jobs and more jobs. Anchorage, Mt. McKinley Publishers, 1968.
113 p. S1029

Graves, S.H.
On the "White Pass" pay-roll. New York, Paladin Press, 1970.
258 p. illus. S1030

Green, Kenneth J
Stampede to Alaska in postage stamps. Skagway, The author, 1972.
1 vol. illus. S1031

Green, Paul, 1901-
I am Eskimo, Aknik my name. By Paul Green aided by Abbe Abbott. With illustrations by George Aden Ahgupuk. Juneau, Alaska Northwest Publishing Co., 1959.
85 p. illus. S1032

Greenwood, Amy
Rolling north. Illustrated by Lombard Jones. New York, Crowell, c1955.
218 p. illus. S1033

Greiner, James
Wager with the wind: the Don Sheldon story. Chicago, Rand McNally, 1974.
256 p. illus. S1034

Griese, Arnold
The way of our people. New York, Thomas Y. Crowell, 1975.
82 p. illus. S1035

Gruening, Ernest Henry, 1887- , comp.
An Alaskan reader, 1867-1967. New York, Meredith Press, 1966.
xvi, 443 p. S1036

Gruening, Ernest Henry
The battle for Alaska statehood. College, University of Alaska Press; distributed by the University of Washington Press, Seattle, 1967.
xi, 122 p. illus. S1037

Gruening, Ernest Henry
Many battles: the autobiography of Ernest Gruening. New York, Liveright, 1973.
x, 564 p. illus. S1038

Gruening, Ernest Henry
The state of Alaska. New York, Random House, 1954.
606 p. maps. S1039

Gruening, Ernest Henry
The state of Alaska. New York, Random House, c1968.
661 p. illus. S1040

Gubser, Nicholas J
The Nunamiut Eskimos, hunters of caribou. New Haven, Yale University Press, 1965.
xv, 384 p. maps. S1041

Hadley, Martha E., 1852-1915
The Alaskan diary of a pioneer Quaker missionary. Dora, Fla., Loren S. Hadley, 1969.
210 p. illus. S1041A

Hadman, Ballard
As the sailor loves the sea. Illustrated by the author. New York, Harper, 1951.
232 p. illus. S1042

Hall, Edwin S., 1939-
The Eskimo storyteller: folktales from Noatak, Alaska. Drawings by Claire Fejes. Knoxville, University of Tennessee Press, 1975.
xi, 491 p. illus. S1043

Hamilton, Walter R., 1872-1964.
The Yukon story. Vancouver, Canada, Mitchell Press, 1964.
261 p. illus. S1044

Hardcastle, Romaine
Alaska day festival, Inc., commemorating the purchase transfer of Alaska from Russia to the U.S.A. Sitka, Alaska Day Festival Committee, 1959.
80 p. illus. S1045

Harkey, Ira B
Pioneer bush pilot: the story of Noel Wien. Seattle, University of Washington Press, 1974.
xviii, 307 p. illus. S1046

Harper, David
The green air. New York, Mason and Lipscomb, 1973.
217 p. S1047

Harrington, Richard (photographer)
The face of the Arctic: a cameraman's story in words and pictures of five journeys into the far north. Maps by Bunji Tagawa. New York, H. Schuman, 1952.
369 p. illus. S1048

Harris, Christie
Raven's cry. Illustrated by Bill Reid. New York, Atheneum, 1966.
193 p. illus. S1049

Harris, Mae Evans
You can Alcan. Middleburg, Va., Denlinger's, 1959.
96 p. S1050

Harris, Walter
Salmon fishing in Alaska: how and where. South Brunswick, N.J., A.S. Barnes, 1967.
143 p. illus. S1051

Hart, Robert G
McKay's guide to Alaska. New York, D. McKay Co., 1959.
330 p. illus. S1052

Hassler, Robert
Traveler's guide to southeastern Alaska: 150 place descriptions, geographical and historical notes, general information for travelers. Altadena, Calif., 1973.
96 p. illus. S1053

Hedla, Lenore
Gardens for Alaskans. n.p., n.p., 1974.
206 p. illus. S1054

Heller, Christine A
Wild flowers of Alaska. n.p., 1966.
104 p. illus. S1055

Heller, Herbert L., 1908- , ed.
Sourdough sagas: the journals, memoirs, tales and recollections of the earliest Alaskan gold miners, 1883-1923, edited by Herbert L. Heller. Cleveland, World Publishing Co., 1967.
x, 273 p. illus. S1056

Helmericks, Constance, 1918-
Our Alaskan winter, by Constance and Harmon Helmericks. 1st ed. Boston, Little, Brown, 1949.
xii, 271 p. illus. S1057

Helmericks, Constance
The flight of the Arctic tern by Constance and Harmon Helmericks. 1st ed. Boston, Little, Brown, 1952.
321 p. illus. S1058

Helmericks, Constance
Our summer with the Eskimos, by Constance and Harmon Helmericks. Boston, Little, Brown, 1950.
239 p. illus. S1059

Helmericks, Harmon, 1917-
The last of the bush pilots. New York, Knopf, 1969.
x, 361 p. illus. S1060

Herbert, Charles F
Alaska mining law manual. College, University of Alaska Mineral Industry Research Laboratory, 1970.
77 p. S1061

Herndon, Booton
The great land. New York, Weybright & Talley, 1971.
241 p. illus. S1062

Herron, Edward Albert, 1912-
Alaska's railroad builder: Mike Heney. New York, Julian Messner, 1960.
192 p. S1063

Herron, Edward Albert
The big country, a story of Alaska, illustrated by W.L. Mars. New York, Aladdin Books, 1953.
190 p. illus. S1064

Herron, Edward Albert
Conqueror of Mount McKinley: Hudson Stuck. New York, J. Messner, 1964.
191 p. S1065

Herron, Edward Albert
Dimond of Alaska, adventurer in the far north. New York, J. Messner, 1957.
190 p. S1066

Herron, Edward Albert
First scientist of Alaska: William Healey Dall, born August 21, 1845 - died March 27, 1927. New York, J. Messner, 1958.
192 p. S1067

Herron, Edward Albert
The return of the Alaskan: mailboat in the outpost. Illustrated by Gene Langley. New York, Aladdin Books, 1955.
190 p. illus. S1068

Herron, Edward Albert
Wings over Alaska, the story of Carl Ben Eielson, born July 10, 1897 - died November 9, 1929. New York, J. Messner, 1959.
192 p. S1069

Hewitt, John Michael
The Alaska vagabond, Doctor Skookum: memories of an adventurous life. 1st ed. New York, Exposition Press, 1953.
284 p. S1070

Higgins, Arthur W
Inside an Alaskan cannery. Juneau, The author, 1972.
53 p. S1071

Hill, Hubert M., 1918-
The golden trek. New York, Pageant Press, 1955.
68 p. S1072

Hilscher, Herbert H., 1902-
Alaska now. With illustrations by the author. Rev. ed. Boston, Little, Brown, 1950.
x, 309 p. illus. S1073

Hilscher, Herbert H
Alaska, U.S.A., by Herb and Miriam Hilscher. With photos. Boston, Little, Brown, 1959.
243 p. illus. S1074

Himmelheber, Hans, 1908-
Eskimokunstler: Ergebnisse einer Reise in Alaska. 2. Aufl. Eisenach, E. Roth, 1953.
136 p. illus. S1075

Hinckley, Kay and Diana Holzmueller
It works for us: a resource list of teaching ideas and materials on Athabascan culture. Fairbanks, University of Alaska Center for Northern Educational Research, 1975.
56 p. S1076

Hinckley, Ted C
The americanization of Alaska, 1867-1897. Palo Alto, Calif., Pacific Books, 1972.
285 p. illus. S1077

Hippler, Arthur E
Eskimo acculturation: a selected annotated bibliography of Alaskan and other Eskimo acculturation studies. College, University of Alaska Institute of Social, Economic and Government Research, 1970.
209 p. illus. S1078

Holmes, William Dayton.
A square in the Artic circle: an Alaskan hunt. Hamden, Conn., The Shoe String Press, Inc., 1960.
168 p. illus. S1079

Hoopes, David
Alaska in haiku, by David Hoopes and Diana Tillion. Illustrated by Diana Tillion. Rutland, Vt., C.E. Tuttle Co., 1972.
72 p. illus. S1080

Hope, Andrew
Founders of the Alaska native brotherhood. n.p.
33 p. illus. S1081

Houston, Alma
Nuki: with drawings by James Houston. Philadelphia, Lippincott, 1953.
150 p. illus. S1082

Houston, James A, 1921-
Akavak: an Eskimo journey. Written and illustrated by James Houston. New York, Harcourt, Brace and World, 1968.
75 p. illus. S1083

Houston, James
Kiviok's magic journey: an Eskimo legend. New York, Atheneum, 1973.
1 vol. illus. S1084

Houston, James A
Tikta'liktak: an Eskimo legend, written and illustrated by James Houston. New York, Harcourt, Brace and World, 1965.
63 p. illus. S1085

Houston, James A
The white archer: an Eskimo legend, written and illustrated by James Houston. New York, Harcourt, Brace and World, 1967.
95 p. illus. S1086

Howay, Frederic William, 1867-1943
A list of trading vessels in the maritime fur trade, 1785-1825. Edited by Richard A. Pierce. Kingston, Ont., Limestone Press, 1973.
208 p. S1087

Hubbard, Bernard Rosecrans, 1888-1962
Alaskan odyssey. London, Robert Hale, 1952.
xii, 198 p. illus. S1088

Hubbard, Charlie
True experiences in Alaska. The author, 1954.
20 p. illus. S1089

Hughes, Charles Campbell
An Eskimo village in the modern world by Charles Campbell Hughes, with the collaboration of Jane M. Hughes. Ithaca, N.Y., Cornell University Press, 1960.
xiv, 419 p. illus. S1090

Hulley, Clarence Charles, 1907-
Alaska, 1741-1953. Portland, Or., Binfords & Mort, 1953.
406 p. illus. S1091

Hulley, Clarence Charles
Alaska: past and present. 3rd ed. Portland, Or., Binfords & Mort, 1970.
477 p. illus. S1092

Hunermann, Wilhelm
De l'Alaska a la terre de feu. By G. Hunermann; traduit par Martin Briem. Mulhouse: Editions Salvator, 1961.
324 p. S1093

Hunke, Naomi Ruth
I have planted thee in this land: the story of the first 25 years of Southern Baptist missions in Alaska. Anchorage, Alaska Baptist Convention, 1971.
334 p. illus. ports. S1094

Hunt, William R
Arctic passage. New York, Scribner, c1975.
xv, 395 p. illus. S1095

Hunt, William R
North of 53°: the wild days of the Alaska-Yukon mining frontier, 1870-1914. New York, Macmillan, 1974.
xvi, 328 p. illus. S1096

Huntington, James
On the edge of nowhere, by James Huntington, as told to Lawrence Elliott. New York, Crown Publishers, 1966.
183 p. S1097

Huntoon, Emery
Intercept and board. Portland, Or., 1975.
101 p. illus. S1098

Hutsuliak, Mykhailo
When Russia was in America: the Alaska boundary treaty negotiations, 1824-25, and the role of Pierre de Poletica. Vancouver, B.C., Mitchell Press, 1971.
xv, 149 p. illus. S1099

Illingworth, Frank, 1908-
Highway to the north. New York, Philosophical Library, 1955.
293 p. illus. S1100

Illingworth, Frank
North of the circle. London, W. Hodge, 1951.
254 p. illus S1101

Ingstad, Helge Marcus, 1899-
Nunamiut: among Alaska's inland Eskimos. New York, W.W. Norton, 1954.
303 p. illus. S1102

An introduction to the native art of Alaska. Anchorage, Anchorage Historical and Fine Arts Museum, 1972.
84 p. illus. S1103

Iroquois Research Institute
A study of archaeological and historic potential along the trans-Alaskan natural gas pipeline routes. Falls Church, Va., The Institute, 1975.
2 vols. illus. S1104

Irwin, Don L.
The colorful Matanuska valley. n.p., 1968.
viii, 148 p. illus. S1105

Isto, Sarah A
Cultures in the north: multi-media resource list. Fairbanks, University of Alaska Center for Northern Educational Research, 1975.
46 p. S1106

Jackson, Basil
Rage under the Arctic. New York, Norton, 1974.
220 p. S1107

Jacobin, Lou
Guide to Alaska and the Yukon. Anchorage, Guide to Alaska, Inc., 1969.
240 p. S1108

Jacquot, Louis Fred
Alaska natives and Alaska higher education, 1960-1972: a descriptive study. Fairbanks, University of Alaska Native Human Development Program, 1974.
255 p. S1109

Janson, Lone E
The copper spike. Anchorage, Alaska Northwest Publishing Co., 1975.
175 p. illus. S1110

Jeffery, Edmond C., ed.
Alaska: who's here, what's doing, who's doing it, 1955. Foreword by B. Frank Heintzleman. Anchorage, Alaska, 1955.
212 p. S1111

Jenness, Aylette
Dwellers of the tundra. New York, Crowell-Collier Press, 1970.
112 p. S1112

Jenness, Diamond, 1886-
Dawn in Arctic Alaska. Illustrated by Giacomo Raimondi. Minneapolis, University of Minnesota Press, 1957.
222 p. illus. S1113

Jenness, Diamond
Eskimo administration. Montreal, Arctic Institute of North America, 1962-1968.
5 vols. illus. S1114

Jensen, Ronald J
The Alaska purchase and Russian American relations. Seattle, Wash., University of Washington Press, 1975.
185 p. illus. S1115

Johannsen, Neil and Elizabeth Johannsen
Exploring Alaska's Prince William Sound, its fiords, islands, glaciers and wildlife. Anchorage, Alaska Travel Publications, Inc., 1975.
306 p. illus. S1116

Johnson, Hugh Albert, 1913-
The land resources of Alaska by Hugh A. Johnson and Harold T. Jorgenson. New York, Published for the University of Alaska by University Publishers, 1963.
xiv, 551 p. maps. S1117

Johnson, Madine (Maddux)
Journey of enchantment: a Texan's tall tale of Alaska. New York, Exposition Press, 1956.
67 p. S1118

Johnson, Paul C
Alaska. New York, Kodansha International, 1974.
130 p. illus. S1119

Johnson, William E
Alaska, through the rhymes of a construction stiff. With narrative inserts by J. Patrick O'Neal. Illustrated by Fred Newman. 2nd ed. rev. and illus. Seattle, Craftsman Press, c1956.
72 p. illus. S1120

Johnston, Dorothy Grunbock
Ginger in Alaska. Wheaton, Ill., Van Kampen Press, 1951.
91 p. S1121

Jones, Laura Buchan
Hearth in the snow by Laura Buchan and Jerry Allen. New York, W. Funk, 1952.
306 p. S1122

Jordan, Jed
Fool's gold: an unrefined account of Alaska in 1899. New York, John Day, 1960.
255 p. S1123

Josephson, Karla
Alaska and the law of the sea: use of the sea by Alaska natives: a historical perspective. Anchorage, University of Alaska Arctic Environmental Information and Data Center, 1974.
95 p. photos. S1124

Kakianak, Nathan
Eskimo boyhood: an autobiography in psychosocial perspective. Edited by Charles C. Hughes. Lexington, Ky., University Press of Kentucky, 1974.
429 p. S1125

Kavanaugh, Ethel, 1909-
Wilderness homesteaders. Caldwell, Idaho, Caxton Printers, 1950.
303 p. illus. S1126

Kawagley, Dolores
Yupik stories. Anchorage, Alaska Methodist University Press, 1975.
84 p. illus. S1127

Keating, Bern
Alaska. Washington, D.C., National Geographic Society, 1969.
207 p. S1128

Keim, Charles J
Aghvook, white Eskimo. College, University of Alaska Press, 1969.
313 p. S1129

Keithahn, Edward Linnaeus, 1900-
Alaskan igloo tales. Illustrated by George Aden Ahgupuk. Edited by Kenneth Gilbert. Seattle, R.D. Seal, c1958.
138 p. illus. S1130

Keithahn, Edward Linnaeus
Eskimo adventure: another journey into the primitive. Seattle, Superior Publishing Co., 1963.
170 p. illus. S1131

Kent, Rockwell, 1882-
Wilderness: a journal of quiet adventures in Alaska. Rev. ed. Los Angeles, Wilderness Press; distributed by W. Ritchie Press, c1970.
xxi, 204 p. illus. S1132

Khlebnikov, Kirill Timofeevich, 1776-1838.
Baranov, chief manager of the Russian colonies in America, by K.T. Khlebnikov. Translated by Colin Bearne. Edited by Richard A. Pierce. Kingston, Ont., Limestone Press, c1973.
xvi, 140 p. illus. S1133

Khromchenko, Vasiley Stepanovich.
V.S. Khromchenko's coastal explorations in southwestern Alaska, 1822. Chicago, Field Museum of Natural History, 1973. (Fieldiana: Anthropology, 64).
95 p. S1134

Kirkland, Lola
Grandma goes to the Arctic, by Alberta L. Weed, as told to her by Lola Kirkland. Philadelphia, Dorrance, 1957.
279 p. illus. S1135

Kitchener, Lois Delano, 1914-
Flag over the north: the story of the Northern Commercial Company. Seattle, Wash., Superior Publishing Co., 1954.
349 p. illus. S1136

Krause, Aurel, 1848-
The Tlingit Indians: results of a trip to the northwest coast of America and the Bering Straits. Translated by Erna Gunther. Seattle, University of Washington Press, 1956.
viii, 310 p. illus. S1137

Kursh, Harry
This is Alaska. Englewood Cliffs, N.J., Prentice-Hall, 1961.
286 p. S1138

Lada-Mocarsgi, Valerian, ed.
Bibliography of books on Alaska published before 1868. New Haven, Conn., Yale University Press, 1969.
567 p. S1139

Languirand, Jacques
Klondyke: action dramatique. Musique de Gabriel Charpentier. Suivi d'une etude: Le Quebec et l'americanite. Montreal, Le Cercle du livre de France, 1971.
237 p. plates. S1140

Lantis, David W
Alaska. Prepared with the cooperation of the American Geographical Society. Garden City, N.Y., Doubleday, 1957.
64 p. illus. S1141

Lantis, Margaret.
Eskimo childhood and interpersonal relationships. Seattle, University of Washington Press, 1960.
219 p. illus. S1142

Lantis, Margaret, ed.
Ethnohistory in southwestern Alaska and the southern Yukon: method and content. Lexington, Ky., University of Kentucky Press, 1970.
311 p. illus. S1143

Larsson, Ernst B
I Alaska: missionsforbundens verksamhet dar. Stockholm, Missionsforbundet, 1953.
5-149 p. illus. S1144

Laurence, Jeanne
An album of Alaskan wildflowers. Seattle, Superior Publishing Co., 1974.
200 p. illus. S1145

Laurence, Jeanne
My life with Sydney Laurence. Seattle, Wash., Salisbury Press Book, 1974.
159 p. illus. S1146

Lauridsen, Peter, 1846-1923
Vitus Bering: the discoverer of Bering Strait. Rev. by the author and translated from the Danish by Julius E. Olson. With an introduction to the American ed. by Frederick Schwatka. Freeport, N.Y., Books for Libraries Press, 1969, c1889.
xvi, 223 p. S1147

Laycock, George
Alaska the embattled frontier. Boston, Mass., Houghton Mifflin, 1971.
205 p. illus. S1148

Lazell, J. Arthur.
Alaskan apostle: the life story of Sheldon Jackson. N.Y., Harper, 1960.
218 p. illus. S1149

Lee, Norman
Klondike cattle drive: the journal of Norman Lee. Prepared for publication by Gordon Elliott with a foreword by Eileen Laurie. Vancouver, B.C., Mitchell Press, 1960.
58 p. illus. S1150

Leopold, Aldo Starker, 1913-
Wildlife in Alaska, an ecological reconnaissance by A. Starker Leopold and F. Fraser Darling. New York, Ronald Press Co., 1953.
129 p. illus. S1151

Les Tina, Dorothy
Alaska: a book to begin on. New York, Holt, 1962. S1152

Lindquist, Willis
Alaska, the forty-ninth state. Foreword by Ernest Gruening. Illustrated by P.A. Hutchison. New York, McGraw-Hill, 1959.
111 p. illus. S1153

Llorente, Segundo
Asi son los eskimales. Introduccion por Jose A. Arroyo. Bilbao, Editorial El Siglo de las Misiones, 1963.
139 p. S1154

Llorente, Segundo
Jesuits in Alaska. Portland, Service Office Supply, 1969.
77 p. map. S1155

Lomen, Carl J
Fifty years in Alaska. Foreword by Richard E. Byrd. New York, D. McKay Co., 1954.
302 p. S1156

Long, John Sherman
McCord of Alaska: statesman for the last frontier. By John Sherman Long with Grace Doering McCord; foreword by Lowell Thomas. Cleveland, Dillon/Liederbach, c1975.
210 p. S1157

Lucia, Ellis
Klondike Kate: the life and legend of Kitty Rockwell, the queen of the Yukon. New York, Hastings House Publishers, c1962.
xi, 305 p. S1158

Luciw, Wasyl
Ahapius Honcharenko and the Alaska Herald: the editor's life and an analysis of his newspaper, by Wasyl Luciw and Theodore Luciw. Toronto, Slavia Library, 1963.
120 p. illus. S1159

Lund, Morten
Inside passage to Alaska. With photos by Clyde Banks and by the author. Philadelphia, Lippincott, 1965.
128 p. illus. S1160

Lung, Edward Burchall, 1867-1956
Black sand and gold: true Alaska-Yukon gold-rush story, by Ella Lung Martinsen as told by her father. Portland, Or., Metropolitan Press, 1967.
419 p. illus. S1161

Lung, Velma D
Trail to north star gold, a sequel to Black sand and gold, true story of the Alaska-Klondike gold rush by Ella Lung Martinsen, as told to her by her mother. Portland, Or., Metropolitan Press, 1969.
359 p. illus. S1162

McCracken, Harold, 1894-
Hunters of the stormy sea. Garden City, N.Y., Doubleday, 1957.
312 p. S1184

McCracken, Harold
The story of Alaska. Illustrated by Earl Oliver Hurst. Garden City, N.Y., Garden City Books, 1956.
57 p. illus. S1185

McDermott, Beverly Brodsky
Sedna: an Eskimo myth, adapted and illustrated by Beverly Brodsky. New York, Viking Press, 1975.
30 p. illus. S1186

Macdonald, Ronald St. J., 1928- , ed.
The Arctic frontier, edited by R. St. J. Macdonald. Toronto, University of Toronto Press, 1966.
311 p. maps. S1187

Macfie, Harry, 1879-
Wasa-wasa, a tale of trails and treasure in the far north by Harry Macfie with Hans G. Westerlund. Translated from the Swedish by F. H. Lyon. New York, Norton, 1951.
288 p. S1188

McGarvey, Lois
Along Alaska trails. N.Y., Vantage Press, 1960.
200 p. S1189

MacGowan, Michael, 1865-1948
The hard road to Klondike. Translated from the Irish by Valentin Iremonger. London, Routledge and K. Paul, 1962.
xiii, 150 p. illus. S1190

Machetanz, Sara
Seegoo: dog of Alaska, photographs by Fred Machetanz. London, Johnson, 1962, c1961.
iii, 204 p. illus. S1191

Machetanz, Sara
Where else but Alaska? Lithographs and photos by Fred Machetanz. New York, Scribner, 1954.
214 p. illus. S1192

Mack, Gerstle, 1894-
Lewis and Hannah Gerstle. New York, 1953.
131 p. illus. S1193

McKennan, Robert Addison, 1903-
The upper Tanana Indians. New Haven Dept. of Anthropology, Yale University, 1959.
226 p. illus. S1194

McKeown, Martha (Ferguson), 1903-
Alaska silver, another Mont Hawthorne story. New York, Macmillan, 1951.
274 p. S1195

McLain, Carrie M., 1895-
Gold-rush Nome. Portland, Or., Graphic Arts Center, 1969.
46 p. illus. S1196

McLain, Carrie M
Pioneer teacher. Portland, Or., Graphic Arts Center, c1970.
70 p. illus. S1197

MacMillan, Miriam (Look)
I married an explorer. London, New York, Hurst & Blackett, 1951.
238 p. illus. S1198

McNeer, May
The Alaska gold rush. New York, Random House, 1960.
186 p. illus. S1199

Madsen, Charles
Arctic trader, by Charles Madsen with John Scott Douglas. New York, Dodd, Mead, 1957.
273 p. illus. S1200

Maher, Ramona
The blind boy and the loon, and other Eskimo myths. New York, John Day Co., 1969.
158 p. illus. S1201

Makarova, Raisa V
Russians on the Pacific, 1743-1799. Translated and edited by Richard A. Pierce and Alton S. Donnelly. Kingston, Ont., The Limestone Press, 1975.
301 p. illus. S1202

Manning, Harvey
Cry crisis!: rehearsal in Alaska. By Harvey Manning, with chapters by Kenneth Brower. Edited by Hugh Nash. San Francisco, Friends of the earth, 1974.
313 p. illus. S1203

Mark Antony, Leo
The Alaskan prospector's short course in introductory prospecting and mining. Rev. ed. College, University of Alaska College of Earth Sciences and Mineral Industry, 1973.
187 p. illus. S1204

Marshall, Robert, 1901-1939.
Alaska wilderness: exploring the Central Brooks range. Edited by George Marshall. 2nd ed. Berkeley, University of California Press, 1970. (First ed., 1956, under title, Arctic wilderness.)
xl, 173 p. illus. S1205

Marston, M.R.
Men of the tundra-Eskimos at war. New York, October House, 1969.
227 p. S1206

Martin, Anna
Around and about Alaska. New York, Vantage Press, 1959.
94 p. map. S1207

Martin, Cy.
Gold rush narrow gauge. Los Angeles, Calif., Trans-Anglo Books, 1969.
illus. S1208

Martin, Fredericka I
Sea bears: the story of the fur seal. Philadelphia, Chilton Co., Book Division, 1960.
201 p. illus. S1209

Martin, Martha, of Alaska
Home on the bear's domain. New York, Macmillan, 1954.
246 p. S1210

Martin, Martha, of Alaska
O rugged land of gold. London, Victor Gollancz, 1956, c1953.
253 p. S1211

Mathews, Richard
The Yukon. Illustrated by Bryan Forsyth. New York, Holt, Rinehart, and Winston, 1968.
313 p. illus. S1214

Matlock, Alma Harwell
Teaching above the Arctic circle. n.p., 196-?
24 p. illus. S1215

Matson, Ruth O.
Happy Alaskans we, by "Ye Olde" of Gostavus. San Francisco, Calif., Goose Cove Press, 1972.
84 p. illus. S1216

Mayokok, Robert
Eskimo life, told by an Eskimo artist. Rev. ed. - s.l.: s.n., 1970.
21 p. illus. S1217

Mayokok, Robert
Eskimo stories. Nome, Alaska, Nome Nugget, 1960.
42 p. S1218

Mekiana, Homer
This is the story about Anaktuvuk Pass village. Barrow, Alaska, Naval Arctic Research Laboratory, 1972.
178 p. S1219

Melin, Margaret
Modern pioneering in Alaska. New York, Pageant Press, 1954.
78 p. illus. S1220

Melzack, Ronald
Raven, creator of the world. Eskimo legends retold. Illustrated by Laszlo Gal. Boston, Little, Brown, 1970.
91 p. illus. S1221

Menager, Francis M
The kingdom of the seal. Chicago, Loyola University Press, 1962.
203 p. illus. S1222

Miers, Earl Schenck, 1910-
Vitus Bering and James Cook discover Alaska and Hawaii. With maps of the voyages by Enrico Arno and with wood engravings by Stefan Martin. Newark, Delaware, Curtis Paper Co., 1960.
28 p. S1224

Mikkelsen, Ejnar, 1880-
Conquering the Arctic ice. With numerous illustrations and maps. Philadelphia, George W. Jacobs, n.d.
xviii, 470 p. illus. S1225

Mikkelsen, Ejnar
Mirage in the Arctic. Translated from the Danish by Maurice Michael. London, Hart-Davis, 1955.
216 p. illus. S1226

Miles, Charles, 1891-
American Indian and Eskimo basketry, a key to identification. Written and compiled by Charles Miles and Pierre Bovis. San Francisco, Calif., P. Bovis, 1969.
144 p. illus. S1227

Miller, Mike and Peggy Wayburn
Alaska: the great land. San Francisco, Calif., Sierra Club, 1974.
152 p. illus. S1228

Miller, Mike
Off the beaten path in Alaska. Juneau, Alaskabooks, 1970.
116 p. S1229

Miller, Orlando W
The frontier in Alaska and the Matanuska colony. New Haven, Conn., Yale University Press, 1975.
329 p. illus. S1230

Miller, Polly
Lost heritage of Alaska: the adventure and art of the Alaskan coastal Indians. Graphics and aesthetic commentary by Leon Gordon Miller. Cleveland, World Publishing Co., 1967.
xv, 289 p. illus. S1231

Mills, James, 1926-
Airborne to the mountains. New York, A.S. Barnes, 1961.
261 p. illus. S1232

Mills, Stephen E
Arctic war birds, Alaska aviation of WW II: a pictorial history of bush flying with the military in the defense of Alaska and America. Seattle, Wash., Superior Publishing Co., 1971.
191 p. illus. S1233

Mills, Stephen E. and James W. Phillips
Sourdough sky-Alaska bush pilots. Seattle, Wash., Superior Publishing Co., 1969.
176 p. illus. S1234

Milotte, Alfred and Elma Milotte
The story of an Alaskan grizzly bear. New York, Alfred Knopf, 1969.
149 p. S1235

Milton, John P
Nameless valleys, shining mountains: the record of an expedition into the vanishing wilderness of Alaska's Brooks range. New York, Walker and Co., 1970.
195 p. illus S1236

Minock, Milo
Drawings and stories. Bethel, Bethel Council on the Arts, 1971.
unp. illus. S1237

Mizony, Paul T
Gold rush, a boy's impression of the stampede into the Klondike during the days of 1898. National City, Calif., 1956.
30 p. S1238

Moody, Joseph P
Arctic doctor, by Joseph P. Moody with W. de Groot van Embden.New York, Dodd, Mead, 1955.
274 p. illus. S1239

Moore, J. Bernard, 1865-1919
Skagway in days primeval. New York, Vantage Press, 1968.
202 p. map. S1240

Moore, Terris
Mt. McKinley: the pioneer climbs. College, University of Alaska Press, distributed by University of Washington Press, 1967.
xv, 202 p. illus. S1241

Moorrees, Coenraad F.A.
The Aleut dentition: a correlative study of dental characteristics in an Eskimoid people. Cambridge, Harvard University Press, 1957.
x, 196 p. illus. S1242

Morenus, Richard
Alaska sourdough, the story of Slim Williams. Chicago, Rand McNally, 1956.
278 p. S1243

Morgan, Lael
And the land provides: Alaskan natives in a year of transition. Garden City, N.Y., Anchor Press/Doubleday, 1974.
325 p. illus. S1244

Morgan, Murray Cromwell, 1916-
One man's gold rush: a Klondike album. Photos by E.A. Hegg. Seattle, University of Washington Press, 1967.
213 p. illus. S1245

Morrow, James Edwin
Illustrated keys to the fresh-water fishes of Alaska. Anchorage, Alaska Northwest Publishing Co., 1974.
78 p. illus. S1246

Munro, John A., 1938- , comp.
The Alaska boundary dispute, edited by John A. Munro. Toronto, Copp Clark Publishing Co., c1970.
169 p. maps S1247

Murie, Adolph
A naturalist in Alaska. New York, Devin-Adair, 1961.
302 p. illus. S1248

Murie, Margaret E
Two in the far north. New York, Knopf, 1962.
438 p. illus. S1249

Murie, Olaus Johan
Journeys to the far north. Palo Alto, Calif., American West Publishing Co., 1973.
255 p. illus. S1250

Murphy, Robert
The haunted journey. Garden City, N.Y., Doubleday, 1961.
212 p. S1251

Nach, James
Alaska in pictures. New York, Sterling Publishing Co., 1970.
64 p. illus. S1252

Naske, Claus-M
An interpretive history of Alaskan statehood. Anchorage, Alaska Northwest Publishing Co., 1973.
xi, 192 p. S1254

Neatby, Leslie H
Conquest of the last frontier. Athens, Ohio University Press, 1966.
xvi, 425 p. maps. S1255

Nelson, Klondy, 1897-
Daughter of the gold rush by Klondy Nelson with Corey Ford. New York, Random House, 1958.
173 p. illus. S1256

Nelson, Richard K
Hunters of the northern forest: designs for survival among Alaskan Kutchin. Chicago, University of Chicago Press, 1973.
xv, 339 p. illus. S1257

Nienhueser, Helen
55 ways to the wilderness in southcentral Alaska. Anchorage, Mountaineering Club of Alaska; Seattle, Wash., The Mountaineers, 1972.
160 p. illus. S1258

Nindorf, Quentin C
The Williwaw cubs. Illustrated by John Jordan. New York Dodd, Mead, 1956.
179 p. illus. S1259

Niven, Frederick
Go north, where the world is young. Seattle, 1969?
1 vol. unp. illus. S1260

Nulsen, Robert Hovey
Trailering to Alaska. Beverly Hills, Calif., Trail R. Club of America, 1960.
112 p. illus. S1261

Oberg, Kalerve
The social economy of the Tlingit Indians. Seattle, Wash., University of Washington Press, 1973.
146 p. illus. S1262

O'Conner, Donald J
Alaska's interior gateway. Vienna, Va., 1953.
46 p. tables. S1263

Okun', Semen Bentsionovich
The Russian-American company. Edited with introduction by B.D. Grekov. Translated from the Russian by Carl Ginsburg. Cambridge, Harvard University Press, 1951.
viii, 311 p. S1264

Olson, Sigurd F., 1899-
Runes of the north. Illustrated by Robert Hines. New York, Knopf, 1963.
xii, 254 p. illus. S1265

Oman, Lela Kiana.
Eskimo legends. Anchorage, Alaska Methodist University Press, 1975.
118 p. illus. S1266

O'Neill, Hester
The picture story of Alaska. Pictures by Ursula Koering. New York, McKay, c1951.
49 p. illus. S1267

Oquilluk, William A and Laurel L. Bland
People of Kauwerak: legends of the northern Eskimo. Anchorage, Alaska Methodist University Press, 1973.
242 p. illus. S1268

Ortzen, Len
Famous Arctic adventures. London, Barker, 1972.
156 p. S1269

Orvik, James and Ray Barnhardt
Cultural influences in Alaskan native education. Fairbanks, University of Alaska Center for Northern Educational Research, 1974.
94 p. S1270

Osgood, Cornelius, 1905-
The Han Indians: a compilation of ethnographic and historical data on the Alaska-Yukon boundary area. 1971. S1271

Oswalt, Wendell H
Alaskan Eskimos. San Francisco, Calif., Chandler Publishing Co., 1967.
xv, 297 p. illus. S1272

Oswalt, Wendell H
Mission of change in Alaska: Eskimos and Moravians on the Kuskokwim. San Marino, Calif., Huntington Library, 1963.
x, 170 p. maps. S1273

Oswalt, Wendell H
Napaskiak: an Alaskan Eskimo community. Illustrated by the author. Tucson, University of Arizona Press, 1963.
xii, 178 p. illus. S1274

Oswalt, Wendell H
Prehistoric sea mammal hunters at Kaflia, Alaska. n.p., 1954?
32 p. illus. S1275

Page, Roger
This is Kodiak. Kodiak, The author, 1970
64 p. illus. S1276

Palmer, Frederick J
Kodiak bear hunt: stalking the giant bears of Alaska. New York, Exposition Press, 1958.
79 p. S1277

Pape, Richard, 1916-
Poles apart: a fast-moving account of his adventures from Alaska to Antartica. With forewords by Lord Rootes and George Dufek. London, Odhams Press, 1960.
256 p. illus. S1278

Parr, Charles H
Preliminary list of early Alaskan imprints, 1869 through 1913. Fairbanks, University of Alaska Elmer E. Rasmuson Library, 1974.
66 p. S1279

Patty, Ernest A
North country challenge. New York, McKay, 1969.
272 p. S1280

Paulsteiner, John
Seward, Alaska, the sinful town on Resurrection Bay. n.p., 1975.
128 p. S1281

Paxton, Duffy
River songs and tales of Alaska. Albuquerque, N.M., McLeod Printing Co., 1972.
218 p. illus. S1282

Pearson, Grant H
My life of high adventure, by Grant H. Pearson with Philip Newill. Englewood Cliffs, N.J., Prentice-Hall, 1962.
234 p. illus. S1283

Peckenpaugh, Harold and Zola Peckenpaugh
Nuggest and beans. New York, Carlton Press, 1973.
122 p. S1284

Pedersen, Elsa
Alaska. Consultant, Roscoe E. Bell. New York, Coward-McCann, 1969.
125 p. illus. S1285

Pedersen, Elsa
Alaska harvest. New York, Abingdon, 1961.
192 p. illus. S1286

Peterson, Leah Jane
This is Alaska. Editor, Alice H. Hayden. Consultants, Madge Gradon and Helen Finlay. Artist, Joan Arend Kickbush. Seattle, Cascade Pacific Books, 1958.
107 p. illus. S1288

Petite, Irving
Meander to Alaska. Garden City, N.Y., Doubleday, 1970.
223 p. S1289

Phebus, George.
Alaskan Eskimo life in the 1890's as sketched by native artists. Washington, D.C., Smithsonian Institution Press, 1972.
168 p. illus. S1290

Phillips, James Wendell
Alaska-Yukon place names. Seattle, Wash., University of Washington Press, 1973.
149 p. S1291

Pierce, Richard A
Alaskan shipping, 1867-1878: arrivals and departures at the port of Sitka. Kingston, Ont., Limestone Press, 1972.
63 p. S1292

Piggott, Margaret H
Discover southeast Alaska with pack and paddle. Seattle, Wash., The Mountaineers, 1974.
268 p. illus. S1293

Pilgrim, Mariette Shaw
Alaska: its history, resources, geography and government. Rev. ed. Caldwell, Idaho, Caxton Printers, 1954.
376 p. illus. S1294

Place, Marian (Templeton)
The Yukon. New York, I. Washburn, 1967.
211 p. map. S1295

Place, Marian (Templeton)
New York to Nome: the first international cross-country flight New York, Macmillan, 1972.
72 p. S1296

Player, Corrie and Sheryl White
Anchorage altogether. Anchorage, The authors, 1972.
136 p. illus. S1297

Poncins, Gontran de Montaigne, (vicomte) de, 1900-
The ghost voyage: out of Eskimo land. Translated from the French by Bernard Frechtman. Garden City, N.Y., Doubleday, 1954.
222 p. illus. S1298

Post, Austin and Edward R. La Chapelle
Glacier ice. Seattle, Wash., The Mountaineers and University of Washington Press, 1971.
110 p. illus. S1299

Potter, Louise, 1895-
Alaska highway flowers. Wasilla, Alaska, 1966.
40 p. S1300

Potter, Louise
Old times on Upper Cook's Inlet. Anchorage, Book Cache, 1967.
43 p. illus. S1301

Potter, Louise
Roadside flowers of Alaska. Thetford Center, Vt., 1962.
590 p. illus. S1302

Potter, Louise
A study of a frontier town in Alaska: Wasilla to 1959. Thetford Center, Vt., 1963.
104 p. illus. S1303

Potter, Louise
Wild flowers along Mt. McKinley Park Road and to westward. Thetford Center, Vt., 1969,
145 p. illus. S1304

Proenneke, Richard and Sam Keith
One man's wilderness: an Alaskan odyssey, from the journals and photo collection of Richard Proenneke. Anchorage, Alaska Northwest Publishing Co., 1973
107 p. illus. S1305

Pruitt, William Obadiah, 1922-
Animals of the north. Drawings by William D. Berry. New York, Harper & Row, 1967.
173 p. illus. S1306

Ray, Dorothy Jean
Artists of the tundra and the sea. Seattle, University of Washington Press, 1961.
170 p. illus. S1307

Redding, Robert H
Mara, an Alaskan weasel. Illustrated by Kiyoaki Komoda. Garden City, N.Y., Doubleday, 1968.
138 p. illus. S1308

Reynolds, Robert and John J. Morris
Alaska. Portland, Or., Charles H. Belding, Printed by Graphic Arts Center, 1971.
187 p. illus. S1309

Richards, Eva Louise Alvey
Arctic mood: a narrative of Arctic adventures. Caldwell, Idaho, Caxton Printers, 1949.
282 p. illus. ports. S1310

Ricks, Melvin B
The earliest history of Alaska. Anchorage, Cook Inlet Historical Society, 1970.
65 p. S1311

Rieder, Keith Kock
Cheechako first class. Manchester, Me., Falmouth Publishing House, 1953.
200 p. illus. S1312

Robarts, Victoria P
Let's go to Alaska: a factual pictorial story for young people and travellers. Los Angeles, Wetzel Publishing Co., c1951.
108 p. illus. S1313

Roberts, David
Deborah: a wilderness narrative. New York, The Vanguard Press, 1970.
188 p. illus. S1314

Robertson, Frank Chester, 1890-
Soapy Smith, king of the frontier con men, by Frank C. Robertson and Beth Kay Harris. New York, Hastings House, 1961.
244 p. illus. S1315

Robins, Elizabeth, 1862-1952
Raymond and I. With a foreword by Leonard Woolf. New York, Macmillan, 1956.
343 p. illus. S1316

Rodahl, Kare, 1917-
Between two worlds: a doctor's logbook of life amongst the Alaskan Eskimos. London, Heinemann, 1964.
208 p. illus. S1317

Rodahl, Kare
The last of the few. Line drawings by Dorothy Robinson. New York, Harper & Row, 1963.
x, 208 p. illus. S1318

Rodahl, Kare
Smilets folk. Oslo, Gyldendal, 1957.
188 p. illus. S1319

Rodli, Agnes Sylvia
North of heaven: a teaching ministry among the Alaskan Indians. Chicago, Moody Press, 1963.
189 p. S1320

Rodney, William
Joe Boyle: king of the Klondike. Toronto, New York, McGraw-Hill Ryerson, 1974.
xiii, 368 p. S1321

Rogers, George William
Alaska in transition: the southeast region. Baltimore, Johns Hopkins Press, 1960.
384 p. illus. S1322

Rogers, George William
The future of Alaska: economic consequences of statehood. Baltimore, Johns Hopkins Press, 1962.
311 p. illus. S1323

Rooth, Anna Eirgitta
The Alaska expedition 1966. Myths, customs and beliefs among the Athabascan Indians and the Eskimos of northern Alaska. Lund, Gleerup, 1971.
xvi, 392 p. illus. S1324

Roseneau, D.G.
Distribution and movements of the porcupine caribou herd in northeastern Alaska, 1972. By D.G. Roseneau and P.M. Stern. Calgary, Canadian Arctic Gas Study; Alaskan Arctic Gas Study Co., 1974.
vi, 209 p. illus. S1325

Ross, Sherwood
Gruening of Alaska. New York, Best Books, 1968.
224 p. illus. ports. S1326

Rossiisko-amerikanskaia kompaniia
Documents on the history of the Russian-American Company. Translated by Mariana Ramsay. Edited by Richard A. Pierce. Kingston, Ont., Limestone Press, c1967.
viii, 220 p. illus. S1327

Ryan, John Joseph, 1922-
The Maggie Murphy. New York, Norton, 1951.
224 p. S1328

Sage, Bryan L
Alaska and its wildlife. New York, Viking Press, 1973.
128 p. S1329

Saint Herman of Alaska. Wilkes-Barre, Pa., The Orthodox Church in America, 1970.
80 p. col. plates. S1330

Salisbury, Oliver Maxson
The customs and legends of the Tlingit Indians of Alaska. New York, Bonanza Books, 1962.
xii, 275 p. illus. S1331

Salisbury, Oliver Maxson
Quoth the raven: a little journey into the primitive. Seattle, Superior Publishing Co., 1962.
275 p. illus. S1332

Samson, Sam, 1869-
The Eskimo princess: a story of a million dollar gold discovery in the Cyrus Noble in Nome, Alaska, as told to Mignon Maynard Chisam by Sam Samson. Boston, Christopher Publishing House, 1951.
50 p. S1333

Satterfield, Archie
Alaska bush pilots in the float country. Seattle, Wash., Superior Publishing Co., 1969.
159 p. S1334

Satterfield, Archie
Chilkoot Pass then and now. Anchorage, Alaska Northwest Publishing Co., 1973.
183 p. illus. S1335

Satterfield, Archie
The Yukon River trail guide. Harrisburg, Pa., Stackpole Books, 1975.
159 p. illus. S1336

Saunders, Dan
Alaska, memoir of a vanishing frontier. New York, Avon Books, c1975.
175 p. S1337

Savage, Alma Helen, 1900-
The forty-ninth star, Alaska. Illustrated by Rus Anderson. New York, Benziger Bros., 1959.
180 p. illus. S1338

Schorr, Alan Edward
Alaska place names. Fairbanks, Elmer E. Rasmuson Library, University of Alaska, 1974.
32 p. S1339

Scudder, H.C.
The Alaska salmon trap: its evoultion, conflicts and consequences. Juneau, Alaska Division of State Libraries, 1970.
25 p. S1340

Senter, Gano E
Kawoo of Alaska. Denver, Sage Books, 1964.
113 p. illus. S1341

Senungetuk, Joseph E
Give or take a century: an Eskimo chronicle. San Francisco, Calif., The Indian Historian Press, 1971.
206 p. illus. S1342

Seveck, Chester Asakak
Longest reindeer herder. A fascinating true life story of an Alaskan Eskimo covering the period from 1890 to 1973. 5th ed. n.p. Rainbow Ventures, 1975.
48 p. illus. S1343

Sgroi, Peter P
The purchase of Alaska, March 30, 1867; a bargain at two cents an acre. New York, Franklin Watts, 1975.
65 p. illus. S1344

Sgroi, Peter P
Why the United States purchased Alaska. College, University of Alaska Press, 1970.
64 p. illus. S1345

Shalkop, R.L.
Russian Orthodox art in Alaska. Anchorage, Anchorage Historical and Fine Arts Museum, 1973.
36 p. S1346

Sherwood, Morgan B., comp.
Alaska and its history. Seattle, University of Washington Press, 1967.
xx, 475 p. illus. S1347

Sherwood, Morgan B
Exploration of Alaska, 1865-1900. New Haven, Yale University Press, 1965.
xiv, 207 p. illus. S1349

Shield, Charles F
My most memorable moments. Eugene, Or., Shield, 1972.
324 p. illus. S1350

Shiels, Archibald Williamson, 1878- comp.
Little journeys into the history of Russian America and the purchase of Alaska. Seattle, Wash., 1964, c1949.
116 p. S1351

Shiels, Archibald Williamson
The purchase of Alaska. College, University of Alaska Press, 1967.
xv, 208 p. S1352

Shimer, R.H.
Squaw Point. New York, Harper & Row, 1972.
225 p. S1353

Shore, Evelyn (Berglund), 1917-
Born on snowshoes. Illustrated with photos and with decorations by Courtney Allen. Boston, Houghton Mifflin, 1954.
209 p. illus. S1354

Short, Wayne
The cheechakoes. Drawings by Peter Parnall. New York, Random House, 1964.
244 p. illus. S1355

Short, Wayne
This raw land. New York, Random House, 1968.
ix, 202 p. map. S1356

Shumaker, Cecil Lee
Do you know? Exploring nature around Prince William Sound, Alaska. New York, Exposition Press, 1967.
82 p. illus. S1357

Siddall, William R
The Yukon waterway in the development of interior Alaska. Berkeley, Calif., University of California, 1959.
1 vol. S1358

Silook, Roger
In the beginning. Anchorage Printing Company, 1970.
illus. S1359

Silver, Connie
Alaska highway sketches: souvenir and travel guide. 3rd ed. Anchorage, 1963.
208 p. illus. S1360

Sleator, William
The angry moon. Boston, Mass., Little, Brown, 1970.
48 p. illus. S1361

Small, Marie
Four fares to Juneau. Illustrated Erna Karolyi. New York, London, Whittlesey House, McGraw-Hill Book Co., Inc., 1947.
237 p. illus. S1362

Smith, Homer
Far north farming: Alaska vs. Scandinavia. Sonora, Mexico, 1971.
40 p. illus. S1363

Smith, Homer
From desert to tundra: what you should know before you pioneer on our "last frontier." Philadelphia, Pa., Dorrance, 1971.
353 p. illus. S1364

Smith, Michael E
Alaska's historic roadhouses. Boulder, Colo., Western Interstate Commission for Higher Education, 1974.
101 p. illus. S1365

Smith, Richard Austin, 1911-
The frontier states: Alaska, Hawaii, by Richard Austin Smith and the editors of Time-Life Books. New York, Time-Life Books, 1968.
192 p. illus. S1366

Snider, Gerrit Heinie
So was Alaska. Anchorage, Color Art Printing Co., 1961.
95 p. illus. S1367

Snyder, Howard H
The hall of the mountain king. New York, Scribner, 1973.
207 p. illus. S1368

Spaulding, Albert Clanton, 1914-
Archaeological investigations on Agattu, Aleutian Islands. Ann Arbor, University of Michigan, 1962.
79 p. illus. tables. S1369

Spring, Norma
Alaska, pioneer state. Photos by Bob and Ira Spring. Camden, N.J., Nelson, 1966.
224 p. illus. S1370

Spring, Norma
Alaska: the complete travel book. New York, Macmillan, 1970.
248 p. S1371

Spring, Norma
Alaska: the complete travel book. New York, Macmillan, 1975.
274 p. photos S1372

Springer, John A., 1911-1961
Innocent in Alaska: the story of Margaret Knudsen Burke. New York, Coward-McCann, 1963.
319 p. S1374

Staender, Vivian
Adventures with Arctic wildlife. Photos by Gilbert Staender. Drawings by Frank Staender. Caldwell, Idaho, Caxton Printers, 1970.
260 p. illus. S1375

Stanton, James B
Ho for the Klondike: a whimsical look at the years 1897-98. Saanichton, B.C., Hancock House, c1974.
64 p. illus. S1376

Starr, Walter Augustus, 1877-
My adventures in the Klondike and Alaska, 1898-1900, written for my grandchildren in 1960. San Francisco, 1960.
68 p. illus. S1377

Stefansson, Evelyn (Schwartz) Baird
Here is Alaska. New York, Scribner, 1973. Rev. ed.
178 p. illus. S1378

Sterling Publishing Company, Inc., New York.
Alaska - the 49th state - in pictures. Introduction by E.L. (Bob) Bartlett. New York, 1958.
64 p. illus. S1379

Stoddard, Gordon
Go north, young man: modern homesteading in Alaska. Portland, Or., Binfords & Mort, 1957.
239 p. illus. S1380

Story, Gillian L. and Constance M. Naish, comps.
Tlingit verb dictionary. College, University of Alaska Native Language Center, 1973.
392 p. illus. S1381

Sunset.
Alaska, by the Sunset editorial staff. 2nd. Rev. ed. Menlo Park, Calif., Lane Books, 1966.
94 p. illus. S1382

Sutton, Ann and Myron
Steller of the north. New York, Rand McNally, 1961.
231 p. S1383

Tales of Eskimo Alaska. Anchorage, Alaska Methodist University Press, 1971.
91 p. illus. S1384

Taylor, Barbara A (Erstein)
Alaska, last frontier. Photos and illustrations by the author. New York, Carlton Press, 1963.
174 p. illus. S1385

Teichmann, Emil, 1845-1924
A journey to Alaska in the year 1868: being a diary of the late Emil Teichmann, edited with an introduction by his son, Oskar. With a foreword by Ernest Gruening. New York, Argosy-Antiquarian, 1963.
272 p. illus. S1386

Tekesky, Pauline, ed.
Seward's folly: the story of Alaska. Chapel Hill, N.C., University of North Carolina Library, 1960.
32 p. S1387

Thomas, Lowell Jackson
The trail of ninety-eight. New York, Duell, Sloan and Pearce, 1962.
191 p. S1388

Thomas, Tay
Cry in the wilderness: "Hear ye the voice of the Lord." Anchorage, Color Art Printing Co., 1967.
125 p. illus. S1389

Thompson, (J. Walter) Company
The Alaskan market, 1958: this concise description of Alaska as a market is an introductory survey. New York, 1958.
39 p. illus. S1390

Tlingit language workshop reader: doo goojee Yeenaa-dei. Book One. Sitka, Sheldon Jackson College Tlingit Language Workshop, 1972.
59 p. S1391

Tourville, Elsie A
Alaska: a bibliography, 1570-1970, with subject index. Boston, Mass., G.K. Hall, 1974.
738 p. S1392

Toye, William
The mountain goats of Temlaham. Pictures by Elizabeth Cleaver. Retold by William Toye. New York, H.Z. Walck, 1969.
32 p. illus. S1393

Tracy, Joseph P
Low man on a gill-netter. Illustrated by the author. Anchorage, Alaska Northwest Publishing Co., 1974.
147 p. illus. S1394

Trefzger, Hardy
My fifty years of hunting, fishing, prospecting, guiding, trading, and trapping in Alaska. New York, Exposition Press, 1964.
118 p. illus. S1395

Tremblay, Kenneth R. and Paul R. Banta
Effects of Immigration in the community of Valdez. Boulder, Colo., Western Interstate Commission for Higher Education, 1974.
63 p. S1396

Trout, Perry
Alaska! By pickup camper. Beverly Hills, Calif., Trail-R- Club of America, 1972.
138 p. illus. S1397

Ungermann, Kenneth A
The race to Nome: the story of the heroic Alaskan dog teams that rushed diphtheria serum to stricken Nome in 1925. Edited by Walter Lord. Illustrated with 25 photos. New York, Harper & Row, 1963.
xiv, 171 p. illus. S1398

Vachon, Andrew William
Ketchikan sketchings. Seattle, R.D. Seal, 1959.
unp. illus. S1399

Van Horne, Bea
The Lake Clark area: planning for people, wildlife and the land. Santa Cruz, Calif., University of California Environmental Studies Program, 1975.
89 p. illus. S1400

VanStone, James W
Akulivikchuk: a nineteenth century Eskimo village on the Nashagak River, Alaska. Chicago, Field Museum of Natural History, 1970. (Fieldiana: anthropology, v. 60).
S1401

VanStone, James W
Athapaskan adaptations: hunters and fishermen of the sub-Arctic forests. Chicago, Aldine Publishing Co., 1974.
145 p. illus. S1402

VanStone, James W
Eskimos of the Nushagak River: an ethnographic history. Seattle, University of Washington Press, 1967.
xxiv, 192 p. maps. S1403

VanStone, James W
Historic settlement patterns in the Nushagak River region, Alaska. Chicago, Field Museum of Natural History, 1971.
149 p. illus. S1404

VanStone, James W
Nushagak: an historic trading center in southwestern Alaska. Chicago, Field Museum of Natural History, 1972.
v, 93 p. illus. S1405

VanStone, James W
Point Hope, an Eskimo village in transition. Seattle, University of Washington Press, 1962.
177 p. illus. S1406

VanStone, James W
Tikchik village: a nineteenth century riverine community in southwestern Alaska. Chicago, Field Museum of Natural History, 1968.
215-368 p. illus. S1407

Vaudrin, Bill
Tanaina tales from Alaska. Norman, Okla., University of Oklahoma Press, 1969.
133 p. S1408

Viereck, Phillip
Eskimo island: a story of the Bering Sea hunters. Illustrated by Ellen Viereck. New York, John Day Co., 1962.
160 p. illus. S1409

Vining, Aidan
The socio-economic impacts of the trans-Alaska pipeline: a strategy for the state of Alaska. Boulder, Colo., Resources Development Internship Program, Western Interstate Commission for Higher Education, 1974.
iii, 57 p. S1410

Wachel, Pat
Oscar Winchell, Alaska's flying cowboy. Minneapolis, T.S. Denison, c1967.
210 p. S1411

Waid, Mrs. Eva (Clark), comp.
Alaska, the land of the totem. New York, Woman's Board of Home Missions of the Presbyterian Church in the U.S.A., 1966?
127 p. S1412

Walker, Franklin Dickerson, 1900-
Jack London and the Klondike: the genesis of an American writer. San Marino, Calif., Huntington Library, 1966.
288 p. illus. S1413

Walker, Theodore J
Red salmon, brown bear: the story of an Alaskan lake. New York, World Publishing Times Mirror, 1971.
226 p. illus. S1414

Wallace, Fern A
The flame of the candle: a pictorial history of Russian Orthodox churches in Alaska. Chillwack, B.C., Sts. Kyril and Methody Society, 1974.
140 p. illus. S1415

Washburn, Bradford, 1910-
Mount McKinley and the Alaska range in literature: a descriptive bibliography. Special advance ed., prepared for the Alaska Science Conference to be held at Mount McKinley National Park, Alaska, Sept.,1951. Boston, Museum of Science, 1951.
88 p. S1416

Washburn, Bradford
A tourist guide to Mount McKinley. Anchorage, Alaska Northwest Publishing Co., 1971.
79 p. illus. S1417

Waxell, Sven Larsson, 1701-1762
The American expedition. Translated with an introduction and note by M.A. Michael. London, W. Hodge, 1952.
236 p. plate. maps. S1418

Webster, Donald H. and Wilfred Zibell
Inupiat Eskimo dictionary. Fairbanks, Summer Institute of Linguistics, 1970.
illus. S1419

Wedbush, Noble, Cooke, Inc.
Alaska: a study of publicly owned companies active in the state. Los Angeles, Calif., the author. 1972. S1420

Weller, Gunter and Sue Ann Bowling
Climate of the Arctic. Fairbanks, University of Alaska Geophysical Institute, 1975.
436 p. illus. S1421

Wells, James K
Ipani Eskimos: a cycle of life in Nature. Anchorage, Alaska Methodist University, 1974.
110 p. illus. S1422

Werstein, Irving
Man against the elements: Adolphus W. Greely. New York, J. Messner, 1960.
191 p. S1423

Western construction
Alaska: a special report on construction by Ralph Whiteker. San Francisco, King Publishers, 1953.
148 p. illus. S1424

Wharton, David
The Alaska gold rush. Bloomington, Ind., Indiana University Press, 1972.
302 p. illus. S1425

Wiggins, Ira Loren
A flora of the Alaskan Arctic slope, by Ira L. Wiggins and John Hunter Thomas. Toronto, University of Toronto Press, 1962.
425 p. illus. S1427

Williams, Jay P
Alaskan adventure. Harrisburg, Pa., Stackpole Co., 1952.
xiii, 299 p. illus. S1428

Williamson, Geoffrey
The young traveller in the far north. London, Phoenix House, c1958.
123 p. plates. S1429

Wilson, Ingeborg
Alaskans I have met. Fairbanks?, 1968.
64 p. S1430

Winchell, Mary Edna, 1878-
Home by the Bering Sea, illustrated with photos. Caldwell, Idaho, Caxton Printers, 1951.
226 p. illus. S1431

Winchell, Mary Edna
Where the wind blows free. Caldwell, Idaho, Caxton Printers, 1954.
176 p. illus. S1432

Winslow, Kathryn
Alaska bound. Decorations by Sylvia Green Johnson. New York, Dodd, Mead, 1960.
281 p. illus. S1433

Wold, Jo Anne
Fairbanks the $200 million gold rush town: historical sketches (1902-1909). Fairbanks, The author, 1971.
42 p. illus. S1434

Wolfe, Ellen
William Beltz. Minneapolis, Dillon Press, 1975.
58 p. illus. S1435

Wood, Peter
Unbelievable years. Playa Del Rey, Calif., Littlepage Press, 1969.
236 p. S1436

Woodworth, Jim
The Kodiak bear. Harrisburg, Pa., Stackpole Co., 1958.
204 p. illus. S1437

Workman, Karen Wood
Alaskan archaeology: a bibliography 2nd ed. Anchorage, Alaska Division of Parks, 1974.
46 p. S1438

Wright, Billie
Four seasons north. New York, Harper & Row, 1973.
x, 278 p. illus. S1439

Yupiktak Bista
A report on subsistence and the conservation of the Yupik life style. n.p., 1974.
80 p. illus. S1440

Zagoskin, Lavrentii Alekseevich, 1808-1890
Lieutenant Zagoskin's travels in Russian America, 1842-1844: the first ethnographic and geographic investigations on the Yukon and Kuskokwim valleys of Alaska, edited by Henry N. Michael. Toronto, University of Toronto Press, 1967.
xiv, 358 p. illus. S1441

Zibell, Akugluk Wilfred, ed.
Unipchaat 3. Animal stories of the Kobuk River Eskimos. Fairbanks, Summer Institute of Linguistics, 1971.
25 p. illus. S1442

BRITISH COLUMBIA

Compiled by Linda Webster
Provincial Archives, British Columbia

Abraham, Dorothy Evelyn (Allarde), 1894-
Lone cone: a journal of life on the West coast of Vancouver Island. 4th ed. Victoria, Diggon-Hibben Ltd., 1952.
103 p. includes postscript.
Also: 5th ed., Vancouver, 1961. S1443

Abraham, Dorothy Evelyn (Allarde)
Old sweats ... heroes all. Victoria, B.C., 1956?
16 p. illus. S1444

Abraham, Dorothy Evelyn (Allarde)
Romantic Vancouver Island: Victoria yesterday and today. Cover designed and donated by Bettie Dunnell. Victoria, B.C., Acme Press, 1947.
118 p. illus. ports.
Also: 2nd ed., Victoria, B.C., published by Diggon-Hibben, 1949. 122 p.
Also: 3rd ed. Victoria, B.C., Hebden Printing Co., Ltd., 1956?
Also: 4th ed. Victoria B.C., Acme-Buckle Printing Co., Ltd., 1964. 120 p.
Also: 5th ed., 1966.
Also: 6th ed., 1968. S1445

Adachi, Ken
A history of the Japanese Canadians in British Columbia 1877-1958. Written under the auspices of the History Committee of the National Japanese Canadian Citizens Association. n.p., National Japanese Canadian Citizens Association, 1958.
43 (1) p. S1446

Adams, John W
The Gitksan potlatch: population flux, resource ownership and reciprocity. Toronto, Holt, Rinehart and Winston, 1973.
132 p. S1447

Affleck, Edward Lloyd, 1924-
Sternwheelers, sandbars and switchbacks: a chronicle of steam transportation in southeastern British Columbia. Vancouver, The author, c1958.
iii, 65 leaves, illus. S1448

Affleck, Edward Lloyd
Sternwheelers, sandbars and switchbacks. Vancouver, Alexander Nicolls Press, 1973.
47 p. illus. S1449

Akrigg, G.P.V. and Helen B. Akrigg
British Columbia chronicle, 1778-1846: adventures by sea and land. Vancouver, Discovery Press, 1975.
429 p. illus. S1450

Akrigg, George Philip Vernon and Helen B. Akrigg
1001 British Columbia place names. Vancouver, Discovery Press, 1969.
195 p. S1451

Along the totem trail, Port Essington to Hazelton, by Sperry Cline and others. Kitimat, B.C., 1961.
44 p. illus. S1452

Anderson, Aili (Sophia), 1906-
History of Sointula. Sointula, B.C., Sointula Centennial Committee, 1958.
16 p. illus.
With supplement by Mrs. Aini Tynjala. Vancouver, Broadway Printers Ltd., 1969.
19 p. S1454

Anderson, Frank Wesley, 1919-
Bill Miner, train robber. Calgary, Frontiers Unlimited, 1963?
56 p. illus. maps. ports. S1455

Anderson, Frank Wesley, ed.
The Dewdney trail, Salmo to Fort Steele. Calgary, Alta., Fronyier, 1972.
48 p. S1456

Anderson, James
Sawney's letters and Cariboo rhymes. Victoria, B.C., Baskerville restoration advisory committee, 1962.
64 p. S1457

Angier, Vena
At home in the woods; living the life of Thoreau today by Vena and Bradford Angier. New York, Sheridan House, c1951.
255 p. illus., ports. S1458

Anglican Young People's Association
The Anglican young people's association golden jubilee, 1902-1952, fifty years "For Christ and the Church." Toronto, A.Y.P.A., Dominion Council, 1951.
80 p. illus. ports. S1459

Angus, Anne Margaret (Anderson), 1901-
Children's aid society of Vancouver, B.C., 1901-1951. Vancouver, 1951?
48 p. illus. S1460

Angus, Henry Forbes, ed.
British Columbia and the United States. New York, Russell and Russell, 1970.
408 p. S1461

Anson, Peter Frederick, 1889-
Abbot extraordinary: a memoir of Aelred Carlyle, monk and missionary, 1874-1955. Foreword by Dame Rose Macaulay. London, the Faith Press, 1958.
310 p. ports.
Also: Foreword by Maisie Ward, New York, Sheed and Ward, 1958.
S1462

Anstey, Arthur, 1847?-1951.
British Columbia, a short history by Arthur Anstey and Neil Sutherland. Illustrated by Huntley Brown. Toronto, W.J. Gage, c1957.
v, 55 p. illus. maps
A revision of his British Columbia, published as an appendix to the Romance of Canada, by A.L. Burt (Toronto, 1946.)
S1463

Antonson, Rick
In search of a legend: the search for the Slumach-Lost Creek gold mine. New Westminster, Western Heritage Supply, 1972.
55p. illus. S1464

Arnott, Ida Janet (Gammage), 1906-
The burning bush in the sagebrush hills: a short history of St. Andrews Presbyterian Church. Kamloops, British Columbia, 1887-1962, by Mrs. D.A. Arnott. North Kamloops, Overland Press Ltd., 1962.
(22) p. illus. S1465

Art, Historical and Scientific Association of Vancouver, B.C.
The great Fraser midden. Vancouver, B.C., The Association (Intro. 1948).
29 p. illus. S1466

Asante, Nadine
The history of terrace. Terrace, Terrace Public Library Association, 1972.
250 p. illus. S1468

Atkinson, Kathy and others.
As it was - Mission City and district. Tsawwassen, Simple Thoughts Press, 1973.
105 p. illus. S1469

Atkinson, Reginald Noel, 1897- , comp.
Historical souvenir of Penticton, B.C., 1908-1958; on the occasion of the city of Penticton's golden jubilee prepared and edited by the Penticton Branch, the Okanagan Historical Society. Penticton, Penticton Herald, Ltd., 1958.
164 p. illus. ports. S1470

Audain, James Guy Payne, 1903-1970
Alex Dunsmuir's dilemma. Victoria, Sunnylane Publishing Co., c1964.
x, 133 p. plates. S1471

Audain, James Guy Payne
From coalmine to castle; the story of the Dunsmuirs of Vancouver Island. New York, Pageant Press, c1955.
213 p. plates. S1472

Audain, James Guy Payne
My borrowed life. Sidney, B.C., Gray's Publishing Ltd., 1963, c1962.
226 p. illus. S1473

Ayre, Robert Hugh
Sketco the raven. Toronto, Macmillan Co., of Canada, 1961.
183 p. illus. S1474

B.C. Air Lines Limited
The story of B.C. Air Lines Limited. Vancouver? The author, 1957?
(11) p. illus. S1475

B.C. Women's Institutes
Modern pioneers, 1909-1959. Vancouver, B.C., Evergreen Press, 1960?
101 p. illus. S1476

Baity, Earl S.
Wilderness welfare: a epic of frontier life. Vancouver, B.C., Mitchell Press, 1966. S1477

Balf, Mary
Kamloops: a history of the district up to 1914. Kamloops Museum, 1969.
144 p. S1478

Balf, Mary
The mighty Company Kamloops and the Hudson's Bay Company. Kamloops Museum, 1973.
15 p. S1479

Balf, Mary
The overlanders and other North Thompson travellers. Kamloops Museum, 1973.
15 p. S1480

Balf, Mary
Ship ahoy! Paddlewheelers of the Thompson waterway. Kamloops Museum, 1973.
12 p. S1481

Banfill, Bessie Jane
With the Indians of the Pacific. Toronto, Ryerson Press, 1966.
S1482

Banks, Charles Arthur, 1885-1961.
British Columbia and Sir James Douglas, K.C.B. (1803-1877). New York, Montreal, The Newcomen Society, 1954.
28 p. illus. S1483

Bannerman, Gary
Gastown: the 107 years. Vancouver, Unity Bank of Canada, Gastown Branch, 1974.
1 vol. illus. S1484

Baptie, Susan
First growth: the study of the British Columbia forest products. Vancouver, J.J. Douglas, 1975.
286 p. illus. S1485

Barlee, N.L.
Gold creek and ghost towns: East Kootenay, Boundary, West Kootenay, Okanagan and Similkameen. Summerland, Canada West Magazine, 1970.
183 p. maps. S1487

Barnett, Homer Garner, 1906-
The coast salish of British Columbia. Eugene, University of Oregon, 1955.
xiii, 320 (12) p. illus. S1488

Barr, James
Ferry across the Harbour. Vancouver, Mitchell Press, 1969.
71 p. illus. S1489

Baynes, George Edgar, 1870-1956
Edgar G. Baynes, pioneer of the West, 1870-1956. Vancouver, B.C., 1957.
(12) p. ports. S1490

Beeson, Edith
Dunlevey: from the diaries of Alex P. McInnes. Lillooet, Lillooet Publishers, 1971.
119 p. illus. S1491

Belsham, Alice Ada (Carroll), 1922- , comp.
History of Fort Fraser. Compiled by Alice Belsham and J. Philip Myers. Fort Fraser, B.C., April, 1958.
12 p. illus. S1492

Bergren, Myrtle
Tough timber; the loggers of British Columbia: their story. Toronto, Progress Books, 1966.
254 p. S1493

Bernsohn, Ken
Prince George area backroads. Sidney, Saltaire Publishing Co., 1975.
S1494

Berton, Pierre Francis deMarigny, 1920-
The mysterious north. 1st ed. New York, Alfred A. Knopf, 1956.
xiv, 345 p. illus. S1496

Bezanson, Ancel Maynard, 1878-
Sodbusters invade the peace. Toronto, The Ryerson Press, c1954.
vi, 209 p. maps. S1497

Bird, George
Tse-ees-tah: one man in a boat. Alberni, Arrowsmith Press, 1971.
240 p. illus. S1498

Bishop, Margaret W
And so they came to Cowichan. Victoria, Robinson Press, 1975.
33 p. illus. S1499

Bissley, Paul Lawrence, 1909-
A history of the Union Club of British Columbia. Victoria, Printed by Colonist Printing, 1956.
43 p. illus. S1500

Bissley, Paul Laurence
History of the Vancouver Club. Vancouver, 1971.
120 p. illus. S1501

Black, Samuel, 1780-1841
A journal of a voyage from Rocky Mountain portage in Peace River to the sources of Finlays Branch and north west ward in summer, 1824, by Samuel Black; edited by E.E. Rich. London, The Hudson's Bay Record Society, 1955.
c, 260, xiii p. fold map. plates (The Hudson's Bay Record Society, Publications 18). S1502

Bloedel, Stewart & Welch, Limited
A tour of the Franklin River logging operation, Sept., 1947. Port Alberni, The Company, 1947.
(24) p. illus. S1503

Blower, James, comp.
Gold rush 1894-1907, a pictorial history. Toronto, McGraw-Hill Ryerson, 1971.
199 p. illus. S1504

Blyth, Gladys
History of Port Edward, British Columbia. Port Edward, 1970.
S1505

Borradaile, John
"Lady of Culzean," Mayne Island. Victoria, 1971.
40 p. illus. S1506

Bowers, Dan and others
Exploring Garibaldi Park. Vol. 1. Vancouver, Gundy's and Bernie's Guide Book, 1972.
96 p. illus. S1507

Bowes, Gordon Emerson, 1914-1971, ed.
Peace River chronicles: eighty-one eye-witness accounts from the first exploration in 1793 of the Peace River region of British Columbia including the Finlay and Parsnip River basins. Selected and edited by Gordon E. Bowes. Vancouver, Prescott Publishing Co., 1963.
557 p. illus. S1508

Bowman, Phyllis
Muskeg, rocks and rain! Prince Rupert, 1973.
unpaged. illus. S1509

Brandis, Maxine van Vollenhoven, 1910-
Land for our sons. London, Hurst & Blackett, 1958.
195 p. illus. ports. S1511

British Columbia. ed. by J. Lewis Robinson. Toronto, University of Toronto Press, 1972.
139 p. illus. S1512

British Columbia. Centennial Committee
Ethnic groups in British Columbia: a selected bibliography based on check-list material in the Provincial Library and Archives. Compiled by Dorothy Blakey Smith. Victoria, The British Columbia Centennial Committee, 1957.
64 l. S1513

British Columbia Cement Company, Limited
The story of the famous "Elk Brand." Victoria, The Company, 1956?
(11) p. illus. ports. S1514

British Columbia centenary: a century to celebrate, 1858-1958. Vancouver, B.C., International Publishing Co., 1957.
352 p. illus. S1515

British Columbia Historical Association. Gulf Islands Branch.
A Gulf Islands patchwork: some early events on the islands of Galiano, Mayne, Saturna, North and South Pender. Sidney, B.C., Peninsula Print Co., 1961.
(7), 190 p. illus. S1516

British Columbia Historical Association. Vancouver Section.
Historic Yale, British Columbia. Vancouver, c1954.
32 p. illus. S1517

British Columbia Liberal Association.
British Columbia at the crossroads: past achievement, the liberal way, progress, stability, development. n.p., The Association, 1951.
(20) p. (part fold.) illus. ports. S1518

British Columbia Medical Association.
Golden jubilee, 1900-1950. Vancouver, Printed by Campbell & Smith, Ltd., 1950.
64 p. illus. S1519

British Columbia Mountaineering Club.
The Mountaineer, fiftieth anniversary, 1907-1957. Vancouver, Printed by Chapman & Warwick, 1957.
23 p. illus. S1520

British Columbia Natural Resources Conference. 1956.
British Columbia: atlas of resources. Editors: J.D. Chapman and D.B. Turner. Vancouver, Smith Lithograph Co., for the British Columbia Natural Resources Conference, 1956.
92 p. illus. maps. S1521

British Columbia Official Centennial Record, 1858-1958, a Century of Progress. Vancouver, B.C., Evergreen Press, Ltd., c1957.
176 p. illus.
Also: Rev. ed., 1957, 182 p. S1522

British Columbia Tree Fruits, Limited.
The British Columbia fruit industry: a short review. Kelowna, British Columbia Tree Fruits, Limited, 1949?
11 p. diagr. map. S1523

British Columbia Tree Fruits, Limited.
The valley of the blossoms. Kelowna, The author, 1947?
15 p. illus. S1524

British Columbia Weekly Newspaper Association. History Committee.
The story of British Columbia weekly newspapers. Mission City, 1972.
106 p. illus. S1525

British Columbia Women's Institute.
Modern pioneers, 1909-1959. Vancouver, 1960.
101 p. illus. S1526

Broadfoot, Anne
Through Lions Gate: a pictorial tour of greater Vancouver. Photographs by Ted Czolowski. Vancouver, B.C., 1966.
94 p. S1527

Broadfoot, Anne
Vancouver Island, a pictorial tour. Photographs by Ted Czolowski. Vancouver, Spectrum Enterprises, 1967.
80 p. S1528

Broadfoot, Barry
Stanley Park: an island in the city. Vancouver, November House, 1972.
unpaged. illus. S1529

Brodie, Steve
Bloody Sunday: Vancouver 1938: recollections of the post office sit down of single unemployed. Vancouver, Young Communist League, 1974.
24 p. S1530

Brooks, Edward Arnold, ed.
Padre Holmes, portrait of a ministry. Hamilton, Ont. Published by the General Board of Religious Education of the Diocese of Niagara, 1958.
66 p. illus. ports. S1531

Brown, Harrison, 1893-
Admirals, adventurers and able seamen: forgotten stories about places on our British Columbia coast and how they got their names. Vancouver, B.C., Keystone Press, 1953.
30 p. illus. S1532

Brown, Wallace William, 1923-
Port Mellon, B.C.: being an account of its first fifty years, by W.W. Brown and J.B. Stewart. Port Mellon, B.C., Port Mellon Community Association, 1958.
36 p. illus. plan. S1533

Bryan, Jack and Liz Bryan
Backroads of British Columbia. Vancouver, Sunflower Books, 1975.
160 p. photos. maps. S1534

Buckland, Frank Morgan, 1873-1953
Ogopogo's vigil: a history of Kelowna and district. Kelowna, c1948.
111leaves. illus. maps.
Also: Ogopogo's vigil; a history of Kelowna and the Okanagan. Kelowna, B.C., Kelowna Branch Okanagan Historical Society, 1966.
124 p. illus. maps. S1535

Bulhak, A. George
Recreational almanac of British Columbia, Canada: with a foreword by Roderick Haig-Brown. Vancouver, B.C., Recreational Almanac, Ltd., 1958.
32 p. illus. S1536

Bulman, T. Alex
Kamloops cattlemen: one hundred years of trail dust! Sidney, Grays Publishing, 1972.
183 p. illus. S1537

Burge, Thomas Ashlee, 1922-
"This is Saltspring." Ganges, B.C., The Spotlight, 1953.
32 p. illus. S1538

Burnes, J. Rodger
Echoes of the ferries: a history of the North Vancouver ferry service. North Vancouver, 1974.
105 p. illus. S1539

Burnes, John Rodger
Saga of a municipality in its formative days 1891-1907. North Vancouver, Carson Graham Secondary School, 1972.
98 p. illus. S1540

Burt, Alfred Leroy, 1888-
The romance of Canada. Toronto, W.J. Gage & Co., Limited, 1944.
400, 64 p. illus.
Also: revision of Anstey's supplement by Neil Sutherland with title, British Columbia, a short history. Illustrated by Huntley Brown. Toronto, W.J. Gage Limited, 1957.
v, 55 p. illus. S1541

Byrnes, Harold
Pioneer days at Cecil Lake, by Slim Byrnes. Fort St. John, Alaska Highway News, 1960.
64 p. illus. S1542

Cail, Robert E
Land, man and the law: the disposal of Crown lands in British Columbia, 1871-1913. Vancouver, University of British Columbia Press, 1974.
333 p. illus. S1543

Canadian Federation of University Women. Maple Ridge.
Maple Ridge, a history of settlement. Written by Sheila Nickols (editor), and others. Maple Ridge, B.C., c1972.
119 p. illus. S1544

Canadian National Railways.
The Jasper way through the majestic Canadian Rockies. Montreal, The author, 1950.
18 p. illus. S1545

Canadian National Steamship Company.
Presenting SS "Prince George," new flagship of the Canadian National Pacific Coast Steamships. Montreal? 1948.
(8) p. illus. S1546

Canadian Pacific Railway Company
Cruise by Canadian Pacific to Alaska and the Yukon. n. p., the author, 1947.
(16) p. illus. S1547

Canoe sport British Columbia. British Columbia canoe routes: a guide to 92 canoe trips in beautiful Columbia. New Westminster. Nunaga Publishing Co., 1974.
112 p. S1548

Carey, Neil G
A guide book to the Queen Charlotte Islands. Anchorage, Alaska, Alaska Northwest Publishing Co., 1975.
71 p. illus. S1549

Carr, Emily, 1871-1945
The heart of a peacock. Edited by Ira Dilworth. Line drawings by the author. Toronto, Oxford University Press, 1953.
xv, 234 p. illus. S1550

Carr, Emily
Hundreds and thousands: the journals of Emily Carr. Toronto, Clarke, Irwin, 1966.
332 p. col. plates S1551

Carroll, Campbell, 1903-1968
Three bar: the story of Douglas Lake. Vancouver, Mitchell Press, 1958.
111 p. illus. ports. S1552

Carrothers, Arthur William Rooke, 1924-
A study of the operation of the injunction in labour-management disputes in British Columbia, 1946-1955, with particular reference to the law of picketing. Toronto, C.C.H. Canadian Limited (Pref. 1956.)
xxvii, 276 p. tables. S1553

Carter, Anthony
Abundant rivers. Chief Dan George, ed. Saanichton, Hancock House, 1972.
144 p. illus. S1554

Carter, Anthony
Somewhere between. Vancouver, Agency Press, 1967.
80 p. S1555

Carter, Anthony
This is Haida. Vancouver, The author, 1969.
139 p. illus. S1556

Cartwright, Edward Rogers, 1883-
A late summer: the memoirs of E.R. Cartwright, C.B.E. London, The Caravel Press, 1964.
x, 224 p. illus. ports. S1557

Case, Victoria
Applesauce needs sugar. Garden City, N.Y., Doubleday, 1960.
232 p. illus. S1558

Cates, Charles Warren, 1899-1960.
Tidal action in British Columbia waters. North Vancouver, 1952.
(51) p. illus.
Also: 1952 (i.e. 1954), 57 p.
S1559

Cavers, Anne Sutherland, 1887-1971
Our school of nursing, 1899-1949. Vancouver, Printed by Ward & Phillips Ltd., 1949?
89 p. illus. S1560

Chambers, Edith Devey
History of Port Coquitlam, our city. 1st ed. Burnaby, Web Press, 1973.
(167) p. illus. S1561

Cherrington, John
Mission on the Fraser: patterns of a small city's progress. Vancouver. Mitchell Press, 1974.
222 p. illus. S1562

Chinese-Canadian Picture Project ad hoc Committee.
Chinese Canadian picture project catalogue. Vancouver, B.C., Vancouver Public Library, 1973.
viii, 159 l. S1563

Christian Community and Brotherhood of Reformed Doukhobors
An open-letter--appeal to the Society of Friends (Quakers) living in Canada and the United States of America. Crescent Valley, B.C., 1954.
51 p. illus. S1564

Christian Community and Brotherhood of Reformed Doukhobors
A public indictment of J.J. Verigin, Secretary of the Orthodox Doukhobors, for his deliberate distortion of the basic principles of the Doukhobor faith. Krestova, B.C., 1954.
22 p. illus. S1565

Christie, James R., 1877-
The story of Okanagan Falls, by Jas. R. Christie and Isabel Christie MacNaughton. Okanagan Falls, Okanagan Falls Centennial Committee, 1958.
44 p. illus. S1566

Christie Indian Residential School, Kakawis
Golden jubilee of Christie Indian residential school, 1900-1950. Victoria, B.C., Acme Press, Ltd., 1950?
(68) p. illus. S1567

Church of England in Canada. Women's Auxiliary. British Columbia Diocesan Board.
Our goodly heritage, 1904-1954. Edited by H. Kathleen Davies. Victoria, 1954.
44 p. ports. S1568

Clark, Cecil
The best of Victoria yesterday and today: a nostalgic 115 year pictorial history of Victoria. Victoria, Victorian Weekly, 1973.
unpaged. illus. S1569

Clark, Cecil
Tales of the British Columbia provincial police. Sidney, Gray's Publishing, 1971.
183 p. illus. S1570

Cleasby, Henry Standley, 1868-1959.
The Nicola valley in review. Merritt, B.C., Printed by the Merritt Herald Ltd., 1958.
48 p. illus. S1571

Clemson, Donovan
Living with logs: British Columbia's log buildings and rail fences. Saanichton, Hancock House, 1974.
95 p. illus. S1572

Clemson, Donovan
Outback adventure: through interior British Columbia. Saanichton, Hancock House, 1974.
224 p. illus. S1573

Clutesi, George C.
Son of raven, son of deer. Sidney, Gray's Publishing, 1967.
126 p. S1574

Clutesi, George C.
Potlatch. Sidney, Grays Publishing, 1969.
188 p. illus. S1575

Cochran, Lutwin Babel (Ulrich), 1880-
The wilderness told me. Quesnel, Aveline Moffat Hill, 1971, c1964.
150 p. illus. S1576

Codere, Helen Frances, 1917-
Fighting with property: a study of Kwakiutl potlatching and warfare, 1792-1930. With tribal and linguistic map of Vancouver Island and adjacent territory drawn and compiled by Vincent F. Kotschar. New York, J.J. Augustin Publisher (pref. 1950).
viii, 136 p. illus.
Also: 2nd printing, Seattle, Univ. of Washington Press, 1966, viii, 135 p.
Also: 3rd printing, 1970; 4th, 1972.
S1577

Collier, Eric
Three against the wilderness: illustrated by Joseph Cellini. Toronto, Clarke, Irwin, 1962.
349 p. illus.
(first published, N.Y., Dutton, 1959). S1578

Community Arts Council of Vancouver.
Gastown revisited. Vancouver, 1970.
34 p. illus. S1579

Connelly, Dolly
Guidebook to Vancouver Island, off the coast of southwest British Columbia. Los Angeles, W. Ritchie Press, 1973.
142 p. illus. S1580

Conover, David
One man's island. Toronto, General Publishing, 1971.
181 p. illus. S1581

Consolidated Mining and Smelting Company of Canada Limited.
The Cominco story. Trail, Printed by Trail Times Ltd., ca. 1953.
36 p. illus.
Also: 1960? 36 p. illus. S1582

Coon, Danny and Gary Ratuskniak, comp.
Ba-Kwum heritage. Courtenay, E.W. Bickle, 1975.
24 p. illus. S1583

Corbitt, Henry Wellington, 1889-1967
The history of Kaleden by H.W. Corbitt with the assistance of Ron King. Kaleden, B.C., Kaleden Centennial Committee, 1958.
61 p. illus. S1584

Corner, John
Pictographs (Indian rock paintings) in the interior of British Columbia. Vernon, The author, 1968.
131 p. illus. S1585

Corner, Raymond Westley, 1894-
Glenmore, the apple valley. Kelowna, Glenmore Centennial Committee, 1958.
57 p. illus. S1586

Coutant, Frank Raymond
Cariboo highway: the great north road to the Fraser River goldfields. Monroe, Conn., The author, 1967.
47 p. S1588

Coutant, Frank Raymond, 1885-
Fraser-Cariboo gold rush: the boom that founded British Columbia. Monroe, Conn., The author, 1967.
52 p. S1589

Coutant, Frank Raymond,
Yankee steamboats on the Fraser River, British Columbia: a story of Yankee participation in building and operating paddlewheelers during the Cariboo gold rush, 1858-1871. Inverness, Fla., 1966.
39 p. illus. S1590

Coutts, Margaret E.
Dawson Creek, past and present: an historical sketch. Dawson Creek, B.C., Dawson Creek Historical Society, 1958.
115 p. illus S1591

Cox, Mary Aline
Saga of a seafarer: the annals of Capt. William Irving. New Westminster, B.C., Irving House Historical Centre, 1966.
37 p. illus. S1592

Cracroft, Sophia, 1816-1892
Lady Franklin visits the Pacific Northwest: being extracts from the letters of Miss Sophia Cracroft, Feb. to April 1861 and April to July, 1870. Victoria, Provincial Archives of British Columbia, 1974. (Provincial Archives, Memoir, no. 11).
xxviii, 157 p. illus. S1593

Cronin, Kay
Cross in the wilderness. Vancouver, B.C., Mitchell Press, c1960.
255 p. illus. S1594

Crown Zellerbach Canada Limited. Richmond Division.
A history of the municipality of Richmond. Vancouver, Evergreen Press, Limited, 1958.
28 p. illus.
Also: with title:A history of Richmond. Richmond, Richmond Centenary Council, 1967. S1595

Crown Zellerbach Canada Limited. Richmond Division.
A history of Richmond. Richmond, B.C., Richmond Historical & Museum Advisory Committee, 1971.
28 (2) p. illus. S1596

Culbert, Dick
Alpine guide to southwestern British Columbia. Vancouver, Alpine Guide, 1974.
441 p. maps. photos S1597

Culbert, Richard
Climber's guide to the coastal ranges of British Columbia. Vancouver, Alpine Club of Canada, 1965.
320 p. illus. S1598

Currie, Laurie
Princeton 100 years, 1867-1967. 1st ed. n.p., Similkameen Spotlight Publishing Co. Ltd., c1967.
96 p. illus. S1599

Currie, William Henry, 1883-1969
Alluring British Columbia. Vancouver, Published by the Vancouver, British Columbia, Club of Printing House Craftsmen, 1949.
58 p. illus. S1600

Curtin, Fred, ed.
Hiking trails. Vancouver, Vancouver Daily Province, 1971.
60 p. illus. S1601

Cyca, Robert and Andrew Harcombe
Exploring Manning Park. Vancouver, Gundy and Bernie's Guide Books, 1970.
96 p. illus. S1602

Czolowski, Ted
British Columbia calling. Vancouver, Tad Publishing, Ltd., 1973.
144 p. illus. S1603

Czolowski, Thaddeus, 1921-
Legacy to behold: famous parks and gardens in or near Vancouver and Victoria, British Columbia. Photographed by Ted Czolowski, with a text by Donald Stainsby. Vancouver, Quest Travelbooks, c1970.
96 p. illus. S1604

Czolowski, Ted
Vancouver calling. Vancouver, B.C., Tad Publishing Enterprises, 1972.
96 p. illus. S1605

Daem, Mary (Bannerman)
A history of early Revelstoke, by M. Daem and E.E. Dickey. Revelstoke, B.C., 1962.
13 p. illus. S1606

Dahl, Ervin
Gateway to the interior: "A brief history of Hope"1971. Chilliwack, 1971.
65 p. illus. S1607

Dakin, Jean L
Kinbasket country: the story of Golden and the Columbia valley. Golden, Golden & District Historical Society, 1973.
88 p. illus. S1608

Dalichow, Fritz
Agricultural geography of British Columbia. Vancouver, Versatile Publishing, 1972.
161 p. illus. S1609

Dalzell, Kathleen E
The Queen Charlotte Islands. Book 2: Of places and names. Prince Rupert, Dalzell Books, 1973.
472 p. illus. S1610

Davies, Marguerite and Cora Ventress
Fort St. John pioneer profiles. Fort St. John, Centennial Committee, 1971.
72 p. illus. S1611

Davis, Chuck
Chuck Davis' guide to Vancouver. Vancouver, J.J. Douglas, 1973.
226 p. illus. S1612

Day, Beth (Feagles), 1924-
Grizzlies in their back yard. New York, Julian Messner, Inc., 1956.
224 p.
Also: with title The world of the grizzlies. Illustrated by Kiyoaki Komoda. Garden City, N.Y., Doubleday & Co., Inc., c1969.
211 p. illus. S1613

De Goutiere, Justin Vernon, 1926-1968.
The pathless way. West Vancouver, Graydonald Graphics, 1968.
193 p. S1614

Deuling, Gertrude Rosemary (McAnany), 1925-
Beyond Shuswap Falls, compiled and written by Rosemary Deuling. Vernon, B.C.,? Printed by Parkland ColorPress, 1973.
117 p. illus. S1615

De Volpi, Charles P
British Columbia: a pictorial record 1778-1891. Toronto, Longman, 1973.
184 plates. S1616

Diespecker, Richard E. Alan, 1907-1973.
Elizabeth by Dick Diespecker. With six drawings by Ron Jackson. Toronto, Vancouver, J.M. Dent & Sons (Canada) Limited, c1950.
170 p. illus S1617

Doe, Ernest, 1911- , comp.
Centennial history of Salmon Arm. Salmon Arm, B.C., Printed by the Salmon Arm observer, 1971.
280 p. illus. S1618

Dougan, Nathan Paul, 1878-1970
Cowichan my valley. Cobble Hill, B.C.: R.I. Dougan, c1973.
284 p. illus. S1619

Downs, Arthur George, 1924-
Paddlewheels on the frontier: the story of B.C. sternwheel steamers, by Art Downs. Cloverdale, B.C., B.C. Outdoors Magazine, c1967-71.
2 vols. illus. S1621

Downs, Arthur George, ed.
Pioneer days in British Columbia: a selection of historical articles from B.C. Outdoors magazine. Edited by Art Downs. Surry, B.C., 1973.
3 vols. illus. ports. S1622

Downs, Art
Wagon road north: the story of the Cariboo gold rush in historical photos. Quesnel, Northwest Digest Ltd., 1960.
80 p. illus. S1623

Drucker, Philip and R.F. Heizer
To make my name good. Berkeley, Calif., University of California Press, 1967.
160 p. S1624

Duncan, Frances Imogene, 1926-
The Sayward-Kelsey Bay saga. Courtnay, B.C., Argus Publishing Co., 1958.
51 p. illus. ports. S1625

Eaton, Leonard A
The architecture of Samuel Maclure. Victoria, Art Gallery of Greater Victoria, 1971.
44 p. illus. S1626

Edwards, Margaret H and John C.R. Lort, comps.
A bibliography of British Columbia: years of growth, 1900-1950. Victoria, University of Victoria Social Science Research Centre, 1975.
446 p. S1627

Edwards, R. Yorke, ed.
Naturalist's guide to the Victoria region. Victoria, Prepared by the British Columbia Nature Council through the Victoria Natural History Society, 1967.
28 p. S1628

Elliott, Gordon Raymond, 1920-
Quesnel, commercial centre of the Cariboo gold rush. Quesnel, B.C., Cariboo Historical Society. Quesnel Branch, 1958.
vii, 190, viii p. illus. S1629

Emery, Maud
A seagull's dry. Surrey, Nunaga, 1975.
152 p. S1630

Evans, Elwood
The re-annexation of British Columbia to the United States right, proper and desirable. Victoria, Morriss Printing Co., 1965.
66 p. illus. S1631

Evans, Mary Augusta (Tappage), 1888-
The days of Augusta. Edited by Jean E. Speare, photography by Robert Keziere. Vancouver, J.J. Douglas, 1973.
79 p. illus. S1632

Fallis, George Oliver, 1885-1952.
A padre's pilgrimage by George O. Fallis, Chaplain of the forces. Toronto, The Ryerson Press, c1953.
xi, 166 p. front. S1633

Farrow, Moira
Nobody here but us: pioneers of the north. Vancouver, J.J. Douglas, 1975.
x, 219 p. illus. S1634

Ferguson, Ted
A white man's country: an exercise in Canadian prejudice. Toronto, Doubleday Canada Limited, 1975.
200 p. illus. S1635

Forbes, Elizabeth Lamont
Wild roses at their feet: pioneer women of Vancouver Island. Vancouver, British Columbia Centenial '71 Committee, 1971.
ix, 147 p. illus. S1636

Forbes, Lurlene Mary
Lac La Hache: historical notes on the early settlers. Quesnel, Big Country Printers, 1970?
34 p. S1637

Forward, Charles Nelson, 1927- , ed.
Residential and neighbourhood studies in Victoria. Victoria, University of Victoria Dept. of Geography, 1973. (Western Geographical Series, 5.)
xv, 230 p. illus. S1638

Fox, Christine Ross
Index to the journals of the Legislative Assembly of the Province of British Columbia, 1872-1971. Victoria, Provincial Library, 1973.
895 p. S1639

Fraser, George Johnston, 1872-1958
The story of Osoyoos, September 1811 to December 1952. Penticton, The Penticton Herald, 1953.
212 p. illus. S1640

Fraser, Simon, 1776-1862
The letters and journals of Simon Fraser, 1806-1808. Edited with an introduction by W. Kaye Lamb. Toronto, Macmillan Co., of Canada, 1960.
292 p. illus. S1641

Freemasons. British Columbia. Grand Lodge.
History of Grand Lodge of British Columbia, 1871-1970. Victoria, 1971.
xvi, 653 p. illus. S1642

Frison-Roche, Roger
Nahanni (trapeurs and prospecteurs du Grand Nord Canadien). Grenoble, Arthaud, 1969.
263 p. illus S1644

Fry, Alan
The ranch on the Cariboo. Garden City, N.Y., Doubleday, 1962.
281 p. maps. S1645

Gabriel, Theresa
Vernon, British Columbia: a brief history. Vernon, B.C., Vernon Centennial Committee, 1958.
63 p. illus. S1646

Galloway, Hazel Frances (Dempsey), 1921-
A history of the Cedar, Bright, Cranberry and Oyster districts on Vancouver Island, B.C. Compiled by Mrs. Allan Galloway and Robert Strachan. Ladysmith, Cedar Centennial Committee, 1958.
26 leaves. illus. S1647

Garrett, Anne Evans
The Bowen Island story. Vancouver, B.C., Mitchell Press, 1957.
16 p. illus. S1648

George, Daniel, 1899-
My heart soars. By Chief Dan George. Saanichton, 1974.
96 p. illus. S1649

Gibson, John Frederic, 1920-
A small and charming world. Toronto, Collins, 1972.
221 p. S1650

Gibson, William C
Wesbrook and his university. Vancouver, University of British Columbia Library, 1973.
xii, 204 p. illus. S1651

Gillespie, Alexander, 1880-1948
Journey through life: biography of Alexander Gillespie, 1880-1948. Victoria, B.C., Published by Victoria Press, Limited, 1954.
143 p. ports. S1652

Gillingham, Donald William
Umiak! London, Museum Press Limited, 1955.
xxv, 27-222 p. illus. S1653

Gilroy, Marion
As we remember it: interviews with pioneering librarians of British Columbia, edited by Marion Gilroy and Samuel Rothstein. Vancouver, University of British Columbia School of Librarianship, 1970.
163 p. maps. S1654

Godman, Josephine
Pioneer days of Port Renfrew. Victoria. Solitaire Publications, 1973.
64 p. illus. S1654A

Golden Centennial Committee, Historical Branch.
Golden memories ... of the town where the turbulent Kicking Horse meets the mighty Columbia. Golden, The Committee, c1958.
91 leaves. illus. ports. S1655

Goodchild, Fred Henry, 1892-1955.
British Columbia, its history, people and industry. Foreword by Byron I. Johnson, Premier of British Columbia. London, George Allen & Unwin Ltd., 1951.
219 p. illus. S1655A

Goodfellow, John Christie, 1890-1968.
The story of Similkameen. Princeton, B.C., Princeton Centennial Committee, 1958.
88 p. maps. ports. S1656

Goudie, St. Clare Clark, 1901-
The wise and foolish virgins, or, the plot that failed. n.p., The author, 1949?
4 pts. in 1 vol. port. S1657

Gould, Edwin Orrin, 1936-
Logging: British Columbia's logging history. Saanichton, Hancock House, 1975.
224 p. illus. S1658

Gould, Jan
Women of British Columbia. Saanichton, Hancock House, 1975.
224 p. illus. S1659

Graham, Clara, 1888-
Kootenay mosaic. Kootenay, 1971.
112 p. illus. S1660

Graham, Clara
Kootenay yesterdays: three first-hand accounts of mining, prospecting, ranching, teaching and trapping in the Kootenay district in pre-World War I times. Clara Graham, Ed Picard, Angus Davis. Vancouver, A. Nicolls Press, foreword, 1976.
iv, 174 p. (16) leaves of plates. illus. maps. S1661

Graham, Clara
This was the Kootenay. Vancouver, B.C., Printed by Evergreen Press Ltd., 1964, c1963.
x, 270 p. illus. S1662

Gray, Arthur Wilfred, 1895-
Kelowna: tales of bygone days. Kelowna, Kelowna Printing Co., 1968.
142 p. S1663

Greene, Ronald Allen, 1938-
Macdonald & Company, bankers, Victoria, Vancouver Island, Vancouver Island, 1859-1864: a numismatic study. Victoria, 1962.
(12) p. facsims. tables. S1664

Greene, Ruth
Personality ships of British Columbia: thirty-seven illustrated sea tales of Canada's western ships. West Vancouver, Marine Tapestry Publications, 1969.
341 p. illus. S1665

Gregson, Harry
A history of Victoria, 1842-1970. Victoria, Observer Publishing, Morriss Printing, 1970.
246 p. S1666

Griffin, Harold John Michael, 1912-
British Columbia: the people's early story. Vancouver, B.C., Tribune Publishing Company, Limited, 1958.
95 p. S1667

Grigg, David Henry, 1883-
From one to seventy. Vancouver, Mitchell Printing & Publishing Co., Limited., 1955, c1953.
199 p. port.
Also: 1st ed. New York, Vantage Press, c1956. 262 p. S1668

Gudlaugson, Magnus G
Three times a pioneer, by ... a Peace River pioneer. Ed. by Holmfridur Danielson. Winnipeg, 1959.
104 p. S1669

Guiltner, James Carl, 1930-
The Peace River country and McKenzie highway: historical and tourist guide. Edmonton, The author, 1963.
336 p. illus.
Also: 1964, 448 p. S1670

Gunn, Sisvan William Aram, 1926-
A complete guide to the totem poles in Stanley Park, Vancouver, B.C. Vancouver, W.E.G. Macdonald, 1965.
24 p. illus. S1671

Gunn, Sisvan William Aram
Haida totems in wood and argillite. West Vancouver, Whiterock Publications, 1967.
24 p. S1672

Gunn, Sisvan William Aram
Kwakiutl house and totem poles at Alert Bay, B.C. West Vancouver, Whiterock Publications, 1966.
24 p. illus. S1673

Gutstein, Donald
Vancouver Ltd. Toronto, James Lorimer, 1975.
192 p. illus. S1674

Hacking, Norman Rupert and W. Kaye Lamb
The princess story: a century and a half of west coast shipping. Vancouver, Mitchell Press, 1975.
360 p. illus. photos. S1675

Hagelund, William Arnold
Flying the chase flag. Toronto, Ryerson, 1961.
ix, 194 p. diagr. S1676

Haig-Brown, Roderick Langmere Haig, 1908-1976.
The farthest shores. Toronto, Longmans, Green, c1960.
127 p. illus. S1677

Haig-Brown, Roderick Langmere Haig
Fisherman's summer. Toronto, W. Collins Sons, 1959.
253 p. S1678

Haig-Brown, Roderick Langmere Haig
Fur and gold: illustrated by Paul Duff. Toronto, Longmans, 1962.
iv, (1), 131 p. illus. S1679

Haig-Brown, Roderick Langmere Haig
The living land: an account of the natural resources of British Columbia. Produced by the British Columbia Natural Resources Conference. Toronto, Macmillan, 1961.
269 p. illus.
Same (Special ed.) Toronto, Macmillan, 1961. S1680

Haig-Brown, Roderick Langmere Haig
Measure of the year. New York, William Morrow & Company, 1950.
x, 260 p.
Also: Toronto, Collins, c1950, 279 p.
Also: Freeport, N.Y., Books for Libraries Press, 1971, c1950.
x, 260 p. (Essay index reprint series.) S1681

Haig-Brown, Roderick Langmere Haig
The whale people: drawings by Mary Weiler. London, Collins, 1962.
184 p. illus. S1682

Hamilton, Beatrice Charlotte
Salt Spring Island. Vancouver, Mitchell Press, 1969.
180 p. illus. S1683

Hamilton, Reuben, 1888-1968
Mount Pleasant early days: memories of Reuben Hamilton, pioneer 1890. Vancouver, City Archives, 1957.
64 p. illus. ports. S1684

Hancock, David and Lyn Hancock
Wild islands: wildlife adventures on North America's West coast. Saanichton, Wildlife Conservation Centre, 1970.
78 p. illus. S1685

Hardwick, Francis Chester, 1905- , ed.
To the promised land: Ukrainians in Canada. Vancouver, Tantalus Research, 1973.
62 p. illus. S1686

Hardwick, Walter Gordon
Vancouver. Toronto, Collier-Macmillan Canada, 1974.
x, 214 p. illus. S1687

Harker, Douglas Edward, 1911-
The dukes: the story of the men who have served in peace and war with the British Columbia Regiment (D.C.O.) 1883-1973. Vancouver? c1974.
487 p. illus. S1688

Harker, Douglas Edward
The story of the British Columbia regiment, 1939-1949. Vancouver? Uneeda Printers? 1950?
85 p. illus. ports. S1689

Harper, Peter
Gold rush in the Cariboo. Toronto, Ginn and Co., 1974.
24 p. illus. S1690

Harrington, Richard Walter, 1911-
British Columbia in pictures. Text by Lyn Harrington. Toronto, T. Nelson, c1958.
1 vol. (unpaged) illus. S1691

Harris, Lorraine
Halfway to the goldfields: a history of Lillooet. Vancouver, J.J. Douglas, 1975.
97 p. illus. S1692

Hastings, Margaret Adelina (Kelly) Lang, 1903-
Where nature dwells: parks of White Rock and South Surrey. White Rock, B.C., White Rock Printers & Publishers, 1966.
40 p. illus. S1693

Hawthorn, Harry Bertram, 1910-
The Indians of British Columbia: a study of contemporary social adjustment, by H.B. Hawthorn, C.S. Belshaw and S.M. Jamieson. Toronto, University of Toronto Press, and the University of B.C., 1958.
ix, 499 p. illus. S1694

Hazlitt, William Carew, 1834-1913
The great gold fields of Cariboo. Vancouver, Klanak Press, 1974.
134 p. illus. S1695

Healey, Elizabeth, 1912- , comp.
A history of Alert Bay and district. Alert Bay, B.C., Alert Bay Centennial Committee, 1958.
101 p. illus. S1696

Hearn, George Robert
"The cordwood limited," a history of the Victoria & Sidney Railway, by George Hearn and David Wilkie. Victoria, British Columbia Railway Historical Association, c1966.
80 p. illus. S1697

Hearn, George Robert
"The cordwood limited": a history of the Victoria & Sidney Railway, by George Hearn and David Wilkie. Rev. 3rd ed. Victoria, British Columbia Railway Historical Association, 1971, c1966.
83 p. illus. S1698

Hearn, George Robert
"The cordwood limited": a history of the Victoria & Sidney Railway by George Hearn and David Wilkie. Rev. 5th ed. Victoria, British Columbia Railway Historical Association, 1976. c1966.
84 p. illus. S1699

Heidmeier, Father Boniface, 1880-1971.
The history of Saint Francis Parish Vancouver. Vancouver, B.C., Alverna distributors, 1959.
174 p. illus. S1700

Heidmeier, Father Boniface
Pioneering in the West. Memories of his life and experiences in the West with the Franciscans. Vancouver, Alverna Distributors, 1957.
xiv, 277 p. illus. S1701

Helmcken, John Sebastian
The reminiscences of Doctor John Sebastian Helmcken, ed. by Dorothy Blakey-Smith. Vancouver, University of British Columbia Press, 1975.
xlii, 373 p. illus. S1702

Hembroff-Schleicher, Edythe
M.E., a portrayal of Emily Carr. Toronto, Clarke, Irwin, 1969.
123 p. S1703

Hendy, Albert Edward, 1905-
St. Paul's Church, Nanaimo, B.C.: a brief history since its foundation, 1859-1952. Nanaimo? 1953.
36 p. illus. S1704

Hickman, Mary
Early history of East Chilliwack. London, Witherby & Co., 1957?
105 p. illus. S1705

Hill, Arnold Victor, 1897-
Tides of change: a story of Fishermen's co-operatives in British Columbia. Prince Rupert, Prince Rupert Fisherman's Co-operative Association 1967.
xii, 279 p. S1706

Hill, Hazel, A.E.
Tales of the Alberni valley. Edmonton, Hamly Press Ltd., 1952.
48 p. illus. S1707

Hilliam,Bentley Collingwood, 1890-
Flotsam's follies: the autobiography of B.C. Hilliam, "Flotsam." London, Arthur Barron, Ltd., 1948.
x, 177, ix-xv p. illus. S1708

History and legends of the Chilcotin. George Terry, comp. Williams Lake, B.C., Caribou Press, Ltd., 1958.
48 p. S1709

Hoagland, Edward, 1932-
Notes from the century before: a journal from British Columbia. New York,Random House, 1969.
272 p. maps. S1710

Hobson, Richmond Pearson, 1907-1966
Grass beyond the mountains: discovering the last great cattle frontier on the North American continent. 1st ed. Philadelphia, New York, J.B. Lippincott Co., c1951.
256 p. map
Also: London, G. Bell and Sons, Ltd., 1952.
Also: Toronto, Montreal, McClelland and Stewart Limited, 1973.
S1711

Hobson, Richmond Pearson
Nothing too good for a cowboy. 1st ed. Philadelphia and New York, J.B. Lippincott Company, c1955.
252 p. map.
Also: London, Hodder & Stoughton, Ltd., 1956.
Also: Toronto, McClelland and Stewart Limited, 1973. S1712

Hobson, Richmond Pearson
The rancher takes a wife. London, G. Bell, 1962.
236 p. map.
Also: Philadelphia, Lippincott, 1961. S1713

Holliday, Charles William, 1870-1955
The valley of youth. Caldwell, Idaho, Caxton Printers, 1948.
357 p. plates. map. S1714

Holloway, Godfrey Fry, 1909-
The Empress of Victoria. Victoria, Pacifica Productions, 1968.
105 p. S1715

Holmes, Rex, 1923-
The last summer: memories of the Peace River country. Illustrated by Jean Redfern. Toronto, Baxter Publishing, 1965.
178 p. illus. S1716

Holt, Simma Milner
Terror in the name of God: the story of the Sons of Freedom Doukhobors. Toronto, McClelland and Stewart Limited, c1964.
312 p. illus. S1717

Hood, Robert Allison, 1880-1958
Vignettes of Vancouver, with illustrations by Harry E. White. Vancouver, Education Services Ltd., 1954.
ix, 84 p. illus. S1718

Horsefly Historical Society
Horsefly ... it's early history, 1859-1915. Horsefly, The Society, 1975.
28 p. illus. S1719

Hou, Charles
To Potlatch or not to Potlatch: an in-depth study of culture-conflict between the British Columbia coastal Indians and the white man. Vancouver, B.C., British Columbia Teachers' Federation, 1973.
81 p. illus. S1720

Houston Centennial '71 Committee
Marks on the forest floor: a story of Houston, British Columbia. Houston, 1971.
152 p. illus. S1721

Howard, Irene
Bowen Island, 1872-1972. Bowen Island, Bowen Island Historians, 1973.
190 p. illus. S1722

Howard, Irene
Vancouver's Svenskar: a history of the Swedish community in Vancouver. Vancouver, Vancouver Historical Society, 1970.
127 p. illus. S1723

Hughes, Ben
History of the Comox valley, 1862 to 1945. Nanaimo, B.C., Evergreen Press, 1962.
58 p. ports. S1724

Hull, Raymond and Olga Ruskin
Gastown's Gassy Jack: the life and times of John Deighton of England, California and early British Columbia. Vancouver, Gordon Soules Economic Research, 1971.
48 p. illus. S1725

Hull, Raymond, ed.
Tales of a pioneer surveyor: Charles Aeneas Shaw. Toronto, Longmans Canada, 1970.
167 p. illus. S1726

Hull, Raymond and others.
Vancouver's past. Seattle, Wash., University of Washington Press, 1974.
96 p. photos maps. S1727

Hutchinson, Bill and Julie Hutchinson
Rockhounding and beachcombing on Vancouver Island. Victoria, Tom & Georgia Vaulkhard, 1971
56 p. illus.
Also: Rev. ed., 1973.
Also: 2nd ed., 1975. S1728

Hutchinson, Bruce, 1901-
The Fraser. Illustrated by Richard Bennett. New York and Toronto, Rinehart & Co., Inc., 1950.
(6) p., 3 l., 368 p. illus. S1729

ILWU Local 500 Pensioners
"Man along the shore!": the story of the Vancouver waterfront as told by longshoremen themselves, 1860's to 1975. ILWU Local 500 Pensioners. Vancouver, B.C., Local 500 Pensioners, 1975.
160 p. illus. ports. S1730

International Publishing Company, Vancouver.
British Columbia centenary: a century to celebrate, 1858-1958. Vancouver, B.C., The Company, 1957.
352 p. illus. S1731

International Woodworkers of America. Western Canadian Regional Council No. 1.
The I.W.A. in British Columbia. Vancouver, 1971.
63 p. illus. S1732

Jackman, Sydney Wayne Anfield, 1925-
The men at Cary Castle: a series of portrait sketches of the Lieutenant-Governors of British Columbia from 1871-1971. Victoria, Morriss Printing Co., 1972.
207 p. S1733

Jackman, Sydney Wayne
Portraits of the Premiers: an informal history of British Columbia. Sidney, Gray's Publishing, 1969.
272 p. illus. S1734

Jackman, Sydney Wayne
Vancouver Island. Toronto, Ont. Griffin House, 1972.
212 p. illus. ports. S1735

Job, Peter Dalzel, (pseud.)
The settlers. London, Constable, c1957.
209 p. illus. S1736

Johnson, Emily Pauline, 1861-1913
Flint and feather, by E. Pauline Johnson (Tekahionwake). Toronto, London, The Musson Book Company, Ltd., 1912.
xx, 156 p. illus. front.
Also: 2nd ed. rev. and enlarged. London, New York, Toronto, Hodder and Stoughton, 1913.
Also: 3rd ed. rev. and enlarged. Toronto, London, the Musson Book Co., Ltd., 1914, xxx, 166 p. illus.
Also: 4th ed. rev. and enlarged, 1916. xxx, 166 p. illus.
Also with title: Flint and feather: the complete poems... 5th ed. rev. and enlarged, 1917, xxi, 176 p. illus. port.
Also: 6th ed. rev. and enlarged, 1920, c1917, xxxi, 166 p.
Also: 7th ed., 1921, c1917
Also: 8th ed. Toronto, The Musson Book Co., Ltd., 1922, c1917. S1737

Johnson, Emily Pauline
Legends of Vancouver, by E. Pauline Johnson (Tekahionwake). Vancouver, Privately printed, 1911.
x, 89 p.
Also: 2nd ed. Vancouver, B.C., Published for Geo. S. Forsyth & Co., 1912, c1911.
Also: 3rd ed. Vancouver, B.C., The Thomson Stationery Company 1912, c1911. xiv, 167 p. illus.
Also: 4th ed. Vancouver, Published for Geo. S. Forsyth & Co., 1912, c1911. xiv, 138 p. illus.
Also: 4th ed. n.p., c1911.
Also: Vancouver, Published for Geo. S. Forsyth & Co., 1913, c1911. xiii, 138 p.
Also: 6th ed. Illustrated. Vancouver, Published by The Thomson Stationery Co., 1913.
Also: 6th ed. Illustrated. Toronto, McClelland & Goodchild, Publishers c1911. S1738

Johnson, Francis Henry, 1908-
A history of public education in British Columbia. Vancouver Publications Centre. University of British Columbia, 1964.
viii, 279 p. diagrs. map. S1739

Johnson, Francis Henry
John Jessop: goldseeker and educator. Vancouver, Mitchell Press, 1974.
190 p. S1740

Johnson, Kate (Bailey), 1885-
Pioneer days of Nakusp and the Arrow Lakes. 1892, Nakusp diamond jubilee, 1952. Nakusp, B.C., The author, c1951.
146 p. illus.
Also: reprinted with additions, 1964. 240 p. S1741

Johnson, Patricia Mary, 1913-
A short history of Nanaimo. Nanaimo, Nanaimo British Columbia Centennial Committee, c1958.
55 p. illus. port. S1742

Johnson, Patricia Mary
Welcome to Nanaimo, British Columbia. Rev. ed. North Vancouver, Trendex Publishers, 1974.
139 p. illus. S1743

Johnson, Wellwood Robert, 1887-
Legend of Langley: an account of the early history of Fort Langley and an intimate story of the lives of some. Langley, Langley Centennial Committee, 1958.
vi, 183 p. illus. S1744

Jupp, Ursula
From Cordwood to campus in Gordon Head, 1852-1959. Victoria, 1975.
186 p. illus. S1745

Jupp, Ursula, ed.
Home port Victoria. Victoria, The author, 1967.
168 p. S1746

Kalman, Harold
Exploring Vancouver: ten tours of the city and its buildings. Vancouver, University of British Columbia Press, 1974.
264 p. maps. photos. S1747

Kaslo. Historical Committee.
History of Kaslo. Kaslo diamond jubilee, 1893-1953. Kaslo, 1953.
64 p. illus. ports. S1748

Kay, David and D.A. MacDonald
Come with me to yesterday: pioneer days in East Kootenay. Cranbrook, B.C., 1965.
72 p. illus. S1749

Keddell, Georgina Matheson (Murray), 1913-
Muskeg maze. Illustrations by Pat Kloepfer. Fort St. John, B.C., Alaska Highway Publications, Ltd., 1963.
88 p. illus. S1750

Keddell, Georgina
The newspapering Murrays. Toronto, McClelland and Stewart, 1967.
224 p. S1751

Keller, Weldon Phillip, 1920-
Canada's wild glory. Photographs by the author. Line drawings by Geraldine Locke. London, Jarrolds, 1961.
336 p. illus.
Also: Toronto, Nelson, Foster and Scott, 1961. S1752

Keller, Weldon Phillip.
Splendour from the sea: the saga of the shantymen. Chicago, Moody Press, c1963.
237 p. illus. S1753

Kelsey, Vera, 1891?-1961
British Columbia rides a star. Illustrated. New York, Harper & Bros. Publishers, c1958.
xviii, 309 p. illus.
Also: Toronto, Vancouver, J.M. Dent & Sons (Canada) Ltd., c1958.
S1754

Kennedy, L.W., and others
Vancouver once upon a time. Vancouver, Radio Station CJOR, 1974.
88 p. illus. S1755

Kennedy, Warnett
Vancouver tomorrow: a search for greatness. Vancouver, Mitchell Press, 1974.
155 p. illus. S1756

Klenman, Allan
British Columbia centennial medal, 1858-1958: a historical record. Victoria, 1960.
39 p. illus. S1757

Knight, Rolf
A very ordinary life. Toronto, New Star Books, 1973. S1758

Knox, Paul and Philip Resnick, eds.
Essays in British Columbia Political Economy. Vancouver, New Star Books, 1974.
83 p. S1759

Kohlstedt, Edward Delor
William Duncan, founder and developer of Alaska's Metlakatla Christian mission. Metlakatla, Alaska, Board of Co-Trustees of the William Duncan Trust, c1957.
iv, 82 p. illus. S1760

Kopas, Cliff
Bella Coola. Vancouver, Mitchell Press, 1970.
269 p. illus. S1761

Kuipers, Aert Hendrik
The Squamish language: grammar, texts, dictionary. The Hague, Mouton, 1967-69. (Janua linguarum. Series practica, 73).
2 vols in 1. maps. port. S1764

Ladner, Leon J.
The Ladners of Ladner: by covered wagon to the welfare state. Vancouver, Mitchell Press, 1972.
161 p. illus. S1765

LaPonce, Jean A
People vs. Politics: a study of opinions, attitudes and perceptions in Vancouver - Burrard, 1963-1965. Toronto, University of Toronto Press, 1969.
219 p. S1766

Large, Richard Geddes, 1901-
Drums and scalpel: from native healers to physicians on the north Pacific coast. Vancouver, Mitchell Press, 1968.
145 p. S1767

Large, Richard Geddes
Prince Rupert, a gateway to Alaska. Vancouver, B.C., Mitchell Press, 1960.
210 p. illus. S1768

Large, Richard Geddes
Prince Rupert, a gateway to Alaska and the Pacific. Rev. 2nd ed. Vancouver, B.C., Mitchell Press, 1973.
230 p. illus. S1769

Large, Richard Geddes
The Skeena, river of destiny. Vancouver, Mitchell Press, Ltd., 1957.
ix, 180 p. illus. S1770

Large, Richard Geddes
Soogwilis: a collection of Kwakiutl Indian designs and legends. Colour drawings by Charlie George. Toronto The Ryerson Press, c1951.
77 (10) p. illus. S1771

Lauriente, Camille, 1874-
The chronicles of Camile. New York, Pageant Press, c1953.
ix, 230 p. S1772

LaViolette, Forrest Emmanuel, 1904-
The Canadian Japanese and World War II: a sociological and psychological account. Toronto, University of Toronto Press, 1948.
x, 332 p. tables. S1773

LaViolette, Forrest Emmanuel
The struggle for survival: Indian cultures and the protestant ethic in British Columbia. Toronto, University of Toronto, 1961.
xi, (1), 201 p. map. S1774

Lawrence, Guy
40 years on the Yukon telegraph. Vancouver, Mitchell Press, 1965.
136 p. illus. S1775

Lawrence, Joseph Collins, 1918-
The south-west coast of Vancouver Island from Metchosin to Bamfield, including Sooke, Otter, River Jordan and Port Renfrew. Sooke, 1959.
73 p. illus. S1776

Lazeo, Laurence Andrew, 1946-
Collector's guide to B.C. Indian artifact sites. Vancouver, 1970.
34 p. illus. S1777

Lazeo, Laurence Andrew
Lost treasure in British Columbia: a history of lost mines and buried or sunken treasure located in British Columbia. Burnaby, Western Heritage Supply, 1973.
48 p. illus. S1778

Lazeo, Laurence Andrew
British Columbia's treasure world: a history of lost mines and buried or sunken treasures located in B.C. New Westminster, 1970.
36 p. illus. S1779

Legg, Herbert, 1891-
Customs services in western Canada, 1867-1925: a history. Creston, B.C., Creston Review Ltd., 1962.
321 p illus. S1780

Lent, Dora Geneva, 1904-
West of the mountains: James Sinclair and the Hudson's Bay Company. Seattle, University of Washington Press, 1963.
xiv p., 2 , 334 p. illus. S1781

Liddell, Kenneth Eric, 1912-
This is British Columbia. Toronto, The Ryerson Press, 1958.
xiv, 250 p. illus. S1782

Lindo, Millicent A., ed.
Making history: an anthology of British Columbia. Victoria, 1975.
235 p. illus. S1783

Lindsay, Frederick Willian, 1903-
The Cariboo dream. Vernon, The author, 1972.
64 p. illus. S1784

Lindsay, Frederick William
The Cariboo story, published in B.C.'s centennial year. Quesnel, B.C., Printed by the Quesnel Advertiser, 1958.
52 p. illus.
Reprinted several times, 5th printing, 1962. S1785

Lindsay, Frederick William
The Outlaws. With pen and ink sketches by Florence Lindsay. Quesnel, B.C., The author, 1963.
64 p. illus. S1786

Lioy, Michele
Social trends in greater Vancouver: a study of a North American metropolis. Vancouver, Gordon Soules Research, 1975.
170 p. illus. S1787

Logan, Harry Tremaine, 1887-1971
Tuum est: a history of the University of British Columbia. With a foreword by N.A.M. Mackenzie. Vancouver, the University of British Columbia, 1958.
xii, 268 p. illus. S1788

Loudon, Robert Peter
The town that got lost, a story of Anyox, British Columbia, with a foreword by Denny Boyd. Sidney, B.C., Grays Pub., 1973.
111 p. illus. S1789

Loughnan, David, 1883-1952
A photographic and descriptive record of my visit to Stanley Park, British Columbia, Canada. Vancouver, Uneeda Printers Ltd., 1948.
72 p. illus.
Also: Rev. 2nd printing, 1950. S1790

Loughnan, David
A photographic and descriptive story of Vancouver, British Columbia, Canada. Vancouver, The author, 1950.
72 p. illus. S1791

Lower, Joseph Arthur, 1907-
Canada on the Pacific rim. Toronto, McGraw-Hill Ryerson, 1975.
225 p. illus. S1792

Lowther, Barbara Joan Sonia (Horsfield), 1932-
A bibliography of British Columbia: laying the foundations, 1849-1889. Victoria, University of Victoria, 1968.
xii, 328 p. S1793

Ludditt, Alfred William, 1907-
Barkerville days. Vancouver, Mitchell Press, 1969.
182 p. illus. S1794

Ludditt, Alfred William
Campfire sketches of the Cariboo. Courtnay, Comox Free Press,1974.
104 p. S1795

Ludditt, Alfred William
Gold in the Cariboo. Vancouver, Evergreen Press, 1958.
(6), 40 p. illus. S1796

Lyons, Chester Peter, 1915-
Milestones in Ogopogo land: in which the many wonders of the land of Ogopogo and sunshine are revealed. Vancouver, Evergreen Press, Ltd., c1957.
xv, 215 p. illus.
Also: Mileposts in Ogopogo land Surrey, B.C., Foremost Publishing Co., Ltd., c1970, 189 p. illus. S1797

Lyons, Chester Peter
Milestones on the mighty Fraser. Victoria, B.C., Toronto, Vancouver, J.M. Dent & Sons (Canada), Ltd., c1950.
xxxvi, 157 p. illus.
Also: Rev. ed. Vancouver, The Wrigley Printing Co., Ltd., 1956. xxii, 130 p. illus.
Also: 3rd ed. Vancouver, Evergreen Press, Ltd., 1958. S1798

Lyons, Chester Peter
Milestones on Vancouver Island: the story of this "island to the west", its past and its present. Vancouver, Evergreen Press, Ltd., 1958.
viii, 314 illus. S1799

Lyons, Chester Peter
Trees, shrubs and flowers to know in British Columbia. 2nd rev. ed. Toronto, Dent, 1966.
194 p. illus. S1800

Lyons, Cicely
Salmon: our heritage. Vancouver, Mitchell Press, 1969.
780 p. illus. S1801

Macaree, David and Mary Macaree
One hundred and three hikes in southwestern British Columbia. West Vancouver, Mountaincraft, 1973. S1802

McClure, Willa
Memories of Marysville. Kimberley, The author, 1973.
139 p. illus. S1803

McDonald, Dougald
Hiking near Vancouver: twenty scenic alpine trails to explore in British Columbia's lower mainland. Vancouver, Mitchell Press, 1971.
103 p. illus. S1804

McGeer, Patrick Lucey, 1927-
Politics in paradise. Toronto, Peter Martin, 1972.
237 p. S1806

McGill, David Earl, 1901-
101 stops of interest in beautiful British Columbia. Vancouver, Agency Press, 1970.
101 p. illus. S1807

MacGill, Elizabeth Muriel Gregory, 1905-
My mother the judge: a biography of Judge Helen Gregory MacGill. Toronto, The Ryerson Press, 1955.
xvi, 248 p. ports. S1808

McGregor, Donald Anderson, 1879-1970
They gave royal assent. Vancouver, Mitchell Press, 1967.
75 p. S1809

MacGregor, James Grierson, 1905-
The land of Twelve Foot Davis (a history of the Peace River country). Edmonton, Alberta, Published by Applied Art Products, Ltd., 1952.
395 p. illus. S1810

MacGregor, James Grierson
Overland by the Yellowhead. Saskatoon, Western Produce Book Service, 1974.
1 vol. illus. S1811

MacGregor, James Grierson
Pack saddles to Tete Juane Cache. Toronto, McClelland and Stewart, c1962.
256 p. maps. S1812

MacInnis, Winona Grace (Woodsworth) 1905-
J.S. Woodsworth. A man to remember. Toronto, The Macmillan Co., of Canada Ltd., 1953.
xiv, 336 p. ports. S1813

McKelvie, Bruce Alistair, 1889-1960.
Tales of conflict, illustrations by C.P. Connorton. Vancouver, The Vancouver Daily Province, 1949.
vii, (3) 99 p. illus. S1814

McKervill, Hugh Wilford, 1931-
Darby of Bella Bella. Toronto, The Ryerson Press, 1964.
159 p. port. S1815

McKervill, Hugh Wilford
The salmon people: the story of Canada's west coast salmon fishing industry. Sidney, Gray's Publishing Co., 1967.
198 p. S1816

McNaught, Kenneth William Kirkpatrick, 1918-
A prophet in politics: a biography of J.S. Woodsworth. Toronto, University of Toronto Press, c1959.
vi, 339 p. front. S1817

Mahood, Ian S
The land of Maquinna. Vancouver, Agency Press, 1971.
128 p. illus. S1818

Marks, William
I saw Ogopogo. Westbank, B.C., Peechland-Okanogan Review, 1971.
48 p. illus. S1819

Marriott, Harry
Cariboo cowboy. Sidney, B.C., Gray's Publishing, 1966. S1820

Marsh, John
A golden guide. Peterborough, Canadian Recreation Services, 1971.
20 p. illus. S1821

Marshall, James Stirrat
The Dominion Construction story, a record of achievements. A recounting of the first fifty years of the Dominion Construction Company Limited. Vancouver, 1960.
73 p. illus. S1822

Matches, Alex
It began with a Ronald. Vancouver, Mitchell Press, 1974.
144 p. illus. S1823

Mather, Barry, 1909-
New Westminster, the royal city, by Barry Mather and Margaret McDonald. Vancouver, J.M. Dent & Sons (Canada), 1958.
xxvii, 192 p. illus. S1824

Matsqui-Sumas-Abbotsford Centennial Society.
Where trails meet: Sumas, Abbotsford, Matsqui. Abbotsford, B.C., The Society, 1958.
62 p. illus. S1825

Melvin, George Henry, 1905-
The post offices of British Columbia, 1858-1970. Vernon, B.C., Wayside Press, c1972.
iv, 189 p. illus. S1826

Merriman, Alec and Taffy Merriman
Logging road travel. Vol. 1: Victoria to Campbell River; Vol. 2: Campbell River to Cape Scott. Sidney, Saltaire Publishing Ltd., 1973.
2 vols. illus. S1827

Merriman, Alec
Outdoors with Alec Merriman. Victoria, Saltaire Publishing Co., 1967.
108 p. S1828

Miller, Edward F., 1903-
Ned McGowan's war. Toronto, MacEachern, 1968.
20 p. S1829

Miller, Laurence A
Memoirs of Moyie. Kamloops, B.C., Sherborne Business Services, Ltd., 1965.
51 p. illus. S1830

Minghi, Julian V., ed.
Peoples of the living land: geography of cultural diversity in British Columbia. Vancouver, Tantalus Research, 1972.
242 p. S1831

Mitchell, Helen A
Diamond in the rough: a history of Campbell River.
Campbell River, B.C., Author, 1966.
158 p. illus. S1832

Mitchell Press Ltd.
Mitchell's Vancouver book. Vancouver, B.C., c1957.
122 p. illus. S1833

Miyazaki, M
My sixty years in Canada. Lillooet, 1973.
137 p. S1834

Monk, Harry Albert Jervis, 1913-
A history of Coquitlam and Fraser Mills, 1858-1958, by H.A.J. Monk and John Stewart. New Westminster, District of Coquitlam-Fraser Mills Centennial Commission, 1958.
76 p. illus. S1835

Morrison, Charles Keith
A book pedlar in British Columbia. Victoria, Library Development Commission, 1969.
93 p. S1836

Morley, Alan Palmer, 1905-
Roar of the breakers: Peter Kelly. Toronto, Ryerson, 1967.
164 p. S1837

Morley, Alan Palmer
Vancouver from milltown to metropolis. Vancouver, Mitchell Press, c1961.
xiii, 234 p. plates, maps. S1838

Morley, Alan Palmer
Vancouver from milltown to metropolis. 3rd ed. Vancouver, Mitchell Press, 1974.
302 p. illus. S1839

Morse, John Jesse, 1906-
Kamloops, the inland capital: a condensed history. Kamloops, B.C., Kamloops Museum Association, 1957.
40 p. illus. S1840

Morton, James
In the sea of sterile mountains: the Chinese in British Columbia. Vancouver, J.J. Douglas, 1974.
280 p. illus. S1841

Morton, James W
Capilano: the story of a river. Toronto, McClelland and Stewart, 1970.
184 p. illus. S1842

Munday, Walter Alfred Don, 1890-1950.
The unknown mountain. London, Hodder and Stoughton Limited Publishers, 1948.
xx, 268 p. illus. S1843

Murphy, Herbert Halliday, 1881-1964
Royal Jubilee Hospital, Victoria, B.C., 1858-1958: the Royal Hospital, 1858-1890, the Provincial Royal Jubilee Hospital, 1890-1938, the Royal Jubilee Hospital 1938-1958. Victoria, Hebden Printing Co., Ltd., 1958.
vii, 160 p. illus. S1844

Myers, Thomas Rathmell, 1884-
90 years of public utility service on Vancouver Island, 1860-1950: a history of the B.C. Electric. Victoria, British Columbia Electric Railway Co., 1954.
359, xxi p. illus. S1845

Myles, Eugenie L
The Emperor of Peace River. Edmonton, Institute of Applied Art, 1965.
310 p. illus. S1846

Neave, Roland Masterman, 1952- , ed.
Hiking the high points. Rev. enl. 2nd ed. Kamloops, Clow Print., 1970.
65 p. maps. S1847

Neave, Roland Masterman
Hiking the high points, edited by Roland Neave. Rev. enl. and illus. 3rd ed. Kamloops, Peerless Printers, 1972.
116 p. illus. S1848

Neave, Roland Masterman
Hiking the high points: a guide to hikes in the interior of British Columbia. 4th ed. New Westminster, Nunaga Publishing, 1974. S1849

Neave, Roland Masterman
Wells Gray Park: a visitor's guide to the park and its environs, by Roland Neave. With contributions on natural history by Trevor Goward, and an account of the Mount Hobson expedition by Hugh Neave. Burnaby? Miocene Press, c1974.
192 (6) fold. p. of maps. illus. S1850

Neering, Rosemary
Emily Carr. Don Mills, Ont., Fitzhenry and Whiteside, 1974.
62 p. illus. S1851

Nesbitt, James Knight, 1908-
Album of Victoria old homes and families. Victoria, B.C., Hebden Printing Co. Ltd., 1956.
63 p. illus. S1852

Newton, Norman Lewis, 1932-
Fire in the raven's nest: the Haida of British Columbia. Toronto, New Press, 1973.
173 p. illus. S1853

Nicholson, George Salier Willis, 1887-
Vancouver Island's west coast, 1762-1962. Victoria, B.C., Morriss Printing, 1962. S1854

Nicol, Eric Patrick, 1919-
Vancouver. Toronto, Doubleday, 1970.
260 p. illus. S1855

Norcross, Elizabeth Blanche, 1920- , and D.F. Tonkin.
Frontier days of Vancouver Island. Courtenay, Island Books, 1969.
128 p. illus. S1856

Norcross, Elizabeth Blanche
The warm land. Duncan, B.C., 1959.
112 p. illus. S1857

Norris, John, ed.
Strangers entertained: a history of the ethnic groups of British Columbia. Victoria, British Columbia Centennial '71 Committee, 1971.
254 p. illus. S1858

Northcote, T.G.
Biology of the lower Fraser River: a review. Vancouver, University of British Columbia Westwater Research Centre, 1974. (Technical Report, 3).
94 p. illus. S1859

Northwest Travel Guide. vols. 1-25. 1945-1969/70. Quesnel, B.C., Northwest Digest Ltd., (etc.) Continued by the Northwest travelguide: British Columbia and The Northwest travelguide: Alaska, Yukon, Alaska Hwy.
25 vols. illus. annual. S1860

Nowell, Iris Winifred, 1939-
Cross-country skiing in British Columbia: how to ski and where to ski in southern and central B.C. Toronto, Greey de Pencier Publications, c1976.
79 p. illus. S1861

Okanagan Historical Society. Penticton Branch.
Historical souvenir of Penticton, B.C., 1908-1958, on the occasion of the city of Penticton's golden jubilee. Penticton, B.C., 1958.
164 p. illus. S1863

O'Kiely, Elizabeth
Vancouver, the golden years, 1900-1910. Vancouver, Vancouver Museum and Planetarium Association, 1971.
52 p. illus. S1864

Olsen, William Henry, 1914-
Water over the wheel. Illustrated by R.L. Ryan. Chemainus, Chemainus Valley Historical Society, 1963.
169 p. illus. S1865

O'Neail, Hazel Irene (Hulls), 1912-
Doukhobor Daze. 4th ed. Sidney, Gray's Publishing, 1974.
143 p. illus. S1866

O'Neill, William John, 1882-1964
Time and place, stories of northern British Columbia. Stories of the west coast, Skeena River, Bulkley Valley, Douglas Channel and the old and new Kitimat. Prince Rupert, Printed by the Prince Rupert Daily News, Ltd., 1958.
53 p. S1867.

Onslow, John, 1906-
Bowler-hatted cowboy. London, Blackwood, 1962.
288 p. S1868

The Optimist, Ladner, B.C.
Tsawwassen legends, collected and printed by the Optimist. B.C., Dunning Press, 1961.
59 p. illus. S1869

Ormsby, Margaret Anchoretta, 1909-
British Columbia: a history. Toronto, Macmillans in Canada, 1958.
x, 558 p. illus. S1870

Ormsby, Margaret Anchoretta
British Columbia, a history. Rev. ed. Toronto, Macmillan of Canada, 1971. c1958.
x, 566 p. illus. S1871

Ossinger, June Eileen
Lamp in the wilderness by June Lydiard Spencer (pseud.) New York, Vantage Press, Inc., c1955.
135 p. S1872

Outdoor Club of Victoria
Hiking trails: southeastern Vancouver Island. Victoria, The Outdoor Club of Victoria Trails Information Society, 1973.
48 p. maps. S1873

Outdoor Club of Victoria
Hiking trails of Victoria and southern Vancouver Island. Victoria, 1972.
32 p. illus. S1874

Outdoor Club of Victoria. Trails Information Society.
Hiking trails 3: central and northern Vancouver Island, including hiking routes of Strathcona Park. Victoria, 1975.
72 p. illus. S1875

Pack, Mary
Never surrender. Vancouver, Mitchell Press, 1974.
256 p. S1876

Page, Frank Christopher
Silvery mists of British Columbia: the loves of science. Vancouver, Lions Publishing Co., 1975.
66 p. illus. S1877

Paterson, Thomas William, 1943-
Ghost town trails of Vancouver Island. Langley, Stagecoach Publishing Co., 1975.
167 p. illus. S1878

Paterson, Thomas William
Treasure British Columbia: true tales of treasure lost and found in B.C., Victoria, B.C., 1971.
79 p. illus. S1879

Patterson, Raymond Murray, 1898-
The dangerous river. London, George Allen and Unwin Ltd., 1954.
260 p. illus.
Also: N.Y., William Sloane Associates, Publishers, c1954. 314 p.
Also: London, Hamilton & Co., (Stafford), Ltd., 1957. 320 p. illus.
Also: 1st Canadian ed. Sidney, Gray's Publishing Ltd., 1966. 272 p. illus. Reprinted 1969, 1972. S1880

Patterson, Raymond Murray
Far pastures. Sidney, B.C., Gray's Publishing Canada, c1963.
290 p. illus. ports.
Also: Sidney, Gray's Publishing Ltd., 1973. S1881

Patterson, Raymond Murray
Finlay's river. Toronto, Macmillan of Canada, 1968.
315 p. S1882

Patterson, Raymond Murray
Trail to the interior. Toronto, Macmillan, 1966.
255 p. illus. S1883

Pattison, Kenneth Manning, 1912-
Milestones on Vancouver Island. Victoria, Milestone Publications, 1973.
256 p. illus. S1884

Peake, Frank Alexander, 1913-
The Anglican Church in British Columbia. Vancouver, Mitchell Press, 1959.
208 p. illus. S1885

Peake, Frank Alexander
History of the Anglican Church in British Columbia. Vancouver, Mitchell Press, 1974.
208 p. S1886

Pearce, Agatha Hunt
Hyak inlet: with illustrations by Patricia F. Wright. London, Blackie, c1961.
188 p. illus. S1887

Pearce, Agatha Hunt
Rattlesnake range: with illustrations by P.F. Wright. London, Blackie, c1961.
190 p. illus. S1888

Pearson, Carol (Williams), 1910-
Emily Carr as I knew her. With a foreword by Kathleen Coburn. Toronto, Clarke, Irwin & Co., Ltd., 1954.
x, 162 p. front. S1889

Pearson, John, 1900-
Land of the Peace arch. Cloverdale, B.C., Surrey Centennial Committee, 1958
xii, 159 p. illus. S1890

Pearsons, Howard Loammi, 1936-
B.C. gem trails. 3rd ed. with maps. Monte Lake, B.C.? 1968?
(65) p. maps S1891

Penlington, Norman
The Alaskan boundary dispute: a critical reappraisal. Scarborough, Ont., McGraw-Hill, Ryerson, 1973.
141 p. illus. S1892

Penner, Peter
Reaching the otherwise unreached: "an historical account of the West Coast Children's Mission of B.C." Clearbrook, B.C., West Coast Children's Mission of British Columbia, Pref., 1959.
125 p. illus. S1893

Pennier, Henry George
Chiefly Indian: the warm and witty story of a British Columbia half breed logger. West Vancouver, Graydonald Graphics, 1972.
130 p. S1894

Peterson, Lester Ray, 1917-
The Cape Scott Story. Vancouver, Mitchell Press, 1974.
134 p. maps. photos. S1895

Peterson, Lester Ray
The Gibson's landing story. Toronto, Peter Martin, 1973.
121 p. S1896

Pethick, Derek William, 1920- , and Susan Im Baumgarten
British Columbia recalled: a picture history 1741-1871. Saanichton, Hancock House, 1974.
96 p. illus. S1897

Pethick, Derek William
First approaches to the Northwest coast. Vancouver, J.J. Douglas, 1975.
268 p. illus. S1898

Pethick, Derek William
James Douglas: servant of two empires. Vancouver, Mitchell Press, c1969.
306 p. illus. S1899

Pethick, Derek William
Men of British Columbia. Saanichton, Hancock House, 1975.
223 p. illus. S1900

Pethick, Derek William
S.S. Beaver: the ship that saved the West. Vancouver, Mitchell, 1970.
160 p. illus. S1901

Pethick, Derek William
Vancouver recalled: a pictorial history to 1887. Saanichton, Hancock House, 1974.
96 p. illus. S1902

Phillips, Paul Arthur, 1938-
No power greater: a century of labor in British Columbia. Vancouver, Federation of Labour, 1967.
xiv, 189 p. S1903

Pohle, Adella
Pioneering in two worlds: the life of Carl and Adella Pohle. Vancouver, 1974.
127 p. illus. S1904

Porter, Lancelot, 1882-
Burton, British Columbia, "Our days before yesterday," as told by Bob Hewatson (pseud.) to Mrs. H.D. McCormack. Burton, B.C., Burton Centennial Committee, 1958.
31 p. illus. S1905

Potterton, Lawrence Albert Newton, 1894-
Northwest assignment. Kelowna, The author, 1973. S1906

Powley, Ellen Frances Gladys (Adams), 1884-1966, comp.
Early days of Winfield, B.C. Winfield B.C., Winfield Women's Institute, 1957.
30 p. illus. S1907

Pugsley, Edmund E
The Great Kicking Horse blunder. Vancouver, Evergreen Press, 1973.
95 p. illus. S1908

Purvis, Ron
Treasure hunting in British Columbia. Toronto, McClelland & Stewart, 1971.
143 p. illus. S1909

Ramsey, Arthur Bruce, 1924-
Barkerville: a guide in word and picture to the fabulous gold camp of the Cariboo. Vancouver, Mitchell Press, 1961.
iv, 92 p. illus. S1919

Ramsey, Arthur Bruce
The big dam country: a pictorial record of the development of the Peace River country. North Vancouver, In Focus Publications, 1969.
160 p. illus. S1920

Ramsey, Arthur Bruce
Britannia: the story of a mine. Britannia Beach, Britannia Beach Community Club, 1967.
x, 177 p. S1921

Ramsey, Arthur Bruce
Ghost towns of British Columbia. Vancouver, Mitchell Press Limited, c1963.
226 p. illus. S1922

Ramsey, Arthur Bruce
A history of the German-Canadians in British Columbia. Winnipeg, National Publishers, 1958.
v, 69 p. illus. S1923

Ramsey, Arthur Bruce
Inn-side British Columbia by automobile: by Bruce Ramsey and Ormond Turner. n.p., Standard Oil Co. of British Columbia and the British Columbia Hotels Association, 1962.
51 p. illus ports. maps. S1924

Ramsey, Arthur Bruce
Historical tour of British Columbia. Vancouver, B.C., The Province, 1966.
49 p. illus. S1925

Ramsey, Arthur Bruce
Mining in focus: an illustrated history of mining in British Columbia. Vancouver, Agency Press, 1968.
vii, 149 p. S1926

Ramsey, Arthur Bruce
Rain people: the story of Ocean Falls, British Columbia, 1871-1971. Ocean Falls, 1971.
233 p. S1927

Rankin, Harry
Rankin's law: recollections of a radical. Vancouver, November House, 1975.
220 p. S1928

Ravenhill, Alice, 1859-1954
The memoirs of an educational pioneer. With a foreword by Norman MacKenzie. Toronto, J.M. Dent & Sons (Canada) Ltd., 1951.
x, 241 p. ports. S1929

Raymond, Steve
Kamloops: an angler's study of the Kamloops trout. New York, Winchester Press, 1971.
218 p. illus. S1930

Reid, Edgar Cameron, 1902-
Fast flows the Fraser. New York, Comet Press Books, 1958.
45 p. illus. S1931

Reid, John Hotchkiss Stewart, 1909-
Mountain, men and rivers, British Columbia in legend and story by J.H. Steward Reid, Professor of history, United College, Winnipeg. Toronto, The Ryerson Press, 1954.
x, 229 p. maps. S1932

Rendall, Evalina Belle, 1889-
Healing waters: history of Harrison Hot Springs and Port Douglas area. Harrison Hot Springs, 1958.
34 p. illus. S1933

Retrospect: the story of St. Philip's Anglican Church, Vancouver, 1925-1975. Edited by R.D. Jamieson. Vancouver, B.C., St. Philip's Anglican Church, 1975.
143 p. illus. S1934

Richmond, Guy, 1904-
Prison doctor: one man's story that must be told in Canada today. Surrey, Nunaga Publishing Co., 1975.
186 p. S1936

Roberts, Eric A
Salt Spring saga. Ganges, B.C. Driftwood Publishers, 1962.
67 p. illus. S1937

Robin, Martin, 1936-
The company province, 1871-1972. Toronto, McClelland and Stewart, 1972-73.
2 vols. illus.
Vol. 1: the rush for spoils, 1871-1933. Vol. 2: pillars of profit, 1934-1972. S1938

Robinson, Gordon, 1918-1953.
Tales of Kitamaat: a selection of legends, folk stories and customs of the Haisla people, a branch of the Kwakiutl Indian language-group who live on the west coast of British Columbia. 3rd ed. Kitimat, B.C., 1961. (1st ed., 1956. 2nd ed., 1957.)
viii, 46 p. illus. S1939

Robinson, John Lewis, 1918- , and Walter G. Hardwick.
British Columbia: one hundred years of geographical change. Vancouver, Talonbooks, 1973.
63 p. illus. S1940

Rodgers, John Eric, 1910-
The birds of Vancouver: an illustrated pocket guide for the amateur birdwatcher. Vancouver, Bryan Publishing, 1971.
170 p. illus. S1941

Rodney, William
Kootenai Brown: his life and times, 1839-1916. Sidney, B.C., Gray's Publishing, 1969.
251 p. illus. S1942

Rogers, Alfred Charles, 1919-
Shipwrecks of British Columbia. North Vancouver, J.J. Douglas, 1973.
256 p. illus. S1943

Rohner, Ronald Preston, 1935- and Evelyn C. Rohner
The Kwakiutl Indians of British Columbia. New York, Montreal, Rinehart & Winston, 1970.
x, 111 p. illus. S1944

Ronayne, Irene
Beyond Garibaldi. Lillooet, Lillooet Publishers, 1971.
167 p. illus. S1945

Rose, T.F.
From shaman to modern medicine: a century of the healing arts in British Columbia. Vancouver, Mitchell Press, 1972.
187 p. S1946

Rothenburger, Mel
We've killed Johnny Ussher: the story of the wild McLean boys and Alex Hare. Vancouver, Mitchell Press, 1973.
210 p. ports. S1948

Roy, Reginald Herbert, 1922-
Sinews of steel: the history of the British Columbia Dragoons. Richter St. Armoury, Kelowna, B.C., B.C. Dragoons, 1965.
xiii, 468 p. plates. S1949

Runnalls, Francis Edwin, 1895-
It's God's country: a review of the United Church and its founding partners, the Congregational, Methodist and Presbyterian churches in British Columbia. Ocean Park, B.C., 1974.
247, 17, 4 p. S1950

Rushton, Gerald Arnold
Whistle up the inlet: the Union Steamship story. Vancouver, J.J. Douglas, 1974.
236 p. photos. maps. S1951

Rutland Centennial Committee.
History of the district of Rutland, British Columbia, 1858-1958. Kelowna, Printed by the Orchard City Press & Calendar Co., Ltd., 1958.
127 p. illus.
Also: Rev., 1971. 171 p. S1952

St. Pierre, Paul H., 1923-
Boss of the Namko drive: a story from the Cariboo country. Toronto, Ryerson Press, 1965.
115 p. S1953

St. Pierre, Paul H
The Chilcotin holiday. Toronto, McClelland and Stewart, 1970.
138 p. illus. S1954

Sandison, James Macleod, ed.
Schools of old Vancouver. Vancouver, Vancouver Historical Society, 1971.
61 p. illus. S1955

Scott, David, 1913- , and Edna H. Hanic
East Kootenay saga. New Westminster, Nunaga Publishing, 1974.
120 p. illus. S1956

Scott, David and Edna Hanic
Nelson: queen city of the Kootenays. Vancouver, Mitchell Press, 1972.
127 p. S1957

Scott, Jack, 1910-
Plunderbund and proletariat. Vancouver, New Star Books, 1975. S1958

Scott, Jack
Sweat and struggle: working class struggles in Canada. Vol. 1: 1789-1899. Vancouver, New Star Books, 1974.
209 p. illus. S1959

Scott, Robert Bruce, 1905-
Barkley Sound, a history of the Pacific Rim National Park area. Victoria, Fleming-Review Printing, Ltd., 1973.
278 p. illus. S1960

Scott, Robert Bruce
Breakers ahead, on the graveyard of the Pacific. Sidney, Review Publishing House, 1970.
176 p. S1961

Scott, Robert Bruce
People of the southwest coast of Vancouver Island: a history of the southwest coast. Victoria, Morriss Printing Co., 1974.
138 p. photos. S1962

Sepass, K'H Halserten, Stalo Chief, 1841?-1943.
Sepass poems, by Eloise Street. Vancouver, B.C., Indian time, 1955?
60, 12 p. illus. port.
Also: Sepass poems: the songs of Y-Ail-Mihth. Recorded by Eloise Street. 1st ed. New York, Vantage Press, c1963. 110 p. ports. S1963

Sepass, K'H Halserten, Stalo Chief, 1841?-1943.
Sepass tales: the songs of Y-Ail-Mihth. Recorded by Eloise Street. 2nd ed. Chilliwack, Sepass Trust, c1974.
110 p. ports. S1964

Sewid, James, 1913-
Guests never leave hungry: the autobiography of James Sewid, a Kwakiutl Indian. Edited by James P. Spradley. New Haven, Conn., Yale University Press, 1969.
310 p. illus. S1965

Shadbolt, Doris (Meisel)
Emily Carr. Vancouver, J.J. Douglas, 1975.
96 p. illus. S1966

Sharcott, Margaret (Brampton), 1928-
A place of many winds. Toronto, British Book Service Canada, 1960.
236 p. illus. S1967

Sharcott, Margaret (Brampton)
Troller's holiday. Illustrated. Toronto, British Book Service (Canada) Ltd., c1957.
221 p. illus. S1968

Shearer, Ronald Alexander, 1932-
Trade liberalization and a regional economy: studies of the impact of free trade on British Columbia. Toronto, University of Toronto Press, c1971. (Canada in the Atlantic economy: 11).
203 p. graphs. S1969

Shelton, William George, ed.
British Columbia & confederation, edited by W. George Shelton. Victoria, B.C., Published for the University of Victoria by the Morriss Printing Co., 1967.
viii, 250 p. illus. S1970

Sherman, Patrick, 1928-
Bennett. Toronto, McClelland & Stewart, 1916.
xii, 316 p. S1971

Shewchuck, Murphy.
Fur, gold and opals: a guide to the Thompson River valleys. Saanichton, Hancock House, 1975.
128 p. illus. S1972

Shier, Morley, 1888-
"Fireside mining": a compendium of mining stories. Vancouver, Printed by Western Miner Press, 1958.
78 p. illus. ports. S1973

Sierra Club of British Columbia.
The West coast trail and Nitinat lakes. West Vancouver, J.J. Douglas, Ltd., 1972.
85 p. illus. S1974

Simeon, John, ed.
Natural history of the Cowichan valley. Duncan, B.C., Cowichan Valley Natural History Society, 1974.
48 p. illus. S1975

Sisters of Saint Ann, Victoria B.C.
Centennial anniversary of the arrival of the pioneer nuns in Victoria, B.C. June 5, 1858 - June 5, 1958. Victoria, B.C., 1958.
63 p. illus. S1976

Sisters of St. Ann, Victoria B.C.
The sisters of St. Ann in British Columbia, Yukon and Alaska, 1858-1958. Victoria, The Acme Press, Limited, 1958.
(100) p. illus. S1977

Skrien, David Albert, 1929-
Countdown to Grey Cup: the story of the B.C. Lions by Dave Skrien and Dick Beddoes. Toronto, McClelland and Stewart, c1965.
144 p. illus. S1978

Smeeton, Miles, 1906-
A change of jungles. London, Hart-Davis, 1962; Toronto, Longmans.
192 p. illus. S1979

Smith, Dorothy (Blakey), 1899-
James Douglas: father of British Columbia. Toronto, Oxford, 1971.
128 p. illus. S1980

Smith, Ian Donaldson, 1939-1977
The unknown island. North Vancouver, J.J. Douglas, 1973.
174 p. illus. S1981

Smyly, John Hamilton, 1924- , and Carolyn Smyly
Those born at Koona. Saanichton, Hancock House, 1973.
120 p. illus. S1982

Spiegel, Ted
Western shore: Canada's Pacific coast. Toronto, McClelland and Stewart, 1975.
128 p. photos. S1983

Stacey, Earl Clifford, 1902-
Peace country heritage. Saskatoon, Western Producer Book Service, 1974.
xi, 173 p. illus. S1974

Stanbury, William Thomas, 1943-
Success and failure: Indians in urban society. Vancouver, University of British Columbia Press, 1975.
xxxi, 415 p. illus. S1985

Stanwell-Fletcher, Theodora Morris (Cope), 1906-
Driftwood valley. Animal sketches by John F. Stanwell-Fletcher. Boston, Little, Brown and Co., 1946.
ix, 384 p. illus.
Also: Driftwood valley: a story of life in a Canadian wilderness. London, George G. Harrap & Co. Ltd., 1949. 287 p. illus.
Also: Driftwood valley. London, Panther Books, 1956. 256 p. illus.
S1986

Steeves, Dorothy Gretchen (Bierstaker), 1895-
The compassionate rebel: Ernest E. Winch and his times. Vancouver, Boag Foundation, 1960.
xi, 227 p. illus. S1987

Stephen, Irene Simmons (Phelan), 1902-
Winged canoes at Nootka and other stories of the Evergreen coast, by Pamela Stephen (pseud.). Illustrations by Annora Brown. Toronto, J.M. Dent & Sons (Canada) Ltd., 1955.
x, 227 p. illus. S1988

Steward, David Edward, 1919-
Okanagan back roads. Vol. 1: south central Okangan; Vol. 2: north Okanagan Shuswap. Sidney, Saltaire Publishing, 1975.
2 vols. illus. S1989

Stewart, Hilary, 1924-
Artifacts of the Northwest coast Indians. Saanichton, Hancock House, 1973.
172 p. illus. S1990

Stokes, Stanley C.W.
Errington, Vancouver Island, British Columbia, Canada. Errington, 1971.
123 p. S1991

Stoochnoff, John Philip
Doukhobors as they are. Toronto, Ryerson Press, 1961.
vii, 102 p. ports. S1992

Stoochnoff, John Philip
Toil and peaceful life: Doukhobors as they are. 2nd ed. Vancouver, Liberty Press, 1971.
118 p. illus. S1993

Stowe, Leland, 1899-
Crusoe of Lonesome Lake. New York, Random House, 1957.
xviii, 234 p. maps. S1994

Strathern, Gloria Margaret, 1928- comp.
Navigations traffiques and discoveries, 1774-1848: a guide to publications relating to the area now British Columbia. Victoria, University of Victoria, Social Science Research Centre, 1970.
xv, 417 p. S1995

Stubbs, Dorothy Isabelle
Courtenay "All about us": a history of the city of Courtenay, 1915-1975. Courtenay, 1975.
127 p. illus. S1996

Sturrock, Sue
All of it was fun. New Westminster, Nunaga Publishing, 1974.
144 p. illus. S1997

Stursberg, Peter
Those were the days. Toronto, Peter Martin, 1973.
169 p. S1998

Sunset.
British Columbia, with Canadian Rocky Mountain national parks, by the editorial staffs of Sunset books and Sunset magazine. Menlo Park, Calif., Lane Publishing Co., c1958.
96 p. illus. S1999

Surtees, Ursula
Lak-la Hai-ee: Shuswap Indian meaning "to tell." Kelowna, Lamont Surtees, 1974-75.
2 vols. illus.
Vol. 1: interior Salish food preparation. Vol. 2: building a winter dwelling. S2000

Symons, Kyrle Charles, 1881-1965
That amazing institution: the story of St. Michael's School, Victoria, B.C., from 1910-1948. Victoria? 1949?
ix, 181 p. illus. S2001

Szczawinski, Adam F
The heather family of British Columbia. 2nd ed. Victoria, British Columbia Provincial Museum of Natural History and Anthorpology, 1970.
205 p. (Handbook Series, 19). S2002

Szczawinski, Adam F
The orchids of British Columbia. 2nd ed. Victoria, British Columbia Provincial Museum of Natural History and Anthropology, 1970.
124 p. (Handbook Series, 16). S2003

Tales from the longhouse, by Indian children of British Columbia. Sidney, B.C., Gray's Publishing Co., c1973.
vii, 112 p. illus. S2004

Tarasoff, Koozma J., 1932-
In search of brotherhood: a history of the Doukhobors. Vancouver, 1963.
3 vols. (iv, 1006 p.) S2005

Tatreau, Doug and Bobbe Tatreau
The parks of British Columbia: a comprehensive guide to British Columbia's provincial and national parks. Vancouver, Mitchell Press, 1973.
133 p. photos. maps. S2006

Taylor, Geoffrey Wilson, 1905-
Timber: a history of the forest industry in British Columbia. Vancouver, J.J. Douglas, 1975.
220 p. illus. S2007

Taylor, Gordon de Rupe, 1923-
Delta's century of progress. Cloverdale, Kerfoot-Holmes Printing Ltd., 1958.
96 p. illus. S2008

Taylor, Phyllis Mary
Buckskin and blackboard. London, Darwen Finlayson Ltd., 1955.
200 p. S2009

Thorington, James Monroe, 1894-
A climber's guide to the interior ranges of British Columbia. Philadelphia, The American Alpine Club, 1937.
xii, 149 p. map.
Also: 2nd ed. New York, The American Alpine Club, 1947, xii, 170 p.
Also: 3rd ed., 1955, c1947, xiv, 231 p.
Also: 4th ed. by William Lowell Putnam, based on previous eds. 1963. xvii, 253 p. illus. maps.
Also: 5th ed., 1971. 323 p. illus. maps. S2010

Thornton, Mildred Valley (Stinson), 1896-1967
Indian lives and legends. Vancouver, B.C., Mitchell Press, 1966.
xvii, 301 p. illus. S2011

The tokens of British Columbia and the Yukon. Vancouver, Vancouver Numismatic Society, 1969.
88 p. S2012

Touchie, Rodger
Vancouver Island: portrait of a past. Vancouver, J.J. Douglas, 1974.
128 p. illus. S2013

Townsend, Arthur Herbert, 1912-
Sod-busters. New York, Toronto, Vantage Press, c1957.
180 p. S2014

Treleaven, Georgia Fern
The Surrey story. Surrey, Museum and Historical Society, 1969-72.
3 vols. illus. S2015

Turnbull, Elsie Grant (Willard), 1903-
Topping's trail. Vancouver, Mitchell Press, Limited, c1964.
65 p. illus. S2016

Turner, Dick, 1911-
Nahanni. Saanichton, Hancock House, 1975.
286 p. illus. S2017

Turner, Robert David, 1947-
Vancouver Island railroads. Vancouver, J.J. Douglas, 1974.
170 p. photos maps.
Also: San Marino, Calif., Golden West Books, 1973. 170 p. S2018

Turpin, Marguerite Eva Jane (Stalker), 1931-
The life and work of Emily Carr (1871-1945): a selected bibliography. Vancouver, School of Librarianship, University of British Columbia, 1965.
20 p. S2019

University of British Columbia. Doukhobor Research Committee.
Report of the Doukhobor research committee: Harry B. Hawthorn, chairman and editor. Vancouver, University of British Columbia, 1952.
ix, 342 p. S2020

University of British Columbia. Indian Research Project.
The Indians of British Columbia: a survey of social and economic conditions. Minister of Citizenship and Immigration. Vancouver, B.C., University of British Columbia, 1955.
3 vols. map.
Also: enlarged ed., 1958, ix, 499 p. S2021

Vallance, James Dunlop, 1903-
Untrodden ways. Dedicated to the pioneers of British Columbia. Victoria, Hebden Print. Co., 1958.
150 p. illus. S2022

Vancouver Art Gallery, Vancouver, B.C.
Arts of the raven: masterworks by the Northwest coast Indian. Catalogue text by Wilson Duff. Vancouver, 1967.
unpaged. S2023

Vancouver Art Gallery, Vancouver, B.C.
Emily Carr: a centennial exhibition celebrating the one hundredth anniversary of her birth. Vancouver, 1971.
96 p. illus. S2024

Vancouver Art Gallery, Vancouver, B.C.
100 years of B.C. art: an exhibition held at the Vancouver Art Gallery to commemorate the British Columbia centennial year, 1958. Compiled and arranged by Robert M. Hume. Vancouver, B.C., 1958.
(132) p. illus. S2025

Victoria Centennial Celebration Society, 1962.
Victoria, British Columbia, Canada, Centennial celebrations, 1862-1962. Victoria, 1962.
(100) p. illus. S2026

Virgin, Victor Ernest, 1892-1964
History of north and south Saanich pioneers and district. Victoria, Saanich Pioneer Society, 1959.
79 p. illus. S2027

Visitors who never left: the origin of the people of Damelahamid. Translated and arranged by Chief Kenneth B. Harris. Vancouver, University of British Columbia Press, 1974.
xxiii, 139 p. illus. S2028

Waite, Donald Ender
Tales of the Fraser canyon. Illustrated. Maple Ridge, Don Waite Photo Center, 1974.
96 p. illus. S2029

Walbran, John Thomas, 1848-1913
British Columbia coast names. Vancouver, The Library's Press, 1971.
546 p. illus. S2030

Walker, Russell Robert, 1888?-
Bacon, beans 'n brave hearts. Lillooet, Lillooet Publishers, 1972.
163 p. S2031

Walker, Russell Robert
Politicians of a pioneering province. Vancouver, Mitchell Press, 1969.
246 p. illus. S2032

Wallace, William Stewart, 1884-
The pedlars from Quebec and other papers on the Nor'westers. Toronto, Ryerson Press, 1954.
xii, 101 p. front. S2033

Walter, Margaret (Shaw)
Early days among the gulf islands of British Columbia. 2nd ed. Victoria, Hebden Printing Co., 1959?
67 p. illus. S2034

Walton, Avis Carroll (Gray), 1911- , ed.
About Victoria: sketches and stories about Victoria, fragments of our colorful past, a few authoritative predictions in regard to our growing future ... factual information. Victoria, New Neighbour Services, 1955.
80 p. illus.
Also: Vol. 2 (i.e. 2nd ed.), 1958. 212 p. illus.
Also: Vol. 3 (i.e. 3rd ed.), 1959. v, 4-216 p.
Also: 4th ed., with sub-title with notations about Port Angeles, Wash., across the Straits of Juan de Fuca. 1960. 224 p.
Also: 5th Rev. ed. Victoria, Felindical publications, c1969.
320 p. illus. maps. S2035

Ware, Reuben
The lands we lost: a history of cut-off lands and land losses from Indian reserves in British Columbia. Vancouver, Union of British Columbia Indian Chiefs Land Claims Research Centre, 1974.
278 p. maps. S2036

Waterfield, Donald Creswell, 1907-
Land grab: one man vs. the authority. Clarke, Irwin, 1973. S1037

Watson, George Albert and Robert Skrill.
Western Canadian bottle collecting. Nanaimo, Hume Compton, 1971.
74 p. illus. S2038

Watson, George Albert
Western Canadian bottle collecting. Book 2, by G. Watson, R. Skrill and J. Heidt. With a special section on ink bottles by Gerald and Joan Bentryn. Vancouver, Evergreen Press, 1972.
113 p. illus. ports. S2039

Watt, Robert D
To the county and beyond: a memoir of Alexander Greer and his descendants. Vancouver, Alison J. Watt, 1975.
138 p. illus. S2040

Watters, Reginald Eyre, 1912- , ed.
British Columbia: a centennial anthology. Toronto, McClelland and Stewart Limited, 1958.
xvi, 576 p. illus
Also: with title: British Columbia. c1961, xv, 576 p. S2041

Webster, Daisy
Growth of the N.D.P. in British Columbia 1900-1970: 81 political biographies. Vancouver, N.D.P., 1970.
103 p. illus. S2042

Wells, Oliver Nelson, 1907-1970
Myths and legends Straw-loh Indians of southwestern British Columbia. Sardis, 1970.
42 p. illus. S2043

Wells, Oliver Nelson
Salish weaving, primitive and modern as practiced by the Salish Indians of southwestern British Columbia. Sardis, The author, 1969.
32 p. S2044

Wells, Oliver Nelson
A vocabulary of native words in the Halkomelem language as used by the native people of the lower Fraser valley, B.C. The author, 1965.
28 p. illus. S2045

Whishaw, Lorna
As far as you'll take me. New York, Dodd, Mead, 1958.
216 p. S2047

White, Elwood Roy, 1918
Shays on the switchbacks: a history of the Lenora, Mt. Sicker railway by Elwood White and David Wilkie. Victoria, British Columbia Railway Historical Association, c1963.
40 p. illus.
Also: Rev. ed. 3rd printing, 1968. c1963. S2048

Whiteside, Richard Vivian, 1893-
The Surrey pioneers. Vancouver, Evergreen Press, 1974.
x, 197 p. illus. S2049

Whittaker, Lawrence Henry, 1913-1968, ed.
Rossland, the golden city: a story of the first half-century of progress and development in the Trail Creek area of west Kootenay. Rossland, Rossland Miner Limited, 1949.
107 p. illus. S2050

Wild, Roland Gibson, 1903-
Amor De Cosmos. Foreword by Hon. W.A.C. Bennett, Premier of British Columbia. Toronto, Ryerson Press, 1958.
xi, 146 p. plates. ports. S2051

Willmot, Jill (Adams), 1937- , comp.
The Indians of British Columbia: a study-discussion text. Vancouver, Department of University Extension, The University of British Columbia, 1963.
290 p. maps. S2052

Willson, Janet
Exploring by bicycle, southwest British Columbia, northwest Washington. Vancouver, Gundy's and Bernie's Guide Books, 1973.
96 p. illus. S2053

Wilson, Amy V
No man stands alone. Sidney, B.C., Gray's Publishing, 1966.
138 p. S2054

Wilson, Neill Compton, 1889- , ed.
Deep roots: the history of Blake, Moffitt & Towne, pioneers in paper since 1855. San Francisco, privately printed, 1955.
112 p. illus. S2057

Wilton, Jean Birch
May I talk to John Howard? The story of J.D. Hobden, a friend to prisoners. Vancouver, John Howard Society, 1973.
241 p. illus. S2058

Windsor, John Best, 1920-
Nowhere else to go. "The man behind the scenes." Sidney, B.C., Gray's Publishing, Ltd., c1964.
138 p. illus. S2059

Wolcott, Harry F., 1929-
A Kwakiutl village and school. New York, Holt, Rinehart and Winston, 1967.
xii, 132 p. S2060

Woodcock, George, 1912-
Amor De Cosmos: journalist and reformer. Toronto, Oxford University Press, 1975.
ix, 177 p. illus. S2061

Woodcock, George
The Doukhobors. By George Woodcock and Ivan Avakumovic. Toronto, Oxford University Press, 1968.
382 p. S2062

Woodland, Alan
New Westminster - the early years, 1858-1898. New Westminster, Nunaga Publishing Co., 1973.
72 p. illus. S2064

Woods, John Jex, 1895-
History and development of the Agassiz-Harrison valley. Agassiz, B.C., Printed by Agassiz-Harrison Advance, 1941.
68 p. illus.
Also: 2nd ed. rev. with title; The Agassiz-Harrison valley, history and development. Sidney, B.C., Peninsula Printing Co., Ltd., 1958. 113 p. illus.
S2065

Worley, Ronald Bruce, 1921-
The wonderful world of W.A.C. Bennett. Toronto, McClelland and Stewart, 1971.
290 p. illus. S2066

Wright, Walter
Men of Medeek, by Will Robinson as told by Walter Wright. Kitimat, B.C. Printed by the Northern Sentinel Press, 1961.
93 p. ports. map. S2067

IDAHO

Compiled by Charles A. Webbert
University of Idaho

Adams, Florence
Idaho City, queen of the gold camps. Idaho City, Idaho. Printed by the Idaho World Publishing Co., 1958.
29 p. illus S2068

Adams, Florence
Idaho City, queen of the gold camps. Idaho City, Idaho, World, 1971.
32 p. S2069

Adams, Mildretta (Hamilton)
Historic Silver City: the story of the Owyhees. Homedale, Idaho, Owyhee Chronicle, c1960.
60 p. illus. S2070

Adams, Mildretta (Hamilton)
Historic Silver City: the story of the Owyhees. Rev. ed. Nampa, Idaho, Schwartz Printing Co., 1969.
82 p. illus. S2071

Adams, Willard
100 years of Jefferson County progress. n.p., 196-?
55 p. illus. S2072

Adkison, Norman B
Indian braves and battles, with more Nez Perce lore. Grangeville, Idaho County Free Press, 1967.
48 p. illus. ports. S2073

Adkison, Norman B
Nez Perce Indian war and original stories, by Norman B. Adkison. Grangeville, Idaho County Free Press, 1966.
47 p. illus. S2074

Aitken, Mickey America Rinehart, 1908-
The saga of Salubria. Weiser, Idaho, Signal American Printers, 1951.
39 p. illus. S2075

Allen, Henry.
From where the sun now stands by Will Henry (pseud.). New York, Random House, 1959. S2076

Allen, William R., 1871-
The chequemegon (shay-wah-me-gon), a narrative of one of the most exciting and colorful periods in our history, from the days of the Civil War aftermath to the present. New York, William-Frederick Press, 1949.
205 p. S2077

Allison, James L
Idaho's gateway to Yellowstone: the Island Park story, by James L. Allison and Dean H. Green. Mack's Inn, Idaho, Island Park-Gateway Publishing Co., 1974.
193 p. illus. S2078

Angelo, C. Aubrey
Idaho: a descriptive tour. Fairfield, Wash., Ye Galleon Press, 1969, (1845).
52 p. S2079

Aoki, Haruo, 1930-
Nez Perce grammar. Berkeley, University of California Press, 1970. (University of California publications in linguistics, v. 62).
xii, 168 p. illus. S2080

Arnold, Lloyd R
High on the wild with Hemingway. Caldwell, Caxton Printers, 1968.
343 p. illus. S2081

Ashby, LeRoy
The spearless leader Senator Borah and the progressive movement in the 1920's. Urbana, Univeristy of Illinois Press, 1972.
x, 325 p. S2082

Backus, Harriet Fish
Tomboy bride. Boulder, Colo., Pruett Press, 1969.
273 p. illus. S2083

Bailey, Bernadine (Freeman), 1901-
Picture book of Idaho. Pictures by Kurt Wiese. Chicago, A. Whitman, c1962.
unpaged. illus. S2084

Bailey, George Cecil, 1883-
Tall trees surround us. Caldwell, Caxton Printers, 1955.
159 p. illus. S2085

Bailey, Paul Dayton.
Wovoka, the Indian messiah. Los Angeles, Westernlore Press, 1957.
223 p. illus. S2086

Bailey, William A., 1895-
Bill Bailey came home: as a farm boy, as a stowaway at the age of nine, a trapper at the age of fifteen, and a hobo at the age of sixteen. Edited by Austin and Alta Fife. Logan, Utah State University Press, 1973.
183 p. illus. S2087

Baker, Bessie M
A history of Idaho for the classroom teacher. Edited by Bessie M. Baker. Caldwell, Idaho, Twin Cities Printing Co., 1964.
72 p. illus. S2088

Balch, Glenn
Horse of two colors. New York, Crowell, 1969.
170 p. S2089

Banks, Eleanor (Macdonald), 1883-
Wandersong: map and drawings by Julia Wallace. Caldwell, Idaho, Caxton Printers, 1950.
309 p. illus. S2090

Bankson, Russell Arden, 1889-
Beneath these mountains, by Russell A. Bankson and Lester S. Harrison. New York, Vantage Press, 1967.
228 p. illus. S2091

Barber, Floyd R
Idaho in the Pacific Northwest, by Floyd R. Barber and Dan W. Martin. Caldwell, Idaho, Caxton Printers, 1956.
433 p. illus. S2092

Barber, Floyd R
First supplement to accompany Idaho in the Pacific Northwest, by Floyd R. Barber and Dan W. Martin. Caldwell, Idaho, Caxton Printers, 1962.
81 p. S2093

Barber, Pearl Eva
Galloping ghosts of Galena. Boise, Idaho, Capitol Lithograph and Printing Co., c1962.
79 p. S2094

Barrett, Glen
The first bank of Troy, 1905-1971: a black diamond history. n.p., 1971.
90 p. S2095

Barrett, Glen
J. Lynn Driscoll: western banker. A black diamond history. Boise, Idaho, Syms-York, 1974.
xiv, 297 p. illus. S2097

Barrett, Glen
Small town banking in the good ol' days. Boise, Boise State University Press, 1975.
110 p. S2098

Beal, Merrill D., 1898-
History of Idaho, by Merrill D. Beal and Merle W. Wells. New York, Lewis Historical Publishing Co., 1959.
3 vols. illus. S2099

Beal, Merrill D
History of Idaho State College. Pocatello?, 1952
216 p. illus. S2100

Beal, Merrill D
"I will fight no more forever"; Chief Joseph and the Nez Perce War. Seattle, University of Washington Press, 1963.
xvii, 366 p. illus. S2101

Beatty, Robert O
Idaho. Boise, Idaho First National Bank, c1974.
207 p. chiefly col. photos. S2102

Beaty, Jeanne Dellar
Lookout wife. New York, Random House, 1953.
311 p. S2103

Beckwith, John A
Gem minerals of Idaho, with drawings and maps by Jane Beckwith. Caldwell, Idaho, Caxton Printers, 1972.
123 p. illus. S2104

Bell, William Gardner
The Snake, a noble and various river. Washington, Potomac Corral, The Westerners, 1969. (The Great western series, no. 4).
20 p. illus. S2105

Bernard, Art
Dog days. Caldwell, Caxton Printers, 1969.
204 p. S2106

Bertram, John L
River street neighborhood plan, by John L. Bertram and Pat Walsh. Boise, EL-ADA Community Action Agency, 1973.
iii, 84 p. illus. S2107

Bigelow, Melvin Jerome, 1926-
IAS: a history of the first decade of Idaho Academy of Science. n.p., 1968.
13 p. S2108

Bird, Annie Laurie
My home town. Caldwell, Idaho, Caxton Printers, 1968.
xviii, 486 p. illus. S2109

Bird, Annie Laurie
Old Fort Boise. Paintings by Arthur Yensen. Parma, Idaho, Old Fort Boise Historical Society, 1971.
90 p. maps. S2110

Blechmann, Clarice E
Hiking around Sun Valley. Sun Valley, Idaho, 1973.
67 p. illus. S2111

Bleeker, Sonia
Horsemen of the western plateaus: the Nez Perce Indians. Illustrated by Patricia Boodell. New York, Morrow, 1957.
157 p. illus. S2112

Bollinger, Wendell LaMar, 1916-
The economic and social characteristics of Idaho's adult population, focusing on recent immigrants and returnees. Caldwell, the College of Idaho, 1972.
15 p. tables. S2113

Bollinger, Wendell LaMar
Personal income in Idaho counties, 1958-1965. Caldwell, Idaho, College of Idaho, 1969.
viii, 195 p. illus. S2114

Bonner County Historical Society
The first home town primer. Sandpoint, Idaho, 1974.
42 p. illus. S2115

Book of Tyhee: fiftieth anniversary of seventh ward, North Pocatello Stake, Pocatello Idaho, June 6, 1964.
28 p. illus. S2116

Boren, Robert R
Wildflowers of the Sawtooth Mountain country, by Robert R. Boren and Marjorie D. Boren. Boise, Idaho, Sawtooth Publishing Co., 1975.
40 p. illus. S2117

Boschken, Herman L
Corporate power and the mismarketing of urban development: Boise Cascade recreation communities. New York, Praeger, 1974.
xiii, 283 p. S2118

Bowen, Gordon S
Street trees of Boise, Idaho. Boise, Boise City Print Shop, 1975.
unpaged. illus. S2119

Bowers, Alfred William, 1901-
Archeological reconnaissance in the Sawtooth Mountain study area. Prepared for National Park Service, Western Region, and Idaho Bureau of Mines and Geology. Moscow, Idaho, 1964.
22 (18) l. maps. plates. S2120

Bradley, Cyprian, 1884-
History of the diocese of Boise, 1863-1952 (i.e., 1953) by Cyprian Bradley and Edward J. Kelly. Boise, Idaho, 1953.
1 vol. illus. S2121

Brink, Carol
Strangers in the forest. New York, Macmillan, 1959.
314 p. S2122

Brockett, Ron
The Moscow opal mines, 1890 to 1893: the first commercial opal mines in the United States. Rangeley, Colo., 1974.
63 p. illus. S2123

Brooks, Juanita
History of the Jews in Utah and Idaho. Salt Lake City, Western Epics, c1973.
252 p. illus. S2124

Brose, Mabel Rosamond
The boy homesteader: true stories of children of the Boise valley during the 1890's. Boise, The author, 1970.
150 p. S2125

Brown, William C
Appraisal, Nez Perce reservation lands ceded to United States of America. Treaty cession 1863-1867. Lewiston, Idaho, 1957.
3 vols. illus. S2127

Brown, William Carey
The sheepeater campaign, 1879. Seattle, Shorey Book Store, 1971. Reprinted from the 10th biennal report,Idaho Historical Society. 1926.
29 p. illus. S2128

Bunker Hill Company, Kellogg, Idaho.
The Bunker Hill Company. Spokane, Wash., Lawton Printing, 1966.
1 vol. unpaged. illus. S2129

Burleigh, Thomas Dearborn, 1895-
Birds of Idaho. Caldwell, Idaho, Caxton Printers, 1972.
xiii, 467 p. illus. S2130

Burt, Olive (Woolley), 1894-
Chief Joseph, boy of the Nez Perce, illustrated by William Moyers. Indianapolis, Bobbs-Merrill, 1967.
200 p. illus. S2131

Burt, Olive (Woolley)
The oak's long shadow: a story of the Basque sheephearders in Idaho. Illustrated by Frederick T. Chapman. Philadelphia, Winston, 1952.
240 p. illus. S2132

Bush, Kenneth W
Crown of terror. Philadelphia, Pa. Dorrance, c1970.
194 p. S2133

Butler, B. Robert
A guide to understanding Idaho archaeology. Pocatello, Idaho State University Museum, 1966.
143 p.
Also: 2nd ed., 1968. 117 p. illus.
S2134

Caldwell, Harry H., ed.
Idaho economic atlas. Moscow, Bureau of Mines and Geology, 1970.
82 p. S2135

Capital's Who's who for Idaho, 1950-51, combined with the pictorial book, Idaho today. Portland, Or., Capitol Publishing Co., c1950.
(240) 227 p. illus. S2136

Carter, Kate B., comp. and ed.
Pioneer irrigation, upper Snake River valley. Daughters of Utah Pioneers, 1955.
xiv, 306 p. illus. S2137

Carter, Kate B
The Salmon River mission. Salt Lake City, Utah Printing Co., c1963.
60 p. map. S2138

Castleford Community Men's Club.
Early history of Castleford, Idaho: supplemented by current information. Castleford, Idaho, c1974.
70 p. illus. S2139

Chadwick, Alta Grete, 1895-1972.
Tales of Silver City. Boise, Idaho, Boise Printing Co., 1975.
vii, 142 p. illus. S2140

Chaffee, Eugene Bernard
Boise College, an idea grows. Boise, Idaho, 1970.
273 p. illus. ports. S2141

Chatterton, Wayne
Vardis Fisher: the frontier and regional works. Boise State College, (Western Writer's Series, 1), 1972.
51 p. S2143

Citizens' Fact-Finding Committee on Farragut.
The Farragut report: a study of the Universal Life Church picnic held at Farragut State Park, and recommendations for legislative action. Nampa, Idaho, Gold Quill, 1972.
143 p. illus. S2144

Clemens, Fred W
Three hundred years along the Rothrock trail... Spokane, Wash., C.W. Hill, c1954.
240 p. illus. S2145

Clements, Louis J
A collection of upper Snake River valley history , plus a complete biography of Andrew Henry. n.p., 196-?
81 p. S2146

Clements, Louis J
History of the upper Snake River area to 1840. Rexburg, Idaho, Eastern Idaho Publishing Co., 1974.
114 p. map. S2147

Clements, Louis J
Pioneering the Snake River fork country, by Louis J. Clements and Harold S. Forbush. Rexburg, Eastern Idaho Publishing Co., 1972.
xxii, 312 p. illus. S2148

Conditt, Paul C., comp.
A union list of serials in Idaho libraries together with a checklist of Idaho serials. Moscow, Idaho, University of Idaho Library, 1969. (Uinversity of Idaho publications, 7).
295, 42p. S2149

Cooke, Edgar Allen
Bingham County, Idaho: premier agriculture district of the upper Snake River valley. Idaho Falls, Register Printing & Publishing Co., 1971.
32 p. S2150

Cornell, Howland, Hayes and Merryfield.
A plan for water pollution control in the south fork Coeur d'Alene River sewer district. Boise, Idaho, 1970.
(95) p. illus. S2151

Cornell, Howland, Hayes and Merryfield/Hill
Planning for Canyon County: introduction and findings. n.p., Canyon County Planning and Zoning Commission, Canyon Development Council, 1972.
188 p. charts. S2152

County Atlas Company
Magic valley atlas. Twin Falls, 1968.
61 p. maps. S2153

Cowling, Cloah (Sebastian), 1886-
The land of Sunrise Mountains: memoirs of Idaho. New York, Vantage Press, 1956.
201 p. illus. S2154

Cowling, Cloah (Sebastian)
Sandy trails. n.p., 1969.
72 p. ports. S2155

Cramer, Howard Ross
Hudspeth's cutoff, southeastern Idaho, a map and composite diary. Prepared for U.S. Bureau of Land Management, Burley District. Burley, Idaho,1969.
v, 55p. tables. maps. S2156

Crossthwaite, E.G.
Water resources of the Goose Creek Rock area, Idaho, Utah, Nevada. Boise, Idaho Dept. of Reclamation, 1969. (It's Water Information Bulletin, 8).
73 p. S2158

Crowder, David Lester
Tendoy, chief of the Lemhis. Caldwell, Idaho, Caxton Printers, 1969.
139 p. illus. S2159

Crowley, Chris
Hiking trails of the Owyhees and Seven Devils Mountains. Caldwell, Idaho, the Sanke River Regional Studies Center, College of Idaho, 1971.
34 p. maps. S2160

Cubit, Jack
Idaho treasure tales and treasure trails, by Jack Cubit and T.R. Glenn. Boise, Id., Alturas Enterprises, 1968.
map 88 x 56 cm. fold. S2161

Darrow, Clarence Seward
Attorney for the damned: edited and with notes by Arthur Weinburg. New York, Simon & Schuster, 1957.
552 p. S2162

Daughters of the American Revolution. Idaho.
History and roster, 1935-1962. Caldwell, Idaho, Shorb Printing Co., 1963.
60 p. illus. S2163

David, Homer
Some recollections of Homer David, 1890-1910. Moscow, Idaho, June 18, 1966.
30 l. S2164

Davis, James W
Aristocrat in burlap: a history of the potato in Idaho. Boise, Idaho Potato Commission, 1975.
209 p. illus. S2165

Davis, Ray Joseph, 1895-
Believe 'em or not: they're true. Pocatello, Id., The author, 1974.
172 p. S2166

Davis, Ray Joseph
Flora of Idaho. Dubuque, Iowa. W.C. Brown, 1952.
iv, 828 p. S2167

Dawson, Alson William
Western saga guide book: Cassia County, cross-trails of the pioneers. Burley, Id., Cassia County Historical Society, 1974.
90 p. illus. S2168

D'Easum, Cedric G
Fragments of villainy. Drawings by Paul B. Evans. Boise, Idaho, Statesman Printing Co., 1959.
246 p. illus. S2169

Declo, my town, my people. Compiled by the Declo History Committee. Burley, Idaho, Burley Reminder, Inc., c1974.
vii, 759 p. illus. S2170

Dorn, Edward
Idaho out. London, Fulcrum Press, 1965.
1 vol. S2171

Douglass, William A
Amerikanuak: Basques in the New World, by William A. Douglass and Jon Bilbao. Reno, University of Nevada Press, 1975.
xiv, 519 p. illus. S2172

Drew, Evalena May
Some of Mama's stories, edited by Hester E. Gittins and Doris H. Peden. Caldwell, Caxton Printers, 1968.
20 p. S2173

Driggs, Benjamin Woodbury, 1858-1930
History of Teton Valley, Idaho. Edited by Louis J. Clements and Harold S. Forbush. Rexburg, Idaho, Eastern Idaho Publishing Co., c1970.
280 p. illus. S2174

Driscoll, Ann Nilsson
They came to a ridge. Edited by Maryann McKie. Moscow, Id., The News Review Publishing Co., 1970.
96 p. illus.
Also: 2nd ed. 1975. 104 p. S2175

Drury, Clifford Merrill, 1897-
The beginnings of Talmaks. "Galloping over the butte." Printed by David H. Crawford, Craigmont, Idaho, 1958.
8 p. S2176

Drury, Clifford Merrill
I, the lawyer. San Rafael, Calif., 1960.
9 p. S2177

Dryden, Cecil Pearl, 1887-
The Clearwater of Idaho. New York, Carlton Press, 1972.
258 p. illus. S2178

Dubois, Fred Thomas, 1851-1930
Fred T. Dubois's the making of a state. Edited by Louis J. Clements. Rexburg, Eastern Idaho Publishing Co., 1971.
207 p. illus. S2179

Dudgeon, Muriel, comp.
John Flynn's memories of Mineral as told to Muriel Dudgeon and other stories of the river... n.p., 1966?
60 p. illus. S2180

Duncombe, Herbert Sydney
Handbook for elected city officials in Idaho. 3rd ed. Moscow, University of Idaho, Bureau of Public Affairs Research, 1971.
S2181

Duncombe, Herbert Sydney and Katherine D. Pell
Handbook for county officials in Idaho. 2nd ed. Moscow, University of Idaho Bureau of Public Affairs Research, 1968. (Its Monograph 7).
137 p. S2182

Duncombe, Herbert Sydney
Idaho election statistics, 1970. Moscow, University of Idaho, Bureau of Public Affairs Research, 1970. (Research Memorandum, 8).
64 p. S2183

Early and present history of Fix Ridge, Latah County, Idaho, 1877-1964. Prepared by the Fix Ridge Club, Juliaetta, Idaho, 1964.
xiv, 117 p. illus. S2184

Eastman, C. Alexander, 1918-
The sin of caring. Portland Or., Metropolitan Press, c1974.
v, 107 p. S2185

Ege, Robert J
Tell Baker to strike them hard: incident on the Marias, 23 Jan. 1870. Introduction by Don Russell. Bellevue, Neb., Old Army Press, 1970.
ix, 146 p. illus. S2186

Ehrenberger, James L
Smoke down the canyons: Union Pacific, Idaho Division by Ehernberger and Gschwind. Callaway, Neb., E. & G. Publications, 1966.
64 p. illus. S2187

Ellis, Erl H
That word "Idaho." Denver, University of Denver Press, 1951. (Denver. University. Publications. Studies in humanities, no. 3).
35 p. S2188

Ellison, Idaho
Last of the breed: an autobiography. My life and times, 1890-1974 as told to Enid C. Howard. St. George, Utah, Dixie Printing, 1975, c1974.
167 p. illus. S2189

Elmore County Historical Foundation, Inc.
A glimpse at early Elmore County: 1963 territorial centennial. n.p., 1963.
96 p. illus. S2190

Elsensohn, Alfreda, Sister, 1897-
A flora of the Camas prairie region in the vicinity of Cottonwood, Idaho. Rev. ed. Cottonwood, Id., The author, 1966.
S2191

Elsensohn, Alfreda, Sister
Idaho Chinese lore. Cottonwood, Id., Benedictine Sisters, 1970.
121 p. illus. S2192

Elsensohn, Alfreda, Sister
Pioneer days in Idaho County. Caldwell, Id., Caxton Printers, 1947-1951.
2 vols. plates. map. S2193

Elsensohn, Alfreda, Sister
Seventy-five years of service, 1884-1959. Fifty years of Cottonwood, 1909-1959. A short historical sketch of the Sisters of St. Gertrude's Community. Cottonwood, Idaho, St. Gertrude's Convent, 1959.
19 p. illus. S2194

Emerson, Tom
Seaplanes from Coeur d'Alene. n.p., 1973.
xiv, 128 p. illus. S2195

Environmental Planning Group, Inc., Boise, Idaho.
Population and economic base study, Caribou County, Idaho. Boise, Id., 1970.
77 p. tables. map. S2196

Estes, James F
Lost mine of Priest Lake. Illustrated by Alfred Skaar. n.p., 1967.
165 p. illus. S2197

Estes, James F
Tales of Priest Lake. Sketches by Alfred Skaar. Spokane, 1964.
159 p. illus. maps.
Also: 4th ed., 1972, 158 p. S2198

Estes, James F
Tales of the Coeur d'Alene. Spokane, Steptoe Publications, 1971.
1 vol. illus S2199

Etulain, Richard W
The Idaho heritage: a collection of historical essays, edited by Richard W. Etulain and Bert W. Marley. Pocatello, ISU Press, 1974.
xvi, 230 p. S2200

Etulain, Richard W. and Merwin Swanson.
Idaho history: a bibliography. Pocatello, Idaho State University Press, 1975.
81 p. S2201

Fahey, John
The ballyhoo bonanza: Charles Sweeny and the Idaho mines. Seattle, Wash., University of Washington Press, 1971.
xiii, 288 p. illus. S2202

Feathers, Joseph J.S.
These are the Coeur d'Alene tribe: featuring Bernard La Sarte and Oswald C. George. Lewiston, Idaho. Lewis-Clark State College Press, 1971.
1 vol (various pagings) illus. maps. S2204

Feathers, Joseph J.S.
These are the Nez Perce nation, featuring Allen P. Slickpoo, Richard A. Halfmoon, Richard M. Ellenwood, and others. Lewiston, Idaho. Lewis-Clark Normal Press, 1970.
142 p. illus. maps. music.S2205

Fichter, Edwon
The amphibians of Idaho, by Edson Fichter and Allan D. Linder. Pocatello, Idaho State University Museum, 1964.
34 p. illus. S2206

Fielder, George
Test excavations at the Coeur d' Alene mission of the Sacred Heart, Cataldo, Idaho, 1973, by George Fielder and Roderick Sprague. Moscow, Idaho, University of Idaho, Laboratory of Anthropology, 1974.
vi, 52 p. illus. S2207

Firman, Robert G
A history of the Boise public school system. Boise, Idaho, 1975.
43 p. illus. S2208

Fisher, Vardis.
Love and death: the complete stories. New York, Doubleday, 1959.
211 p. S2209

Folz, William Edward, 1906-
An analysis of the income structure of Idaho. Boise, 1951.
117 p. diagrs. S2211

Foote, Morris, comp.
One hundred years in Middleton. Middleton, Idaho, Boise Valley Hearld, 1963.
80 p. illus. S2212

Foster, Annie Jane (Biggers) Elliott
Annie Jane's journal, 1904. Glen E. Biggers, 1974.
60 p. illus. S2213

Fraser, Joseph H
A survey of the recreation and tourism resources in the Nez Perce country. Chicago, Armour Research Foundation of Illinois Institute of Technology, 1963.
2 vols. illus. S2214

Frederickson, Lars, 1857-1939
History of Weston, Idaho. Edited by A.J. Simmonds. Logan, Utah State University Press, 1972.
78 p. illus. S2215

Freemasons. Idaho. Grand Lodge.
100 years, 1867-1967. centennial of the grand lodge of Idaho, A.F. & A.M. Boise, Id., The Lodge, 1967.
16 p. illus. S2216

Garst, Doris Shannon, 1899-
Chief Joseph of the Nez Perces: illustrated by Douglas Gorsline. New York, J. Messner, 1953.
184 p. illus. S2217

Gem State Authors' Guild
Starlight and syringa. Written by members of the ... guild. Pocatello, Idaho. Gateway Printers, Inc., c1959.
116 p. illus. S2218

Genesee, Idaho. St. Mary's Church.
St. Mary's diamond jubilee and dedication, Genesee, Idaho, 1890-1965. Genesee, Idaho, 1965.
19 p. illus. S2219

Gerassi, John
The boys of Boise: furor, vice and folly in an American city. New York, Macmillan, 1966.
xciii, 328 p. S2220

Gibbs, Rafe
Beacon for mountain and plain: story of the University of Idaho. Moscow, University of Idaho, 1962.
x, 420 p. illus. S2221

Glenn, T.R.
Ghost towns and mining camps of Idaho. n.p., 1967.
map 87 x 56 cm. fold. S2222

Goertzen, Dorine
Boise basin brocade. Illustrated by Vic Goertzen. Boise, Idaho, Capitol Lithograph and Print, c1960.
(24) p. illus. S2224

Goldsmith, Claire, 1891-
In the shadow of the squaw: the history and development of the New Plymouth community in Idaho as told in records, reminiscences, and pioneer stories. New Plymouth, Idaho, 1953.
99 p. S2225

Groefsema, Olive De Ette (Jenson), 1894- , comp.
Elmore County, its historical gleanings: a collection of pioneer narrative, treasured family pictures and early clippings about the settling of Elmore County, Idaho. Mountain Home? Idaho, 1949.
xvii, 453 p. illus. S2226

Grover, David Hubert
Debaters and dynamiters: the story of the Haywood trial. Corvallis, Or., Oregon State University Press, 1964. (Oregon State monographs: Studies in history, no. 4).
viii, 310 p. S2227

Grover, David Hubert
Diamondfield Jack: a study in frontier justice. Reno, University of Nevada Press, 1968.
xi, 189 p. illus. S2228

Gulick, Grover C
Bend of the Snake. Boston, Houghton Mifflin, 1950.
274 p.
Also: London; Museum Press, 1952.
192 p. S2229

Gulick, Grover C
Snake River country. Photography by Earl Roberge. Caldwell, Idaho, Caxton Printers, 1971.
xvi, 195 p. illus. S2230

Gulick, Grover C
They came to a valley. Garden City, N.Y., Doubleday, 1966.
474 p. S2231

Hagen C.L. and Boyd Henry
Consumer finance industry in Idaho: a study of the growth and operations of the industry, an analysis of its borrowers and a comparison of operations with those of other related industries. Caldwell, Idaho, College of Idaho, 1960.
79 p. S2231A

Haines, Francis
Indians of the Great Basin and Plateau. New York, Putnam, 1970.
223 p. illus. S2232

Haines, Francis
The Nez Perces: tribesmen of the Columbia Plateau. Norman, University of Oklahoma Press, 1955.
xvii, 329 p. illus. S2233

Haines, Francis
Red Eagle and the Absaroka. Illustrated by Arthur Kenneth Yost. Caldwell, Idaho, Caxton Printers, 1960.
191 p. illus. S2234

Hall, Lucille (Peterson) Hathaway, 1883-
Memories of old Alturas County, Idaho. Denver, Big Mountain Press, 1956.
72 p. illus. S2235

Hall, William Webster, 1903-
The small college talks back: an intimate appraisal. New York, R.R. Smith, 1951.
214 p. S2236

Hammes, JoJane, ed.
Living, 1906-1908. St. Maries, Idaho, Western Historical, Inc., 1962.
(28) p. illus. S2237

Hammes, Robert M., ed.
The way it was: being ... the photographic efforts primarily of the decades of 1890 to 1900 to 1910 ... the St. Maries and St. Joseph river valleys. Comp. and edited by Robert M. Hammes and E. Mark Justice. St. Maries, Idaho., Western Historical Inc., c1962.
(84) p. illus. S2238

Harmsworth, Harry C
Population trends in Idaho, 1950-1960. Moscow, Idaho, University of Idaho. Dept. of Social Sciences, 1964.
58 p. illus. S2239

Harmsworth, Harry C
Sixty years of population growth in in Idaho, 1890-1950. Moscow, Id., University of Idaho. Dept. of Social Sciences, 1952.
85 p. illus. S2240

Harmsworth, Harry C
Vital statistics and population projections for Idaho: 1960-1980. Moscow, Id., University of Idaho, Dept. of Social Sciences, 1967.
40 p. tables, graphs. S2241

Hart, Newell, ed.
Hometown album: a pictorial history of Franklin County, Idaho, horse and buggy days and early auto era. Preston, Id., Cache Valley Newsletter Publishing Co., 1973.
843 plates. S2242

Hawes, Adelaid (Turner), 1875-
The valley of tall grass. Bruneau, Idaho, 1950.
244 p. illus. S2243

Heady, Eleanor B
Sage smoke: tales of the Shoshoni-Bannock Indians. Illustrated by Arvis Stewart. Chicago, Follett Publishing Co., 1973.
96 p. illus. S2244

Heady, Eleanor B
Tales of the Nimipoo from the land of the Nez Perce Indians. Illustrated by Eric Carle. New York, World Publishing Co., 1970.
124 p. illus. S2245

Herndon, Ellen (Boulton)
I remember Idaho: my childhood on Boulton farm. Claremont, Calif., Published by Esther Boulton Black, 1972.
40 p. illus. S2246

Hiking trails of the Owyhees and Seven Devils Mountains. Caldwell, College of Idaho Regional Studies Center, 1973. S2247

Historic houses of Boise's Warm Springs Avenue. Boise, Bishops House Preservation Society, 1975.
30 p. illus. S2248

History of Idaho Territory. Fairfield, Wash., Ye Galleon Press, 1973. (Reprint of 1884 ed.)
302 p. illus. S2249

History of Latah County. Provo, Utah, Somon Benson, 1973. (Reprint of Latah County portion of Illustrated History of North Idaho, 1903). S2250

History of the First United Presbyterian Church, Coeur d'Alene, Idaho. 1888-1963. Coeur d'Alene, Idaho, 1963.
(5), 28 p. illus. S2251

Hogsett, Vernetta (Murchison), 1897-
The golden years: a history of the Idaho Federation of Women's Clubs, 1905-1955. Caldwell? Idaho, 1955.
377 p. illus. S2252

Holbrook, Stewart Hall
The Rocky Mountain revolution. New York, H. Holt, 1956.
318 p. maps. S2253

Holenbaugh, Kenneth M
The evaluation of geologic processes in the Boise foothills that may be hazardous to urban development. Boise, Ada Council Of Governments, 1973.
88 p. illus. S2254

Horr, David A
Nez Perce Indians. New York, Garland, 1974.
621 p. S2255

Horsley, Albert E., 1866-1954
Harry Orchard: the man God made again, by Harry Orchard in collaboration with LeRoy Edwin Froom. Nashville, Southern Publishing Association, 1952.
200 p. illus. S2256

Hovey, Paul E
Presbyterian yesterdays in Northern Idaho: an address delivered at Coeur D'Alene, Id., March 18, 1963 ... Lewiston, Id., Presbytery of Northern Idaho, 1964.
13 p. S2257

Hult, Ruby El, 1912-
Steamboats in the timber. Illustrated by photos. Caldwell Id., Caxton Printers, 1952.
209 p. illus.
Also: 2nd ed. Portland, Or., Binfords & Mort, 1968. 209 p. S2259

Hyde, Dayton O.
The last free man: the true story behind the massacre of Shoshone Mike and his band of Indians in 1911. New York, Dial Press, 1973.
264 p. illus. S2260

Idaho. Dept. of Commerce and Develop.
Manufacturing Directory of Idaho, 1971. Boise, Id., 1971.
1 vol. S2261

Idaho. Secretary of State.
Idaho Blue Book: "The Gem State" 1971-1972. Boise, 1971.
196 p. S2262

Idaho Falls Chapter of the Retired Teachers' Association
The way we were: a history of early schools in Idaho. Idaho Falls, Idaho, 1975.
218 p. S2263

Idaho First National Bank (Boise).
A national bank 100 years, 1867-1967. Boise, 1967.
1 vol. S2264

Idaho Genealogical Society
Idaho Territory: federal population schedules and mortality schedules, 1870. Boise? Williams Print., 1973.
218 p. illus. S2265

Idaho. Historical Society.
Architecturally significant and historic buildings of Boise. Boise, 1970. S2266

Idaho. Historical Society.
A short history of Idaho. Boise, 1974.
100 p. S2267

Idaho Poets' amd Writers' Guild.
The Idaho story. Iona, Ipas Publishing Co., 1967-68.
2 vols. S2268

Idaho Poets' and Writers' Guild.
Songs to Idaho: centennial edition, 1962. Shelley, Idaho, Printed by the Shelley Pioneer, Publishers, 1962.
88 p. S2269

Idaho Poets' and Writers' Guild.
These to remember. Centennial ed. n.p., 1962.
158 p. illus. S2270

Idaho Power Company
Water on the land: private enterprise development of irrigation in the Snake River valley. Boise, Idaho, 1964.
24 p. illus. S2271

Idaho Republican State Central Committee.
The Idaho review, 1965-66. Boise, Syms-York, 1965.
126 p. S2272

Idaho Wildlife Federation.
Idaho Environmental issues. Boise, Idaho, 1974.
100 p. illus. S2273

Idaho Writers' League.
Idaho, legend and story. Pocatello, The league, 1961.
161 p. S2274

Idaho Writers' League. Boise Chapter.
The sign post-to places of interest in and out of Boise. Boise, Intermountain Observer, 1969.
32 p. S2275

Idaho Writer's League. Boise Chapter.
Silhouettes of Boise. Boise, Capital Lithography and Print Co., 1963.
32 p. S2276

Johnson, Claudius O
Borah of Idaho. Seattle, Wash., University of Washington Press, 1967. (Reissue with a new introduction by the author, of 1936 ed.)
544 p. S2277

Johnson, Donald Ralph, 1931-
Unique, rare and endangered raptorial birds of northern Idaho: nesting successes and management recommendations by Donald R. Johnson and Wayne E. Melquist. Moscow, University of Idaho, 1972.
ii, 42 l. illus. S2278

Johnson, Lynn Eric, comp.
Wilford, Idaho, sketches of a pioneer community. n.p., 1965.
illus. S2279

Jones, George R
Bruneau as I knew it, 1912 to 1945. Boise, Id., Syms-York, c1963.
50 p. S2280

Jordan, Grace (Edgington), ed.
Idaho reader. Boise, Id., Syms-York, 1963.
x, 406 p. illus. S2281

Jordan, Grace (Edgington)
The king's pines of Idaho: a story of the Browns of McCall. Portland, Or., Binfords & Mort, 1961.
295 p. illus. S2282

Jordan, Grace (Edgington)
The unintentional senator. Boise, Syms-York Co., 1972.
xii, 318 p. illus. S2283

Junk, Frank Stanley
Boundary County, and Bonners Ferry, Idaho: comprehensive plan, water and sewage. Moscow, Idaho, 1969.
69 p. tables. maps. S2285

Kappholz, Lowell
Gold! with contemporary accounts and illustrations. New York, McBride, 1959.
214 p. illus. S2286

Keeling, Alma Taylor-Lauder
The un-covered wagon: a glimpse of pioneer days in Moscow, Idaho. Moscow, Id., Keeling, 1975.
vi, 151 leaves, (8) leaves of plates. illus. S2287

Kinucan, K.W.
Wildlife communities of Sun Valley: an ecological interpretation, by K.W. and E.S. Kinucan. Sun Valley, Id., Sun Valley Creative Arts Center, c1972.
155 p. illus. S2288

Kirkwood, Charlotte M., 1836-1926
The Nez Perce Indian war under war chiefs Joseph and Whitebird. Grangeville, Idaho County Free Press, n.d.
58 p. S2289

Klages, Karl Henry William, 1898-
Climate of the Palouse area of Idaho: a summary of 70 years of climatological data collected at the University of Idaho. Moscow, Idaho Agricultural Experiment Station, 1965. (Its Bulletin 448).
40 p. S2290

Knight, Gladys Bowman, 1899-
A biographical sketch of Earl Wayland Bowman, "the ramblin' kid." Council, Id., 1967.
48 p. illus. S2291

Knight, Gladys Marie Bowman
Letters to the editor. Council, Idaho, 1970.
57 p. S2292

Kreizenbeck, Helen
A history of the Idaho First National Bank. Boise, Idaho, 1949.
24 p. illus. ports. S2293

Lafferty, J.B., 1875-
My eventful years. Weiser, Idaho, Signal American Printers, 1963.
53 p. illus. S2294

Lame, C.C.
Star garnet and opal from Idaho - The Gem state: how to find and cut them. A guide for the gem hunter. Lewiston, Id., Commercial Printing Co., 1953.
16 p. maps. S2295

Larrison, Earl Junior, 1919-
Guide to Idaho birds, by Earl J. Larrison and Jerry L. Tucker, and Malcom T. Jollie. Moscow? Idaho, 1967. (Journal of the Idaho Academy of Sciences, v. 5).
220 p. tables. S2296

Larrison, Earl Junior
Guide to Idaho mammals. Illustrated by Norma Donaldson. Pocatello, Id., Idaho Academy of Science, 1967. (Journal of the Idaho Academy of Science, v. 7).
166 p. illus. S2297

Larrison, Earl Junior
Owyhee: the life of a northern desert. Illustrated by Don Fritts. Caldwell, Id., Caxton Printers, 1957.
357 p. illus. S2298

League of Women Voters, Boise.
Here is Boise, Idaho. n.p., 1958?
S2299

League of Women Voters, Boise.
Who's in charge here: government of Ada County and Boise City. 1969. S2300

League of Women Voters, Idaho.
A brief look at the constitution of the state of Idaho, 1889-1972. Boise, 1972. (Its Publication, no. 30).
22 p. illus. S2301

League of Women Voters, Idaho.
Equality of opportunity for education and employment in Idaho. Boise, Id., 1965.
7 (10) p. tables. S2302

League of Women Voters, Idaho.
A look at Idaho's constitution, then and now, 1889-1962. Boise, 1962. (Its Publication no. 8).
35 p. illus. organizational chart. S2303

League of Women Voters, Lewiston
A roundup of information about Lewiston. Lewiston, 1973.
24 p. tables. maps. S2304

League of Women Voters, Moscow.
This is Moscow, U.S.A. Moscow, 1965.
21 p. S2305

Lee, Shirley W
A survey of acculturation in the inter-mountain area of the United States. Pocatello, Idaho State University Museum, 1967. (Museum Occasional Papers, 19).
57 p. S2306

Lenard, Charles A
Lewiston-Clarkston area manpower survey. Pullman, Wash., Washington State University, Bureau of Economic and Business Research, 1969.
41 p. illus. S2307

Liljeblad, Sven Samuel, 1899-
The Idaho Indians in transition, 1805-1960. With a preface by Earl H. Swanson, Jr. Pocatello, Idaho State University Museum, 1972.
xi, 112 p. maps. S2308

Livingstone-Little, Dallas Eugene, 1916-
An economic history of north Idaho, 1800-1900. Cartography by George Bowditch. Los Angeles, Carroll Spear Morrison, Publishers, 1965.
xvii, 133 p. illus. maps. S2310

Lockwood, Sarah (McNeil)
The elbow of the Snake. New York, Doubleday, 1959.
251 p. S2311

Loeffler, Fred
The avenging innkeeper: the Magruder party murder. n.p., 1972.
58 p. S2312

Lord, Walter
The good years: from 1900 to the first World War. New York, Harpers, 1960.
369 p. S2313

Lovell, Edith Haroldsen
Captain Bonneville's county. Idaho Falls, Eastern Idaho Farmer, 1963.
275 p. illus. S2314

Lyon, Ruth B., 1910-
Valley of plenty. Boise, Capitol Lithograph and Printing Co., 1968.
107 p. illus. S2315

McBride, Leroy, comp.
History of the View Ward, 1904-1954. n.p., n.d.
88 p. illus. S2316

McDermott, John Dishon
Forlorn hope: a study of the battle of White Bird Canyon, Idaho, and the beginning of the Nez Perce Indian war. Washington, D.C., National Park Service, 1968.
xi, 370 (21) p. illus. S2317

McKenna, Marian Cecilia, 1926-
Borah. Ann Arbor, University of Michigan Press, 1961.
450 p. illus. S2318

MacLane, John Fisher, 1878-
A sagebrush lawyer. New York, Pandick Press, Inc., c1953.
177 p. illus. S2319

McLeod, George A., 1857-1949
History of Alturas and Blaine counties, Idaho. 3rd ed. Hailey, Idaho, The Hailey Times, 1950.
216 p. S2320

McWhorter, Lucullus Virgil, 1860-1944.
Hear me, my chiefs! Nez Perce history and legend: edited by Ruth Bordin: illustrated with photos. Caldwell, Caxton Printers, 1952.
xxiv, 640 p. illus. S2321

Madden, Richard B
"Tree farmers and wood converters": the story of Potlatch Corporation. n.p. Newcomen Society, 1975.
S2322

Madsen, Brigham D
The Bannock of Idaho. Illustrated by Maynard Dixon Stewart. Caldwell, Caxton Printers, 1958.
382 p. illus. S2323

Magnuson, Richard G.
Coeur d'Alene diary: the first ten years of hard rock mining in north Idaho. Portland, Or., Metropolitan Press, c1968.
xiv, 319 p. illus. S2324

Malone, Michael Peter, 1940-
C. Ben Ross and the new deal in Idaho. Seattle, University of Washington Press, 1970.
xxiii, 191 p. ports. S2325

Maps of early Idaho: old gold mines, Indian battle grounds, old military roads, old forts, overland stage routes, early towns. Preparation: R.N. Preston. Corvallis, Or., Western Guide Publishers, 1972.
59 p. (chiefly maps.) S2326

Markham, John, 1916-
The Ashton, Idaho-Moran, Wyoming horse and wagon freight line, mid-July of 1910 to October 15, 1927. Turlock, Calif., Turlock Printing Co., 1972.
40 p. illus. S2327

Mathieson, Theodore
The Nez Perce Indian war: the compelling true saga of a valiant people who were forced into war to stay alive. Derby, Conn., Monarch Books, 1964.
156 p. S2328

Mayo, Roy E
Gold and strychnine. Manchester, Wash., 1975.
74 p. illus. S2329

Metsker Maps. Atlas of Bonner County, Idaho. Tacoma, Wash., 1974.
55 leaves. S2330

Midmore, Joe
Middle fork history. With photos by Kern Adams. Reno, Nev., Harrah's Club, 1970.
82 p. illus. S2331

Miller, John B
The trees grew tall. Moscow, Idaho, The New Review Publishing Co., 1972.
214 p. illus. S2333

Mills, Nellie B. (Ireton), 1880-
All along the river. Territorial and pioneer days on the Payette. n.p. B.C. Payette, 1963.
320 p. illus. S2334

The Minidoka story: the land and the people, in words and pictures. Rupert, Idaho, The Minidoka County News, 1963.
42 p. illus. S2335

Minobras
Idaho industrial minerals. Santa Ana, Calif., Minobras, 1975.
55 p. map. S2336

Mitchell, Anna (Smith), comp.
Homesteaders and early settlers of the Cedar Creek Ridge area, Latah County, Idaho, n.p., 1961.
107 p. S2337

Montgomery, Richard Calvin
Canyon County: the economic geography of a southwestern Idaho irrigated area. Lincoln, 1951.
120 p. maps. S2338

Montpelier, Paris and the Bear Lake country of Idaho. n.p., 1963.
(10) p. illus. S2339

Morrow, Jack O
So firm thy faith in Odd Fellowship, 1864-1971: history of Pioneer Lodge no. 1, Independent Order of Odd Fellows, Idaho City, Idaho. By Jack O. and Waletta S. Morrow. Caldwell, Id., Grand Lodge Printing Press, I.O.O.F., 1971.
196 p. illus. S2340

Morrow, Waletta S., comp.
Idaho's century of triple links: a history of Idaho's 100 years of Odd Fellowship. Compiled and written by Waletta S. Morrow. Caldwell, Id., Published by the Grand Lodge of Idaho, I.O.O.F., 1963.
147 p. illus. S2341

Moscow, Idaho. First Presbyterian Church.
Diamond jubilee of the First Presbyterian Church, Moscow, Idaho. Moscow, 1955.
30 p. illus. music. S2342

Moscow, Idaho. St. Mark's Church.
75th anniversary 1889-1964, St. Mark's Church, Moscow, Idaho. Moscow, 1964.
14 p. illus. S2343

Mountain States Telephone & Telegraph.
Idaho base maps (West zone). Denver, Colo., 1973.
1 vol. S2345

Mullen, William J
Lost River wilderness. Pocatello, Studio Press, 1970.
18 p. S2346

Murphy, Robert Francis, 1924-
Shoshone-Bannock subsistence and society, by Robert F. and Yolanda Murphy. Berkeley, University of California Press, 1960. (Anthropoligical records, v. 16, no. 7).
293-338 p. map. S2347

Nelson, Elsie
Today is ours. n.p., 1972.
130 p. illus. S2348

Nettleton, Helen
Interesting buildings in Silver City, Idaho. n.p., 1974.
unpaged. illus. S2349

Newell, Helen Marie, 1909-
Idaho's place in the sun. Boise, Syms-York, 1975.
vi, 180 p. illus. S2350

Nez Perce Indians. Aboriginal territory of the Nez Perce Indians by Stuart A. Chalfant. Ethnohistory of the Joseph band of Nez Perce Indians: 1805-1905 by Verne F. Ray. New York, Garland Publishing Inc., 1974.
453 p. maps. S2351

Nichols, Glenn W
Handbook for elected city officials in Idaho, 2nd ed. Moscow, University of Idaho Bureau of Public Affairs Research, 1969. (Its Public Affairs Series, 6).
102 p. S2352

Nichols, Glenn W. and others.
Idaho election statistics, 1968. Moscow, University of Idaho Bureau of Public Affairs Research, 1969. (Its Research Memorandum, 7).
61 p. S2353

Nixon, L. Wesley
Bald mountain vision. Des Moines, Iowa, Garner Publishing Co., 1957.
viii, 207 p. illus. S2354

North Idaho access. Moscow, Idaho, North Idaho Access, c1975.
54 p. illus. S2355

Norton, Boyd
Snake wilderness. San Francisco, Sierra Club, c1972.
159 p. illus. S2356

Nuxoll, Sister M. Ildephonse, O.S.B., 1906-
Idaho Benedictine: St. Gertrude's Convent, Cottonwood, Idaho. Cottonwood, Id., 1974.
56, 5 p. illus. S2357

Oberg, Pearl M
Between these mountains: history of Birch Creek Valley, Idaho. New York, Exposition Press, 1970.
199 p. illus. S2359

Ogden, Peter Skene, 1794-1854
Snake country journals, 1824-25 and 1825-26, edited by E.E. Rich. London, Hudson's Bay Record Society, 1950. (Hudson's Bay Record Society Publications, 13.)
lxxix, 283 p. maps. S2360

Ogden, Peter Skene
Snake country journal, 1826-27. London, Hudson's Bay Record Society, 1961.
255 p. S2361

Ojala, Gary L
The fabulous Coeur d'Alene mining district. Cataldo, Id., 1972.
46 p. illus
Also: 2nd ed. rev. Coeur d'Alene, 1973. 46 p. S2362

Olson, Joe M
Just reminiscing: a true adventure story. Coeur d'Alene, J.M. Olson, c1972.
236 p. illus. S2362A

Opinion Research of California.
Public opinion image and attitude survey concerning the city of Boise, n.p., 1967.
unpaged S2363

Orlich, Donald C
Teacher mobility in Idaho, by Donald C. Orlich, Evelyn M. Craven and R.D. Rounds. Boise, Distributed by the Idaho Education Association, 1968.
vii, 160 p. S2364

Otter, Myrtle Elizabeth Hubbard, 1872-
From covered wagon to space ships. Boise? n.p., 1961.
60 l. photo S2365

Pacific Power & Light Co., Industrial Development Department.
Sandpoint, Bonner County, Idaho: indsutrial survey. Portland, Or., 1964.
27 p. illus. S2366

Painter, Rex
Idaho's bonanza years: ghost towns, their history and how to find them. Original oil paintings by Rex Painter. Stories by Dorothy Povey. n.p., 1966
46 p. illus. S2367

Palladino, Lawrence Benedict
The Coeur d'Alene reservation, and our friends the Coeur d' Alene Indians. Fairfield, Wash., Ye Galleon Press, 1967.
26,21 p. S2368

Panhandle Planning and Development Council.
Overall economic development plan for the Panhandle economic development district ... By the Panhandle Planning and Development Council, counties of Benewah, Bonner, Boundary, Kootenai, and Shoshone. Coeur d'Alene, Id., 1974.
136 (21) p. tables. maps. S2369

Parke, Adelia Lettie (Routson)
Memories of an old timer. Weiser, Idaho, Signal-American Printers, 1955.
65 p. illus. S2370

Parke, Adelia Lettie (Routson)
Ramblings in retrospect. Fruitland, Idaho, Strange Printing Service, 1968.
65 p. illus. S2371

Parker, A.F. and others.
Sheepeater Indian campaign. Grangeville, Idaho County Free Press, 1968. S2372

Parkins, Mac
Ballads of Owyhee mine days. Homedale, Idaho, c1964. S2373

Parsons, Donna L
Characteristics of the Snake River basin. Caldwell, Snake River Regional Studies Center, College of Idaho, 1973.
12 L. S2373A

Parsons, Donna L
Idaho: an outdoor classroom. Nyssa, Or., Blue Star Advertising and Publishing, 1968.
224 p; illus. S2374

Paul, Elliot Harold, 1891-
Desperate scenery. New York, Random House, 1954.
302 p. S2375

Peebles, John J
Lewis and Clark in Idaho. Boise, Idaho State Historical Society, 1966. (Idaho Historical Series, 16).
40 p. S2377

Peltier, James
The banditti of the Rocky Mountains and vigilance committee in Idaho: an authentic record of startling adventures in the gold mines of Idaho. Notes and bibliography by Jerome Peltier. Minneapolis, Ross & Haines, 1964.
190 p. illus. S2378

Peltier, Jerome
Manners and customs of the Coeur d'Alene Indians: with some comparative studies. Illustrated by Mary Parker, LeRoy Green Eagle. Spokane, Peltier Publications, 1975.
vi, 84 p. S2379

Peterson, Frank Ross, 1941- , ed.
History of Bear Lake pioneers. Compiled by Edith Parker Haddock and Dorothy Hardy Matthews. Edited by F. Ross Peterson, Edith Parker Haddock, Dorothy Hardy Matthews. Salt Lake City, Published by Daughters of Utah Pioneers, Bear Lake County, 1968.
xiv, 915 p. illus. S2380

Peterson, Frank Ross,
Prophet without honor: Glen H. Taylor and the fight for American liberalism. Lexington, University Press of Kentucky, 1974.
216 p. S2381

Peterson, Harold, 1939-
The last of the mountain men. New York, Scribner, 1969.
160 p. illus. S2382

Peterson, Philip E
Idaho estate administration. Edited by Philip E. Peterson. Boise, Idaho State Bar, 1974.
v, 378 p. forms. S2383

Phipps, Maude (Pefley)
Peter Jackson Pefley, my father ... 1953.
51 p. ports. S2384

Pierce, Elias Davidson
The Pierce chronicle: personal reminiscenses of E.D. Pierce. Edited by J. Gary Williams and Ronald W. Stark. Moscow, Idaho Research Foundation, 1975.
127 p. illus. S2385

The pioneer history and development of the Milo Ward, 1880 to 1960. Idaho Falls, Idaho, printed by Typo-Press Commercial Printers, 1960.
162 p. illus. ports. S2386

Platt, John A
Whispers from "Old Genesee," and echoes of the Salmon River. Kendrick, Idaho, 1959.
67, 46 p. illus. S2388

Platt, John A
Whispers from old Genesee and echoes of the Salmon River. Memorial ed. Fairfield, Wash., Ye Galleon Press, 1975.
xix, 184 p. illus. S2389

Pollock, Dean, 1897-
Joseph, chief of the Nez Perce. Pictures and text by Dean Pollock. Portland, Or., Binfords & Mort, c1950.
62 p. illus. S2390

Pollock, Robert Westly, 1906-
Grandfather, Chief Joseph, and psychodynamics. Baker? Or., 1964.
107 (2) p. S2391

Pottenger, Cynthia E
My Roseberry: original and personal accounts of life in and around once-flourishing town of Roseberry, Idaho. Cascade and McCall, Idaho, The Star-News, 1972.
83 p. illus. S2392

Prather, Wylie A
The American iron curtain. Boise, The author, 1967.
215 p. S2393

Price, Juanita
Pictorial primer of Idaho Territory. Photos by John Price. Weiser Id., 1963.
16 p. illus. S2394

Proulx, Calra
Early history of the upper Lemhi valley. Junction, The author, 1973.
35 p. S2395

Public Administration Service, Chicago.
Idaho highways: a report of a study for the Idaho Highway Study Committee. Chicago, Public Administration Service, 1949.
1 vol. (various pagings) illus. S2396

Rabe, Fred W. and David G. Flaherty.
River of green and gold: a pristine wilderness dramatically affected by man's discovery of gold. Moscow, Idaho Research Foundation, 1974.
98 p. illus. S2397

Ramsey, Guy Reed, comp.
Postmarked Idaho: a list of Idaho post offices. Boise, Idaho State Historical Society, 1975.
unpaged. S2398

Ranney, Agnes (Johnson)
The valley I remember: Meadows Valley, Idaho. Portland Or., 1973.
116 p. illus. S2399

Ravitz, Abe C., ed.
The Haywood case: materials for analysis, selected and edited by Abe C. Ravitz and James N. Primm. San Francisco, Chandler Publishing Co., c1960.
viii, 244 p. S2400

Rawlins, Jennie Brown
Exploring Idaho's past. Salt Lake City, Deseret Book Co., 1963.
166 p. illus. S2401

Rawlins, Jennie Brown
High button shoes. Salt Lake City, Deseret Book Co., 1962.
185 p. S2402

Ray, Verne Frederic, 1905-
Lewis and Clark and the Nez Perce Indians. Washington, D.C., Potomac Corral, The Westerners, 1971.
26 p. illus. S2403

Rea, Thelma M
Living in Idaho. Pen sketches by Avis Thompson. Caldwell, Idaho, Caxton Printers, 1955.
315 p. illus. S2404

Redfield, Francis Mylon, 1842-1929
Reminiscences of Francis Mylon Redfield, pioneer of Oregon and Idaho. Edited by Ethel E. Redfield. Pocatello, Idaho, Private print., 1949.
124 p. port. S2405

Rees, John E., 1868-
Idaho: chronology, nomenclature, bibliography. Chicago, W.B. Conkey, 1918. Seattle, Shorey Book Store, 1965.
125 p. S2406

Rees, John E
Madame Charbonneau: the Indian woman who accompanied the Lewis and Clark Expedition, 1804-6. How she received her Indian name and what became of her. David G. Ainsworth, editor. Salmon, Id., Published by the Lemhi County Historical Society, 1970.
27 p. S2407

Reid, Agnes Just, 1886-
Letters of long ago. Introduction by Brigham D. Madsen. Rev. ed. Salt Lake City, Tanner Trust Fund, c1973.
xviii, 93 p. illus. S2408

Rhodenbaugh, Edward Frnaklin, 1872-
Sketches of Idaho geology. Caldwell, Id., Caxton Printers, 1953.
267 p. illus. S2409

Rhodenbaugh, Edward F.
Sketches of Idaho geology. 2nd ed. Caldwell, Caxton, 1961.
293 p. S2410

Rice, Allen C., ed.
The Idaho oldtime fiddlers. Boise, Idaho Old Time Fiddlers' Association, 1963.
101 p. illus. S2411

Rich, Russell R
Land of the sky-blue water: a history of the L.D.S. settlement of the Bear Lake valley. Provo, Ut., Brigham Young University Press, 1963.
213 p. illus. S2412

Riedesel, Edna Pember, 1904-
Magic valley pioneers: an account of the lives and genealogies of Hebard and Emma Pember, pioneers of Buhl, Idaho. By Edna and Gerhard Riedesel. Pullman, Wash., 1973.
iv, 95 p. illus. S2413

Riedesel, Gerhard A., comp.
Arid acres: a history of the Kimama-Minidoka homesteaders, 1912 to 1932. Pullman, Wash., G.A. Riedesel, 1969.
79 p. illus. S2414

Roberts, Frank Wesley, 1886-1964
Adventures of an oldtimer, as told to his wife, Lela Hudson Roberts. New York, Vantage Press, 1972.
89 p. illus. S2415

Robertson, Frank Chester, 1890-
Fort Hall, gateway to the Oregon country. New York, Hastings House, 1963.
318 p. illus. S2416

Robertson, Frank Chester
Ram in the thicket, an autobiography. New York, Abelard Press, 1950.
357 p. illus.
Also: Rev. ed. N.Y., Hastings House, 1959. 311 p. S2417

Rockwell, Irvin Elmer, 1862-
Buried mines of the Wood River district, Idaho. Bellevue, Idaho, 1949?
11 p. front. S2418

Rockwell, Irvin Elmer
Sketch portraits of men who made Idaho. Boise, Id., Boise Junior College, c1949.
35 p. S2419

Ross, Sylvia H
Introduction to Idaho caves and caving. Moscow, Idaho Bureau of Mines and Geology, 1969.
54 p. S2420

Rowland, Frank P
Founding of McCall, Idaho. Boise, Idaho, 1960.
24 p. illus. S2421

Ryan, John Francis, 1891-1970
A history of Camas prairie. Fairfield, Id., Published by the Camas County Historical Society in cooperation with the Idaho State Historical Society, 1975.
119 p. illus. S2422

Ryan, William J
Pronunciation guide for the state of Idaho. Pocatello, Idaho State University Press, 1974.
1 vol. S2423

Salem, L.D.S. Ward history, 1883-1972. Salem, Idaho, 1972.
103 p. illus. ports. S2424

Sappington, Roger Edwin, 1929-
The brethren along the Snake River: a history of the Church of the Brethren in Idaho and western Montana. Elgin, Ill., Brethren Press, 1966.
158 p. illus. S2426

Savage, C.N.
Economic geology of central Idaho. Blacksand placers. Idaho Bureau of Mines and Geology. Moscow, 1961. (Bulletin no. 17).
160 p. S2427

Schad, Georgia (LaFollette)
Mary E. Hatfield LaFollette, my pioneer mother. Weiser, Idaho. Commercial Printers & Publishers, 1954.
154 p. illus. S2428

Scheffer, Martin
Boise citizens survey, 1975: final report. Boise, Id., Boise Center for Urban Research, 1975.
ii, 92 p. S2429

Schell, Frank R
Ghost towns and live ones: a chronology of the post office dept. in Idaho, 1861-1973. Twin Falls, Id.
ii, 109 p. illus. S2430

Schell, Frank R
Idaho merchants' tokens (1865-1967). Twin Falls, Idaho, 1967.
(102) p. illus. S2431

Schell, Frank R
Idaho merchants' tokens, 1865-1970. 2nd ed. Twin Falls, Idaho, 1970.
x, 56, (16) p. illus. S2432

Schill, William J
An analysis of the role of Lewis-Clark Normal School in Idaho higher education, with recommendations by William J. Schill, Omar L. Olson, and Henry M. Reitan. Seattle, Center for the Development of Community College Education, University of Washington, 1968.
22 p. tables. S2433

Schwarze, David M
Geology of the Lava Hot Springs area. Idaho State College, Pocatello, 1960. (ISC Museum, Occasional papers no. 4).
51 p. S2434

Scott, Edith C., ed.
Settling of Emmett Valley and history of Emmett LDS wards from 1861-1959. n.p., n.d.
97 l. illus. S2435

Scott, Orland A
Pioneer days on the shadowy St. Joe. Coeur d'Alene, Idaho, 1967.
xiv, 372 p. illus. S2436

Sears, Roebuck and Company
We the people: the Sears candidate guide book for the 1970 Idaho state and congressional elections. Chicago, Ill., 1970.
48 p. S2437

Sheepeater Indian campaign, Chamberlain Basin country. Grangeville, Idaho County Free Press, 1968.
72, 29 p. illus. S2438

Shoup, George E
History of Lemhi County. Boise, Idaho State Library, 1969.
34 p. S2439

Sierra Club, San Francisco
Idaho primitive area: report of exploration and reconnaissance. San Francisco, 1964.
65 p. illus. S2440

Sierra Club, San Francisco
River of No Return wilderness: a report of Sierra Club wilderness studies of the Idaho and Salmon River breaks primitive areas and adjacent lands. By Peter Morrison. San Francisco? 1972.
1 vol. maps. S2441

Slickpoo, Allen P., ed.
Noon nee-me-poo, we the Nez Perces: culture and history of the Nez Perces. Lapwai, Idaho? Nez Perce Tribe of Idaho, 1973.
1 vol. illus. S2442

Slickpoo, Allen P., comp.
Nu mee poom tit wah tit (Nez Perce legends) 2nd ed. Lapwai? Idaho, Nez Perce Tribe of Idaho, 1972.
xxii, 214 p. illus. S2443

Small, Albert E., 1878-
Cape Cod and return. Boston, House of Edinboro, 1953.
215 p. illus. S2444

Smith, Pauline Udell
Captain Jefferson Hunt of the Mormon Battery. Salt Lake City. Nicholas G. Morgan, Sr. Foundation, 1958.
308 p. S2445

Smith, Robert S., 1906-
Idaho surgeon: an autobiography. Boise, Idaho, Syms-York, 1974.
viii, 151 p. (21) plates illus.
S2446

Smith, Robert Wayne, 1903-
The Coeur d'Alene mining war of 1892: a case study of an industrial dispute. Corvallis, Or., Oregon State College, c1961. (Oregon State monographs. Studies in history, no. 2).
131 p. illus. S2447

Sonnenkalb, Oscar, 1847-1928
Reminiscences of Oscar Sonnenkalb, Idaho surveyor and pioneer. Edited by Peter T. Harstad. Pocatello, Idaho State University Press, 1972.
66 p. illus. S2448

Sorensen, Arthur H
Age and mode of origin of the Coeur d'Alene ore deposits, Idaho. New York, Carlton Press, c1972.
85 p. illus. S2449

Space, Ralph S
Lewis and Clark through Idaho, 1805-1806. Lewiston, Idaho, Tribune Publishing Co., 1964?
15 (1) p. illus. S2450

Space, Ralph S
The Lolo trail: a history of events connected with the Lolo trail since Lewis and Clark. Lewiston, Idaho, Printed by Printcraft Printing, 1970.
65 p. illus. S2451

Space, Ralph S
Pioneer timbermen: a history of the rush to acquire the white pine forests of the Clearwater country in Idaho. Lewiston, Printcraft Printing, 1972.
61 p. illus. S2452

Sparling, Wayne C
Southern Idaho ghost towns. Caldwell, Idaho, Caxton Printers, 1974.
135 p. illus. S2453

Spencer, Betty Goodwin
The big blowup: illustrated with photos. Caldwell, Idaho, Caxton Printers, 1956.
286 p. illus. S2454

Spencer, Layne Gellner
And five were hanged: and other historical short stories of Pierce and the Oro Fino mining district. Cover design and map by Robert W. Spencer. Lewiston, Printcraft Printing, 1968.
60 p. illus. S2455

Speth, Rudoply Lynn, 1936-
Water quality study on the Salmon River between north fork and Salmon Falls. By R. Lynn Speth, Lewis M. Mulkay and others. Rexburg, Idaho, Dept. of Biological Sciences, Ricks College, 1970.
41 p. tables. S2456

Stafford, K.R. and others
The economic impact of the University of Idaho on the community of Moscow, Idaho. Moscow, Idaho Research Foundation, 1974.
33 p. S2457

Stanford, Omer N
Owyhee county corral dust. n.p., 1963.
48 p. illus. S2458

Stanke, Jerry E., ed.
Owyhee County Historical Society. Nampa, Schwartz Printing Co., 1969. S2459

State and local government in Idaho: a reader. Moscow, University of Idaho Bureau of Public Affairs Research, 1970.
259 p. S2460

Statham, Wilma Lewis, comp.
Owyhee county gleanings. Boise, The Idaho Genealogical Society and the Idaho Historical Society, 1964.
v, 45 p. illus. S2461

Steiner, Dan
The history of the Boise Police Department, prepared by Dan Steiner and Larry A. Paulson. Boise, Id., 1971?
i, 29 p. S2462

Steuenberg, Frank W
The martyr of Idaho. College Place? Wash., 1974.
109 p. illus. S2463

Strong, Benton J
A look into Hells Canyon. By Benton J. Strong and Leland Olds. Washington, D.C., Public Affairs Institute, 1953.
31 p. illus. S2464

Strachan, John
Blazing the Mullan Trail: connecting the headwaters of the Missouri and the Columbia Rivers, and locating the great overland highway to the Pacific Northwest. Rockford, Ill., 1952.
59 p. map. S2465

Stringham, Miranda C
Basalt-Firth since 1900, a locality history of the two communities of people. Illustrated by Peggy C. Cromwell. Idaho Falls, Hansen Printing, 1972.
557 p. illus. S2466

Stringham, Miranda C
History of the Cedar Point, dedicated to Cedar Point community. n.p., Daughters of Utah Pioneers, 1970.
114 p. illus. S2467

Strong, Clarence C
White pine: king of many waters by Clarence C. Strong and Clyde S. Sebb. Missoula, Mont., Mountain Press Publishing Co., c1970.
xii, 212 p. illus. S2468

Sundahl, Carrol Vernon
Municipal (city) bond laws in Idaho. Moscow, Idaho, University of Idaho, Dept. of Social Sciences, 1954.
81 p. diagrs. tables. S2469

Sunset travel guide to Idaho. Menlo Park, Calif., Lane Books, 2969.
80 p. illus. S2470

Swank, Gladys Rae, 1925- , ed.
Tsceminicum. (Meeting of the waters) The Clearwater and Snake Rivers. Edited by Gladys Swank and Nellie Woods. Lewiston, Idaho, Lewiston Chapter, Idaho Writer's League, 196-?
127 p. illus. S2471

Swanson, Earl Herbert, Jr. and Paul G. Sneed.
Birch Creek papers no. 3: the archeology of the shoup rockshelters in east central Idaho. Pocatello, Idaho State University Museum, 1966. (Occasional papers, no. 17).
50 p. S2472

Swanson, Earl Herbert, Jr.
The emergence of plateau culture. Pocatello, Idaho State College Museum, 1962. (Occasional papers, no. 8).
89 p. S2473

Swanson, Earl Herbert, Jr.
Prehistoric Idaho, a report of recent archeologist discoveries. Boise, Idaho State Historical Society, 1966. (Idaho Historical Series, 14).
8 p. S2474

Swanson, Earl Herbert, Jr.
Types and distribution of site features and stone tools, by E. H. Swanson, Dr. R. Tuohy and A.L. Bryan. Pocatello, Id., Idaho State College, 1959. (Idaho St. College Museum, Occasional papers, no. 2).
104 p. illus. S2475

Swinney, H.J.
The establishment of Idaho. Boise, State Historical Society, 1963.
13 l. S2476

Talbott, Clarence Elzy
Memories of Clarence Elzy Talbott, 1875-1900. n.p., 1950?
99 p. S2477

Taylor, Margaret Watson, 1875-
Memories of a wagon trip and pioneer life on Weiser Flat. Weiser, Idaho. Signal-American Printers, c1954.
56 p. S2478

Thomas, Janet
This side of the mountains: stories of eastern Idaho. Idaho Falls, KID Broadcasting Corp., 1975.
102 p. illus. S2479

Thompson, Bonnie
Folklore in the Bear Lake Valley. Salt Lake City, Granite Publishing Co., 1973.
219 p. illus. S2480

Thompson, Erwin N
Fort Lapwai, Nez Perce National Historical Park, Idaho. Denver, Denver Service Center, National Park Service, 1973.
206 p. illus. S2481

Throckmorton, Annie Theresa B
Across the years: "my diary of memories." Rupert, Idaho, 1973.
375 p. S2482

Tompkins, Linda Davidson and others
Idaho fiscal sourcebook. 3rd ed. Moscow, University of Idaho Bureau of Public Affairs Research, 1973.
261 p. S2483

Torgeson, Lenora Barr
Snake River hills. Lacrosse, Wash., 1975.
56 p. illus. S2484

Trenholm, Virginia Cole, 1902-
The Shoshonis, sentinels of the Rockies, by Virginia Cole Trenholm and Maurine Carley. Norman, University of Oklahoma Press, 1964. (The Civilization of the American Indian series, 74).
xiii, 367 p. illus. S2487

Tuohy, Donald R
Archaeological survey in southwestern Idaho and northern Nevada. Carson City, 1963. (Nevada State Museum. Anthropological papers, no. 8).
136 p. illus. S2488

Turner, Faith.(Bailey)
The golden dream - being a story of the beginnings and growth of the public library system in Boise. Boise, The Idaho Statesman, 1955.
36 p. illus. S2489

Turner, Faith (Bailey), ed.
Silhouettes of Boise. Boise, Boise Chapter of the Idaho Writers' League, 1963.
32 p. illus. S2490

Twin Falls County, Idaho. Territorial Centennial Committee.
A folk history of Twin Falls County. Illustrated by Mrs. Donald Lambert. Twin Falls, Standard Printing Co., 1962.
110 p. illus. S2491

U.S. Forest Service.
A history of the Salmon National Forest. 1973.
174 p. S2492

Valentine, Dan
Spirit of Idaho. Illustrated by James Valentine. Salt Lake City, Dan Valentine Publications, 1974.
(67) p. illus. S2493

Walgamott, C.S.
Reminiscences of early days: a series of historical sketches and happenings in the early days of Snake River valley. 2nd ed. Seattle, Shorey Book Store, 1971.
127 p. S2494

Walker, Deward E., Jr.
American Indians of Idaho. Moscow, University of Idaho, 1971. (Anthropological monographs of the University of Idaho, no. 2).
1 vol. illus. S2495

Way, Mary, comp.
The history of Red River Hot Springs. n.p., 1974.
(20) p. illus. S2497

Webbert, Charles A
The Basque collection: a preliminary checklist. Moscow, University of Idaho, 1971. (University of Idaho Library, 9).
100 p. S2498

Webbert, Charles A., comp.
Checklist of western Americana in the Day-NW collection, University of Idaho Library, July 1969. Moscow, University of Idaho Library, 1970. (University Publication, 8).
664 p. S2499

Weber, Tena A., comp.
Parma ward history, 1944-1969. Parma, Idaho, 1969.
346 p. ports. S2500

Wells, Merle W
Gold camps and silver cities. Moscow, 1963. (Idaho Bureau of Mines and Geology. Bulletin no. 22).
86 p. S2501

Wells, Merle W
Idaho: a students' guide to localized history. New York, Bureau of Publications, Teachers College, Columbia University, 1965.
x, 28 p. S2502

Wells, Merle W
Rush to Idaho. With a supplementary section entitled, Only a few struck it rich: economic conditions in the early north Idaho mines. Idaho Bureau of Mines and Geology, Moscow, 1960. (Bulletin no. 19).
57 p. S2503

Wetter, Karl, ed.
Tales of early Plummer. Plummer, Idaho, Plummer High School, 1962.
1 vol. illus. S2504

Williams, E.L.
The sawmilling industry of northern Idaho. Moscow, 1964. (Idaho Agricultural Experiment Station Bulletin, no. 430). S2505

Williams, Thomas Horton, 1894-
Miracle of the desert: a history of the Thomas ward and surrounding communities. Blackfoot, Idaho, 1957.
xiv, 617 p. illus. S2506

Williams, Viva
Hannah K. Lewiston, Idaho, 1972.
80 p. illus. S2507

Willson, Earl
Thunder Mountain story: Thunder Mountain "Tome Up." n.p., c1962.
(12) p. illus. S2508

Wilson, Elijah Nicholas
Among the Shoshones. Medford, Or., Pine Cone, 1971. (Facsimile printing of 1910 ed.).
222 p. S2509

Woods, Helen Gee
The upper eighty. Idaho Falls, Mer-Jons Publishing Co., 1967.
270 p. illus. S2512

Woods, Jewell M
Lives to live by. Council, Idaho, 1968.
182 p. illus. S2513

MONTANA

Compiled by Minnie Paugh,
Montana State University

Aasheim, Magnus
Sheridan's daybreak: a story of Sheridan County and its pioneers. Compiled and collated by Magnus Aasheim. Great Falls, Mont., Blue Print and Letter, Co., Printers, c1970.
vi, 1007 p. illus. S2515

Adams, Alexander B
Sitting Bull, an epic of the plains. New York, Putnam's, 1973.
446 p. ports. S2516

Adams, Andy
The log of a cowboy: a narrative of the old trail days. Lincoln, University of Nebraska Press, 1964.
387 p. S2517

Adams, Paul
When wagon trails were dim. Montana Conference Board of Education of the Methodist church. c1957.
165 p. S2518

Adams, Ramon Frederick
The old-time cowhand. Illustrated by Nick Eggenhofer. New York, Macmillan, 1961.
354 p. illus. S2519

Aldrich, Lanning, ed.
The western art of Charles M. Russell. New York, Ballantine, 1975.
47 leaves (chiefly illus.) S2520

Allison, Janet S
Trial and triumph: 101 years in north central Montana. Art work by Beth Mundt. Chinook? Mont., North Central Montana CowBelles, 1968.
iv, 211 p. illus. S2521

Ambrose, Stephen E
Crazy Horse and Custer: the parallel lives of two American warriors. Garden City, N.Y., Doubleday, 1975.
486 p. illus. S2522

Anaconda Company
This Anaconda. New York, c1960.
59 p. illus. S2523

Anaconda copper etchings: diamond jubilee: 1883-1958. Butte, Mt., n.p., 1958.
136 p. illus. S2524

Anderson, John C
Mackinaws down the Missouri: John C. Anderson's journal of a trip from Saint Louis, Missouri to Virginia City, Montana, and return, 1866. Edited by Glen Barrett. Logan, Utah, Western Text Society, 1973.
105 p. illus. S2525

Andrews, Ralph Warren.
Indians, as the Westerners saw them. Seattle, Superior Publishing Co., 1963.
176 p. ports. S2526

Annin, James
The gazed on the Beartooths. Columbus, Mont., 1964.
3 vols. S2527

Armstrong, J.B.
The big north. Missoula, University of Montana, c1965.
70 p. S2528

Armstrong, J.B.
The raw edge. Missoula, Montana State University Press, 1964.
90 p. S2529

Aronson, J. Hugo
The galluping Swede. Missoula, Mountain Press, 1970.
180 p. illus. S2530

Athearn, Robert G.
Forts of the upper Missouri. Englewood, N.J., Prentice Hall, 1967.
339 p. S2531

Athearn, Robert G
Union Pacific country. New York, Rand McNally, 1971.
480 p. illus. S2532

Avon Youth Association
Brand book, 1957, of the following counties: Deer Lodge, Granite, Lewis and Clark. Avon, Mont., The Association, 1957.
131 p. S2533

Bailey, Ralph Edgar
Indian fighter: the story of Nelson A. Miles. Maps by James Macdonald. New York, Morrow, 1965.
224 p. S2534

Bard, Floyd C
Horse wrangler: sixty years in the saddle in Wyoming and Montana, by Floyd C. Bard as told to Agnes Wright Spring. Norman, University of Oklahoma Press, 1960.
296 p. map. S2535

Barsness, Larry
Gold camp: Alder Gulch and Virginia City, Montana. New York, Hastings House, 1962.
312 p. S2536

Bartlett, Alice Wiles
Montana meadow star: illustrated by Jim Padgett. Nashville, Tenn., Southern Publishing Co., 1965.
198 p. S2537

Beidler, John Xavier
X. Beidler: vigilante; edited by Helen Fitzgerald Saunders. Norman, University of Oklahoma Press, 1957.
165 p. illus. S2538

Bell, Edward Janes, Jr.
Montana agriculture and the State University, 1893-1968. Bozeman, Montana State University, 1968.
23 p. S2539

Bell, Edward Janes
Homesteading in Montana 1911-1923: Life in the Blue Mountain country. Bozeman, Big Sky Books, 1975.
68 p. illus. S2540

Bennett, Edward Earl
The Congregational Church in Missoula, 1891-1966, a chronological sketch. Missoula, Mountain Press, 1966?
46 p. illus. S2541

Bennett, Edward Earl
One hundred years of Masonic history, 1868-1968. Missoula Lodge, No. 13, A.F. & A.M. Missoula, Delaney's 1969.
69 p. illus. S2542

Berry, Gerald L
The whoop-up trail; Alberta-Montana relationships. Edmonton, Applied Arts Products, 1953.
143 p. illus. index S2543

Berthold, Mary Paddock
Big Hole journal: notes and excerpts. Detroit, Mich., Harlo Press, 1973.
215 p. S2544

Berthold, Mary Paddock
Turn here for the Big Hole. Detroit, Mich., Harlo Press, 1970.
206 p. S2545

Bigart, Robert, comp.
Environmental pollution in Montana Missoula, Mountain Press Publishing Co., 1972.
xiv, 216 p. illus. S2546

Blacker, Bertha M
When we get where we're going: a story of the Sullivan family from Ireland to the West. Seattle, Trade Printery, 1967.
168 p. S2547

Boesh, Mark
John Colter, man who found Yellowstone. New York, Putnam, 1959.
189 p. S2548

Bozeman, Montana. First Presbyterian Church.
First Presbyterian Church, Bozeman, Montana. June 1872-June 1972. Bozeman, Mt., 1972.
1 vol. illus. S2550

Brad, Jacoba (Bakker) Boothman
Homestead on the Kootenai. Caldwell, Idaho, Caxton Printers, 1960.
180 p. illus. S2551

Bradley, James H., 1877-1944
The march of the Montana Column: a prelude to the Custer disaster. Edited by Edgar I. Steward. Norman, University of Oklahoma Press, 1961.
182 p. illus. S2552

Brier, Warren Judson, 1931- , comp.
A century of Montana journalism. Edited by Warren J. Brier and Nathan B. Blumberg. Missoula, Mountain Press Publishing Co., 1971.
352 p. S2553

Brier, Warren J
The frightful punishment. Missoula, University of Montana, 1969.
113 p. illus. S2554

Brimlow, George Francis
Good old days in Montana territory: reminiscences of the Harrington and Butcher families. Billings, Mont., McKee Publishing Co., 1957.
16 p. S2555

Broome, Harvey, 1902-1968
Faces of the wilderness. Missoula, Mt., Mountain Press Publishing Co., 1972.
xiii, 271 p. illus. S2556

Brothers, Beverley J
Sketches of Walkerville: the high and the mighty. Butte, Mt., Ashton, 1973.
83 p. illus. S2557

Brown, C.J.D.
Fishes of Montana. Bozeman, Montana State University, 1971.
S2558

Brown, Dee
Showdown at the Little Big Horn. New York, Putnam's 1964. S2559

Brown, Kimberly Rice
Historical overview of the Dillon District. Boulder, Colo., Western Interstate Commission for Higher Education, 1975.
177 p. illus. S2560

Brown, Margery H
Montana: a student's guide to localized history by Margery H. Brown and Virginia G. Griffing. New York, Teachers College Press, 1971.
45 p. map. S2561

Brown, Mark Herbert, 1900-
The plainsmen of the Yellowstone: a history of the Yellowstone basin. New York, Putnam, 1961.
480 p. illus. S2562

Bruner, Kith
The Bruner bunch, by Kith and Kin. Great Falls, Blue Print and Letter Co., 1973.
93 p. illus. S2563

Bryde, John F
The Sioux Indian student, a study of scholastic failure and personality conflict. Pine Ridge, S.D., John F. Bryde, 1966.
196 p. S2564

Buchholtz, Curtis Walter
Man in Glacier. West Glacier, Mt., Glacier Natural History Association, Inc., 1976.
88 p. illus. S2565

Bue, Olaf J
A guide to pronunciation of place names in Montana. Missoula, Mt., Bureau of Press & Broadcasting Research, Montana State Unviersity, 1959.
28 p. illus. S2566

Burk, Dale A
The clearcut crisis: controversy in the Bitterroot. Missoula, Montana Missoulian, 1970.
204 p. S2567

Burk, Dale A
New interpretations: 25 Montana Artists. Great Falls, The author, 1969.
204 p. illus. S2568

Burlingame, Merrill Gildea
Gallatin century of progress. Bozeman, Mont., Country Book Shop, 1964. S2569

Burlingame, Merrill Gildea
Gallatin County heritage: a report on progress, 1805-1976. Bozeman, Gallatin County Bicentennial Committee, 1976.
106 p. illus. S2570

Burlingame, Merrill Gildea, and K. Ross Toole, eds.
A history of Montana. New York, Lewis Hist. Pub., 1957.
3 vol. S2571

Burlingame, Merrill Gildea
John M. Bozeman, Montana trailmaker. 2nd rev. ed. Bozeman, The author, 1971.
36 p. ports. S2572

Burt, Mrs. Olive (Woolley)
Jim Beckwourth, Crow chief. New York, Messner, 1957.
192 p. S2573

Bye, John O.
Back trailing in the heart of the short grass country. Everett, Wash., n.p., 1956.
392 p. illus. S2574

Byerly, Ken
Central Montana communities. Lewistown, Central Montana Publishing Co., 1975. S2575

Call, Hughie (Florence)
Golden fleece. With illustrations by Paul Brown and an introduction by A.B. Guthrie, Jr. New York, Crown Publishers, 1961.
250 p. illus. S2576

Callaway, Llewellyn Link
Two true tales of the wild West. Oakland, Calif., Maude Gonne Press, 1973.
130 p. illus. S2577

Campbell, William C
From the quarries of Last Chance Gulch. Helena, Mont., Bell-Arm Corp., 1964.
2 vols. S2578

Carling, Mary Ann, comp.
Butte commemorative. Butte, Mt., The author, 1974.
96 p. illus. S2579

Carroll, John M., ed.
The Benteen-Goldin letters on Custer and his last battle. New York, Liveright, 1974.
312 p. S2580

Carroll, John M., ed.
The two battles of the Little Big Horn. New York, Liveright, 1974.
214 p. S2581

Carroll, John M. and Byron Price, comps.
Roll call on the Little Big Horn: 28 June, 1876. Fort Collins, Colo., Old Army Press, 1974.
168 p. S2582

Chaffin, Glenn
The last horizon, the rambling Chaffin clan settles in western Montana in 1864 ... Sommerset, Calif., Pine Trail Press, 1971.
105 p. illus. S2584

Changing West, compiled by James and Mildred Speiser, Johnnie and Gertrude Gilman. Miles City, H. & T Quality Printing, 1975.
186 p. illus. S2585

Charlton, Waivie and Elsie Cummings
Survival, pioneer, Indian and wilderness lore. Hot Springs, The author, 1971.
208 p. illus. S2586

Cheney, Roberta Carkeek
Names on the face of Montana: the story of Montana's place names. Missoula, Printed by the printing Dept., University of Montana, 1971.
275 p. maps. S2587

Chittenden, Hiram Martin
The Yellowstone National Park. Edited and with an introduction by Richard A. Bartlett. Norman, University of Oklahoma Press, 1964.
208 p. S2588

Christopherson, Edmund
Adventures among the glaciers: the story of America's most exciting scenery. Glacier National Park, Missoula, Mt., Earthquake Press, 1966.
88 p. S2589

Christopherson, Edmund
The night the mountain fell: the story of the Montana-Yellowstone earthquake. Cover by Elwood Averill. Missoula? Mt., 1960.
88 p. illus. S2590

Christopherson, Edmund
This here is Montana. Illustrated by Elwood Averill. Missoula, Mt., 1961.
88 p. illus. S2591

Christopherson, Edmund
"Westward I go free": the story of J.F.K. in Montana. Missoula, Earthquake Press, c1964.
88 p. S2592

Clarke, W.B.
Dusting off the old ones. Miles City, Mt., n.p., 1963.
158 p. illus. S2593

Clay, John
My life on the range. With an introduction by Donald R. Ornduff. new ed. Norman, University of Oklahoma Press, 1962.
372 p. illus. S2594

Clinch, Thomas A., 1927-
Urban populism and free silver in Montana: a narrative of idology in political action. Missoula, University of Montana Press, 1970.
xiii, 190 p. illus. S2595

Coburn, Walt, 1889-
Pioneer cattleman in Montana: the story of the Circle C. Ranch. Norman, University of Oklahoma Press, c1968.
xii, 338 p. illus. S2596

Coburn, Walt
Stirrup high. New York, Messner, 1957.
190 p. S2597

Cockhill, Brian E. and Dale L. Johnson, eds.
Guide to manuscripts in Montana repositories. Missoula, University of Montana Library, 1973.
unpaged. S2598

Cook, Charles W., 1839-1927
The valley of the upper Yellowstone: an exploration of the headwaters of the Yellowstone River in the year 1869, as recorded by Charles W. Cook, David E. Folsom, and William Peterson. Edited and with an introduction by Aubrey L. Haines. Norman, University of Oklahoma Press, 1965.
xxxii, 79 p. illus. S2599

Cooley, Myra
Meet me on the green: the saga of beads and buckskin: historical incidents of the early West. New York, William-Frederick Press, 1960.
240 p. S2600

Cottonwood Home Demonstration Club
In the years gone by. n.p., The author, 1964.
254 p. illus. S2602

Crowell, Dave
Montana's own. Missoula, Gateway Press, 1970.
64 p. illus. S2603

Cushman, Dan
Montana: the gold frontier. Great Falls, Mont., Stay Away Joe Publishers, 1973.
293 p. maps. S2604

Cushman, Dan
Plenty of room and air. Great Falls, Stay Away Joe Publishers, 1975.
260 p. S2605

Davis, Jean (Walton), 1909- , comp.
Shallow diggin's: tales from Montana's ghost towns. Caldwell, Id., Caxton Printers, 1962.
375 p. illus. S2606

Davis, William Lyle, 1893-
A history of St. Ignatius Mission, an outpost of Catholic culture on the Montana frontier. Spokane? Wash., 1954.
147 p. illus. S2607

DeHaas, John N. and Bernice W. DeHaas
Footlights and fire engines: the story of Bozeman's glorious old opera house-city hall. Bozeman, Mt., Museum of the Rockies, 1967.
18 p. S2608

Dempsey, Hugh Aylmer, 1929-
Crowfoot, chief of the Blackfeet. Foreword by Paul F. Sharp. Norman, University of Oklahoma Press, 1972.
xix, 226 p. S2609

Denig, Edwin Thompson.
Five Indian tribes of the upper Missiouri: Sioux, Arickaras, Assiniboines, Crees, Crows. Edited and with an introduction by John C. Ewers. Norman, University of Oklahoma Press, 1961.
217 p. illus. S2610

Denning, Frances
Growing pains. Bozeman, Color World of Montana, Inc., 1975.
114 p. S2611

Diacon, Lois
Grip of the bear paws. Big Sandy, Mont., Mountaineer Press, 1962.
353 p. S2612

Dimsdale, Thomas Josiah, d. 1866
The vigilantes of Montana: or, popular justice in the Rocky Mountains. Being a correct and impartial narrative of the chase, trial, capture and execution of Henry Plummer's road agent band ... With an introduction by E. DeGolyer. New ed. Norman, University of Oklahoma Press, 1953.
268 p. S2613

Donald, Alma P.
Love and three squares a day in Montana: a pictorial autobiography. New York, Exposition, c1964.
287 p. S2614

Donovan, Roberta
Ike - boy of the breaks. Raynesford, T.H.A.R. Institute, 1975.
177 p. illus. S2615

Du Bois, Charles G., 1919-
Kick the dead lion, a case book of the Custer battle. 2nd rev., and enl. ed. Billings, Mont., The Reporter Printing & Supply Co., 1961.
77 p. illus. S2616

Du Mont, John S
Custer battle guns. Fort Collins, Colo., Old Army Press, 1974.
113 p. S2617

Duncan, David
The long walk home from town. Garden City, New York, Doubleday, 1964.
233 p. S2618

Dunlap, Kate, 1837-1901
The Montana gold rush diary of Kate Dunlap. Edited and annotated by S. Lyman Tyler. Denver, Colo., F.A. Rosenstock Old West Publishing Co., 1969.
1 vol. illus. S2619

Durham, G. Homer
The administration of higher education in Montana: a study of the University of Montana system. Helena, Montana Legislative Council, 1958.
153 p. S2620

Dusenberry, Verne
The Montana Cree: a study in religious persistence. Stockholm, Almquist and Wilsell, 1962.
280 p. S2621

Dyck, Paul
Brule' Sioux people of the rosebud. Flagstaff, Ariz., Northland Press, 1970.
366 p. illus. S2622

Dykeman, Wilma
Too many people, too little love: Edna Rankin McKinnon, pioneer for birth control. New York, Hold, Rinehart and Winston, 1974.
276 p. S2623

Dyson, James Lindsay, 1912-
The geologic story of Glacier National Park. West Glacier, Mont., 1953.
24 p. illus. S2624

Eckelberry, Henry
Down memory lane in the Flathead. Kalispell, Thomas Printing, 1972.
55 p. illus. S2625

Eckelberry, Henry
Yesterday was Demersville. Kalispell, The author, 1974.
42 p. illus. S2626

Edwards, J. Gordon
A climber's guide to Glacier National Park. San Francisco, Cal., 1960.
141 p. maps. S2627

Ege, Robert J
Settling the dust: a brief for a much-maligned cavalryman. Chinook, Chinook Opinion, 1968.
40 p. S2628

Egly Country Club, Chouteau County.
Trails, trials and tributes. Great Falls, Mt., 1958.
112 p. illus. S2629

Eliel, Frank and others
Southwestern Montana: Beaverhead revisited. Dillon, Finefrock Publishing, 1969.
90 p. illus. S2630

Engen, Orrin A
Writer of the plains, a biography of B.M. Bower. Culver City, Cal., Pontine Press, 1973.
56 p. illus. S2632

Erlanson, Charles B
Battle of the Butte: General Miles' fight with the Indians on Tongue River, January 8, 1877. n.p., 1963.
32 p. illus. S2633

Eunson, Dale
Up on the rim. New York, Farrar,1970.
242 p. S2634

Evans, C. Burt
Another Montana pioneer. Spokane, The author, 1960.
139 p. S2635

Ewers, John Canfield
The Blackfeet: raiders on the Northwestern plains. Norman, University of Oklahoma Press, 1958.
xviii, 348 p. plates. maps. S2636

Ewers, John C
Indian life in the upper Missouri. Norman, Okla., University of Oklahoma, 1968.
336 p. S2637

Faber, Lorney
Next year country. Denver, Colo., Forum Publishing Co., 1975.
137 p. S2638

Feraca, Stephen E
Wakinyan: contemporary Teton Dakota religion. Browning, Mont., Museum of the Plains Indian, 1963.
72 p. S2640

Flannery, Regina, 1904-
The Gros Ventres of Montana. Washington, Catholic University of America. Press, 1953-57. Vol. 1: social life, Vol. 2: religion and ritual, by John M. Cooper.
2 vols. plates. S2641

Fletcher, Ellen Gordon
A bride on the Bozeman trail: the letters and diary of ... 1866, edited by Francis D. Haines, Jr., Medford, Or., Gandee Printing Center, 1971.
139 p. illus. S2642

Fletcher, Robert Henry
Free grass to fences: the Montana cattle range story. Illustrated by Charles M. Russell. New York, Published for the Historical Society of Montant by University Publishers, c1960.
233 p. illus. S2643

Fletcher, Robert Henry
Montana's historic markers. Missoula, Mt., Earthquake Press, 1970.
120 p. S2644

Fletcher, Robert Henry
Virginia City, Montana. Butte, Mt., 1953.
1 vol. unpaged. illus. S2645

Floerchinger, Dorothy
To speak of love was not enough: a biography of Reverend and Mrs. Daniel McCorkle. Conrad, The author, 1974.
70 p. illus. S2646

Foote, Stella
Pompeys pillar of the Lewis and Clark trail. Billings, Mont., The author, 1971.
16 p. illus. S2647

Francis, Bertha Agnes (Wraton)
The land of big snows. Illustrated with photos. Butte, Mt., n.p., 1955.
299 p. illus. S2648

Frink, Maurice and Casey E. Barthel Barthelmess.
Photographer on an army mule. Norman, University of Oklahoma Press, 1965.
151 p. S2649

From God's country to the Atlantic: we came, we saw and we loved it, words and pictures of the fabulous Montana Territorial Centennial Train. Butte, Mt., Ashton's, 1965.
48 p. S2650

Fulmer, Genie Philbrick
Cabins and campfires in southeastern Montana. Forsyth, Mt., The author, 1973.
109 p. illus. S2651

Garst, Doris Shannon
Cowboy-artist: Charles M. Russell. New York, Messner, 1960.
192 p. S2653

Gitchel, Jay W
We bet our lives. New York, Vantage Press, 1962.
159 p. S2654

Goble, Paul and Dorothy Goble.
Red Hawk's account of Custer's last battle. New York, Pantheon, 1969.
59 p. illus. S2655

Godfrey, Edward Settle, 1843-1932.
An account of Custer's last campaign, and the battle of the Little Big Horn, by Captain E.S. Godfrey, who commanded Co. K in the fighting. Palo Alto, Cal., Lewis Osborne, 1968.
86 p. illus. S2656

Godfrey, Edward Settle
The field diary of Lt. Edward Settle Godfrey, commanding Co. K, 7th Cavalry Regiment under Lt. Colonel George Armstrong Custer in the Sioux encounter at the battle of the Little Big Horn. Edited with an introduction and notes by Edgar I. Stewart and Jane R. Stewart. Together with a note on the Kicking Bear pictograph by Carl S. Dentzel. Portland, Or., Champoeg Press, 1957.
ix, 74 p. illus. S2657

Gold, Douglas
A schoolmaster with the Blackfeet Indians. Caldwell, Idaho, Caxton Printing Co., 1963.
287 p. S2658

Golden Valley County Bicentennial Committee.
Bicentennial Golden Valley County heritage, 1976. Ryegate, Roundup Record Tribune, 1975.
30 p. illus. S2659

Gordon, Albie and others
Dawn in Golden Valley, a county in Montana. Ryegate, Mt., n.p., 1971.
375 p. illus. S2660

Goyins, Blair Allen
Snake tracks. New York, Carlton Press, 1970.
96 p. S2661

Graff, James R.
Historic Helena, 1864-1964. Helena, Mont., Home Building and Loan Association, 1964. S2662

Graham, William Alexander, 1875-
The Custer myth, a source book of Custeriana. To which is added some important items of Custeriana and a complete and comprehensive bibliography of Fred Dustin. Harrisburg, Pa., Stackpole Co., 1953.
413 p. illus. S2663

Graham, William Alexander
The story of the Little Big Horn: Custer's last fight. 2nd ed. New York, Collier Books, 1962, c1926.
159 p. S2664

Green, Charles
Montana memories. Coram, Mt., The author, 1971-72.
4 vols. illus. S2665

Greene, Jerome A
Evidence and the Custer enigma: a reconstruction of Indian-military history. Kansas City, Mo., Kansas City Possee of the Westerners, 1973.
56 p. illus. S2666

Grinnell, George Bird
Pawnee, Blackfoot and Cheyenne: history and folklore of the plains, from the writings of George Bird Grinnell. Selected with an introduction by Dee Brown. New York, Scribner, 1961.
301 p. S2667

Grinnell, George Bird
Blackfoot lodge tales: the story of a prairie people. Lincoln, University of Nebraska Press, 1962.
310 p. S2668

Grinnell, George Bird
By Cheyenne campfires. With photos by Elizabeth C. Grinnell. New Haven, Conn., Yale Press, 1962.
305 p. illus. S2669

Guthrie, Alfred Bertram
The blue hen's chick: a life in context. New York, McGraw-Hill, c1965.
261 p. S2670

Hafen, LeRoy Reuben, ed.
Powder River campaigns and Sawyers' expedition of 1865: a documentary account comprising official and personal narratives: edited with introductions and notes by LeRoy R. Hafen and Ann W. Hafen. Glendale, Cal., A.H. Clark Co., 1961.
386 p. ports. maps. S2671

Haines, Aubrey L
Yellowstone National Park: its exploration and establishment. Washington, D.C., U.S. National Park Service, 1974.
218 p. illus. S2672

Halseth, James A
Cowboy ways on and about the E-Y of Chinook, Montana. Havre, Bear Paw Printers, 1975.
124 p. S2673

Hamaker, Dorothy
Napi's lookout: the story of Willow Rounds. Kalispell, Mont., Thomas Printing, 1967.
74 p. S2674

Hamilton, James McLellan
From wilderness to statehood: a history of Montana, 1805-1900. Foreword by A.L. Strand: edited by Merrill G. Burlingame. Portland, Or., Binfords & Mort, 1957.
620 p.
Also: 2nd rev. ed., 1970. 704 p. illus. S2675

Hampton, H. Duane.
How the U.S. Cavalry saved our national parks. Bloomington, Ind., University of Indiana Press, 1971.
256 p. illus. S2676

Hansen, Virginia
Fabulous past of Cooke City, by Virginia Hansen and Al Funderburk. Billings, Mt., Billings Printing Co., c1962.
22 p. illus. S2677

Hardin, Floyd
Campfires and cowchips. n.p., The author, 1972.
119 p. illus. S2678

Hargreaves, Mary Wilma N
Dry farming in the northern Great plains, 1900-1925. Cambridge, Harvard University Press, 1957.
587 p. S2679

Harlowton Women's Club
Yesteryears and pioneers. Harlowton, 1972.
417 p. illus. S2680

Harrod, Howard L., 1932-
Mission among the Blackfeet. Norman, University of Oklahoma Press, 1971.
xxi, 218 p. illus. S2681

Haynes, Jack Ellis.
Yellowstone stage holdups. Bozeman, Mt., Haynes Studio, Ind., 1959.
30 p. illus. S2682

Henry, Ralph Chester, 1912-
The people of Montana: a study of Montana government for students in Montana schools. 2nd ed. Helena, Mt., State Publishing Co., c1958.
237 p. illus. S2683

Henry, Ralph Chester
Our land Montana. Helena, State Publishing Co., 1962.
437 p. illus. S2684

Herndon, Sarah Raymond
Overland days to Montana in 1865: the diary of Sarah Raymond and journal of Dr. Waid Howard, edited by Raymond W. Settle and Mary Lund Settle. Glendale, Cal., A.H. Clark, 1971.
232 p. illus. S2685

Highland, Geneva
Big dry country. Jordan, Mont., Printed by the author, c1960.
171 p. illus. S2686

Hill, J.L.
The end of the cattle trail. Austin, Tex., Jenkins Publishing Co., 1971.
120 p. S2687

Hoebel, Edward Adamson
The Cheyennes: Indians of the Great Plains. New York, Holt, 1960.
103 p. ports. map. S2688

Holgren, Beryl
Frank Baney: forty years a Montana law enforcer. New York, Vantage Press, 1965.
190 p. S2689

Hollingshead, Lillie Hall
The years of no return. Havre, The author, 1974.
118 p. illus. S2690

Homesteaders Golden Jubilee Association.
A brief historical review of life and times on the northeastern Montana prairies, 1913-1963. Scobey, Mont., 1963.
96 p. S2691

Hoopes, Alban W
The road to the Little Big Horn — and beyond. New York, Vantage Press, 1975.
336 p. S2692

Howard, Joseph Kinsey, 1906-1951
Montana: high, wide and handsome. Pref. by A.B. Guthrie, Jr. Drawings by Peter Hurd. New Haven, Yale University Press, 1959.
347 p. S2693

Hudson, Wilson Mathis.
Andy Adams, his life and writings Dallas, Southern Methodist University Press, 1964.
274 p. S2694

Hungry Wolf, Adolf
Charlo's people: the Flathead tribe of Montana. Invermere, B.C., Good Medicine Books, 1974.
64 p. S2695

Hungry Wolf, Adolf
Good medicine in Glacier National Park. Golden, B.C., Good Medicine Books, 1971.
32 p. illus. S2696

Huntington, Bill
Both feet in the stirrups. Illustrated by J.K. Ralston. Billings, Mont., 1959.
408 p. S2697

Huntley, Chet, 1911-1971
The generous years: rememberences of a frontier boyhood. New York, Random House, 1968.
215 p. S2698

Huntsberger, Eleanor Fraser
Mouth full of toes. New York, Carlton Press, 1975.
103 p. S2699

Hutchens, Alice S. Jackman
The gift of little things. Caldwell, Idaho, Caxton Printers, 1968.
152 p. S2700

Hutchens, John K., 1905-
One man's Montana: an informal portrait of a state. Philadelphia, Lippincott, 1964.
221 p. S2701

The Hutterian Brethren of Montana. Augusta, Mont., 1965.
41 p. S2702

Innis, Benjamin
Bloody Knife, Custer's favorite scout. Fort Collins, Colo., Old Army Press, 1973.
201 p. illus. S2703

Iverson, Ronald J
The princess of the prairie. Bozeman, Montana State University, 1965. S2704

Jackson, Donald Dean
Custer's gold: the United States Cavalry expedition of 1874. New Haven, Yale University Press, 1966.
152 p. S2705

James, Don
Butte's memory book. Caldwell, Idaho, Caxton Printers, 1975.
295 p. photos. S2706

Jensen, Margaret
Looking back. Denver, Big Mountain Press, 1967. S2707

Johnson, Barry C
Case of Marcus A. Reno. London, English Westerner's Society, 1969.
92 p. S2708

Johnson, Dorothy Marie
The bloody Bozeman: the perilous trail to Montana's gold. New York, McGraw-Hill, 1971.
xx, 366 p. illus. S2709

Johnson, Dorothy Marie
Warrior for a lost nation, a biography of Sitting Bull. Philadelphia, Pa., Westminister Press, 1969.
173 p. S2710

Johnson, Florence Riddle
Ghost trails country. Anaconda, Mont., c1964.
106 p. S2711

Johnson, Maxine C
Beef cattle in the Montana economy. Missoula, Mont., 1961.
30 p. S2712

Johnson, Olga Weydemeyer
Bears in the Rockies. Illustrated by John R. Hennersy. Fortine, Mont., The author, 1960.
85 p. S2713

Johnson, Olag Weydemeyer
Early Libby and Troy, Montana. n.p., 1958.
110 p. illus. S2714

Johnson, Olga Weydemeyer
Flathead and Kootenay: the rivers, the tribes and the region's traders. Glendale, Cal., A.H. Clark, Co., 1969.
392 p. illus. S2715

Johnson, Virginia Weisel
The long, long trail. Boston, Houghton Mifflin, 1966.
184 p. S2716

Jones, Agens L. (Schock)
Crow country. Billings, Mont., Rocky Mountain College Print Shop, 1959?
77 p. S2717

Jones, Evan Henry
Keeper of the peace pipe and other stories. Ulm, Mont., Homes Sales Associates, 1967.
180 p. S2718

Jones, Evan Henry
Tales from the Teton: three Indian folklore stories. Fort Benton, Mt., Homes Sales Associates, c1965.
123 p. S2719

Joralemon, Ira B
Copper. Berkeley, Cal., Howell-North, 1973.
400 p. illus. S2720

Josephson, Hannah
Jeannette Rankin, first lady in congress: a biography. Indianapolis, Ind., Bobbs-Merrill, 1974.
227 p. illus. S2721

Judith Basin Livestock Association.
Brand book. Judith Basin County. Judith Basin Press, May, 1958.
56 p. S2722

Kain, Robert C
In the valley of the Little Big Horn, the 7th and the Sioux. New Fane, Vt., Vermont Printing Co., 1969.
xiii, 128 p. illus. S2723

Kair, Anita and J.M. Moynahan
The Ace Powell etching catalogue. Kalispell, 1973.
83 p. illus. S2724

Karlin, Jules A
Joseph M. Dixon of Montana. Missoula, University of Montana, c1974.
2 vols. illus. S2725

Kellar, Kenneth C
Seth Bullock: frontier marshall. Aberdeen, S.D., North Plains, Press, 1972.
191 p. illus. S2727

Koelbel, Lenora
Missoula the way it was: "a portrait of an early Western town." Missoula, Mt., Gateway Printing and Litho., c1972.
ix, 128 p. illus. S2728

Konizeski, Richard L
The Montanans' fishing guide. 3rd ed. Missoula, Mountain Press Publishing Co., 1975.
310 p. illus. S2729

Koury, Michael J
Diaries of the Little Big Horn. Papillion, Neb., The author, 1968. S2730

Koury, Michael J
Military posts of Montana. Illustrated by Derek Fitz James. Photography by Clark Babcock. Bellevue, Neb, Old Army Press, 1970.
96 p. illus. S2731

Kraenzel, Carl F
Montana farm and ranch organizations directory. Bozeman, Montana State University, 1966.
1 vol. S2732

Kuhlman, Charles
Custer and the gall saga. Bellevue, Neb., Old Army Press, 1969.
46 p. S2733

Kuhlman, Charles
Did Custer disobey orders at the battle of the Little Big Horn? Harrisburg, Stackpole, c1957.
56 p. illus. S2734

Kurz, Rudolph Fredrick
The journal of Rudolph Fredrick Kurz. Pullman, Wash., Washington State University, 1969.
382 p. illus. S2735

Larson, Helen Kay Brander
Brander sisters let 'er buck. Fountain, Colo., The author, 1975.
35 p. illus. S2737

Lawrence, Lou
Pioneer days at Big Sandy, Montana. Big Sandy, Mountaineer, 1963.
90 p. S2738

League of Women Voters of Montana.
Check and balance, a study of the effective reorganization of the administrative branch of state government. Great Falls, Mont., 1962.
24 p. S2739

League of Women Voters of Montana.
A guide to Montana's custodial and rehabilitative institutions. Great Falls, Mt., 1971.
43 p. S2740

League of Women Voters of Montana.
Know your state, a survey of Montana state government. 2nd ed. Washington, D.C., Published by the League of Women Voters Education Fund, 1968.
62 p. tables.
Also: 1973 ed. 59 p. S2741

League of Women Voters of Montana.
Series on state laws affecting local governments. Missoula, Mt., 1964.--no. 1: local government in an urban era. (6) p.-no 2: restrictions on local taxation and debt. (6) p.-no. 3: state-local approaches to urbanization 8 p.-no. 4: state and locan finance. 6 p. S2742

Lemmon, Ed
Boss cowman: the recollections of Ed Lemmon, 1857-1946, edited by Nellie Snyder Yost. Lincoln, Neb., University of Nebraska, 1969.
321 p. S2743

Lewis, Wade V
Arthritis and radioactivity: a story of Montana's free enterprise uranium-radon mine. Rev. ed. Boston, Christopher, c1955, 1964.
153 p. S2744

Liberty, Margot
Fights with the Shoshone, 1855-1870: a northern Cheyenne Indian narrative by Margot Liberty in cooperation with John Stands-in-Timber. Missoula, Montana State University Press, 1965? S2745

Limbaugh, Ronald H., ed.
Cheyenne and Sioux: the reminiscences of four Indians and a white soldier. Compiled by Dr. T.B. Marquis. Stockton, Cal., Pacific Center for Western Historical Studies, 1974.
79 p. S2746

Lind, Robert W
From the ground up: The story of "Brother Van," Montana pioneer minister, 1848-1919. n.p., Treasure State Publishing Co., 1961.
182 p. illus. S2747

Linderman, Frank Bird
Montana adventure: the recollections of Frank B. Linderman. Edited by Harold G. Merriam. Lincoln, Neb., University of Nebraska, 1968.
224 p. S2748

Linderman, Frank Bird
Recollections of Charley Russell, edited and with an introduction by Dr. H.G. Merriam with drawings by Charley Russell. Norman, University of Oklahoma Press, 1963.
148 p. ports. S2749

Link, Louis W
The great Montana earthquake, Hebgen Lake and Madison Canyon, Montana, August 17, 1959, 11:37 p.m. Cardwell, Mont., 1964.
119 p. illus. S2750

Link, Louis W
Lewis and Clark Cavern, Montana. New York, The author, Montana Exhibition. N.Y. World's Fair, c1964.
112 p. S2751

Little Big Horn biographies: Edward S. Luce memorial edition, revised 1965: Custer Battlefield Historical and Museum Association.
55 p. S2752

Loble, Judge Lester H
Delinquency can be stopped. McGraw-Hill, 1967.
148 p. S2753

Lodgegrass Public School
A history of the Crow Indians based on written sources. Lodge Grass, 1971.
1 vol. S2754

Long, Philip S
The great Canadian range. Vancouver, B.C., Cypress Publishing Limited, 1970.
178 p. S2755

Long, T.B.
70 years a cowboy. Regina, Sask., Western Printers Association, c1960?
62 p. S2756

Lowery, Geraldine
The American Legion in Montana. Billings, Mt., Reporter Printing and Supply Co., c1965.
257 p. S2757

Lowie, Robert Harry, ed. and tr.
Crow texts: collected, translated and edited by Robert H. Lowie. Berkeley, University of California Press, 1960.
550 p. S2758

Lowie, Robert Harry
Crow word lists: Crow-English and English-Crow vocabularies. Berkeley, University of California Press, 1960.
411 p. S2759

Luce, Edward S
Custer battlefield. National Park Service, 1967. S2760

Luther, Tal
High spots of Custer and battle of the Little Big Horn literature (and a few low spots). Kansas City, Kansas City Posse of the Westerners, 1967.
36 p. illus. S2761

Lyback, Johanna R.M.
Indian legends of the great West. Color illustrations and map ornamentation by Dick West. Chicago, Lyons and Carnahan, 1963.
180 p. maps. S2762

McAlear, J.F., 1894-
The fabulous Flathead. As told to Sharon Bergman. Polson, Mont., Treasure State Publishing Co., 1962.
224 p. illus. S2763

McAuslan, Helen
Helen McAuslan drawings. Bozeman Museum of the Rockies, 1972.
Portfolio. S2764

McBride, Genevieve
The bird tail. New York, Vantage Press, 1974.
220 p. illus. S2765

McCarthy, Don
Afternoons in Montana. Aberdeen, S.D., North Plains Press, 1971.
116 p. illus. S2766

McClernand, Edward John, 1848-1926
With the Indian and the buffalo in Montana, 1870-1878: including an account of the Sioux expedition of 1876 and the rescue of the remnant of Custer's command at the Little Big Horn. With introduction by Carroll Friswold. Glendale, Calif., A.H. Clark, 1969. S2767

McCracken, Harold
The Charles M. Russell book: the life and work of the cowboy artist. Garden City, N.Y., Doubleday, 1963, c1957.
236 p. plates. S2768

MacDonald, Marie Peterson
After barbed wire: a pictorial history of the homestead rush into the northern Great Plains, 1900-1919. Glendive, Mont., Frontier Gateway Museum, c1963.
128 p. S2769

MacDonald, Marie Peterson.
Glendive: the history of a Montana town Glendive, Mt., Gateway Press, 1968.
120 p. illus. ports. S2770

McFee, Malcolm
Modern Blackfeet: Montanans on a reservation. New York, Holt, Rinehart and Winston, 1972.
134 p. illus. S2771

McKinney, Patricia M
Presbyterianism in Montana: its first hundred years. Helena, Centennial Celebration Committee, 1972.
135 p. illus. S2772

McNelis, Sarah
Copper king at war, the history of Augustus Heinze. Missoula, University of Montana, 1968.
230 p. S2773

Magnussen, Daniel O
Peter Thompson's narrative of the Little Big Horn campaign, 1876: a critical analysis of an eyewitness account of the Custer debacle. Glendale, Calif., A.H. Clark, 1974.
339 p. illus. S2774

Malone, Michael P. and Richard B. Roeder.
Montana as it was, 1876: a centennial overview. Bozeman, Montana State University, 1975.
63 p. illus. S2775

Malone, Michael Peter, 1940- , comp.
The Montana past: an anthology. Michael P. Malone and Richard B. Roeder, editors. Missoula, Mont., University of Montana Press, 1969.
xii, 376 p. illus. S2776

Malone, Michael Peter
Montana's past: selected essays. Michael P. Malone and Richard B. Roeder, Editors. Missoula, University of Montana Press, 1973.
529 p. illus. S2777

Malouf, Carling Isaac, ed.
Symposium on buffalo jumps. Carling Malouf and Stuart Conner, eds. Missoula, Mt., Montana Archaeological Society, 1962.
3 p.l. 58 p. illus. S2778

Marcosson, Isaac Frederick, 1876-
Anaconda. New York, Dodd, Mead, 1957.
370 p. illus. S2779

Marquis, Thomas Bailey, 1869-1935
Custer on the Little Bighorn. Lodi, Cal., J.L. Hastings, 1967.
56 p. illus. S2780

Martin, Mildred Albert
The Martins of Gunbarrel. Pen and ink drawings by Paul Reese Martin. Caldwell, Idaho, Caxton Printers, 1959.
280 p. S2781

Mattes, Merrill J
Colter's hell and Jackson's hole. Yellowstone Park, Wyo. Yellowstone Library and Museum Association, c1962.
87 p. illus. S2782

Meagher, Margaret Mary
The bison of Yellowstone National Park. Washington, D.C., U.S. National Park Service, 1973.
161 p. illus. S2783

Meagher County Historical Society
Meagher County: an early-day pictorial history, 1867-1967. Material gathered by Centennial Pictorial History Committee. White Sulpher Springs, Mt., Meagher County News, 1968.
76 p. illus. S2784

Merriam, Alan P.
Ethnomusicology of the Flathead Indians. Aldine, 1967.
403 p. S2785

Merriam, Harold G.
The University of Montana, a history. Missoula, University of Montana Press, 1970.
340 p. illus. S2786

Michaelson, Brad
John Melcher, Democratic representative from Montana. Washington, D.C., Grossman Publishers, 1972.
24 p. S2787

Micka, Helen Kranick
A history of the Parent Teacher Association in Montana, 1915-1965. Helena, 1965.
282 p. S2788

Miller, Alice Stewart
Virgil Stewart, self-made dentist of the Judith Basin. Seattle, Wash., 1963.
94 p. S2789

Miller, David Humphreys
Custer's fall: the Indian side of the story. Illustrated by the author. New York, Duell, Sloan and Pearce, 1957.
271 p. S2790

Miller, David Humphreys
Ghost dance. New York, Duell, Sloan and Pearce, 1959.
318 p. S2791

Miller, Don C
Ghost towns of Montana. Boulder, Colo., Pruett Publishing Co., 1974.
xiii, 177 p. illus. S2792

Miller, Harriet and Elizabeth Harrison.
Coyote tales of the Montana Salish, from tales narrated by Pierre Pichette. Illustrated by Frederick E. Roullier. Browning, Museum of the Plains Indian, 1974.
79 p. illus. S2793

Miller, James Knox Polk, 1845-1891
The road to Virginia City: the diary of James Knox Polk Miller. Edited by Andrew F. Rolle. Norman, University of Oklahoma Press, 1960.
143 p. illus. S2795

Miller, Max
Shinny on your own side and other memories of growing up. Drawings by Ray Houlihan. New York, Doubleday, 1958.
240 p. S2796

Miller, Robert E
The hands of the workmen: a history of the first 100 years of the Grand Lodge of Montana Ancient, Free and Accepted Masons. Helena, State Publishing Co., 1966.
278 p. S2797

Miller, Robert E
190 years of Scottish Rite in Montana. Helena, Scottish Rite Publications, 1972.
174 p. illus. S2798

Minneota Friendly Club, Minneota Mt.
Tumbleweeds and tar paper shacks. Iowa Falls, Iowa, General Publishing and Binding, 1971.
312 p. illus. S2799

Mockel, Myrtle Simpson
Dusty Corrals. Billings, Western Printing, 1972.
148 p. illus. S2800

Mockel, Myrtle Simpson
Half-wild and half-breed. Billings, Western Printing and Lithography, 1974.
105 p. S2801

Mockel, Myrtle Simpson
Montana: an illustrated history. Chicago, Sage Books, 1969.
102 p. S2802

Molinario, Manya
So told the Gypsy. Carter, Mt., 1968.
378 p. S2803

Mondak Historical and Art Society.
Courage enough. Sidney, MonDak Family Histories, 1975.
1078 p. illus. maps. S2804

The Montana almanac. 1957. Missoula, Montana State University, c1957.
392 p. S2805

The Montana almanac, 1959-60 edition. Missoula, Montana State University, c1958.
469 p. S2806

Montana. Fish and Game Commission
A guide to hunting and fishing in Montana. Butte, McKee Printing Co., 1958.
44 p. S2807

Montana Historical Society.
The life and times of Olaf C. Seltzer, 1877-1957. Helena, Mont., n.d.,
24 p. illus. S2808

Montana Historical Society.
Open range days in old Montana and Wyoming. Helena, Mont., n.d.
32 p. S2809

Montana Institute of the Arts. Libby Writer's Group
Times we remember in and around Libby, Montana. Libby, 1974.
104 p. illus. S2810

Montana State Highway Commission.
Montana county maps, including revisions to Dec. 31, 1964: issued in cooperation with the U.S. Bureau of Public Roads. Helena, 1965?
unpaged. illus. S2811

Montana. State University. Bureau of Government Research.
Directory of executive and administrative agencies of the state of Montana. Missoula, Montana State University, July, 1958.
24 p. S2812

Montana, The magazine of Western history. Cowboys and cattlemen: a roundup, selected and edited by Michael S. Kennedy. New York, Hastings House, 1964.
xii, 364 p. illus. S2813

Moore, Jean M
Treasure state treasure tales: a handbook for treasure hunters. White Sulphur Springs, Western Life Publishing Co., 1970.
72 p. S2814

Mountains and meadows, a pioneer history of the Cascade, Chestnut valley, Hardy, St. Peter's Mission and Castner Falls, 1805-1925. Compiled and collated by Mrs. Clarence J. (Conrad) Rowe. Great Falls, Mont., Blue Print and Letter Co., 1970.
301 p. illus. S2815

Mountjoy, Lucille
Our family. Los Angeles, Cal., The author, 1973.
72 p. S2816

Moynahan, J.M.
The Ace Powell book. Kalispell, Ace Powell Art Galleries, 1974.
184 p. illus. S2817

Moynahan, J.M.
Ace Powell's Montana. Cheney, Wash., Art of the Northwest, 1974.
99 p. S2818

Moynahan, J.M.
Montana impressions: the Western art of Nancy McLaughlin, who specializes in painting Montana Indians. Cheney, Wash., The author, 1970.
69 p. S2819

Moynahan, J.M.
The West of Sandy Ingersoll. Cheney, Wash., Art of the West, 1975.
94 p. S2820

Moynahan, J.M. and Robert O. Rich
The Western art of Sheryl Bodily. Cheney, Wash., 1971.
94 p. illus. S2821

Musselshell Valley Pioneer Club. Musselshell Valley History Committee.
Horizons o'er the Musselshell. The author, 1974.
182 p. illus. S2822

Musselshell Valley Historical Museum, Roundup, Montana.
Roundup on the Musselshell: pieces of the past. Roundup, 1974.
84 p. illus. S2823

Myers, Rex
Montana's trolleys. South Gate, Cal., Ira Swett, 1970.
3 vols. illus. S2824

Neils, Paul
Julius Neils and the J. Neils Lumber Company. Seattle, Wash., Frank McCaffrey Publishers, 1971.
87 p. illus. S2825

Noyes, Alva Josiah
The story of Ajax: life in the Big Hole basin. New York, Buffalo-Head Press, 1966.
158 p. S2826

Nye, Elwood I
Marching with Custer: a day-by-day evaluation of the uses and abuses, and conditions of the animals on the ill-fated expedition of 1876. Glendale, Cal., A.H. Clark, 1964.
53 p. illus. S2827

O'Fallon Historical Society.
O'Fallon flashbacks. Baker, O'Fallon Historical Society, 1975.
549 p. map. S2828

Oliver, George A.
Joliet: its pioneers and early days. Huntsville, Ala., n.p., c1973.
223 p. illus. S2829

Olson, James C
Red Cloud and the Sioux problem. Lincoln, University of Nebraska Press, 1965.
375 p. S2830

O'Malley, Richard K
Mile high, mile deep. Missoula, Mountain Press Publishing Co., 1971.
304 p. S2831

One hundred years under the big sky in Montana, 1864-1964. The record of accomplishment: the vision of opportunity. Kalispell, Mont., O'Neil Printers, 1964.
1 vol. unpaged. S2832

O'Neil, Clinton DeWitt
Timber n'injuns. Pen sketches by Jean Allen Robocker. Kalispell, Mont., Kalispell News-Farm Journal Print., 1955. S2833

Ostberg, Jake
Sketches of old Butte. Butte, The author, 1972.
124 p. S2834

Overfield, Loyd J., comp
The Little Big Horn, 1876: the official communications, documents and reports, with rosters of the officers and troops of the campaign. Compiled and annotated by Loyd J. Overfield II. Glendale, Cal., A. H. Clark Co., 1971.
203 p. S2835

Ovitt, Mable, 1896-
Golden treasure. Dillon, Mt., 1952.
252 p. illus. S2836

Owings, Ralph E
Montana directory of public affairs, 1864-1960. Ann Arbor, Mich., Edward Brothers, Inc., c1960.
345 p. S2837

Pace, Dick
Golden gulch: the story of Montana's fabulous Alder Gulch, being a true, quite partial, and somewhat humorous history ... With sketches by Sindy Cosens. Virginia City? Mont., 1962.
106 p. illus.
Also: 2nd rev. ed., 1970 96 p. S2838

Paladin, Vivian A
Catalog of Bob Scriver bronzes. Helena, Montana Historical Society, 1972.
32 p. S2839

Paladin, Vivian A
From buffalo bones to sonic boom, compiled and edited by ... 75th anniversary souvenir. Glasgow, Mt., Glasgow Jubilee Committee, 1962.
102 p. illus. S2840

Paulding, Holmes Offley
Surgeon's diary with the Custer relief column. Edited by W. Boyes. Rockville, Md., WJBM Associates, 1974.
36 p. S2841

Perrin, Sandra
Organic gardening in Montana. Missoula, Borrowed Times Media Action Group, 1975.
46 p. S2842

Perry, Eugene Sheridan
Montana in the geologic past. Butte, Mt., Montana School of Mines, 1962. vi, 78 p. maps. S2843

Peterson, Karen
Howling Wolf: a pictorial history of the Cheyenne Indians. Palo Alto, Cal., American West Publishing Co., 1968. S2844

Petkas, Peter J
Lee Metcalf, Democratic senator from Montana. Washington, D.C., Grossman Publishers, 1972.
23 p. tables. S2845

Pfaller, Lewis
Father DeSmet in Dakota. Richarton, N.D., Assumption Abbey Press, 1962.
79 p. illus. S2846

Phillips, Paul Chrisler, 1883-1956.
Medicine in the making of Montana. Missoula, Montana State University Press, 1962.
564 p. illus. S2847

Picton, Harold D. and Irene E. Picton
Saga of the Sun: a history of the Sun River elk herd. Helena, Mt., Dept. of Fish and Game, 1975.
55 p. S2848

Pictorial features of Flathead County: past, present, future. Kalispell, Trippet Publishers, 1972.
63 p. illus. S2849

Pioneers of the Tobacco Plains country. The story of the Tobacco Plains country: the autobiography of a community. Editor, Olga Weydemeyer (Mrs. Pete) Johnson. Rexford? Mt., 1950.
x, 273 p. illus. S2850

Place, Marion (Templeton)
Buckskins and buffalo: the story of the Yellowstone River. Illustrated by Paul Laune. New York, Holt, c1964.
122 p. S2851

Place, Marian (Templeton)
The copper kings of Montana. Illustrated by Ernest Kurt Barth. New York, Random House, 1961.
184 p. illus. S2852

Plate, Robert
Palette and tomahawk: the story of George Catlin, July 27, 1796-Dec. 23, 1872. Illustrated from drawings by George Catlin. New York, D. McKay Co., 1962.
248 p. S2853

Pleasant Valley Home Demonstration Club.
Chouteau County. Footprints through the valley. Great Falls, Mont., 1958.
48 p. illus. S2854.

Plentywood: golden years, 1912-1962. Plentywood, Mont., 1962.
108 p. S2855

Portage Historical Society
Prairie pioneers: a narrative of Montana homestead days. n.p., 1966.
183 p. S2856

Porter, Roy
Kootenai Valley inundated. 1971.
1 vol. illus. S2857

Powder River County. Echoing footsteps. Butte, Montana, Ashton Printing and Engraving Co., 1967.
xxiv, 719 p. S2858

Powell, Peter J
Sweet medicine, the continuing role of the Sacred Arrows, the Sun Dance and the Sacred Buffalo Hat in northern Cheyenne history. Norman, University of Oklahoma, 1969.
560 p. S2859

Prairie County Historical Society, Terry, Montana.
Wheels across Montana's prairie. n.p., 1974.
691 p. illus. S2860

Quay-lem u en-chow-men: a collection of hymns and prayers in the Flathead-Kalispell-Spokane Indian language. Recorded, transcribed and edited by Thomas E. Connoly, S.J. Spokane, Wash., Accurate Letter Shop, c1958.
58 p. S2861

Quinn, Larry D
Politicians in business: a history of the liquor control system in Montana. Missoula, University of Montana Press, 1970.
171 p. tables. S2862

Radtke, Hans D
The Hutterites in Montana: an economic description. Bozeman, Montana Agricultural Experiment Station, 1971.
58 p. charts. S2863

Raining Bird, Art
Wi-sah-ke-chah-k and the Closing-eyes Dance, told in Cree by Art Raining Bird, Translated by Pat Chief Stick. Rocky Boy Reservation, Mont., Bilingual Education Center, 1971.
1 vol. illus. S2864

Ralston, J.K.
Rhymes of a cowboy. Billings, Mt., Rimrock Publishing Co., 1969.
112 p. illus. S2865

Ralston, William N
Open range in rhyme. Great Falls, Mt., Blue Print and Letter Co., 1972.
100 p. illus. S2866

Randall, Leslie Watson, 1893-
Footprints along the Yellowstone. San Antonio, Naylor Co., 1961.
186 p. illus. S2867

Range Riders.
Fanning the embers. Miles City, Range Riders Museum, 1971.
580 p. illus. S2868

Red Fox, William
The memoirs of Chief Red Fox, edited by Cash Asher. New York, McGraw Hill, 1971.
208 p. illus. S2869

Redgate, John
Barlow's Kingdom. New York, Trident Press, 1969.
160 p. S2870

Renner, Frederic G
Charles M. Russell. New York, Harry N. Abrams, 1974.
illus. S2871

Reno, Marcus Albert, 1835-1889, defendant
Abstract of the official record of proceedings of the Reno Court of Inquiry, convened at Chicago, Illinois, 13 January 1879, to investigate his conduct at the battle of the Little Big Horn, 25-26 June 1876. With a preface by W.A. Graham. Harrisburg, Pa., Stackpole Co., 1954.
xxx, 303 p. illus. S2872

Reynolds, Ann
Richard G. Shoup, Republican representative from Montana. Washington, D.C., Grossman Publishers, 1972.
18 p. tables. S2873

Rhone, John
Wild horse prairie. Plains, Plains Historical Association, 1969.
80 p. S2874

Rinehart Collection of Indian Photographs. Face of Courage. Ft. Collins, Colo., Old Army Press, 1971.
1 vol. unpaged. plates. S2875

Risley, Ephretta J
The golden triangle: an account of homeseatding in Montana by one who lived it. White Sulpher Springs, The Meagher County News, 1975.
31 p. S2876

Robertson, Mary S
Rodeo, standard guide to the cowboy spirit. Berkeley, Cal., Howell-North, 1961.
163 p. photos S2877

Robinson, Donald H
Through the years in Glacier National Park. West Glacier Mt., Glacier Natural History Association, 1960.
111 p. illus. - S2878

Ronan, Mary, 1852-
Frontier woman: the story of Mary Ronan as told to Margaret Ronan. Edited by H.G. Merriam. Missoula, University of Montana, c1973.
viii, 172 p. illus. S2879

Ronish, Henry G
Homesteaders in the Judith Basin. Denton, The author, 1974.
45 p. illus. S2880

Rosenberg, Bruce A
Custer and the epic of defeat. University Park, Pennsylvania State University Press, 1974.
313 p. S2881

Rounds, Glen
Cowboy trade. New York, Holiday House, 1972.
95 p. illus. S2882

Ruffcorn, Andrea Lanegraff
History of the Baylor community from 1910-1937. Glasgow, The author, 1970.
24 p. illus. S2883

Ruhle, George C
The Ruhle handbook: roads and trails of Waterton-Glacier National Parks. Minneapolis, Minn., John W. Forney, 1972.
164 p. illus. S2884

Russell, Austin
C.M.R., Charles M. Russell, cowboy artist. New York, Twayne, 1957.
247 p. illus. S2885

Russell, Charles M
Boyhood Sketchbook. Text by R.D. Warden, introduction by Frederic G. Renner. Bozeman, Treasure Products Inc., 1972.
34 p. illus. S2886

Russell, Don
Custer's last, or the battle of the Little Big Horn. Ft. Worth, Tex., Amon Carter Museum of Western Art, 1968.
67 p. S2887

Russell, Don
Sioux buffalo hunters. Illustrated by Bob Glaubke. Chicago, Encyclopedia Britannica Press, 1962.
unpaged. S2888

Russell, Jim
Bob Fudge: Texas trail driver, Montana-Wyoming cowboy, 1862-1933. Denver, Big Mountain Press, 1962.
135 p. S2889

Ryan, J.C.
Custer fell first, the adventures of John C. Lockwood. Edited and compiled by J.C. Ryan. San Antonio, Tex., Naylor Co., 1966.
119 p. S2890

Ryden, Hope
America's last wild horses. New York, Dutton, 1970.
311 p. S2891

Sales, Reno H
Underground warfare at Butte. Butte, Mont., World Museum of Mining, 1964.
77 p. illus. S2892

Samson, A'Delbert.
Church groups in four agricultural settings. Bozeman, 1958.
43 p. illus. S2893

Sandoz, Mari, 1907-1966.
The battle of the Little Bighorn. Philadelphia, Lippincott, 1966.
191 p. map. S2894

Schafer, Betty
Stump town to ski town: the story of Whitefish, Montana by Betty Schafer and Mabel Engelter. Whitefish, Mont., Whitefish Library Association, 1973.
286 p. illus. S2895

Scharff, Robert
Glacier National Park, edited by Robert Scharff. New York, David McKay, 1967.
184 p. S2896

Scharff, Robert
Yellowstone and Grand Teton National Parks. Edited by Robert Scharff. New York, David McKay, 1966.
209 p. S2897

Schillreff, Fern E. and Jessie M. Shawver.
Twenty five years of Garfield County High School, 1914-1939. The author, 1975.
200 p. S2898

Schoenberg, Wilfred P
Jesuits in Montana 1840-1960. Portland, Or., The Oregon-Jesuit, 1960.
120 p. illus. S2899

Schultz, James Willard, 1859-1947
Blackfeet and buffalo: memories of life among the Indians, by James Willard Schults (Apikuni) Edited by Keith C. Seele. Norman, University of Oklahoma Press, 1962.
384 p. illus. S2900

Schultz, James Willard
Why gone those times? Blackfoot tales, by James Willard Schultz, (Apikuni). Edited by Eugene Lee Silliman. Norman, University of Oklahoma Press, 1973, c1974.
xiii, 271 p. illus. S2901

Scriver, Bob
An honest try. Kansas City, Mo., The Lowell Press, 1975.
91 p. illus. S2902

Scudder, Ralph E
Custer country. Portland, Or., Binford & Mort, 1963.
63 p. S2903

Seltzer, Olaf C
Montana in miniature: with pictures of Olaf C. Seltzer. Edited by Dr. Van Kirke Nelson and Cato K. Butler. Kalispell, Mont., O'Neil Printers, 1966.
206 p. S2904

Shatraw, Milton, 1901-
Thrashin' time: memories of a Montana boyhood. Illustrated by Jody Primoff. Palo Alto, Cal., American West Publishing Co., 1970.
188 p. illus. S2906

Shaudys, Vincent K
Published maps of Montana, an annotated bibliography. Missoula, 1958.
55 p. S2907

Shaw, Charlie
The Flathead story. Kalispell, U.S. Forest Service, 1967.
145 p. illus. S2908

Shawver, Jessie
Dusty trails. Miles City, Mt., 1965.
S2909

Shelby History Society
Shelby backgrounds. Shelby, Mont., The Society, 1965.
304 p. S2910

Shelton, Lola
Charles Marion Russell: cowboy, artist, friend. New York, Dodd, Mead, 1962.
230 p. S2911

Sheridan County Historical Association
Sheridan's daybreak. Plentywood, 1970.
600 p. S2912

Shiffman, William F
Winter of the sleeping giants: Glacier National Park. Missoula, Shiffman and Shiffman Enterprises, 1972.
64 p. illus. S2913

Shiflet, Kenneth E
The convenient coward. Harrisburg, Pa., Stackpole Co., 1961. S2914

Skaar, Palmer David
Montana bird distribution: preliminary mapping by Latilong. Bozeman, Mt., The author, 1975.
56 p. illus. S2915

Smith, Helena Huntington
The war on Powder River. New York, McGraw, 1966.
320 p. S2916

Smurr, John Welling, ed.
Historical Essays on Montana and the Northwest. In honor of Paul C. Phillips. Edited by J.W. Smurr and K. Ross Toole. Helena, Mont., Western Press, 1957.
iv, 304 p. port. S2917

Sollid, Roberta Beed
Calamity Jane: a study in historical criticism, correlated and edited by Vivian A. Paladin. Helena, Western Press of the Historical Society of Montana, 1958.
147 p. 26 plates. S2918

Stands in Timber, John
Cheyenne memories. New Haven, Yale University Press, 1967.
330 p. S2919

Stanfield, Howard Stillwell
The diary of Howard Stillwell Stanfield, edited by Jack J. Detzler, Bloomington, Ind., University of Indiana, 1969.
232 p. S2920

Staunton, Ruth and Dorothy Keur
Jerkline to jeep: a brief history of the Upper Boulder. Harlowton, The Times Clarion, 1975.
85 p. S2921

Stearns, Harold Joseph
A history of the upper Musselshell Valley of Montana (to 1920). 2nd ed. Harlowton, Mt., Times Clarion, 1966.
205 p. S2922

Stearns, Harold Joseph
On the trail with Lewis and Clark in Montana. Harlowton, Harlowton Times Clarion, 1972.
41 p. S2923

Stegner, Wallace Earle
Wolf willow: a history, a story and a memory of the last plain frontier. New York, Viking Press, 1962.
306 p. S2924

Stevens, Christian D
Meagher of the sword. Dodd, Mead, 1967.
xii, 275 p. S2925

Stevensville Historical Society
Montana genesis: a history of the Stevensville area of the Bitterroot Valley. Missoula, Mt., Mountain Press Publishing, 1971.
289 p. illus. S2926

Stork, Byron Claude
Rawhide and haywire: true tales of the old West, recalled and illustrated by Spokane's painter of western scenes. New York, William Frederick Press, 1959.
146 p. S2927

Stuart, Colin
Shoot an arrow and stop the wind. New York, Dial, 1970.
248 p. S2928

Stuwe, Jane Willits
East base, 1940-1946. n.p., The author, 1974.
137 p. illus. S2929

Sunder, John Edward
The fur trade on the upper Missouri, 1840-1865. Norman, University of Oklahoma Press, 1965.
xiv, 295 p. illus. S2930

Templeton, Sardis W
Lame captain: the life and adventures of Pegleg Smith. Los Angeles, Ca., Westernlane Press, 1965.
239 p. S2933

Terrell, John Upton
Black Robe: the life of Pierre-Jean De Smet, missionary, explorer and pioneer. Garden City, N.Y., Doubleday, 1964.
381 p. S2934

Terrell, John Upton and George Walton
Faint the trumpet sounds: the life and trial of Major Reno. New York, D. McKay, 1966.
332 p. S2935

Terry, Alfred H
The field diary of General Alfred H. Terry: the Yellowstone expedition, 1876. Bellevue, Neb., Old Army Press, 1969.
32 p. S2936

Thompson, David, 1770-1857
Journals relating to Montana and adjacent regions, 1808-1812. Edited with an introduction by M. Catherine White. Missoula, Mt., Montana State University Press, 1950.
cixi, 345 p. illus. S2937

Tolman, Newton F
Search for General Miles. New York, Putnam, 1968.
252 p. S2939

Toman, J. Fred
Powder River Congressional Church, a history of the first 50 years. Broadus, Powder River Congressional Church, 1970.
81 p. illus. S2940

Toole, Kenneth Ross, 1920-
Montana: an uncommon land. Norman, University of Oklahoma Press, 1959.
278 p. illus. S2941

Toole, Kenneth Ross
Twentieth-century Montana: a state of extremes. Norman, University of Oklahoma Press, 1972.
xix, 307 p. illus. S2942

Towle, Virginia Rowe
Vigilante woman. South Brunswick, N.J., Barnes, 1966.
182 p. illus. S2943

Townsend, Elsie Doig
Always the frontier. Independence, Mo., Hearld Publishing House, 1972.
256 p. S2944

Townsend, Elsie Doig
If you would learn--Go teach. Independence, Mo., Herald Publishing House, 1973.
246 p. S2945

Trippet, Edgar W
Historical information concerning the upper Flathead valley. Kalispell, The author, 1971.
96 p. illus. S2946

Truchot, Theresa
The black wind. Lake Oswego, Or., The author, 1974.
69 p. S2947

Truchot, Theresa
Chips. Lake Oswego, Or., The author, 1975.
149 p. S2948

Turner, Judy and Robert Fellmeth
Mike Mansfield: Democratic senator from Montana. Washington, D.C., Grossman Publishers, 1972.
28 p. S2949

Two Leggings.
Two Leggings, the making of a Crow warrior. Interview by William Wildschat, (1919-1923). New York, Crowell, 1967.
226 p. S2950

U.S. Dept. of the Interior
Natural resources of Montana, "the treasure state." Washington, U. S. Govt. Printing Office, 1964.
68 p. S2951

Upton, Richard, 1933- , comp.
The Custer adventure as told by its participants. Fort Collins, Colo., Old Army Press, 1975.
119 p. S2952

Upton, Richard, comp.
Fort Custer on the Big Horn, 1877-1898: its history and personalities as told and pictured by its contemporaries. Glendale, Cal., A.H. Clark Co., 1973.
316 p. illus. S2953

Urban Management Consultants of San Francisco, Inc.
Profile of the Montana native American. San Francisco, 1974.
247 p. charts. S2954

Utley, Robert Marshall, 1929-
Custer and the great controversy: the origin and development of a legend. Los Angeles, Westernlore Press, 1962.
184 p. illus.
Also: 2nd ed., 1971. 184 p. S2955

Utley, Robert Marshall
The Reno Court of Inquiry: the Chicago Times account. Fort Collins, Colo., Old Army Press, 1971.
500 p. illus. S2956

Utterback, Gretchen and Isabella Murphy
Pioneers of old Dawson County. Glendrive, Mt., Review Publishing Co., 1965.
40 p. S2957

Van Orsdel, William Wesley
In March month I started. Ft. Benton, River Press, 1972.
1 vol. illus. S2958

Vaughn, Jesse Wendell
The Reynolds campaign on Powder River. Norman, University of Oklahoma Press, 1961.
239 p. S2959

Von Richthofen, Walter Baron
Cattle-raising on the plains of North America. With an introduction by Edward Everett Dale, new ed. Norman, University of Oklahoma Press, c1964.
120 p. S2960

Waldron, Ellis L., comp
Montana politics since 1864: an atlas of elections. Compiled with maps by Ellis L. Waldron. Missoula, Montana State University Press, 1958.
x, 428 p. maps. tables. S2961

Warden, Richard D
Metcalf of Montana: how a senator makes government work, with a foreword by Paul H. Douglas. Washington, Acropolis Books, c1965.
92 p. S2962

Warner, Charles
Old coins of the Sweet Grass hills and some shreds of wire gold. Kalispell, Mt., Thomas Printing & Engraving, c1965.
83 p. S2963

Watkins, J. Spencer
Lucky Montana cowpoke. New York, Vantage Press, 1958.
87 p. S2964

Watson, Art H
Devil man with a gun. White Sulpher Springs, Mt., Meagher County News, 1967.
197 p. S2965

Watt, Phyllis McKeever
Livestock brands of Garfield County, Montana. Brusett, Mt., The author, 1957.
122 p. S2966

We called them back: Montana homesteaders and pioneers of the old Wilson Post Office country, by Lloyd and Mabel Johnston, et al. Fairfield, Mt., Fairfield Times, 1974.
176 p. illus. S2967

Weisel, George Ferdinand
Ten animal myths of the Flathead Indians. Missoula, Mt., 1959.
15 p. S2969

West, Helen B
Meriwether Lewis in Blackfeet country. Browning, Mt., Blackfeet Agency, Museum of Plains Indians, 1964.
18, 10 p. illus. S2970

Wheeler, Burton Kendall, 1882-
Yankee from the West: the candid, turbulent life story of the Yankee born U.S. senator from Montana, by Burton K. Wheeler with Paul F. Healy. Garden City, N.Y., Doubleday, 1962.
436 p. illus. S2971

White Bull, Joseph
The warrior who killed Custer: the personal narrative of Chief Joseph White Bull, edited by James H. Howard. Lincoln, Neb., University of Nebraska, 1969.
84 p. S2972

Whithorn, Bill and Doris Whithorn
Photo history from Yellowstone Park: nature's wonderland. Livingston, Park County News, 1970.
1 vol. illus. S2973

Whithorn, Bill
A photo history of Aldridge: coal camp that died a-bornin', by Bill and Doris Whithorn. Pray, Mt., The author, 1965.
200 p. S2974

Whithorn, Bill and Doris Whithorn
Photo history of Chico Lodge: early resort area: a country doctor; oldest town in Park County. Pray, The authors, 1968.
1 vol. illus. S2975

Whithorn, Bill and Doris Whithorn
Photo history of Gardiner, Jardine, Crevasse; entrance to Yellowstone National Park wonderland (Centennial-1972); Gold mining world for a hundred years. Pray, The author, 1968.
1 vol. illus. S2976

Whithorn, Bill
Photo history of Livingston-Bozeman coal country; Cokedale, Timberline, Chestnut, Storrs, Hoffman, Maxey lived on coal. Pray, Mt., Livingston Enterprises, 197-?
48 p. illus. S2977

Whithorn, Bill and Doris Whithorn
Photo history of Shields Valley. Livingston, Park County News, 1970.
1 vol. illus. S2978

Whithorn, Bill and Doris Whithorn
Pics and quotes of Yellowstone. Livingston, Park County News, 1972.
48 p. illus. S2979

Whithorn, Bill
60 miles of photo history: upper Yellowstone Valley. Livingston, Park County News, 1965.
unpaged. S2980

Whithorn, Doris
Montana in the good old days. The Wan-i-gan, Pray, Montana, 1972.
2 vols. S2981

Whithorn, Doris
Photo history of Livingston, Montana. The Wan-i-gan, Pray, Mt., n.d.,
1 vol. S2982

Wiley, Frank W
Montana and the sky: the beginning of aviation in the land of the shining mountains. Minneapolis, Holden Publishing Co., 1966.
343 p. S2983

Willard, John
Adventure trails in Montana. Sponsored by Montana Historical Society, Helena, 1964.
243 p. S2984

Willard, John
The Charles M. Russell book. Seattle, Wash., Salisbury Press, 1970.
64 p. S2985

Williams, Kim
Wildflowers of these Missoula hills. Missoula, University of Montana School of Education, 1974.
54 p. S2986

Williams, Lyle K
Historically speaking: stories of the men and women who explored and settled the Missouri River headquarters. Three Forks, The author, 1975.
80 p. S2987

Wilson, Sonja
Castle on the prairie. Boston, Branden Press, 1972.
unpaged S2988

Wolf, James R
Guide to the Continental Divide trail in Montana. Missoula, Mt., Mountain Press, 1974.
200 p. S2989

Wolle, Muriel Vincent Sibell, 1898-
Montana pay dirt: a guide to the mining camps of the treasure state. Denver, Sage Books, c1963.
436 p. illus. S2990

Wolstad, George R
The schoolmarm and the saddle tramp. Missoula, Gateway Printing, 1972.
53 p. illus. S2991

Wooden Leg, Cheyenne Indian, 1858-
Wooden Leg, a warrior who fought Custer. Interpreted by Thomas B. Marquis. Lincoln, University of Nebraska Press, 1962, c1957.
384 p. illus. S2992

Woodson, Warren
Pioneering tales of Montana. New York, Exposition Press, c1965.
169 p. S2993

Wright, Don and William Pedersen
Some things are forever. Missoula, Telemark of Montana, 1970.
38 p. illus. S2994

Wright, Robert C
Montana, territory of treasures: people, places, events by Bob and Kathryn Wright. Billings, Mont., Gazette Printing Co., 1964.
92 p.
Also: 2nd ed. Ft. Collins, Colo., Old Army Press, 1970. 89 p. illus.
Also: 3rd ed., 1972. 89 p. S2995

Yost, Karl and Frederic G. Renner
A bibliography of the published works of Charles M. Russell. Lincoln, Neb., University of Nebraska Press, 1971.
317 p. plates. S2996

OREGON

Compiled by Nadine H. Purcell
Jackson County (Ore.) Library System

Aamodt, David A
Oregon's prime agricultural lands: an area of critical state concern. Portland, Oregon Student Public Interest Research Group, 1973.
37 p. illus. S2997

Adams, W. Claude, 1873-
History of dentistry in Oregon. Portland, Or., Binfords & Mort, c1956.
343 p. illus. S2998

Alexander, Maud
Uncle Dave discovers gold. Pendleton, East Oregonian Publishing Co., 1972.
76 p. S2999

Apsler, Alfred
Northwest pioneer: the story of Louis Fleischner. Illustrated by Morton Garchik. N.Y., Farrar, Straus & Cudahy, 1960.
180 p. illus. S3000

Armstrong, Chester
Oregon state parks: history, 1917-1963, compiled by Chester H. Armstrong. Salem, Oregon State Highway Dept., 1965.
x, 269 p. illus. S3001

Atkeson, Ray and Paul M. Lewis
Beautiful Oregon. Eugene, Beautiful Oregon Publications, 1974.
64 p. illus. S3002

Atkeson, Ray
Oregon. Portland, Or., C.H. Belding, 1968.
187 p. illus. S3003

Atkeson, Ray and Archie Satterfield
The Oregon coast. Portland, C.H. Belding, 1972.
124 p. photos. S3004

Atkeson, Ray and Archie Satterfield
Oregon II. Portland, C.H. Belding, 1974.
192 p. illus. S3006

Atterbury, Vivian Corbett
The Oregon story. Portland, Or., Binfords & Mort, 1959.
128 p. illus. S3007

Atwood, Kay
Jackson County conversations. Medford, Jackson County Intermediate Education District, 1975.
173 p. illus. S3008

Avshalomoff, Jacob
Music is where you make it, a panoramic view of the Portland Junior Symphony. Portland, Or., Portland Junior Symphony Association, c1959.
52 p. ports. S3009

Babb, Douglas E
Oregon real estate division and subdivision control problems. Portland, Oregon Student Public Interest Research Group, 1973.
100 p. S3010

Bachelder, Horace Lyman
Liberal church at the end of the Oregon Trail. Oregon City, Atkinson Memorial Congregational Church, 1969. S3011

Bailey, Barbara
Upper Mill Creek community: an illustrated history. Illustration by Mary Howell. Photographic reprints by A.F. Procter. The Dalles, Or., The author, 1973.
37 p. illus. S3012

Baker, Oregon. Centennial Committee.
Baker City centennial album: 100 years of Baker City, 1874-1974.
51 p. illus. S3013

Bakken, Lavola J
Land of the north Umpquas: peaceful Indians of the West..Grants Pass, Or., Te-Cum-Tom Publications, 1973.
40 p. illus. S3014

Bakken, Lavola J
Lone rock free state: a collection of historical adventures and incidents in Oregon's north Umpqua valley, 1850-1910. Myrtle Creek, Myrtle Creek Mail, 1970.
156 p. illus. S3015

Balch, Frederic Homer
Bridge of the gods. Portland, Or., Binfords & Mort, 1968. (Reprint of 1890 ed.)
326 p. S3016

Baldwin, Ewart Merlin
Geology of Oregon. Eugene, Or., University of Oregon. Coop Book Store, 1959.
136 p. illus.
Aslo: 2nd ed., 1964. 165 p. S3017

Barchus, Agnes
Eliza R. Barchus, the Oregon artist, 1857-1959. Portland, Binfords & Mort, 1974.
166 p. illus. S3018

Barette, Leonore (Gale)
Thumbpapers: sketches of pioneer days Eugene, Or., Picture Press Printers, 1950.
59 p. illus. S3019

Barlow Road: Bicentennial edition, 1974-1975. The Dalles, Wasco County Historical Society, 1975.
90 p. illus. S3020

Barry, Bob
From shamrocks to sagebrush. Lakeview, Or., Examiner Publishing Co., 1969.
193 p. illus. S3021

Bartlett, Grace
Wallowa, the land of winding waters, rev. ed., 1967.
40 p. S3022

Beaulieu, John D
Geologic hazards of the Bull Run watershed, Multnomah and Clackamas Counties, Oregon. Portland, Oregon Dept. of Geology and Mineral Industries, 1974. (Bulletin 82.)
77 p. illus. S3023

Beckham, Stephen Dow
Coos Bay: the pioneer period, 1851-1890. Coos Bay, Arago Books, 1973.
70 p. illus. S3024

Beckham, Stephen Dow
Lonely outpost: the Army's Fort Umpqua. Portland, Oregon Historical Society, 1971.
24 p. illus. S3025

Beckham, Stephen Dow
Oregon's coast country: a literary landscape. McMinnville, Linfield College, 1970.
18 p. S3026

Beckham, Stephen Dow
Requiem for a people: the Rogue Indians and the frontiersmen. Norman, University of Oklahoma Press, 1971.
214 p. illus. S3027

Beckham, Stephen Dow
The Simpsons of Shore Acres. Coos Bay, Arago Books, 1971.
37 p. photos S3028

Bedingfield, Nancy
Oregon's 100 years in pictures: 1859-1959. Portland, Or., Binfords & Mort, 1958.
48 p. illus. S3029

Bedwell, Stephen Ferguson
Fort Rock Basin: Prehistory and environment. Eugene, University of Oregon Books, 1973.
189 p. illus. S3030

Beebe, Ralph K., 1932-
A garden of the Lord: a history of Oregon yearly meeting of Friends Church. Illustrated by Stan Putman. Newberg, Or., Barclay Press, 1968.
vii, 288 p. illus. S3031

Belknap, George N
Oregon imprints: 1845-1870. Eugene, Or., University of Oregon Books, 1968.
305 p. S3032

Belshaw, George
The diary of George Belshaw (Oregon Trail-1853). Eugene, Or., Lane County Pioneer-Historical Soceity, 1960.
(3) 52 l. photo. S3033

Benner, Richard
The Oregon coast and the Oregon Coastal Conservation and Development Commission: why not classify estuaries? Portland, Oregon Student Public Interest Research Group, 1973.
105 p. S3034

Bennett, Joseph W
Vandals wild. Portland, Bennett Publishing Co., 1969.
238 p. illus. photos. S3035

Bensell, Royal Augustus
All quiet on the Yamhill: the Civil War in Oregon, (his) journal, edited by Gunther Barth. Eugene, University of Oregon, 1959.
xx, 226 p. illus. S3036

Benson, Robert
Pioneer landmarks in Washington County Oregon. Hillsboro, Washington County Historical Society, 1967. S3037

Bettis, Stand and Jon Doornink
Place called Oregon. Palo Alto, Cal., Pacific Books, 1972. S3038

Beyler, Cecelia Mae
America calls from castle walls. Portland, Or., Metropolitan Press, 1957.
128 p. illus. S3039

Bianco, Joe
Seeing Portland, a guide to points of interest in the Portland area. Portland? Oregon Cattlemen's Association, 1964? S3040

Blacker, George Walter
One way journey: the cultivation of the Grande Ronde valley in northeastern Oregon and the trials and tribulations of the Nodine family. Halfway, Kenray Enterprises, 1969. S3041

Blair, Harry C
Lincoln's constant ally: the life of Colonel Edward D. Baker, together with four of his great orations, by Harry C. Blair and Rebecca Tarshis. Portland, Oregon Historical Society, c1960.
233 p. illus. S3042

Bleything, Dennis and Susan Hawkins
Getting off on 96 and other less traveled roads: drives and hikes in the Trinity Alps, Redwoods and Siskiyous. Beaverton, Touchstone Press, 1975.
79 p. illus. S3043

Blodgett, Beverley
A picture or two: the story of Ray Eyerly. With foreword by Tom McCall. McMinnville, Oakwood Press, 1974.
124 p. illus. S3044

Boege, Lila
Tillamook memories. Tillamook Pioneer Association, 1972.
218 p. illus. S3045

Booth, Percy T
The legend of Indian Mary and Umpqua Joe. Grants Pass, Or., Josephine County Historical Society, 1975.
54 p. illus. S3046

Booth, Percy T
Valley of the Rogues. Kerby, Or., Josephine County Historical Society, 1971.
72 p. photos S3047

Bowmer, Angus L
As I remember, Adam: an autobiography of a festival. Ashland, Or., Oregon Shakespearean Festival Association, 1975.
272 p. illus. S3048

Boyington, Mildred S. and others
A history of St. Paul's Episcopal Church, Oregon City, Oregon, 1847-through 1973. Oregon City, St. Paul's Episcopal Church, 1973.
52 p. illus. S3049

Boyle, William Henry
Personal observations on the conduct of the Modoc War. Los Angeles, Dawson's Book Shop, 1959.
80 p. S3050

Boylen, Eugene Norval
Episode of the West: the Pendleton Round-up, 1910-1951. Pendleton, The author, 1975.
92 p. illus. S3051

Brimlow, George Francis
Harney County, Oregon, and its range land. Portland, Binfords & Mort, c1951.
316 p. illus. S3052

Bristow, Elijah Lafayette
The letters of Elijah Lafayette Bristow. Oregon pioneer of 1848. From his original manifold letter writer by which he retained a copy of each letter written between 1857 and 1864. Eugene, Or., Lane County Pioneer-Historical Society, 1961.
(159) p. photo. S3053

Brogan, Phil F
East of the Cascades: a history of of central Oregon. Portland, Or., Binfords and Mort, 1963.
425 p. illus. S3054

Brogan, Phil F
Story of the Deschutes National Forest. Washington, D.C., U.S. Forest Service, 1969. S3055

Brooks, Howard C
Gold and silver in Oregon by Howard C. Brooks and Len Ramp. Portland, Or., Oregon State Dept, of Geology and Mineral Industries, 1968. (Bulletin no. 55)
337 p. illus. S3056

Brown, Cecil Muriel
A right to dream. Vantage Press, 1968.
185 p. S3057

Brown, Wilfred H
This was a man: something about the life and times of Jesse Applegate, wagon train captain, trail blazer, statesman, diplomat, sage of Yoncalla. North Hollywood, Cal., The Camas Press, 1971.
162 p. illus. S3058

Burrell, Orin Kay
Gold in the woodpile: an informal history of banking in Oregon. Eugene, University of Oregon Books, 1967.
333 p. S3059

Burton, Robert E
Democrats of Oregon: the pattern of minority politics, 1900-1956. Eugene, University of Oregon, 1970.
158 p. S3060

Bushnell, James Addison
Autobiography of James Addison Bushnell (1826-1912). Eugene, Oregon Lane County Pioneer-Historical Society, 1959.
25 l. photos. S3061

Carlson, Jennie Stowe
Wagon trains lead to roses in December: a pioneer history of Drain, Oregon. Drain, Or., Drain Enterprises, 1959.
56 p. illus. S3062

Carlson, William Hugh, 1898-
In a grand and awful time: essays from the librarian's desk on 20th century man and his books. Corvallis, Oregon State University Press, 1967.
157 p. S3063

Carlson, William Hugh
The library of Oregon State University: its origins, management and growth, a centennial history. Corvallis, Or., 1966.
94 p. S3064

Carpenter, Allan
Oregon: from its glorious past to the present, illustrated by Phil Austin Chicago, Children's Press, 1965.
95 p. S3065

Carson, Ginnia G
The Swamp Fox of the Willamette. Portland, Ryder Press, 1968.
43 p. illus. S3066

Case, Victoria
A finger in every pie. New York, Doubleday and Co., 1962.
254 p. S3067

Chase, Don Marquis
He opened the West and led the first white explorers through northwest California, May-June, 1828. Crescent City, Cal., Del Norte Triplicate Press, c1958.
36, 3 p. ports. S3068

Chase, Don Marquis
Pack saddles and rolling wheels: the story of travel and transportation in southern Oregon and northwestern California from 1852, by Don M. Chase and Marjorie Neill Helms. Crescent City, Cal., Del Norte Triplicate, c1959.
64 p. illus. S3069

Chenowith, J.V.
The making of Oakland. Oakland, Oakland Printing Co., 1970.
S3070

Chipman, Art
History of KMED radio. Medford, Or., Pine Cone Press, 1972.
64 p. S3071

Churchill, Sam
Big Sam. New York, Doubleday, 1965.
184 p. illus. ports. S3072

Clackamas County Historical Society
Clackamas County historical. Oregon City, Or., Clackamas County Historical Society, 1960.
60 p. illus. S3073

Clark, Ava Milam and Kenneth Munford
Adventures of a home economist. Corvallis, Oregon State University Press, 1969.
432 p. illus. ports. S3074

Clark, Malcolm, Jr. and Kenneth W. Porter
War on the Webfoot Saloon and other tales of feminine adventures. Portland, Oregon Historical Society, 1969.
53 p. photos. S3075

Clark, Ronald Keith
Terrible trail: the Meek Cutoff, 1845, by Keith Clark and Lowell Tiller. Caldwell, Idaho, Caxton Printers, 1966.
224 p. illus. S3076

Clarke, Samuel A
The Samuel A. Clarke papers. Klamath Falls, Or., Guide Printing Co., 1960. (Klamath County Museum, Research paper, no. 2)
33 p. S3077

Clough, Bess A
One hundred years in Canyonville, n.p., Douglas Fir Printing Co., c1958.
35 l. illus. S3078

Cole, David L. and LeRoy Johnson, Jr.
A bibliographic guide to the archaeology of Oregon and adjacent retions. Eugene, University of Oregon Museum of Natural History, 1969. (Its Special Publication).
41 p. S3080

Cole, David L
Report on archaeological research in the John Day dam reservoir area, 1965-1967. Interim report 1965/66-1967/68. Eugene, University of Oregon Museum of Natural History, 1966-68.
4 vols. S3081

Cole, Maude E
Away back when. Drain, Or., The Drain Enterprise, 1961.
163 p. illus. S3082

Combs, Welcome M
God made a valley, by Welcome M. Combs and Sharon C. Ross. Empire, Or., Empire Charleston Builder, 1962.
75 p. S3083

Constance, Clifford L
Chronology of Oregon schools, 1834-1958. Eugene, University of Oregon Books, 1960. (University of Oregon Monographs, Studies in Education, no. 2).
vii, 80 p. S3085

Coos-Curry Pioneer and Historical Association
Glancing back. North Bend, Coos-Curry Museum, 1971. S3086

Corning, Howard McKinley, 1896- , ed.
Dictionary of Oregon history, compiled from the research files of the former Oregon Writers' Project with much added material. Portland, Binfords & Mort, c1956.
281 p. facsim. S3087

Corning, Howard McKinley
Willamette landings: ghost towns of the river. 2nd ed. Portland, Oregon Historical Society, 1973.
224 p. illus. S3088

Cottage Grove, Oregon. Writers' Discussion Group.
Golden was the past. Cottage Grove, Sentinel Press Shop, 1970.
224 p. illus. S3089

Cour, Robert M
The plywood age: a history of the fir plywood industry's first fifty years. Portland, Or., Binfords and Mort, c1955.
171 p. illus. S3090

Cowles, John
Cougar Mountain cave in south central Oregon. Rainier, Or., The author, 1959.
50 p. illus. S3091

Cox, Herbert Joseph, 1891-
Random lengths: forty years with "timber beasts" and "sawdust savages". Eugene, Or., 1949.
310 (14) p. illus. S3092

Cressman, Luther Sheeleigh
Cultural sequences at The Dalles, Oregon, a contribution to the Pacific Northwest prehistory. Philadelphia, American Philosophical Society, 1960.
108 p. illus. S3093

Cressman, Luther Sheeleigh
The sandal and the cave: the Indians of Oregon. Portland, Or., Champoeg Press, Inc., 1961.
81 p. illus. S3094

Creswell Area Historical Society
Creswell's centennial, 1873-1973: Oregon history in pictures. Creswell, 1973.
50 p. illus. S3095

Crockatt, Ernest L
The murder of Til Taylor ... a great Western sheriff. Philadelphia, Pa., Dorrance & Co., 1970.
194 p. illus. S3096

Crook, Laura S
The Crook book. Portland, Center Press, 1974.
148 p. illus. S3097

Crow, Rankin, 1900-
Rankin Crow and the Oregon country, by Rankin Crow as told to Colleen Connaughy. Ironside, Or., 1970.
242 p. illus. S3098

Culp, Edwin D
Stations West: the story of the Oregon railways. Caldwell, Idaho, Caxton Printers, 1972.
265 p. illus. S3099

Dallas, Neva
Lamplighters: leaders in learning. Portland, Or., Binfords & Mort, 1959.
208 p. S3100

Dart, John Olney
From Portland to the Pacific: an environmental-Studies tour via the Wilson River Highway. Portland, Portland State University, Dept. of Geography, 1973.
83 p. illus. S3101

Daughters of the American Revolution. Oregon Society.
Oregon historic landmarks. Portland, The Society, 1957.
64 p. illus. S3102

Daughters of the American Revolution. Oregon Society.
Oregon historic landmarks, eastern Oregon. Portland, 1959.
illus. S3103

Davis, Harold Lenoir
The distant music. New York, Morrow, 1957.
311 p. S3104

Davis, Lenwood G
Blacks in the state of Oregon, 1788-1974: a bibliography of published works and of unpublished source materials on the life and achievements of black people in the beaver state. 2nd ed. Monticello, Ill., Council of Planning Librarians, 1974.
85 p. S3105

Deady, Matthew P
Pharisee among Philistines: the diary of Judge Matthew P. Deady, 1871-1892. Edited and with introduction by Malcolm Clark, Jr. Portland, Oregon Historical Society, 1975.
2 vols. illus. S3106

Decker, Fred William
The weather of Oregon. 2nd ed. Corvallis, Oregon State University Press, 1961. (Oregon State University Science Series no. 2).
47 p. illus. S3107

Dennis, La Rea J
Name your poison: a guide to the cultivated and native Oregon plants toxic to humans. Corvallis, Oregon State University Bookstore, 1972.
76 p. illus. S3108

Devin, Ira H
The flora country: the hardships and struggles of the Matt Devin family as pioneers in northern Wallowa County, Oregon. Edited by Carl Devin. Longview, Wash., Published by Lower Columbia College, 1971.
168 p. illus. S3109

DeWolfe, Fred
Portland west. Portland, Press-22, 1973.
unpaged. illus. 3110

Dicken, Samuel N
Oregon geography: the people, the place and the time. 5th ed. Ann Arbor, Mich., Edwards Brothers, 1973.
147 p. S3111

Dicken, Samuel N
Pioneer trails of the Oregon coast. Portland, Oregon Historical Society, 1971.
77 p. illus. S3112

Dodds, Gordon Barlow, 1932-
The salmon king of Oregon: R.D. Hume and the Pacific fisheries. Chapel Hill, University of North Carolina Press, 1963, c1959.
257 p. illus. S3113

Dodge, Nicholas A
A climber's guide to Oregon. Portland, Mazamas, 1968.
154 p. illus. S3114

Dodge, Nicholas A
A climbing guide to Oregon. Beaverton, Touchstone Press, 1975.
160 p. illus. S3115

Dodge, Orvil
Pioneer history of Coos and Curry Counties, Oregon: heroic deeds and thrilling adventures of the early settlers. Bandon, Western World, 1969. 2nd ed.
468 p. illus. ports. S3116

Drawson, Maynard C
Treasures of the Oregon country. Salem, Dee Publishing Co., 1975.
212 p. illus. S3117

Drew, Harry J
Early transportation on Klamath waterways. Klamath Falls, Or., Klamath County Museum, 1974.
100 p. illus. S3118

Due, John Fitzgerald.
Rails to the Ochocco country: the City of Prineville railway by John F. Due and Frances Juris. San Marino, Cal., Golden West Books, 1968.
236 p. illus. S3120

Duncan, Ray
The big ditch: a story of gold mining in Malheur County, Oregon. Portland, The author, 1970 S3121

Duniway, David C
Salem state centennial guide, 1859-1959. Salem, Or., Statesman Publishing Co., 1959.
36 p. illus. S3122

Edson, Christopher Howard
The Chinese in eastern Oregon, 1860-1890. San Francisco, R.D. Reed, 1974.
84 p. illus. S3123

Ehernberger, James L
Smoke along the Columbia: Union Pacific, Oregon division, by Ehernberger and Gschwind. Callaway, Neb., E.G. Publications, 1968.
64 p. illus. S3124

Emmerson, Irma L. and Jean Muir
The woods were full of men. New York, David McKay Co., 1963.
242 p. S3125

Eubanks, Bernard M
The story of the pump and its relatives. Portland, Metropolitan Press, 1971.
185 p. S3126

Farrell, Allie M., comp.
Jefferson County reminiscences by Many Hands. Portland, Binfords & Mort, 1957.
384 p. illus. S3127

Ferguson, Gail Broderick
Wildflowers of spring in Portland. Portland, Bardalone, Ltd., 1973.
22 p. illus. S3128

Feris, Charles M
Hiking the Oregon Skyline (the Pacific Crest National Scenic Trail). Beaverton, Touchstone Press, 1973.
160 p. illus. S3129

Ferrell, Mallory Hope
Rails, sagebrush and pine: a garland of railroads and logging days in Oregon's Sumpter Valley. San Marino, Cal., Golden West Books, 1967. S3130

First Methodist Church, Salem, Oregon.
History of the First Methodist Church of Salem, Oregon. Salem, First Methodist Church, 1962. S3131

Florin, Lambert
Oregon Ghost towns. Seattle, Superior Publishing Co., c1970
89 (7) p. illus. S3135

Fowler, Ronald R
Soda: the Oregon bottlers. Aloha, The author, 1975.
91 p. illus. S3137

French, Giles L
Cattle country of Peter French. Portland, Binfords & Mort, 1964.
370 p. map. S3139

French, Giles L
Cattleman, Peter French. Portland Or., Binfords & Mort, 1963.
250 p. illus. S3140

French, Giles L
The golden land: a history of Sherman County, Oregon. Portland, Oregon Historical Society, 1958.
237 p. illus. S3141

French, Giles L
Homesteads and heritages: a history of Morrow County, Oregon. Portland, Binfords & Mort, 1971.
127 p. illus. S3142

Friedman, Ralph
Oregon for the curious. Portland, Or., Pars Publishing Co., 1965.
134 p.
Also: 2nd ed., 1967. 153 p. illus.
Also: 3rd ed., Caldwell, Caxton, 1972. 246 p. illus. S3144

Friedman, Ralph
Tales out of Oregon. Portland, Pars Publishing Co., 1967.
242 p.
Also: 2nd ed., N.Y., Ballantine Books, 1973. 242 p. S3145

Friedman, Ralph
A touch of Oregon. Portland, Pars Publishing Co., 1970.
234 p.
Also: 2nd ed., N.Y., Ballantine Books, 1974. 218 p. S3146

Garren, John
Oregon river tours. Portland, Binfords & Mort, 1974.
120 p. illus. S3147

Gassaway, Carolyn
Oregon plans the land: a guide to 1973-74 Land Use law. Portland, The author, 1974.
50 p. illus. S3148

Gault, Vera Whitney
Walking tour of Astoria, Oregon: featuring historic homes of Franklin and Grand Avenues. Illustrated by Gale Hubbell. Astoria, Clatsop County Historical Society, 1975.
unpaged. illus. S3149

Gelb, Barbara
So short a time: a biography of John Reed and Louise Bryant. New York, Norton, 1973
304 p. S3150

Gillette, Martha Hill
Overland to Oregon: and in the Indian wars of 1853. With an account of earlier life in rural Tennessee. Ashland, Or., Lewis Osborne, 1971.
77 p. illus. S3151

Gleeson, George W
The return of a river: the Willamette River, Oregon. Corvallis, Oregon State University, Water Resources Research Institute, 1972.
103 p. S3152

Glimpses of Wheeler County's past: an early history of north central Oregon. Edited by F. Smith Fussner. Portland, Published by Binford & Mort for the Wheeler County Historical Commission, 1975.
134 p. illus. S3153

Goldhammer, Keith.
Jackson County revisited: a case study in the politics of public education by Keith Goldhammer and Richard J. Pellegrin, edited by Joanne M. Kitchel. Eugene, University of Oregon Center for the Advanced Study of Educational Administration, 1968.
91 p. S3154

Goodall, Mary
Oregon's iron dream: a story of old Oswego and the proposed iron empire of the West. Portland, Binfords & Mort, 1958.
156 p. illus. S3155

Grauer, Jack
Mount Hood: a complete history. Gresham, The author, 1975.
296 p. illus. S3156

Gregg, Jacob Ray, 1871-
Pioneer days in Malheur County, perpetuating the memory of prominent pioneers and preserving an authentic history of the county. Los Angeles, Privately printed by L.L. Morrison, 1950.
442 p. illus. ports. S3157

Gregg, Robert
Chronicles of Willamette. Salem, Willamette University Book Store, 1970.
238 p. illus. S3158

Griffeth, Ross John
Crusaders for Christ: a history of Northwest Christian College, 1895-1971. Eugene, Northwest Christian College, 1971. S3159

Guillou, Charles F.B.
Oregon and California drawings, 1841 and 1847. With a biographical sketch by Emily Blackmore. and a commentary by Elliot A.P. Evans. San Francisco, Book Club of California, 1961.
28 p. plates. S3160

Haines, Francis D., Jr. and Vern S. Smith
Gold on Sterling Creek. Medford, Or., Gandee Printing Co., 1964.
104 p. S3161

Haines, Francis D., Jr.
Jacksonville: biography of a gold camp. Medford, Gandee Printing Co., 1967.
164 p. S3162

Hall, Don Alan
On top of Oregon. Corvallis, Or., Golden West Press, 1975.
180 p. illus. S3163

Hall, Eli S
Then to now with Roseburg schools, 1854-1970. Portland, Metropolitan Press, 1970.
241 p. illus. S3164

Harpham, Josephine Evans
Doorways into history. Eugene, A.K. Briggs Co., 1966.
55 p. S3165

Hart, John
Hiking the bigfoot country: exloring the wildlands of northern California and southern Oregon. San Francisco, Sierra Club, 1975.
398 p. maps. S3166

Hatfield, Mark O
Not so simple. New York, Harper, 1968. S3167

Havighurst, Walter
The first book of the Oregon Trail: pictures by Helen Borton. New York, F. Watts, 1960.
60 p. S3168

Haw, Frank and others.
Oregon saltwater fishing guide. Seattle, Stan Jones Publishing Co., 1972.
200 p. S3169

Hendrickson, James K
Joe Lane of Oregon: machine politics and the sectional crisis, 1849-1861. New Haven, Yale Universtiy Press, 1967.
274 p. S3170

Hermann, Binger
The Baltimore colony and pioneer recollections: taken from the original notes of the Honorable Binger Hermann. Coos Bay, Baltimore Colony Centennial Committee, 1959.
83 p. S3171

Hewlett, LeRoy, ed.
Indians of Oregon ... a bibliography of materials in the Oregon State Library. Salem, Oregon State Library, 1969.
125 p. S3172

Highsmith, Richard Morgan, Jr.
Atlas of Oregon agriculture. Corvallis, Agricultural Experiment Station, Oregon State College, 1958.
42 p. illus. S3173

Hill, D.D.
They broke the trail ... In collaboration with E.R. Jackman. Pendleton, Oregon. Oregon Wheat Commission, 1960.
16 p. illus. S3174

Hilleary, William M., 1840-1917
A webfoot volunteer: the diary of William M. Hilleary, 1864-1866. Edited by Herbert B. Nelson and Preston E. Onstad. Corvallis, Oregon State University Press, c1965. (Oregon State monographs, Studies in history, no. 5).
viii, 240 p. illus. S3175

Hiltz, Ivy E. and others, eds.
Nutritive values of native foods of Warm Spring Indians. Corvallis, Oregon State University Extension Service, 1972.
23 p. S3176

Ho, Franklin Y.H.
Small lumber companies in western Oregon: prepared by the University of Portland. Project directors: Franklin Y.H. Ho and Joseph A. Kehoe. Portland, 1963.
119 p. maps. tables. S3177

Hoffman, Helen Epley
Gold and silver and precious stones. Klamath Falls, Craft Printers, 1973.
unpaged S3178

Hoffstetter, William F
Geologic hazards to excavation, grading and foundations in the Portland area. Portland, Oregon Student Public Interest Research Group, 1974.
25 p. illus. S3179

Holbrook, Stewart Hall
Mr. Otis: with an introduction by Stewart H. Holbrook. New York, Macmillan, 1958.
70 p. illus. S3180

Holden, Arnold G. and Bruce Shepard
Migration and Oregon, 1970: patterns and implications. Corvallis, Oregon State University, 1974.
112 p. S3181

Holm, Don
101 best fishing trips in Oregon. Portland, Caxton, 1970. S3182

Holmes, Llewellyn Perry
Modoc: the last sundown. New York, Dodd, Mead, 1957.
213 p. S3183

Holmgren, Virginia C
Chinese pheasants, Oregon pioneers. Portland, Oregon Hist. Soc., 1964.
38 p. S3184

Holmgren, Virginia C
The war lord. Chicago, Follett Publishing Co., 1969.
128 p. illus. S3185

Howe, Carrol B
Ancient tribes of the Klamath country. Portland, Binfords & Mort, 1968.
262 p. illus. S3186

Howorth, Richard, comp.
Twelve Oregon photographers: a collection of their works. Eugene, Early Worm Productions, 1974.
unpaged. illus. S3187

Huckleberry, E.R.
The adventures of Dr. Huckleberry, Tillamook County. Portland, Oregon Historical Society, 1970.
242 p. illus. S3188

Hug, Bernal D., ed.
The history of Union County, Oregon. Edited and compiled for the Union County Historical Society, La Grande, The Society, 1961.
249 p. illus. S3189

Hug, Bernal D., Sr.
Salt of the earth. Elgin, Or., Elgin Recorder, 1964.
64 p. S3190

Huot, Leland and Alfred Powers.
Homer Davenport of Silverton: life of a great cartoonist. Bingen, Wash., West Shore Press, 1973.
260, 189 p. illus. S3191

Hussey, John A
Champoeg, place of transition: a disputed history. Portland, Oregon Historical Society, 1967.
424 p. S3192

Huston, Henry Clay
Henry Clay Huston journals, 1856-1860. Eugene, Or., Lane County Pioneer Historical Society, 1960.
39 l. photo. S3193

Hyde, Dayton O
Cranes in my corral. New York, Dial Press, 1971.
86 p. illus. S3194

Hyde, Dayton O
Sandy: the true story of a rare sand hill crane who joined our family. New York, Dial Press, 1968.
214 p. illus. S3195

Indian Festival of Arts, Inc.
Te-Yok-Keen (hear ye). La Grande, Or., Indian Festival of Arts, 1964. S3196

Ingram, Stan and others.
Anthony, a tale of two skis. Baker, Or., Record-Courier, 1971. S3197

Irving, Washington.
Astoria, or anecdotes of an enterprise beyond the Rocky Mountains. Edited with an introduction by Edgeley W. Todd. Norman, University of Oklahoma Press, 1964.
552 p. illus. S3198

Irving, Washington
Astoria. Portland, Binfords & Mort, 1967.
494 p. S3199

Jackman, Edwin Russell and R.A. Long
The Oregon desert. Caldwell, Idaho, Caxton Printers, 1964.
407 p. illus. S3200

Jackman, Edwin Russell and John Scharff
Steen's Mountian in Oregon's high desert country. Caldwell, Idaho, Caxton Printers, 1967.
203 p. S3201

Jackson, Kenneth T
The Ku Klux Klan in the city, 1915-1930. New York, Oxford University Press, 1967.
326 p. S3202

Jacobs, Melville, 1902-
Clackamas Chinook texts. Bloomington, Ind., 1958. (Indiana University. Research Center in Anthropology, Folklore and Linguistics. Publication 8).
vi, 293 p. S3203

Jacobs, Melville
The content and style of an oral literature: Clackamas Chinook myths and tales. Chicago, University of Chicago Press, 1959.
285 p. S3204

Jacobs, Melville, ed.
Nehalem Tillamook tales: recorded by Elizabeth Derr Jacobs. Eugene, University of Oregon, 1959.
216 p. S3205

Jankowski, Nick and Else Jankowski
55 Oregon bicycle trips. Beaverton, Touchstone Press, 1973.
127 p. S3207

Jensen, Veryl M
Early days in the upper Willamette. Oakridge, Upper Willamette Pioneer Association, 1970. S3208

Jensen, Virginia.
Astoria of the fur traders: a chronology, 1542-1846. Astoria, The author, c1959, 1961.
(10) p. S3209

Jessett, Thomas E
Christian missions to the Indians of Oregon. Seattle, 1959.
12 p. S3210

Johnson, Steve and others.
Chinook Centrex: Portland access directory. Portland, Chinook Centrex, 1973.
456 p. S3214

Jonasson, Jonas A
100 years of witnessing: a history of the First Baptist Church, Mc-Minnville, Oregon, 1857-1967. Mc-Minneville, 1967. S3215

Jones, Hathaway
Tall tales from Rogue River: the yarns of Hathaway Jones. Edited by Stephen Dow Beckham. Bloomington, Ind., Indiana University Press, 1974.
178 p. S3216

Judson, Lewis E
Reflections on the Jason Lee Mission and the opening of civilization in the Oregon country. Salem, Wynkoop-Blair, 1971.
55 p. S3218

Juris, Frances
Old Crook County: the heart of Oregon. Prineville, The author, 1975.
31 p. illus. S3219

Kassell, Larry
Silverton sampler. Silverton, The author, 1972.
44 p. illus. S3220

Keenan, Charles J
The railroad saga of Jeff Keenan. Portland, Binford & Mort, 1975.
152 p. illus. S3221

Keller, Paul and Jack Pement.
Oregon historical vignettes. Portland, Binfords & Mort, 1974.
104 p. illus. S3222

Kemp, K. Larry
Epitaph for the giants: the story of the Tillamook burn. Portland, Touchstone Press, 1967.
110 p. S3223

Kirk, Ruth
Exploring Crater Lake country. Seattle, Wash., University of Washington Press, 1975.
74 p. illus. S3224

Kirkpatrick, John M., 1825-1910
The hero of Battle Rock, compiled and edited by Bert Webber. Fairfield Wash., Ye Galleon Press, 1973.
25 p. illus. ports. S3225

Kittleman, Laurence R
Guide to the geology of the Owyhee region of Oregon. Eugene, University of Oregon, 1973.
61 p. illus. S3226

Knowles, Margie Young
Honeymoon on horseback. New York, Carleton Press, 1970.
102 p. S3227

Knuth, Priscilla
"Picturesque" frontier: the Army's Fort Dallas. Portland, Oregon Historical Society, 1967.
104 p. S3228

Labarre, Mary
Through brush and briar. Portland, Or., Good Samaritan Hospital, 1975.
72 p. illus. S3229

Lampman, Ben Hur
The Lampman papers. Edited by V.S. Hidy. Portland, Touchstone Press, 1965.
109 p. illus. S3230

League of Women Voters of Beaverton. Milwaukie, Oswego and Portland. A tale of three counties, one metropolitan community. Portland, Oregon, 1959.
32 p. maps. S3231

League of Women Voters of East Washington County.
Washington County: its government and resources. Hillsboro, Or., 1969.
S3232

League of Women Voters of Eugene and Springfield.
Eugene and its government. Eugene, Or., City of Eugene, 1962.
65 p. illus. S3233

League of Women Voters of Eugene and Springfield.
Lane County government. Eugene, Or., 1959.
74 p. illus. S3234

League of Women Voters of Grants Pass
Know your town. Grants Pass, Oregon, 1959. S3235

League of Women Voters of McMinnville, comp.
McMinnville, the first hundred years. McMinnville, Daily News-Reporter, 1957.
40 p. illus. S3236

League of Women Voters of The Dalles.
The Dalles, 100 years and more. The Dalles, Oregon, 1958. S3237

Lee, Mabel (Barbee)
The rainbow years: a happy interlude. Garden City, N.Y., Doubleday, 1966.
viii, 159 p. S3238

Leonard, Helen
Fun along the way. Portland, Western Lithograph, 1970. S3239

Lewis, Oscar
The story of Oregon. Illustrated by John N. Barron. Garden City, N.Y., Garden City Books, 1957.
56 p. illus. S3240

Libbey, F.W.
The Ameda mine, Josephine County. Salem, Oregon State Dept, of Geology and Mineral Industries, 1967.
53 p. S3241

Linfield College, McMinnville, Ore.
Linfield's hundred years: a centennial history of Linfield College, McMinneville, Oregon. Edited by Kenneth L. Holmes. Portland, Binfords & Mort, 1956.
ix, 198 p. illus. ports. S3242

Lockley, Fred
Captain Sol Tetherow, wagon train master. Fairfield, Wash., Ye Galleon Press, 1971. S3243

Lockley, Fred
Recollections of Benjamin Franklin Bonney. Fairfield, Wash., Ye Galleon Press, 1971. S3244

Lockley, Fred
To Oregon by ox-team in 1847. Fairfield, Wash., Ye Galleon Press, 1971 S3245

Lomax, Alfred Lewis
Later woolen mills in Oregon: a history of the woolen mills which followed the pioneer mills. Portland, Binfords & Mort, 1974.
301 p. illus. S3246

Lorenz, Claudia Spink
The times of my life. Klamath Falls, Klamath County Museum, 1969.
113 p. illus. S3247

Lowe, Don and Roberta Lowe
Mount Hood: portrait of a magnificent mountain. Caldwell, Idaho, Caxton Printers, 1975.
119 p. illus. S3248

Lowe, Don and Roberta Lowe
100 Oregon hiking trails. Portland, Touchstone Press, 1969.
240 p. illus. S3249

Lowe, Don and Roberta Lowe
70 hiking trails: northern Oregon Cascades. Beaverton, Touchstone Press, 1974.
160 p. illus. S3250

Loy, William G., ed.
Atlas of Oregon. Eugene, University of Oregon Cooperative Bookstore, 1972. S3251

Lucia, Ellis
Cornerstone: the story of St. Vincent: Oregon's first permanent hospital, its formative years. Portland, St. Vincent Medical Foundation, 1975.
119 p. illus. S3252

Lucia, Ellis
Don't call it Or-e-gawn, a view of Oregon today. Portland, Overland West Press, 1964.
80 p. illus. S3253

Lucia, Ellis
Sea wall, adventuring along the rugged Oregon coast. Portland, Overland West Press, 1966.
104 p. illus. S3254

Lynch, Vera Martin
Free land for free men: a story of Clackamas County. Portland, Artline Printing, 1973.
680 p. illus. S3255

McAfee, Don
Visitors' guide to the Oregon coast. McMinnville, Oregon Guide Publishers, 1967. S3256

McArthur, Lewis Ankeny
Oregon geographical names. 3rd ed. Portland, Oregon Historical Society, 1952.
Also: 4th ed. Portland, Binfords & Mort, 1964. 800 p. S3257

McCall, Dorothy Lawson
The copper king's daughter: from Cape Cod to Crooked River. Portland, Binfords & Mort, 1972.
190 p. S3258

McCall, Dorothy Lawson
Ranch under the Rimrock. Portland, Binfords & Mort, 1968.
208 p. illus. S3259

Mackey, Harold
The Kalapuyans: a sourcebook on the Indians of the Willamette Valley. Salem. Or., Mission Mill Museum Association, 1974.
165 p. illus. S3260

McLeod, Rev. William
Souvenir, 1958-1959. Medford, Or., 1959.
48 p. illus. S3261

McMillan, Sam G
The bunchgrassers: a history of Lexington, Morrow County, Oregon. Portland, Irwin-Hodson Co., 1974.
167 p. illus. S3262

McMullen, D.E.
Oregon under foot. Edited by Robert B. Pamplin, Jr. and Thomas K. Worcester. Portland, OMSI Press, 1975.
60 p. illus. S3263

McMurtrie, Douglas Crawford, 1888-1944.
Oregon imprints, 1847-1870. Eugene, University of Oregon Press, 1950. (University of Oregon Library, Studies in bibliography, no. 2).
xxi, 206 p. facsims. S3264

MacNab, Gordon G
A century of news and people in the East Oregonian, 1875-1975. Pendleton, Or., East Oregonian Publishing Co., 1975.
397 p. illus. S3265

McNamee. Sister Mary Dominica
Willamette interlude. Palo Alto, Ca., Pacific Books, 1959.
302 p. illus. S3266

McNeal, Roy Wilson
Southern Oregon College cavalcade. Ashland, Or., Southern Oregon College Foundation, 1973.
30 p. illus. S3267

McNeal, William H
A brief history of the old Wasco County, Oregon Pioneers Association. The Dalles, The author, 1975.
188, 6 p. illus. S3268

McNeal, William H
The Dalles High School, 1921-1971. The Dalles, The author, 1971. S3269

McNeal, William H
A history of the centennial churches of the Dalles. The Dalles, The author, 1969.
illus. S3270

McNeal, William H
History of Wasco Lodge No. 15, A.F. & A.M. and Allied Orders. The Dalles, 1969.
103 p. illus. S3271

Mahaffy, Charlotte S
Coos River echoes: a story of the Coos River Valley. Portland, Or., Interstate Press, 1965. S3272

Mallett, Mary Powell
Courageous people. Portland, Printed by Del Brumble, 1972.
140 p. illus. S3273

Marlitt, Richard
Nineteenth street. Portland, Oregon Historical Society, 1970.
128 p. illus. S3274

Marshall, David B
Endangered plants and animals of Oregon. III Birds. Corvallis, Oregon Agricultural Experiment Station, 1969.
23 p. S3275

Mattila, Walter, ed.
The theater Finns. Portland, Finnish-American Historical Society of the West, 1972.
66p. illus. S3276

Maybee, Lottie
Days and ways of old Damascus, Oregon, By Lottie Maybee and Forrest Dale Forbes. Calimesa, Cal., Damascus Road Press, 1962.
64 p. S3277

Medford League of Women Voters.
How much do you know about Jackson County? Medford, Or., 1969. S3278

Metzler, Ken
Confrontation: the destruction of a college president. Los Angeles, Nash Publishing, 1973.
337 p. S3279

Miller, Clifford R
Baptists and the Oregon frontier. Portland, Oregon Baptist Convention, 1967.
225 p. illus. S3280

Miller, Clifford R
Shining light: the story of Moses Williams, pioneer preacher, father of Presbyterianism in southern Oregon. Ashland, Or., Presbytery of S.W. Oregon, 1972.
164 p. illus. S3281

Miller, Emma Gene
Clatsop County, Oregon: a history. Portland, Binfords & Mort, 1958.
291 p. illus. S3282

Miller, May McCollough
Golden memories of the Paulina area. Redmond, Midstate Printing, Inc., 1974.
69 p. illus. S3283

Mills, Randall Vause, 1907-
Railroads down the valleys: some short lines of the Oregon country. Palo Alto, Cal., Pacific Books, 1950.
ix, 151 p. illus. S3284

Minter, Harold A
Umpqua Valley, Oregon, and its pioneers. Portland, Binfords & Mort, 1967.
306 p. S3285

Mintonye, Edna A., comp.
They laughed, too. San Antonio, Tex., Naylor Co., 1968.
222 p. illus. S3286

Monaghan, Robert
Pronunciation guide of Oregon place names. Eugene, Oregon Association of Broadcasters, 1961.
81 p. illus. S3287

Montague, Martha F.
Lewis and Clark College: 1876-1967. Portland, Or., Binfords & Mort, 1968.
xiv, 244 p. illus. ports. S3288

Mooberry, Lester C
The gray nineties. Portland, Or., Binfords & Mort, 1957.
167 p. illus. S3289

Mooberry, Lester C
History of the Hillsboro Methodist Church, 1843-1959. Hillsboro, Or., 1959.
63 p. illus. S3290

Moore, Earl F
Silent arrows: Indian lore and artifact hunting. Trail, Muse Press, 1973.
196 p. illus. S3291

Moore, Maple Dell
Afterglow: Memories of a pioneer's daughter. New York, Vantage Press, 1972.
207 p. ports. S3292

Morgan, A.W.
Fifty years in Siletz timber. McMinnville, News-Register Printing Co., 1959.
xiii, 82 p. illus. S3293

Mullen, Floyd
The land of Linn. Lebanon, Dalton's Printing, 1971.
352 p. photos. S3294

Munger, Thornton T
History of Portland's Forest-Park. by Thornton T. Munger in collaboration with C. Paul Keyser. Portland, Or., Forest-Park Committee of Fifty, 1960.
37 p. illus. S3295

Murray, Keith A
The Modocs and their war. Norman, University of Oklahoma Press, 1959.
346 p. illus. S3296

National Board of Fire Underwriters.
The Roseburg, Oregon fire, explosion and conflagration, August 7, 1959. Portland, Oregon Ins. Rating Bureau, 1959.
20 p. S3297

Nelson, Lee H
Century of Oregon covered bridges. Portland, Oregon Historical Society, 1960.
211 p. illus. S3298

Nelson, Ray
Facts and yarns of the Bohemia gold mines. Cottage Grove, Or., Cottage Grove Sentinel, 1959.
30 p. map. S3299

Newman, Doug and Sally Sharrard
Oregon ski tours: 65 cross-country ski trails. Beaverton, Touchstone Press, 1973.
160 p. illus. S3300

Newton, Dwight Bennett
The Oregon rifles. Garden City, N.Y., Doubleday and Co. Inc., 1962
184 p. S3302

Newton, Sid
The early history of Independence, Oregon. Independence, Enterprise-Hearld, 1971.
120 p. illus. S3303

Nickerson, Dorothy
The cornerstone of North Clackamas County. Oak Grove, Or., The Oak Leaf, c1959.
1 vol. unpaged. illus. S3304

Noble, Iris
Oregon. New York, Coward, 1966.
127 p. illus. ports. S3305

Nodel, Julius J
The ties between: a century of Judaism on America's last frontier. The human story of Congregation Beth Israel. Portland, Temple Beth Israel, c1959.
194 p. illus. S3306

Nyden, Evangeline
Old Sellwood. Portland, Sellwood-Moreland Bee, 1971.
104 p. illus. S3307

O'Callaghan, Jerry Alexander
The disposition of the public domain in Oregon. Washington, G.P.O., 1960.
113 p. S3308

O'Connor, Richard and Dale L. Walker
The lost revolutionary: a biography of John Reed. New York, Harcourt, 1967.
328 p. S3309

Oliver, Herman
Gold and cattle country. Edited by E.R. Jackman. Portland, Binfords & Mort, 1961.
312 p. illus.
Also: 2nd ed., 1962. 320 p. S3310

Olson, Charles Oluf
History of Milwaukie, Oregon. Milwaukie, Or., Milwaukie Historical Society, 1965. S3311

Olson, Joan and Gene Olson
Oregon times and trails: a historical account for junior high school Grants Pass, Or., Windy-ridge Press, 1965.
201 p. illus. S3312

Onstine, Burton W
Oregon votes, 1858-1972: election returns, by county, from statehood to 1972 for U.S. President, Governor, U.S. Senator and U.S. Representative. Portland, Oregon Historical Society, 1973.
395 p. maps. S3313

The Oregon almanac and book of facts, 1961/62. Portland, Binfords & Mort, 1961.
607 p. illus. ports. maps. S3314

Oregon Archaeological Society
Wakemap mound and nearby sites on the Long Narrows of the Columbia River. Portland, Oregon Archaeological Society, 1959.
40 p. illus. S3315

Oregon. Dept. of Geology and Mineral Industries.
The Oregon King mine, Jefferson County, Oregon, by F.W. Libbey and R.E. Corcoran. Portland, The Dept., 1962.
49 p. S3316

Oregon, Dept. of Geology and Mineral Industries
Quicksilver in Oregon. by Howard C. Brooks. Portland, The Dept., 1963. (Its Bulletin, no. 55).
223 p. S3317

The Oregon experiment, by Christopher Alexander and others. New York, Oxford University Press, 1975.
190 p. illus. S3318

Oregon Historical Society, Portland.
Manuscripts collection. Portland, 1971.
264 p. S3319

Oregon Historical Soceity, Portland
Pacific Northwest Americana catalog. Portland, Or., 1961.
unpaged. S3320

Oregon, State Library, Salem.
Oregon: frontier of the future. Read about Oregon. Oregon centennial publication. Compiled by Hazel E. Mills. Salem, 1959.
66 p. S3321

Oregon. State Library
Oregon newspapers. Edited by Loretta G. Fisher. Salem, Oregon State Library, 1963.
70 p. S3322

Oregon. State Library
State archives. Pioneer families of the Oregon territory, 1850. Salem, Or., 1961.
64 p. S3323

Oregon. State University, Corvallis. Centennial Committee.
Centennial lectures, 1968-1969. The second hundred years. Corvallis, 1969.
126 p. S3324

Oregon Student Public Interest Research Group.
Nursing home patients: who protects them? Portland, 1974.
175 p. S3325

Oregon. University. Department of Geography
Som recent physical changes of the Oregon coast, by Samuel N. Dicken. Eugene, The Department, 1961.
151 p. S3326

Oregon. University. Library
Inventory of the papers of John T. Flynn. Eugene, 1966. (University of Oregon Occasional paper no. 3). "Prepared by Martin Schmitt."
32 l. S3327

Oregon. University. Library
Inventory of the papers of Senator Wayne L. Morse, 1919-1969. Prepared by Martin Schmitt. Eugene, 1974.
257 p. front. S3328

Overton, John
The Oregon clean river handbook. Portland, Oregon Student Public Interst Research Group, 1974.
60 p. S3330

Paine, Lauren Bosworth, 1916-
Oregon guns by James Glen (pseud.) London, Gresham, 1966.
160 p. S3331

Pamplin, Robert B., ed.
A portrait of Oregon. Paintings: Howard Snapp. Photographs: Robert Reynolds. Text: Thomas K. Worcester. Beaverton, OMSI Press, 1973.
1 vol. illus. S3332

Pander, Henk
Views of Mount Hood. Portland, Press 22, 1971. S3333

Payne, Doris Palmer
Captain Jack, Modoc renegade. Portland, Binfords & Mort, 1959. 3rd ed.
268 p. illus. S3334

Peale, Titian Ramsey
Diary of Titian Ramsey Peale: Oregon to California, overland journey September and October, 1841. Edited by Clifford Merrill Drury. Los Angeles. Glen Dawson, 1957. (Early California Travels series, xxxvi).
85 p. illus. S3335

Peck, Morton Eaton
A manual of the higher plants of Oregon. 2nd ed. Portland, Binfords & Mort, 1961.
936 p. illus. S3336

Pennington, Levi Talbott
Rambling recollections of ninety happy years. Portland, Metropolitan Press, 1967.
187 p. S3337

Peterson, Emil R
A century of Coos and Curry: history of southwest Oregon, by Emil R. Peterson and Alfred Powers. Portland, Binfords & Mort, 1952.
599 p. illus. S3338

Phillips, Mary E. and Catherine Lauris
Public libraries in Oregon. Eugene, University of Oregon Press, 1962.
126 p. charts. maps. biblio. S3339

Phipps, D.L.
Log brands registered with the state forester for the period October 1, 1961 to September 30, 1966. Salem, Or., Office of the State Forester.
340 p. S3340

Pierce, Lois A
Lost immigrants of 1845 and the Blue Bucket gold. Shelton, Wash., Shelton-Mason County Journal, 1962.
59 p. illus. S3341

Pilcher, William W
The Portland longshoremen: a dispersed urban community. New York, Holt, Rinehart and Winston, 1972.
128 p. illus. S3342

Place, Howard and Marian Place
The story of Crater Lake National Park. Caldwell, Idaho, Caxton Printers, 1974.
84 p. illus. S3343

Poling, Daniel A
Mine eyes have seen: an autobiography. New York, McGraw, 1959.
320 p. illus. S3344

Polk County Centennial Book Committee.
A century of Polk County, 1859-1959. Dallas, Or., Curry Print Shop, 1959?
4 l. illus. S3345

Portland's terrific Timbers. Portland Oregon Journal, 1975. S3346

Potter, Miles F
Oregon's golden years: bonanza of the West. Caldwell, Idaho, Caxton Printers, 1975.
185 p. S3347

Pratt, Laurence
I remember Portland, 1899-1915. Portland, Or., Metropolitan Press, 1965. S3348

Pratt, Laurence
An Oregon boyhood. Worthly Lake Press, 1968. S3349

Pratt, Laurence
Portland, my city: a new Portland book, years 1915-2017. Portland, Worthylake Press, 1967.
94 p. S3350

Prichard, Lewis G
Oregon's first century, 1859-1959. Portland, First National Bank, 1959.
16 p. charts. S3351

Purvine, Mary B
Mary B. Purvine pioneer doctor. Santa Barbara, Cal., Privately printed, 1958.
60 p. illus. S3352

Rand, Helen B
Gold, jade and elegance. Baker, The author, 1974.
79 p. illus. S3353

Randall, Warren R
Manual of Oregon trees and shrubs. Corvallis, Oregon State College Cooperative Association, 1960.
234 p. illus. S3354

Reed College, Portland, Oregon. The Behavioral Science Research Institute.
A social profile of northwest Portland, 1958. Portland, Reed College, 1959.
31 p. tables. S3355

Reed College, Fiftieth anniversary: 1911-1961. Portland, Reed College, 1961?
56 p. illus. S3356

Richmond, Henry R
The Oregon coast and the Oregon coastal conservation and Development Commission: the fox guarding the chickens? Portland, Oregon Student Public Interest Research Group, 1973.
91 p. S3357

Ringhand, Harry E
Marie Dorion and the trail of the pioneers. Milton-Freewater, Or., Valley Hearld, 1971.
68 p. photos. map. S3358

Roberts, Phyllis Pugh, comp.
Francis Asbury and Ruth Jessup Pugh, pioneers of 1846 in the Oregon country, n.p., 1958?
116 p. photos. S3359

Rodakowski, Albert A
A century of Polk County history: 1859-1959. Dalles, Or., Polk County Centennial Book Committee, 1959.
66 p. S3361

Rogue River Valley railroads. An album of old photos of railroading in Jackson, Josephine and Curry Counties, spanning about seventy years. Jacksonville, Or., Jacksonville Museum, 1959.
33 p. S3362

Rosenstone, Robert A
Romantic revolutionary: a biography of John Reed. New York, Knopf, 1975.
430 p. illus. S3363

Ross, Charles R
Trees to know in Oregon. Artist High Hayes. Corvallis, Oregon State University, 1966. Revised.
96 p. illus. S3364

Ross, Marion Dean
A century of architecture in Oregon: 1859-1959. Eugene, University of Oregon, School of Architecture and Allied Arts, 1959.
24 p. S3365

Ruby, Robert H. and John A. Brown
The Cayuse Indians: imperial tribesmen of old Oregon. Norman, University of Oklahoma Press, 1972.
345 p. illus. S3366

Sanderson, William
The acid test, cartoons from the Oregonian. Portland, 1967. S3368

Sauter, John and Bruce Johnson
Tillamook Indians of the Oregon coast. Portland, Binfords & Mort, 1974.
196 p. illus. S3369

Savage, John F. and Henry R. Richmond
Oregon's bottle bill: a riproaring success. Portland, Oregon Student Public Interest Research Group, 1974
1 vol. S3370

Schlesser, Norman Dennis
Bastion of empire, the Hudson's Bay Company's Fort Unpqua: being a narrative of the early explorations and the fur trade in Douglas County. Oakland, Oakland Printing Co., 1973.
44 p. illus. S3371

Schmitt, Martin
Catalogue of manuscripts in the University of Oregon Library. Eugene, University of Oregon Books, 1971.
355 p. S3372

Schoenberg, Rev. Wilfred P
The Jesuits in Oregon, 1844-1959. Portland, Oregon Jesuit, 1959.
64 p. S3373

Schwind, Dick
West coast river touring: Rogue River Canyon and south. Beaverton, Touchstone Press, 1974.
224 p. illus. S3374

Scofield, Winifred M
Oregon's historical markers. Pleasant Hill, Or., Souvenir Publishing, 1966.
104 p. illus. S3375

Scott, John D
We climb high, a chronology of the Mazamas, 1894-1964. Portland, The author, 1969.
94 p. illus. S3376

Scott, Walter Lee, 1882-
Pan bread 'n jerky: an autobiography. Introduced by E.R. Jackmsn. Caldwell, Idaho, Caxton Printers, 1968.
174 p. illus. photos. S3377

Seaman, N.G.
Stone age on the Columbia River. 2nd ed., rev. and enl. Portland, Binfords & Mort, 1967.
256 p. S3378

Searcy, Mildred
Way back when. Pendleton, East Oregonian, 1972.
189 p. bibl. S3379

Searcy, Mildred
We remember. Pendleton, East Oregonian Publishing Co., 1973.
176 p. illus. S3380

Seligman, Lester G
Patterns of recruitment: a state chooses its lawmakers. Chicago, Rand McNally, 1974.
269 p. S3381

Sharpe, Grant and Wenonah Sharpe
101 wildflowers of Crater Lake National Park. Seattle, University of Washington Press, 1959.
50 p. illus. S3382

Shaw, James Gerard
Edwin Vincent O'Hara: American prelate. Foreword by Matthew F. Brady. New York, Farrar, Straus & Cudahy, 1957.
274 p. illus. S3383

Shotwell, J. Arnold
The Juntura Basin: studies in earth history and paleoecology. With contirbutions by R.G. Bowen and others. Philadelphia, American Philosophical Society, 1963.
77 p. S3384

Sigurdson, Clarence
Raised by the sea. Astoria, Consolidated Printing, 1973.
105 p. illus. S3385

Smith, Arthur Robert
The tiger in the Senate: a biography of Wayne Morse. Garden City, N.Y., Doubleday and Co., 1962.
455 p. S3386

Smith, Earl R
The Westfall country: the story of an eastern Oregon community and the people who settled and lived there. New York, Exposition Press, 1963.
288 p. S3387

Smith, Edesse Perry
The pokes of gold. New York, Dodd, Mead, 1958.
207 p. S3388

Smith, Helen Krebs
The presumptuous dreamers: a sociological history of the life and times of Abigail Scott Duniway (1834-1915). Lake Oswego, Smith, Smith and Smith Publishing Co., 1974.
303 p. S3389

Snow, Berkeley
The history of the Deschutes Club. Portland, Touchstone Press, 1966.
S3390

Snyder, Eugene E
Early Portland or Stumptown triumphant. Portland, Binfords & Mort, 1970.
182 p. S3391

Snyder, Eugene E
Skidmore's Portland: his fountain and its sculptor, from buckboards to bustles. Portland, Binfords & Mort, 1973.
152 p. illus. S3392

Soher, Hubert J
Oregon, today and tomorrow: an economic study of the quality state. Portland, Pacific Power and Light Co., 1962.
56 p. S3393

Sorenson, Pete
Annotated bibliography of the Coquille Valley area, southern Coos County. Eugene, OSPRIG, 1972.
31 p. map. S3394

Southern Oregon Library Federation.
A guide to the State of Jefferson: a union list of Historical materials relating to northern California and southern Oregon. Portland, Oregon Historical Society, 1972. (Research and Bibliography Series, 2).
209 p. S3395

Southern Oregon Library Federation.
Union list of serials, 1973. Richard E. Moore, Project Coordinator. Medford, Jackson County Library System, 1973.
302 p. S3396

Spangler, Harrison E
The record of Wayne Morse. Portland, Meriwether Book Co., 1962.
128 p. S3397

Spencer, Arthur C
Historical notes on Trinity Episcopal Church, Portland, Oregon. Begun for the 125th Parish anniversary, 1976. Portland, The author, 1975.
135 l. S3398

Spooner, Ella Brown
Tabitha Brown's western adventures: a grandmother's account of her trek from Missouri to Oregon. New York, Exposition Press, 1958.
102 p. illus. S3399

Spring, Robert and others
Crater Lake National Park, Klamath Basin National Wildlife Refuges, Lava Beds National Monument. Seattle, Wash., Superior Publishing Co., 1975.
unpaged. illus. S3400

Spring, Robert
This is Oregon. Photos by Bob and Ira Spring, text by Ron Fish. Seattle, Superior Publishing Co., 1957.
72 p. illus. S3401

Sproull, Harry V
Modoc Indian War. Yreka, Cal.? Lava Beds Natural History Association, 1975.
(45) p. illus. S3402

Stearns, Marjorie Ruth, 1898-
The history of the Japanese people in Oregon. San Francisco, R and E Research Associates,1974.
iii, 106 p. S3403

Stebbins, Ellis A
The OCE story. Monmouth, Oregon College of Education, 1973.
150 p. illus. S3404

Stern, Theodore
The Klamath tribe: a people and their reservation. Seattle, Wash., University of Washington Press, c1966.
xvi, 356 p. illus. ports. S3405

Stone, Buena Cobb
Fort Klamath, frontier post in Oregon, 1863-1890. Dallas, Tex., Royal Publishing Co., 1964.
91 p. illus. S3406

Stone, Buena Cobb
Ninety years of Klamath schools, 1870-1960. Compiled by Buena Cobb Stone, Marjorie Reeder Howe and Isabelle Tyrell Brixner. Klamath Falls, 1960.
84 p. illus. S3407

Stone, Buena Cobb
Son of the lakes: a story of the Klamath Indians. Klamath Falls, Or., Smith Bates Printing Co., 1967
50 p. illus. S3408

Stonehill, Arthur and others.
The Oregon ski area study, 1967-1968 winter season. Corvallis, Oregon State University, 1969.
45 p. S3409

Stout, Sally Reed
Saint Helen's Hall--the first century, 1869-1969. Portland, St. Helen's Hall, 1969. S3410

Stovall, Charles Roscoe
Charley's heaven. New York, Pageant Press, 1958.
238 p. S3411

Street, Willard and Elsie Street.
Sailors' diggings. Wilderville, Wilderville Press, 1973.
44 p. S3412

Strong, Emory M
Stone Age in the Great Basin. Portland, Binfords & Mort, 1969.
274 p. maps. bibl. S3413

Strong, Henry
Stone Age of the Columbia River, the history of a remarkable culture. Portland, Binfords & Mort, 1968.
256 p. illus. index. S3414

Stuart, Reginald R
Calvin B. West of the Umpqua: an obscure chapter in the history of southern Oregon. Stockton, Ca., California History Foundation, 1961.
115 p. illus. S3415

Sunset.
Sunset discovery trips in Oregon. Menlo Park, Ca., Lane Publishing Co., 1959.
94 p. illus. maps.
Also: Rev. ed., 1968. S3416

Sutton, Jack
Golden years of Jacksonville, a pictorial walking tour. Jacksonville, Or., The author, 1961.
12 p. illus. S3417

Sutton, Jack and Dorothy Sutton, eds.
Indian wars of the Rogue River. Kirby, Josephine County Historical Society, 1969.
illus. maps. bibl. S3418

Sutton, Jack
The mythical State of Jefferson: a pictorial history of early northern California and southern Oregon. (In the 1964 yearbook of the Josephine County Historical Society, The Oldtimes). Grants Pass, The Josephine County Historical Society, 1964.
110 p. S3419

Sutton, Jack
One day of southern Oregon history, a pictorial motor tour guide of Jackson and Josephine Counties. Grants Pass, Or., Bulletin Publishing Co., 1960.
9 p. illus.
Also: rev. ed., 1962. S3420

Sutton, Jack
110 years with Josephine: the history of Josephine County, Oregon, 1856-1966. Medford, Or., Klocker Printers, 1966.
206 p. illus. S3421

Sutton, Jack
A pictorial history of southern Oregon and northern California. Grants Pass, Or., Grants Pass Bulletin Publishing Co., Inc., 1959.
100 p. S3422

Swanson, Rev. Fred L
The centennial jubilee history. First Presbyterian Church, Brownsville, Oregon, 1857-1957. Portland, Schoppe Printing Service, 1964.
illus. S3423

Swartz, B.K.
A bibliography of Klamath Basin anthropology, with excerpts and annotations. Klamath Falls, Or., Guide Printing Co., 1960. (Klamath County Museum, Research Papers, no. 3).
117 p. S3424

Tartar, Lena Belle
Chronicles from Pedee, Oregon. Corvallis, Or., 1974.
104 p. illus. S3426

Taylor, Arthur S. and Hugh G. Simpson.
A history of Southern Oregon College, 1872-1959. Eugene, Oregon State Board of Higher Education, 1959.
16 p. S3427

Taylor, Herbert Cecil and Robert J. Suphan.
Anthropolological investigation of the Tillamook Indians. Anthropological investigation of the Chinook Indians. The identity and localization of certain native peoples of northwestern Oregon. New York, Garland Publishing, 1974.
326 p. illus. S3428

Tetlow, Roger T
The Astorian: the personal history of DeWitt Clinton Ireland, pioneer newspaperman, printer and publisher. Portland, Binfords & Mort, 1975.
178 p. illus. S3429

Thompson, Erwin N
Modoc war: its military history and topography. Sacramento, Argus Books, 1971.
188 p. illus. S3430

Throckmorton, Arthur L
Oregon argonauts: merchant adventurers on the western frontier. Portland, Oregon Historical Society, 1961.
300 p. illus. S3431

Tillamook County Pioneer Association.
List of all Tillamook County cemeteries and private burials. Tillamook, The author, 1967.
443 p. S3432

Tillamook history: sequel to Tillamook memories. Tillamook, Tillamook Pioneer Association, 1975.
262 p. illus. S3433

Trullinger, Susan and Judith Ann Rose. eds.
Portland and the Pacific Northwest. Portland, Fox Publishing, 1975.
84 p. illus. S3434

Turnbull, George Stanley, 1882-
Governors of Oregon. Portland, Binfords & Mort, 1959.
112 p. illus. S3435

Turnbull, George Stanley
Journalists in the making: a history of the School of Journalism at the University of Oregon. Eugene, Oregon School of Journalism, University of Oregon, 1965.
162 p. S3436

Turnbull, George Stanley
An Oregon crusader. Portland, Binfords & Mort, 1955.
246 p. illus. S3437

U.S. National Park Service.
Champoeg State Park, Oregon: a summary report of its history and a proposed plan for its development by John A. Hussey. San Francisco, Ca., 1962.
3 vols. S3438

Vaughan, Thomas
Bybee-Howell House on Sauvie Island: The Oregon territorial farmstead. Portland, Oregon Historical Society, 1974.
unpaged. illus. S3439

Vaughan, Thomas and George A. McMath
A century of Portland architecture. Portland, Oregon Historical Society, 1967.
226 p. S3440

Walsh, Frank K. and William R. Halliday.
Discovery and exploration of the Oregon Caves. Grants Pass, Te-Cum-Tom Enterprises, 1971.
27 p. illus. S3441

Walsh, Frank K.
Indian battles along the Rogue River 1855-1856. Grants Pass, Te-Cum-Tom Enterprises, 1972.
28 p. S3442

Walsh, Frank K
Indian battles of the lower Rogue. Grants Pass, The author, 1970.
maps. illus. S3443

Ward, Harriet
Gold saga of the Umpqua. Portland, Or., Binfords & Mort, 1966.
199 p. S3444

Wardin, Albert W
Baptists in Oregon. Portland, Judson Baptist College, 1969.
635 p. maps. S3445

Warren, Mary Phraner and Don Kirkendall.
Botton high to the crowd. New York, Walker, 1973.
222 p. S3446

Waters, Aaron C
Moon craters and Oregon volcanoes. Eugene, University of Oregon Books, 1967.
70 p. S3447

Watson, Donald A. and Robert Loring Allen.
Oregon economic and trade structure. Eugene, University of Oregon, 1969.
112 p. S3448

Weatherford, Marion T
Things I see. Corvallis, Distributed by Oregon State University Press, 1974.
32 p. illus. S3449

Weatherford, Mark V
Rogue River Indian war. The author? 1962.
103 p. S3450

Webb, Billee Snead
Martin Christopher Randleman: his kin and heirs, 1754-1964: two hundred and ten year history of a pioneering American family. North Bend, Or.? The author, 1964.
750 p. S3451

Webber, Ebbert T
Oregon's great train holdup: the DeAutremont case, no. 57893-0, compiled and edited by Bert Webber. Fairfield, Wash., Ye Galleon Press, c1973.
viii, 24 p. S3452

Webber, Ebbert T
What happened at Bayocean? Is Salishan next? Fairfield, Wash., Ye Galleon Press, 1973.
40 p. illus. S3453

White, James Seeley
The Hedden's store handbook of proprietary medicines. Portland, The author, 1974.
94 p. illus. S3454

Wiard, Harry Leonard
Memoirs of Harry Leonard Wiard. Klamath Falls, Guide Printing Co., 1958.
vi, 88 p. S3456

Wieman, John S.
History of English holly (Ilex aquifolium) in Oregon and the Northwest. Portland, The author, 1961.
39 p. S3457

Will, Clark M
Story of old Aurora in pictures and prose, 1856-1883. Salem, The author, 1972.
26 p. illus. S3458

Willis, Lois Athel (Devine)
The family of Silas and Jane Ann (Blair) Brown, Oregon pioneers. Gaston, Or., The author, c1960.
18 p. S3459

Willis, Lois Athel (Devine)
The William Shields family at the end of the Oregon Trail. Hillsboro, The author, 1970.
53 p. S3460

Wilson, Fred W. and Earl K. Stewart.
Steamboat days on the river. Portland, Oregon Historical Society, 1969.
119 p. photos. S3461

Wilson, Tillie Davidson and Alice Scott.
That was yesterday: a history of the town of Sisters, Oregon, and the surrounding area. Sisters, The author, 1974.
113 p. illus. S3462

Wisdom, Loy Winter
John William Wisdom, pioneer. Baker, The author, 1974.
40 p. S3463

Wood, Elizabeth Lambert
Peter French, cattle king. Portland, Binfords & Mort, 1959. 2nd ed.
240 p. illus. S3464

Woodward, Arthur
Indian trade goods. Portland, Oregon Archaeological Society,1965.
38 p. illus. S3465

Wooldridge, Alice H
Pioneers and incidents of the upper Coquille Valley. Myrtle Point, The author, 1971.
photos. S3466

Wooley, Ivan M
Off to Mt. Hood, an auto biography of the old road. Portland, Oregon Historical Society, 1959.
109 p. illus. S3467

Workman, Gladys
Only when I laugh. Englewood Cliffs, N.J., Prentice Hall, 1959.
236 p. S3468

Yarnes, Thomas D
History of Oregon Methodism. Edited by Harvey E. Tobie, Portland, Oregon Methodist Conference Historical Society, n.d.
352 p. S3469

WASHINGTON

Compiled by Nancy Pryor
Washington State Library

Ackley, Daisy
Wagon wheels a'rollin': an autogiography. n.p., 1966, c1960
156 p. ports. S3470

Adams, Sally
WSU, the hill: a collection of pen-and-ink illustrations and an essay highlighting seventy-five years in the history of Washington State University. Illustrations and design by Richard S. Thornton. Pullman, Washington State University, 1963.
128 p. illus. S3471

Albi, G.G.
The artists of Puget Sound by G.G. Albi and G.B. Peck. Seattle, Metropolitan Press and Western, c1962.
32 p. illus. S3472

Allen, Terry D
Doctor in buckskin. New York, Harper, 1951.
227 p. S3473

Allison, Guy Selwin
Forgotten great man of Washington history, James G. Swan: a biographical account. Longview, Wash., Longview Daily News, 1951.
24 p. port. S3474

American Alpine Club
Climber's guide to the Cascade and Olympic mountains of Washington. New York, American Alpine Club, 1961.
386 p. illus. S3475

American Friends Service Committee.
Uncommon controversy: fishing rights of the Muckleshoot, Puyallup and Nisqually Indians. Seattle, University of Washington Press, 1970.
232 p. illus. S3476

American Institute of Architects. Spokane Chapter.
A selection of notable architects in Spokane. Spokane, Wash., 1967.
1 vol. unpaged. illus. S3477

Anderson, Eva Greenslit
C. Clarence Ward, pioneer surveyor: the remarkable life story of one who has seen and played an important part in the development of north central Washington. Wenatchee, Wenatchee Daily World, 1956.
24 p. illus. S3478

Anderson, Eva Greenslit
Charles F. Keiser: the pioneer with a yen for work. Wenatchee, Wenatchee Daily World, 1954.
24 p. illus. S3479

Anderson, Eva Greenslit
E.T. Pybus; the ingenious pioneer. Wenatchee, Wenatchee Daily World, 1954.
32 p. illus. S3480

Anderson, Eva Greenslit
Jacob H. Miller ... perennial pioneer. Wenatchee, Wenatchee Daily World, 1953.
46 p. illus. ports. S3481

Anderson, Eva Greenslit
Rails across the Cascades. Wenatchee, Wenatchee Daily World, 1952.
64 p. illus. S3482

Anderson, Eva Greenslit
The spirit of the Big Bend: the interesting life story and experiences of William F. Schluenz. With which is incorporated an autobiography by Etta Marie Schluenz. Wenatchee, Wenatchee Daily World, 1955.
48 p. illus. S3483

Anderson, Florence Mary Bennett
Leaven for the frontier: the true story of a pioneer educator. Boston, Christopher, 1953.
437 p. bibl. S3484

Anderson, Helen McReavy
How, when and where on Hood Canal. Everett, Wash., Puget Press, 1960.
83 p. illus. S3485

Anderson, Josephine Goldman
Golden reflections of by-gone-days. Tumwater, H.J. Quality Printing, 1973.
147 p. illus. S3486

Anderson, Richard C
Portraits of Bainbridge Island. Port Blakely, Siegel-Anderson, 1970.
24 p. illus. S3487

Anderson, Richard C
Portraits of the Olympic Peninsula. Bainbridge Island, Island Productions, 1971.
unpaged. illus. S3488

Anderson, Richard C
Portraits of Vashon Island. Port Blakely, Siegel-Anderson, 1970.
24 p. illus. S3489

Anderson, Richard C
Portraits of Whidbey Island. Port Blakely, Siegel-Anderson, 1970.
24 p. illus. S3490

Andrews, Ralph W
The Seattle I saw. Seattle, Superior Publishing Co., 1964.
99 p. illus. S3492

Appelo, Carlton E
Altoona, Wahkiakum County, Washington. Deep River, The author, 1972.
88 p. illus. S3493

Appelo, Carlton E
Bookfield--the Joe Megler story (Wahkiakum County) Washington. Deep River, Wash., Carlton E. Appelo, 1966.
40 p. illus. S3494

Appelo, Carlton E
Frankfort on the Columbia (Pacific County) Washington. Deep River, Wash., 1965.
28 p. illus. S3495

Appelo, Carlton E
Knappton, the first 50 years: Pacific County, Washington. Deep River, Western Wahkiakum County Telephone Co., 1975.
88 p. illus. S3496

Appelo, Carlton E
Wahkiakum County, Washington. Deep River, 1969.
40 p. illus. S3497

Atkeson, Ray
Beautiful Washington. Photographs by Ray Atkeson. Text by Paul M. Lewis. Eguene, Or., Beautiful West Publishing Co., 1974.
72 p. illus. S3498

Atkeson, Ray
Washington. Photography by Ray Atkeson. Text by Carl Gohs. Portland, Or., C.H. Belding, 1969.
iv, 188 p. illus. S3499

Atkeson, Ray and Archie Satterfield, Washington II. Portland, Or., C.H. Belding, 1973.
124 p. photos. S3500

Attwell, Jim
Tahmahnaw: the bridge of the gods. Chicago, Ill., Adams Press, 1973.
63 p. illus. S3501

Avery, Mary Williamson
Government of Washington state. Seattle, University of Washington Press, 1967, c1966.
320 p. illus.
Also: rev. ed., 1973. 329 p. S3502

Avery, Mary Williamson
History and government of the state of Washington, Seattle, University of Washington Press, 1961.
583 p. illus. S3503

Bacon, George H
Booming and panicking on Puget Sound. Bellingham, Watcom Museum of History and Art, 1970.
50 p. illus. S3504

Baker, Gordon E
The politics of reapportionment in Washington state. N.Y., Holt, Rinehart and Winston, 1960.
16 p. illus. S3505

Ball, Thomas and Harriet Ball
Life of Peter Cook, known as "Captain Cook." Portland, Metropolitan Press, 1959.
illus. S3506

Ballou, Robert
Early Klickitat Valley days. Portland, Or., Binfords & Mort, 1960, c1938.
496 p. illus. S3507

Bard, Mary
The doctor wears three faces. Philadelphia, J.B. Lippincott, 1949.
254 p. S3508

Barksdale, Julian D
Geology of the Methow Valley, Okanogan County, Washington. Olympia, Washington State Dept. of Natural Resources, 1975. (Bulletin, 68).
72 p. illus. S3509

Barrow, Susan H.L. and J. Allan Evans
Green gold: a history of logging and its products. Bellingham, Wash., Whatcom Museum of History and Art, 1970. S3510

Barrow, Susan H.L.
Whatcom seascapes: the influence of the sea on Whatcom County. Bellingham, Whatcom Museum of History and Art, 1970.
78 p. illus. S3511

Barto, Harold E
History of the state of Washington. By Harold E. Barto and Catherine Bullard. 2nd ed. Boston, Heath, 1953.
320 p. illus. S3512

Beach, Raymond Virgil
The history of Waterman from the coming of the first white settler in 1882 to the time of the present writing, January 1, 1951. Manchester, Wash., Century Press, 1951.
48, 5 p. illus. S3513

Beal, Zoe M
Bainbridge Island in battened buildings and clipper days. Seattle, Dickson, Fletcher Printing Co., 1960.
143 p. S3514

Bean, Margaret
Spokane's age of elegance. Spokane, The Campbell House Committee of the Eastern Washington State Historical Society, 1961.
22 p. S3515

Beatty, Patricia
Indian canoe-maker. Caldwell, Idaho, Caxton Printers, 1960.
194 p. illus. S3516

Beaver, Lowell J
Historic memories from monuments and plaques of western Washington. Puyallup, Wash., Historic Memories, Press, 1964.
275 p. illus. S3517

Becher, Edmund T
Spokane corona: eras and empires. Spokane, C.W. Hill Printers, 1974.
319 p. illus. S3518

Beck, Ethel Fyles
Lummi Indian how stories. Illustrated by Elizabeth Sykes Michaels. Caldwell, Id., Caxton Printers, 1955.
124 p. illus. S3519

Becker, Ethel Anderson
Here comes the Polly. Seattle, Superior Publishing, 1971.
127 p. illus. S3520

Beckett, Paul Louis, 1913-
From wilderness to enabling act: the evolution of the state of Washington. Pullman, Washington State University Press, 1968.
111 p. S3521

Beckey, Fred W
Cascade alpine guide: climbing and high routes, Columbia River to Stevens Pass. Seattle, Mountaineers, 1973.
341 p. illus. S3522

Beckey, Fred W
Challenge of the north Cascades. Seattle, the Mountaineers, 1969.
280 p. illus. S3523

Beckey, Fred W
Climber's guide to the Cascade and Olympic Mountains. New York, American Alpine Club, 1969.
271 p. illus. S3524

Beckey, Fred W. and Eric Bjornstad
Guide to Leavenworth rock-climbing areas. Seattle, The Mountaineers, 1965.
86 p. map. S3525

Bell, Richard C
Partners in progress: the story of Washington Cooperative Farms Association. Seattle, 1956.
132 p. illus. S3526

Benton County Historical Association
Benton County, Washington — a glimpse of the past. Kennewick, Wash., 1967.
61 p. S3527

Berg, Norah (Sullivan)
Lady on the beach. New York, Prentice-Hall, 1952. S3528

Bertholf, John Rossman
Men and mutuality: 50 years. Seattle, Metropolitan Press, 1951.
223 p. illus. S3529

Biddle, Henry J
Beacon Rock on the Columbia: legends and traditions of a famous landmark. Seattle, Frontiersman Press, 1973.
11 p. illus. S3530

Binns, Archie
The enchanted islands. New York, Duell, Sloan and Pearce, 1956.
239 p. illus. S3531

Binns, Archie
The headwaters. New York, Duell, Sloan and Pearce, 1957.
280 p. S3532

Binns, Archie
Sea in the forest. Garden City, N.Y., Doubleday, 1953.
256 p. S3533

Birkeland, Torger
Echoes of Puget Sound: fifty years of logging and steamboating. Caldwell, Idaho, Caxton Printers, 1960.
251 p. illus. S3534

Blackwell, Ruby Chapin, 1876-
A girl in Washington territory. Tacoma, Washington State Historical Society, c1972.
x, 31 p. illus. S3535

Blair, Harry C
Dr. Anson G. Henry, physician, politician, friend of Abraham Lincoln. Portland Or., 1950. S3536

Blanchard, Leslie F
The street railway era in Seattle: a chronicle of six decades. Forty Fort, Pa., Harold E. Cox, 1968.
151 p. S3537

Blanchard, Leslie F
Trolley days in Seattle: the story of the Seattle and Rainier Valley railroad. Los Angeles, Trans-Anglo Books, 1965.
49 p. illus. S3538

Blankenship, Georgina
Early history of Thurston County, Washington: together with biographies and reminiscences of those identified with pioneer days. Seattle, Shorey Book Store, 1972. (Facsimile reproduction of 1914 ed.)
396 p. illus. S3539

Boeing Company
Pedigree of champions: Boeing since 1916. Seattle, The company, 1963.
80 p. illus. S3540

Bonn, Marjorie Faulkner
Hogback. New York, Vantage Press, 1954.
85 p. illus. S3542

Bonnell, E. Marion
Scenic, historic Olympia, Washington "the evergreen state". Olympia, Wash., Quick Print, 1948.
28 p. illus. S3543

Bowers, Dawn
Expo '74 World's Fair, Spokane. Spokane, Expo '74 Corporation, 1974.
127 p. illus. S3544

Bowers, Peter M
Boeing aircraft since 1916. New York, Putnam, 1966.
464 p. illus. S3545

Bradley, Stuart B., ed.
The big smoke, 1969. Chicago, 1969.
48 p. illus. S3546

Bradner, Enos
The inside on the outdoors: an outdoor editors 26 year scrapbook. Seattle, Superior Publishing, 1973.
256 p. illus. S3547

Brockman, Christian Frank
Trees of Mount Rainier National Park. Seattle, University of Washington Press, 1949.
49 p. illus. S3548

Broderick, Henry
The "H B" story: Henry Broderick relates Seattle's yesterdays with some thoughts by the way. Seattle, Frank McCaffrey, 1969.
238 p. illus. S3549

Broderick, Henry
Mirrors of Seattle's old hotels. Seattle, Dogwood Press, 1965.
1 vol. unpaged. illus. S3550

Broderick, Henry
A slice of Seattle history: gravy train of 1906. Seattle, Dogwood Press, 1960.
12 p. S3551

Brown, Joseph C., ed.
The night the mountain fell and other stories of north central Washington history. Wenatchee, 1973.
95 p. illus. S3552

Brown, Joseph C
The rainbow seekers: stories of Spokane, the Expo city, and the inland empire. Wenatchee, Westcoast Publishing Co., 1974.
127 p. illus. bibl. S3553

Brown, Joseph C
Valley of the strong: stories of Yakima and central Washington history. Wenatchee, Westcoast Publishing Co., 1974.
111 p. illus. S3554

Brown, Milton W
Jacob Lawrence. New York, N.Y., Whitney Museum of American Art, 1974.
64 p. illus. S3555

Brown, William Compton
Early Okanogan history. Fairfield, Ye Galleon Press, 1968. (Reprint of 1911 ed.). S3556

Bruce, Richard L., ed.
Logging managed forests. Pullman, Washington State University, 1966.
271 p. S3558

Buchanan, Nina
Tall tales of a teacher. New York, Vantage Press, 1962.
243 p. illus. S3560

Buell, Robert Kingery and Charlotte Northcote Skladal.
Sea otters and the China trade. New York, David McKay Co., 1968. S3561

Bullitt, Stimson
To be a politicain. New York, Doubleday, 1959.
190 p. S3562

Butler, B. Robert
Contributions to the prehistory of the Columbian plateau: a report on excavations in the Palouse and Craig mountain sections. Pocatello, Idaho State College Museum, 1962.
86 p. illus. S3563

Butler, Maude Kimball
Cathlamet pioneer: the paintings of Maude Kimball Butler. Descriptive notes by Julia Butler Hanson. Tacoma, Washington State Historical Society, 1973.
39 p. illus. S3564

Cain, Harvey Thomas
Petroglyphs of central Washington. Seattle, University of Washington Press, 1950.
57 p. illus. S3565

Calhoun, Bruce
Cruising the San Juan Islands. Newport Beach, Ca., Sea Publications, 1973.
216 p. illus. S3566

Calkins, Rutherford Birchard Hayes
High tide: the drama and tragedy of Seattle's waterfront, produced of a permanent record of the men and ships the author has known during many years as a waterfront newsman. Seattle, Marine Digest Publishing Co., 1952.
356 p. illus. S3567

Callahan, Kenneth
Kenneth Callahan: universal voyage. Edited by Michael R. Johnson. Seattle, Published for the Henry Art Gallery by University of Washington Press, 1973.
79 p. illus. S3568

Cammon, Betsey Johnson
Island memoir: a personal history of Anderson and McNeil Islands. Puyallup, The Valley Press, 1969.
221 p. illus. S3569

Camp, Oscar A. and Paul C. McGrew
History of Washington's soil and water conservation districts. n.p., March, 1969.
103 p. illus. S3570

Campbell, Ernest Howard
Washington voters' handbook. By Ernest H. Campbell and George D. Smith. Seattle, University of Washington Press, 1950.
71 p. illus. S3571

Canaday, Lewis
Cloud country: crossing America's last frontier. By Lewis Canaday and Jan S. Doward. Mountain View, Ca., Pacific Press Pub. Association, 1953.
151 p. illus. S3572

Cannon, Bart
Minerals of Washington. Mercer Island, Cordilleran, 1975.
184 p. illus. S3573

Carey, Roland Nelson
The sound and the mountain. Seattle, Alderbrook Publishing Co., 1970.
123 p. illus. ports. S3574

Carey, Roland Nelson
The sound of steamers. Seattle, Alderbrook Publishing Co., 1965.
109 p. illus. S3575

Carey, Roland Nelson
The steamboat landing on Elliott Bay. Seattle, Alderbrook Publishing Co., 1962.
73 p. illus. S3576

Carson, Joan
Tall timber and the tide. Poulsbo, Kitsap Weeklies, 1971.
113 p. illus. S3577

Cartwright, Calhoun.
Barns of Puget Sound country as seen through the sketches of William Nelson and Al Logdahl. Port Townsend, Cartwright's Oldtime Print Shop, 1975.
49 p. illus. S3478

Carver, Mrs. Fred E., ed.
Records of Yakima County, Washington: 1869-1907 and Benton County Washington: 1905-1907. Yakima, Yakima Valley Genealogical Society, 1975.
4 vols. S3579

Caryl, Delmar H
With angels to the rear: an informal portrait of early Meadowdale. Edmonds, Wash., The Dilemma Press, 1960.
159 p. illus. S3580

Central Electric Railfans' Association.
The electric railroads of Washington state. Chicago, 1951.
90 p. illus. S3581

The Centralia case: three views of the Armistice Day tragedy at Centralia, Washington, November 11, 1919: the Centralia conspiracy, by Ralph Chaplin; Centralia: tragedy and trial, by Ben Hur Lampman; and The Centralia case, a joint report. New York, Da Capo, 1971.
143, 79, 48 p. illus. S3582

Chalfant, Stuart A. and others.
Ethnohistorical reports on aboriginal land use and occupancy: Spokan Indians, Palus Indians, Columbia Salish, Wenatchi Salish ... New York, Garland, 1974.
718 p. maps. S3583

Chalfant, Stuart A. and William N. Bischoff
Historical material relative to Coeur d'Alene Indian ... New York, Garland, 1974.
328 p. maps. S3584

Chambers, Andrew Jackson and Margaret White Chambers
Recollections, by Andrew Jackson Chambers: Reminiscences by Margaret White Chambers. Fairfield, Ye Galleon Press, 1975. (Recollections was first published in limited edition in 1947; Reminiscences was first published in 1903.)
59 p. illus. S3585

Chance, David H
Influences of the Hudson's Bay Company on the native cultures of the Colvile district. Moscow, University of Idaho Dept, of Sociology/Anthropology, 1973.
166 p. map. bibl. S3586

Charles and Emma Frye Free Public Art Museum, Seattle.
An introduction to the Charles and Emma Frye collection, important current in nineteenth century art. Seattle, 1952.
118 p. illus. S3587

Chase, Cora G
Unto the least: a biographic sketch of Mother Ryther, founder of Seattle's own Ryther Child Center. Seattle, Shorey Book Store, 1972.
75 p. illus. ports. S3588

Chin, Doug and Art Chin
Up hill: the settlement and diffusion of the Chinese in Seattle, Washington. Seattle, Shorey Book Store, 1973.
70 p. illus. S3589

Chittenden, Hiram M
H.M. Chittenden, a western epic. Being a selection from his unpublished journals and reports. Edited by Bruce LeRoy. Tacoma, Washington State Historical Society, 1961.
136 p. illus. S3590

Clancy, Frank J
Doctor come quickly. Seattle, Superior Publishing Co., 1950.
248 p. S3591

Clark, Donald Hathaway
18 men and a horse. Seattle, Metropolitan Press, 1949.
217 p. illus. S3592

Clark, Norman H
The dry years: prohibition and social change in Washington. Seattle, University of Washington Press, 1965.
304 p. illus. S3593

Clark, Norman H
Mill town: a social history of Everett, Washington, from its earliest beginnings on the shores of Puget Sound to the tragic and infamous events known as the Everett massacre. Seattle, University of Washington Press, 1970.
267 p. illus. S3594

Clarridge, David and June Clarridge
A ton of gold: the Seattle gold rush 1897-98. Seattle, The author, 1972.
24 p. illus. S3595

Clayson, Edward
Historical narratives of Puget Sound, Hood's Canal, 1865-1885. Fairfield, Ye Galleon Press, 1969. (Reprint of 1911 ed.)
104 p. illus. S3596

Cleland, Lucile Horr, comp.
Trials and trails of the pioneers of the Olympia Peninsula. Hoquiam, Wash., Humptulips Pioneer Association, 1959.
312 p. S3597

Clevinger, Woodrow R
Cascade mountain clan: the Clevingers and Stilners and related families. Seattle, Seattle University Bookstore, 1971.
42 p. illus. S3598

Cloud, Ray Verner
Edmonds, the gem of Puget Sound: a history of the city of Edmonds. Edmonds, Wash., Edmonds Tribune-Review Press, 1953.
227 p. illus. S3599

Collins, June McCormack
Valley of the spirits: the upper Skagit Indians of western Washington. Seattle, University of Washington Press, 1974.
267 p. illus. S3600

Colson, Elizabeth
The Makah Indians, a study of an Indian tribe in modern American society. Minneapolis, University of Minnesota, 1953.
308 p. maps. S3601

Coman, Edwin Truman
Time, tide and timber: a century of Pope & Talbot. By Edwin T. Coman, Jr. and Helen M. Gibbs. Stanford, Stanford University Press, 1949.
480 p. illus. S3602

Conant, Roger
Mercer's belles: the journal of a reporter. Edited by Lenna A. Deutsch. Seattle, University of Washington Press, 1960.
xiii, 190 p. illus. S3603

Cook, Beatrice Gray
More fish to fry. New York, Morrow, 1951.
280 p. illus. S3604

Cook, Beatrice Gray
Till fish do us part: the confessions of a fisherman's wife. New York, Morrow, 1949.
249 p. S3605

Cook, Francis H., 1851-1920
The territory of Washington. Fairfield, Wash., Ye Galleon Press, 1972.
38 p. port. S3606

Cook, Fred S., ed.
Washington state travel book. Co-edited by Fred S. Cook and Barlow Hardy. Yakima, Wash., Franklin Press, c1962.
299 p. illus. S3607

Cooley, Leland Frederick.
God's high table: a contemporary adventure romance of the Pacific Northwest. New York, Doubleday, 1962.
552 p. S3608

Corliss, Margaret McKibben
Fall City in the Valley of the Moon. Fall City, The author, 1972.
214 p. illus. maps. plans. S3609

Cornish, Nellie C
Miss Aunt Nellie: the autobiography of Nellie C. Cornish. Seattle, University fo Washington Press, 1964.
260 p. illus. S3610

Countryman, Vern
Un-American activities in the state of Washington: the work of the Canwell Committee. Ithaca, Cornell University Press, 1951.
403 p. S3611

Crain, Jim and Terry Milne
Camping around Washington. New York, Random House, 1974.
94 p. illus. S3613

Craine, Bessie Wilson
Squak Valley (Issaquah). Seattle, King County Library System, 1963.
51 p. port. S3614

Cranston, Paul
To heaven on horseback: the romantic story of Narcissa Whitman. New York, Messner, 1952.
255 p. S3615

Crawford, Jeanne R., comp.
As the valley was. Yakima, Yakima Federal Savings and Loan, 1968.
1 vol. S3616

Crawford, Jeanne R., comp.
Wheels led the way: horse-drawn vehicles, plain and fancy, 1820-1920. Yakima Valley Museum, 1973.
87 p. illus. S3617

Crithfield, June
Of yesterday and the river. Colton, Wash., The author, 1964.
110 p. illus. S3618

Crowder, Dwight F. and Rowland W. Tabor
Routes and rocks: hiker's guide to the north Cascades... Seattle, The Mountaineers, 1965.
235 p. illus. S3619

Cunningham, Imogen
Imogen! Imogen Cunningham photographs, 1910-1973. Seattle, University of Washington Press, 1974.
110 p. illus. S3620

Cutter, James W
Puget Sound and Northwest waterways: boating, fishing, hunting. Menlo Park, Ca., Lane Publishing, 1953.
48 p. maps. S3621

Dalquest, Walter W
Mammals of Washington. Lawrence, University of Kansas, 1948.
444 p. illus. S3622

Danner, Wilbert Roosevelt
Geology of Olympic National Park. Seattle, University of Washington Press, 1955.
68 p. illus. S3623

Darvill, Fred T
North Cascades National Park and associated areas. Mount Vernon, 1972.
2 vols. illus. S3624

Darvill, Fred T., Jr. and Louise B. Marshall
Winter walks: a pocket guide to lowland trails in Whatcom, Skagit, San Juan and Island Counties. Lynnwood, Signpost Publications, 1970.
68 p. illus. S3625

Daugherty, James Henry
Marcus and Narcissa Whitman, pioneers of Oregon. Story and pictures by James Daugherty. New York, Viking Press, 1953. S3626

Davis, Norman
Fine arts exhibition. Seattle World's Fair, April 21-October 21, 1962. Seattle, Seattle World's Fair, 1962.
various paging. illus. S3627

Davis, William J
A pictorial sketch of the Puget Sound area and its builders. Seattle, Davis Publishing Co., 1960.
120 p. illus. S3628

Deegan, Harry W
History of Mason County, Washington. Rev. ed. Shelton, The author, 1971.
140 p. illus. S3629

Demoro, Harre W
The evergreen fleet: a pictorial history of Washington state ferries. San Marino, Ca., Golden West Books, 1971.
136 p. illus. S3630

Demoro, Harre W
Seattle trolley coaches. South Gate, Ca., Interurban Magazine, 1971.
124 p. illus. S3631

Dennis, Mae E., ed.
Pioneers of the Columbia. Colville, Washington, Greenwood Park Grange, 1965.
110 p. illus. S3632

Denny, Arthur Armstrong
Pioneer days on Puget Soung. With an introduction by William Katz. Fairfield, Wash., Ye Galleon Press, 1965. (Reprint of 1888 ed.).
83 p. S3633

Densmore, Frances
Nootka and Quileute music. New York, De Capo Press, 1972. (Reprint of 1939 ed.).
358 p. illus. S3634

Desmarteau, David M
The Washington wine industry. Olympia, Dept. of Commerce and Economic Development, 1970. S3635

Desmond, Gerald Raymond
Gambling among the Yakima. Washington, Catholic University of America Press, 1952.
58 p. map. S3636

Dill, Clarence Cleveland
Where water falls. Spokane, C.W. Hill, Printer, 1970.
275 p. illus. S3637

Dionne, Emil
Reminiscing. Spokane, The Evergreen Press, 1952.
64 p. illus. S3638

Dodds, Gordon Barlow
Hiram Martin Chittenden, His public career. Lexington, Ky., University Press of Kentucky, 1973.
220 p. illus. S3639

Douglas, William Orville
Go east, young man: the early years: the autobiography of William O. Douglas. New York, Random House, 1974.
492 p. illus. S3640

Douglas, William Orville,
Washington and manifest destiny: address at the opening of the Library of Congress exhibition commemorating the centennial of the Territory of Washington, May 14, 1953. Washington, Library of Congress, 1953.
35 p. S3641

Draper, Melanie Elsner
Timber, tides and tales, a history of the Des Moines area. The author, 1975.
157 p. illus. ports. S3644

Drury, Dlifford Merrill, 1897-
A tepee in his front yard: a biography of H.T. Cowley, one of the four founders of the city of Spokane, Washington. Portland, Or., Binfords & Mort, 1949.
ix, 206 p. ports. S3645

Dryden, Cecil Pearl, 1887-
Dryden's history of Washington. Portland, Or., Binfords & Mort, 1968.
412 p. illus. S3646

Dryden, Cecil
Light for an empire: the story of Eastern Washington State College. Cheney, Eastern Washington State College, 1965.
369 p. illus. S3647

Durham, George William
Indian canoes of the Northwest coast. Seattle, Copper Canoe Press, 1960.
82 p. illus. S3648

Durham, Nelson Wayne
Lake Chelan in the 1890's: 1891 steamboat trip to Stehekin on Lake Chelan's first steamer. Stehekin, Robert Byrd, 1972.
30 p. illus. S3649

Dwelley, Joseph Franklin
The story of a Skagit pioneer: 1839, Boston-1939, LaConner: the autobiography of Joseph Franklin Dwelley. LaConner, 1974.
31 l. illus. S3650

Dyar, Ralph E
News for an empire: the story of the Spokesman-Review of Spokane, Washington, and the field it serves. Caldwell, Idaho, Caxton Printers, 1952.
404 p. illus. S3651

Early Washington. Corvallis, Or., Western Guide Publishers, 1973.
unpaged. S3652

Easterbrook, Don J. and David A. Rahm.
Landforms of Washington: the geologic environment. Bellingham, Western Washington State College, 1970.
156 p. illus. S3653

Edson, Lelah Jackson
The fourth corner: highlights from the early Northwest. Bellingham, 1951.
208 p. illus. S3654

Edson, Lelah Jackson
The fourth corner: highlights from the early Northwest, with an introduction by Alfred B. Loop. Bellingham, Whatcom Museum of History and Art, 1969.
298 p. illus. S3655

Eells, Myron
Ten years of missionary work among the Indians at Skokomish, Washington Territory, 1874-1884. Seattle, Shorey Book Store, 1972. (Facsimile reprint of 1886 ed.).
271 p. illus. ports. S3656

Eklund, Donald D.
Washington's "wild Scotsman": the early aeronautical adventures of L. Guy Mecklem, 1897-1910. Bellingham, Western Washington State College Center for Pacific Northwest Studies, 1974.
57 p. illus. S3658

Elmendorf, William Welcome and June McCormack Collins.
Structure of Twana culture: a study of religious change among the Skagit Indians of Washington. New York, Garland, 1974. (Reprint of the 1960 ed.).
763 p. S3659

Elmore, Helen Troy
This isle of Guemes. Caldwell, Idaho, Caxton Printers, 1973.
139 p. S3660

Ely, Arline
Our foundering fathers: the story of Kirkland. Kirkland, Kirkland Public Library, 1975.
128 p. illus. S3661

Emmons, Della Gould
Leschi of the Nisqualies. Minneapolis, T.S. Denison, 1965.
416 p. map. S3662

Emmons, Della Gould
Nothing in life is free: through Naches Pass to Puget Sound. Minneapolis, Northwestern Press, 1953.
315 p. S3663

Engstrom, Emil
The vanishing logger. New York, Vantage Press, 1956.
135 p. S3664

Essex, Alice
Stanwood story. Stanwood, Stanwood News, 1971-75.
2 vols. illus. S3665

Evans, Brock
The alpine lakes. Seattle, University of Washington Press, 1971.
128 p. illus. S3666

Evans, Lynette and George Burley
Roche Harbor: a saga of the San Juans. Everett, B & E Enterprises, 1972.
95 p. illus. S3667

Eyler, Melba and Eleanor Yeager
The many roads to Highline. Seattle, The author, 1972.
92 p. illus. S3668

Faber, Jim
An irreverent guide to Washington state. Garden City, N.Y., Doubleday, 1974.
175 p. S3669

Fahey, John
Inland empire: D.C. Corbin and Spokane Seattle, University of Washington Press, 1965.
270 p. illus. S3671

Fargo, Lucile Foster
Spokane story. New York. Columbia University Press, 1950.
276 p. illus. S3672

Fargo, Lucile F
Spokane story. Minneapolis, The Northwest Press, 1957, c1950
xi, 276 p. illus. S3673

Fashion Groups, Inc.
The heritage of Seattle hotels. Seattle, 1970.
24 p. illus S3674

Feagans, Raymond J
The railroad that ran by the tide: Ilwaco Railroad and Navigation Co., of the state of Washington. Berkeley, Ca., Howell-North Books, 1972.
146 p. illus. S3675

Field, Virgil
The Camp Murray story, the command post. Camp Murray, Tacoma, Washington (State) Adjutant General's Office, 1959.
65 p. illus. S3676

Fish, Byron
Adventuring on Puget Sound. Photos by Bob and Ira Spring. Seattle, Superior Publishing Co., 1955.
70 p. photos. S3677

Fish, Byron
Adventuring on the Columbia. Photos by Bob and Ira Spring. Seattle, Superior Publishing Co., 1957.
72 p. illus. S3678

Fish, Byron
Guidebook to Puget Sound, the water world that the Indians called Whulge. Los Angeles, W. Ritchie Press, 1973.
126 p. illus. S3679

Fish, Byron
Washington. Seattle, Superior Publishing Co., 1969.
157 p. illus. S3681

Fish, Edward R
The past at present in Issaquah, Washington. Kingsport, Tenn.,Kingsport Press, 1967.
186 p. illus. S3682

Flaherty, David G
The Yakima Basin and its water. Pullman, State of Washington Water Research Center, 1975.
29 p. illus. S3683

Fleming, Douglas K
Views of Washington State. Charles E. Ogrosky, cartographic editor. Seattle? Association of American Geographers, 1974.
122 p. maps. S3684

Flowers, Ralph
The education of a bear hunter. New York, Winchester Press, 1975
277 p. illus. S3686

Fort Vancouver Historical Society.
Clark County history. Vancouver, Wash., The Society, 1960-1971.
12 parts. S3687

Frare, Aleua L
Magnolia yesterday and today. Seattle, Magnolia Community Club, 1975.
126 p. illus. S3688

Frear, Gordon S., ed.
100 years of progress: Seattle, America's evergreen playground. Seattle, Wood & Reber, 1952.
1 vol. unpaged. illus. S3689

Freeman, Otis Willard and Rolland Upton
Washington state resources. 2nd ed. Seattle, Washington State Resources Commission, 1957.
210 p. S3690

Friedheim, Robert L
The Seattle general strike. Seattle, University of Washington Press, 1964.
224 p. illus. S3691

Fries, Mary A
Wildflowers of Mount Rainier and the Cascades. Seattle, The Mountaineers, 1970.(Photos by Bob and Ira Spring).
208 p. illus. S3692

Fries, Ulrich Englehart
From Copenhagen to Okanogan: the autogiography of a pioneer. Portland, Binfords & Mort, 1972. (Essentially a reprint of 1949 ed.).
437 p. illus. S3693

Fronek, Minnie Turner
Pioneering in the Palouse and LaCrosse country. LaCrosse, 1951.
46 l. illus. port. S3694

Fuller, Alice Marie
Memoirs of Mrs. Andrew B. Fuller. Seattle, The author, 1970.
61 p. illus. S3695

Furrer, Werner
Kayak and canoe trips in Washington. Lynnwood, Signpost Publications, 1971.
32 p. maps. illus. S3696

Furrer, Werner
Water trails of Washington. Lynnwood, Signpost, 1973.
31 p. illus. S3697

Gaffney, Joseph W
A history of Sprague, 1880-1962. Spokane, 1962.
96 p. illus. S3698

Gaines, Xerpha M. and D.G. Swan
Weeds of eastern Washington and adjacent areas. Davenport, Camp-Na-Bor-Lee Association, 1972.
349 p. illus. S3699

Ganders, Harry S
Pioneering Ganders: a genealogy of John and Leah Ganders on the Bickleton frontier of the territory and State of Washington, 1884-1974. Syracuse, N.Y., 1974.
126 p. illus. ports. S3700

Gates, Charles M
The first century at the University of Washington, 1861-1961. Seattle, University of Washington Press, 1961.
252 p. illus. S3701

Gauld, Charles Anderson
America's first General overseas: the story of Thomas M. Anderson. Vancouver, Fort Vancouver Historical Society, 1973
24 p. illus. S3702

Gay, Elliott
Yesterday and the day before. Colfax, The author, 1975.
illus. S3703

Gee, Nancie, 1940-
Reflections in Pike Place markets. Seattle, Superior Publishing Co., 1968.
128 p. (chiefly illus.) S3704

Gellatly, John A
A history of Wenatchee, the apple capital of the world. Wenatchee, Wash., The author, 1962.
392 p. illus. S3705

Gibbs, George
Alphabetical vocabularies of the Clallam and Lummi. New York, AMS Press, 1971. (Reprint of 1863 ed.)
40 p. S3706

Gibbs, George
A dictionary of the Niskwalli (Nisqually) Indian language--western Washington. Seattle, The Shorey Book Store, 1970. (Facsimile reprint of 1877 ed.)
76 p. S3707

Giboney, Ezra P
The life of Mark A. Matthews, "tall pine of the Sierras." Grand Rapids, W.B. Eerdmans, 1948.
134 p. illus. S3708

Gilbert, Kenneth
Challenge of the wild. Seattle, Superior Publishing Co., 1949.
240 p. S3709

Glauert, Earl T. and Merle H. Kunz, eds.
The Kittitas Indians. Ellensburg, Ellensburg Public Library, 1972.
105 p. illus. S3710

Goff, Willard F
Seattle's pioneer hospitals. Seattle, The author, 1970. S3711

Granger Library Club
Granger: the town...the land... the people. Compiled from many sources by the Granger Library Club. Granger, 1975.
153 p. illus. S3712

Grant County (Washington) Public Utility District.
Back through the pages of history. Ephrata, Public Utility District of Grant County, 1967.
35 p. illus. S3713

Grater, Russell K
Guide to Mt. Rainier National Park. Portland, Binfords & Mort, 1959.
S3714

Gray, Alfred O
Not by might: the story of Whitworth College, 1890-1965. Spokane, Whitworth College, 1965.
279 p. illus. S3715

Gray, Henry Lilburn
The famous ride of Queen Marie. Seattle, The author, 1967.
13 p. illus. S3716

Gray, Henry Lilburn
Historic railroads of Washington. Seattle, The author, 1971.
26 p. illus. S3717

Gray, Henry Lilburn
The metropolitan tract story. Seattle, 1964.
321 p. map. S3718

Green, Roger H
South Slav settlement in western Washington: perception and choice. San Francisco, E & R Research Associates, 1974.
ix, 111 p. illus. S3718

Guberlet, Muriel Lewin
The windows to his world: the story of Trevor Kincaid. Palo Alto, Ca., Pacific Books, 1975.
287 p. illus. S3720

Guie, Heister Dean
Bugles in the valley: Garnett's Fort Simcoe. Yakima, 1956.
144 p. illus.
Also: Rev. ed., Portland, Oregon Hist. Society, 1977. 196 p. S3721

Gustafson, Egill Oscar and Mike Bathum.
The Pike Place market. Puyallup, the Valley Press, 1971.
unpaged illus. S3722

Gutohrlein, Adolf
Rayonier, Inc.: railroading in the Northwest pines. Los Angeles, Trans-Anglo Books, 1964.
32 p. illus. S3723

Haines, Aubrey Leon
Mountain fever: historic conquests of Rainier. Portland, Oregon Historical Society, 1962.
255 p. illus. S3724

Halliday, William R. and Charles H. Anderson.
The Paradise ice caves of Mt. Rainier National Park. Seattle, Cascade Grotto of the National Speleological Society, 1972.
maps. S3725

Hanify, Mary Lou and Craig Blencowe.
Guidebook to the Hoh rain forest: an interpretive handbook. Port Angeles, Pen-Print, 1974.
32 p. illus. S3726

Hanify, Mary Lou
The light in the mansion: a collection of stories about first ladies of the state of Washington and their families. Port Angeles, The author, 1971.
60 p. illus. S3727

Hansen, Kent M
Fishing King County mountain lakes. Lynnwood, Signpost Publications, 1971. (Reprint of 1962 ed.)
48 p. illus. S3728

Hansen, Kent M
Fishing Kittias County mountain lakes. Lynnwood, Signpost Publications, 1971. (Reprint of 1962 ed.)
36 p. illus. S3729

Hansen, Kent M
Fishing Snohomish County mountain lakes. Lynnwood, Signpost Publications, 1971. (Reprint of 1962 ed.)
48 p. illus. S3730

Hardy, Martha
Skyo. Seattle, Superior Publishing Co., 1949.
256 p. illus. S3732

Harris, Mary Powell
Goodbye White Bluffs. Yakima, The Franklin Press, 1972.
155 p. illus. S3733

Harvey, Paul W
Tacoma headlines: an account of Tacoma news and newspapers from 1873 to 1962. Tacoma, Wash., Tacoma News Tribune, 1962.
134 p. illus. ports. S3734

Haskett, Patrick J
The Wilkes expedition in the Puget Sound, 1841. Olympia, 1974.
60 p. illus. S3735

Hatch, Melville Harrison
Studies honoring Trevor Kincaid. Seattle, University of Washington Press, 1950.
167 p. illus. S3736

Haw, Frank
Saltwater fishing in Washington. Seattle, Stanley N. Jones, 1971.
192 p. illus. S3737

Hawley, Lowell Stillwell
Council for the damned: a biography of George Francis Vanderveer. By Lowell S. Hawley and Ralph Bushnell Potts. Philadelphia, Lippincott, 1953.
320 p. S3738

Hawley, Robert Emmett
Sqee Mus, or pioneer days on the Nooksack ... Being a series of personal memoirs. Bellingham, Whatcom Museum of History and Art, 1971. (Reprint of 1945 ed.).
189 p. illus. S3739

Hays, Finley
Crown Zellerback loggers. Chehalis, Loggers World, Inc., 1970.
143 p. illus. S3740

Hazard, Joseph Taylor, 1879-
Companion of adventure: a biography of Isaac Ingalls Stevens, first governor of Washington Territory. Portland, Binfords & Mort, 1952.
238 p. illus. S3741

Hazard, Joseph Taylor
Pioneer teachers of Washington. Seattle, Retired Teachers Association, 1955.
144 p. illus. S3742

Hazeltine, Jean
The historical and regional geography of Willapa Bay area, Washington. South Bend, South Bend Journal, 1956.
308 p. illus. S3743

Hebner, Ethel Provan
Avondale. Spokane, Koetch & Associates, 1971, c1966.
68 p. illus. S3744

Heckman, Hazel
Island in the Sound. Drawings by Helen Hiatt. Seattle, University of Washington Press, 1967.
284 p. illus. S3745

Heckman, Hazel
Island year. Seattle, University of Washington Press, 1972.
255 p. illus. S3746

Hewitt, John and others.
How to live in Tacoma, Washington, and love it: the Tacoma guide. Tacoma, Ho-Ho Press, 1975.
160 p. S3748

Higman, Harry Wentworth
Pilchuck, the life of a mountain. By Harry W. Higman and Earl J. Larrison. Seattle, Superior Publishing Co., 1949.
288 p. illus. S3749

Higman, Harry Wentworth
Union Bay, the life of a city marsh. By Harry W. Higman and Earl J. Larrison. Seattle, University of Washington Press, 1951.
315 p. illus. S3750

Hillstrom, Edith
Manchester memories (1871-1971). Port Orchard, Wyatt's Colonial Printery, 1971.
113 p. illus. S3751

Hitchman, James H.
The port of Bellingham, 1930-1970. Rev. Bellingham, Western Washington State College Center for Pacific Northwest Studies, 1974.
126 p. maps. S3752

Hitchman, James H
Yacht racing on Bellingham Bay, 1877-1973. Bellingham, Western Washington State College, 1974.
87 l. S3753

Holm, Bill
Northwest coast Indian art: an analysis of form. Seattle, University of Washington Press, 1965.
115 p. illus. S3754

Holman, Eloise
The Washington beachcomber. Seattle, The Washington Beachcomber, 1974.
1 vol. S3755

Hoonan, Charles E
Neah Bay, Washington: a brief historical sketch. Crown Zellerbach Corporation, 1964.
29 p. illus. S3756

Hope, Nelson W
Atomic town. New York, Comet Press Books, 1954.
125 p. illus. S3757

Howard, Grace Elizabeth
Lichens of the state of Washington. Seattle, University of Washington Press, 1950.
191 p. illus. S3758

Hughes, Glenn Arthur
The dream and the deed: a stage cavalcade of Seattle's hundred years. The official play of the Seattle centennial. Seattle, School of Drama, University of Washington, 1952.
59 p. S3759

Hult, Ruby El
The untamed Olympics: the story of a peninsula. 2nd ed. Portland, Or., Binfords & Mort, 1971.
267 p. illus. S3760

Hussey, John Adam
Chinook point, and the story of Fort Columbia. Olympia, Wash., State Parks and Recreation Commission, 1957.
30 p. S3761

Hussey, John Adam
The history of Fort Vancouver and its physical structure. Tacoma, Washington State Historical Society, 1957.
xx, 256 p. illus. S3762

Hussey, John Adam
A short history of Fort Casey, Washington. San Francisco, Region Four, National Park Service, 1955.
49 l. S3763

Hynding, Alan
The public life of Eugene Semple, promoter and politician of the Pacific Northwest. Seattle, University of Washington Press, 1973.
195 p. illus. ports. S3764

Ingersoll, Rex E
Seattle ... at this moment. Seattle, Wash., 1962.
unpaged. illus. S3765

Irving, Wells P., ed
Bars on the sound: the history of McNeil Island. McNeil Island, Wash., U.S. Penetentiary, 1964.
84 p. illus. S3766

Jackson, Bob and Kay Jackson
The rockhound's guide to Washington. Renton, Jax Products, 1975.
45 p. illus. S3767

Jackson, Gary L
Remembering Yakima by those who were there. Yakima, Golden West Publishing Co., 1975.
128 p. illus. S3768

Jeffcott, Percival Robert
Blanket Bill Jarman: Northwest Washington mystery man. Ferndale, P.R. Jeffcott, 1958.
xii, 202 p. S3769

Jeffcott, Percival Robert
Chechaco and sourdough: being an account of hectic pursuit of gold in the Mt. Baker mining district of Whatcom County, Washington, 1858-1960. Bellingham, Pioneer Printing Co., 1963.
181 p. illus. S3770

Jeffcott, Percival Robert
Nooksack tales and trails, being a collection of stories and historical events ... Whatcom County, Washington ... between 1848 and 1895. Ferndale, Wash., Sedro-Woolley Courier-Times, 1949.
436 p. illus. S3771

Jefferson County Historical Society.
With pride in heritage: history of Jefferson County. Port Townsend, Wash., Jefferson County Historical Society, 1966.
422 p. illus. S3772

Jensen, Hazel Addie
Across the years: pioneer story of southern Washington. n.p., 1951.
124 p. illus. S3773

Jessett, Thomas E
Pioneering God's country: the history of the diocese of Olympia: 1853-1967. 2nd ed. Seattle, The Diocese of the Olympia Press, 1967.
55 p. S3775

Jewett, Stanley Gordon
Birds of Washington state. By Stanley G. Jewett, Walter P. Taylor, William T. Shaw, and John W. Aldrich. Seattle, University of Washington Press, 1953.
767 p. illus. S3776

Jewitt, John R
Narrative of the adventures and sufferings of John R. Jewitt, only survivor of the crew of the ship Boston, during a captivity of nearly three years among the savages of Nootka Sound. Fairfield, Ye Galleon Press, 1967. (Facsimile reproduction of 1815 ed.)
161 p. illus. S3777

Jimmy come lately, history of Clallam County. A symposium. Edited by Jervis Russell. Port Angeles, Wash., Clallam County Historical Society, 1971.
xxvi, 631 p. illus. S3778

Johns, Helen
Twenty-five years of the Washington Library Association. Palo Alto, Ca., Pacific Books, 1956.
176 p. S3779

Johnson, Randall A
May 17, 1958: the ordeal of the Steptoe Command. Spokane, the author, 1972.
33 p. illus. S3780

Johnston, Gene
Seattlewash. Edmonds, Seattlewash Press, 1973.
43 p. illus. S3781

Jones, Alden H
From Jamestown to Coffin Rock: a history of Weyerhaeuser operations in southwest Washington. Tacoma, Weyerhaeuser Co., 1974.
346 p. illus. S3782

Jones, Nard
Northwest narratives: stories of Washington history. Seattle, 1959. S3783

Jones, Nard
Seattle. N.Y., Doubleday, 1972.
371 p. illus. S3784

Jones, Roy Franklin
Boundary town: early days in a northwest boundary town. Vancouver, Wash., Fleet Printing Co., 1958.
viii, 306 p. illus. S3785

Jones, Stan
Washington state fishing guide. 2nd ed. Edmonds, Alaska Northwest Publishing Co., 1968. S3787

Jones, Sylvia Case
From cabin to cupola: an illustrated story of the county courthouse and the counties of Washington. Seattle, Shorey Book Store, 1971.
135 p. illus. S3788

Jordan, Josee
You're at liberty here--mines and miners of the Swauk. Yakima, Wash., Franklin Press, 1967.
103 p. illus. S3789

Jordan, Ray
Yarns of the Skagit country: Ray's writin's. La Conner, Wash., Sedro Woolley, 1974.
406 p. illus. S3790

Kalez, Jay J
Saga of a western town ... Spokane: a collection of factual incidents and anecdotes relating to the pioneer past ... Washington, Spokane, Lawton Printing Inc., 1972.
136 p. illus. S3793

Kalez, Jay J
This town of ours ... Spokane: a chronological anthology of Spokane's historical past from Indian trading post to trading center of an inland empire, 1804-1974. Spokane, Lawton Printing Co., 1973.
136 p. illus. S3794

Karolevitz, Robert P
Everything's green ... but my thumb! Aberdeen, S.D., North Plains Press, 1971.
118 p. illus. S3795

Kendrick, R.H.
Washington state composers. Seattle, Washington State Federation of Music Clubs, 1963.
34 p. S3796

Kimmel, Thelma
The Fort Simcoe story. Toppenish, Wash., Toppenish Review, 1954.
24 p. S3797

Kimmel Thelma
The red house. Goldendale, Goldendale Sentinel, 1972.
16 p. illus. S3798

Kincaid, Garret D. and A.H. Harris
Palouse in the making. Palouse, Wash., 1967.
28, 56 p. illus. S3799

Kincaid, Tom and Wendelborg 'Ole' Hansen.
Cruising Nor'west waters with Norwesting. Edmonds, Nor'westing Inc., 1969.
54 p. illus. S3800

Kincaid, Trevor
The oyster industry of Willapa Bay, Washington. Ilwaco, Wash., Tribune, 1951.
45 p. illus. S3801

Kingston, C.S., ed.
Grass root cuttings, sources of the history of the Territory of Washington. Longview, Wash., Longview Daily News, 1954.
27 p. S3802

Kip, Lawrence
Indian council at Walla Walla, Washington Territory. Fairfield, Ye Galleon Press, 1970. (Reprint of 1897 ed.). S3803

Kirk, Ruth
Exploring Mount Rainier. Seattle, University of Washington, 1968.
104 p. S3804

Kirk, Ruth
Exploring the Olympic Peninsula. Seattle, University of Washington Press, 1964.
188 p. illus. S3805

Kirk, Ruth
The Olympic rain forest. Seattle, University of Washington Press, 1966.
86 p. illus. S3806

Kirk, Ruth
Olympic seashore. Port Angeles, Olympic Natural History Assoc., 1962.
80 p. illus. S3807

Kirk, Ruth
Washington state national parks, historical sites, recreation areas and natural landmarks. Seattle, University of Washington Press, 1974.
63 p. illus. S3808

Kitchin, Edward Alexander
Birds of the Olympic peninsula... Port Angeles, Olympic Stationers, 1949.
262 p. illus. S3809

Kloke, Dallas M
Boulder and cliffs: climbers' guide to lowland rocks in Skagit and Whatcom County. Lynnwood, Signpost Publications, 1971.
illus. maps. S3810

Kolde, Endel Jakob
Energy base of the Pacific Northwest economy: a regional analysis... Seattle, University of Washington 1954.
282 p. maps. S3811

Kondo, Kara, ed.
Profile, Yakima Valley Japanese community, 1973. Yakima, 1974.
42 p. illus. S3812

Kozloff, Eugene N
Keys to the marine invertebrates of Puget Sound, the San Juan Archipelago and adjacent regions. Seattle, University of Washington Press, 1974.
226 p. S3813

Kozloff, Eugene N
Seashore life of Puget Sound, the Strait of Georgia and the San Juan Archipelago. Seattle, University of Washington Press, 1973.
282 p. illus. S3814

Krenmayr, Janice
Footloose around Puget Sound: 100 walks on beaches, lowlands and foothills. Seattle, The Mountaineers, 1969.
222 p. illus. S3814A

Krenmayr, Janice
Footloose in Seattle. Seattle, A-1 Litho Type, 1963-66.
2 vols. illus. S3815

Kuykendall, Elgin V
Historic glimpses of Asotin County, Washington: with supplement of myths, legends and curious beliefs of Indians of the Northwest... Clarkston, Wash., Clarkston Herald, 1954.
70 p. S3817

Laidlaw, Ellis and Elvira Ellen Laidlaw.
Wait's Mill: the story of the community of Waitsburg, Washington. Chicago, Adams Press, 1970.
214 p. illus. S3819

Lambert, Patricia
A guide to water research information sources in the state of Washington. Pullman, Washington State University Water Research Center, 1973.
238 p. S3820

Landerholm, Carl
Vancouver area chronology 1784-1958. Vancouver, Wash., Rasmussen's Book and Stationery Co., 1960.
unpaged. S3821

Larrison, Earl Junior
Field guide to birds of Puget Sound. Seattle, Seattle Audubon Society, 1952.
112 p. illus. S3822

Larrison, Earl Junior
A field guide to the birds of the Seattle area. Seattle, Seattle Audubon Society, 1952.
112 p. illus. S3823

Larrison, Earl Junior and Klaus Sonnenberg.
Washington birds: their location and identification. Seattle, Seattle Audubon Society, 1968.
258 p. S3824

Larrison, Earl Junior
Washington mammals: their habits, identification and distribution. Seattle, Seattle Audubon Society, 1970.
243 p. illus. S3825

Larrowe, Charles Patrick
Shape-up and hiring hall: a comparison of hiring methods and labor relations on the New York and Seattle waterfronts. Berkeley, University of California Press, 1955.
250 p. illus. S3826

Lartigue, Weston and Carrie Lartigue, comps.
Tombstone inscriptions, Lincoln County, Washington. Spokane, Eastern Washington Genealogical Society, 1974.
181 p. S3827

Latshaw, Ross
Roosevelt came West: reforms--past and future. Sequim, The author, 1971.
73 p. S3828

League of Women Voters of Chelan County.
Chelan County. Wenatchee, 1970.
38 p. illus. S3829

League of Women Voters of Lake Washington East.
East side: a description of the structure, powers and services of its governmental units. Bellevue, 1969?
104 p. illus. S3830

League of Women Voters of Seattle.
King County Government. Seattle, 1959.
42 p. S3831

League of Women Voters of Seattle.
Seattle city government. 3rd ed. Seattle, League of Women Voters, 1962.
25 p. charts. map S3832

League of Women Voters of Thurston County
A look at Olympia, Wash.. Sherwood Press, 1966.
42 p. illus. S3833

League of Women Voters of Yakima.
Profile: Yakima County government. Yakima, 1967. S3834

Leavel, Willard H.
Campaign, an old play with a new cast. Seattle, University of Washington, 1959.
17 p. S3835

Lee, W. Storrs, ed.
Washington: a literary chronicle. New York, Funk & Wagnalls, 1969. 514 p. illus. S3836

Leissler, Frederick
Roads and trails of Olympic National Park. Seattle, University of Washington Press, 1957. 84 p. S3837

Leissler, Frederick
Roads and trails of Olympic National Park; rev. ed. Seattle, University of Washington Press, 1965. 84 p. illus. S3838

Leissler, Frederick
Roads and trails of Olympic National Park. 2nd rev. ed. Seattle, University of Washington Press, 1971. 84 p. illus. S3839

Levy, Newman
The Nan Patterson case. N.Y., Simon & Schuster, 1959. 245 p. S3840

LeWarne, Charles Pierce
Utopias on Puget Sound, 1885-1915. Seattle, University of Washington Press, 1975. 325 p. illus. S3841

Lindquist, Emory Kempton
An immigrant's American odyssey: a biography of Ernest Skarstedt. Rock Island, Ill., Augustana Historical Society, 1974. 240 p. illus. S3842

Livingston, Vaughn E., Jr.
Geologic history and rocks and minerals of Washington. Olympia, Department of Natural Resources Division of Mines and Geology, 1969. 42 p. illus. S3843

Lofgren, Svante E
Barth Ar-Kell (the White Bear). Seattle, Publications Press, 1948. 208 p. ports. S3844

The long road to self-government: the history of Richland, Washington, 1943-1968. Richland, 1968. 1 vol. S3845

Loutzenhiser, Richard
The story of Yelm, the little town with the big history, 1848-1948. Yelm, 1951. 47 p. S3846

Lowry, Ed and Mary Lowry
Museum excursions in Washington state. Tacoma, Erco, 1973. 2 vols. illus. S3847

Ludwig, Charles H
A brief history of Waldron Island. Seattle, Wash., The author, 1959. 44 p. S3848

Lummi Tribe of the Lummi Reservation (Marietta).
Nooh-whLummi, a brief history of the Lummi. Marietta, 1974. 20 p. illus. S3849

Lyons, B.J.
Thrills and spills of a cowboy rancher. New York, Vantage Press, 1959. 172 p. S3850

Lyons, Chester Peter
Trees, shrubs and flowers to know in Washington. Toronto, Dent, 1957. 211 p. illus. S3851

McCaffrey, Frank, 1894-
Old days in Seattle. Seattle, The Seattle Club of Printing House Craftsmen, 1949. 63 p. illus. S3852

McCallum, John and Lorraine Wilcox Ross
Port Angeles, U.S.A. The panorama of American growth. Seattle, Wood and Reber, Inc., 1961
197 p. illus. S3853

McClelland, John Morris, Jr.
Cowlitz corridor. Longview, Longview Publishing Co., 1958.
64 p. illus. S3854

McClelland, John Morris, Jr.
Lewis and Clark in the Fort Columbia area. Ilwaco, Tribune Publishing Co., 1955.
26 p. maps. S3855

McClelland, John Morris, Jr.
Longview, the remarkable beginnings of a modern western city. Portland, Binfords & Mort, 1949.
158 p. illus. S3856

MacConnell, James David
Moses Lake: a new frontier. By James D. MacConnell and William R. Odell. Stanford, Stanford University, 1952.
85 p. illus. S3857

McCormick, John A
Cruise of the Calcite. Everett, B & E Enterprises, 1973.
63 p. illus. S3858

McCurdy, James G
The collected works of James G. McCurdy. Vancouver, B.C., Evergreen Press, 1972.
144 p. illus. S3859

McCurdy, James G
Indian days at Neah Bay. Edited by Gordon Newell. Superior Publishing Co., 1961.
123 p. illus. S3860

MacDonald Betty (Bard)
Who me? The autobiography of Betty MacDonald. Philadelphia, Lippincott, 1959.
352 p. S3861

MacDonald Dougald
Puget Sound regional ski guide: 1966-67 edition. Seattle, Bradley, Printing and Lithograph Co., 1966.
36 p. illus. S3862

McDonald, Lucile Saunders, 1898-
Coast country: a history of southwest Washington. Portland, Binfords & Mort, 1966.
184 p. illus. S3863

McDonald, Lucile Saunders and Werner Lenggenhager.
The look of old time Washington. Seattle, Superior Publishing Co., 1971.
159 p. illus. S3864

McDonald Lucile Saunders
Washington's yesterdays (before there was a Territory) 1775-1853. Pictures by Parker McAllister. Portland, Binfords & Mort, 1953.
191 p. illus. S3866

McDonald, Lucile Saunders
Where the Washingtonians lived: interesting early homes and the people who built and lived in them. Photos by Werner Lenggenhager. Seattle, Superior Publishing Co., 1969.
224 p. illus. S3867

McDowell, Esther.
Unitarians in the state of Washington, 1870-1960: a history of the churches and fellowships. Seattle, Frank McCaffrey, 1966.
319 p. illus. S3868

McGillivray, Donald E
Autobiographical anecdotes. Port Angeles, Wash., 1950.
112 p. S3869

McLaughlin, Inez
We grew up together. Seattle. L & H Printing Co., 1959.
62 p. illus. S3870

McVay, Alfred and Iris Meyers
Doctor Baker's railroad: the Walla Walla & Columbia River RR, completed October 23, 1875. Walla Walla, City-County Bicentennial Committee, 1975.
unpaged. illus. S3871

McVay, Alfred, ed.
The Walla Walla story: an illustrated anthology of the history and resources of the valley ... Walla Walla, Chamber of Commerce, 1953.
61 p. illus. S3872

McWilliams, Mary
Seattle Water Department history. 1854-1954: operational data and memoranda. Seattle, 1955.
262 p. illus. S3873

Majors, Harry M
Exploring Washington. Holland, Mich., Van Winkle, 1975.
176 p. illus. S3874

Manning, Harvey
The north Cascades National Park. Seattle, Superior Publishing Co., 1969.
143 p. illus. S3875

Manning, Harvey
The wild Cascades, forgotten parkland. Photos by Ansel Adams and others. San Francisco, Sierra Club, 1965.
128 p. illus. S3877

Mansfield, Harold
Billion dollar battle: the story behind the "impossible" 727 project. New York, McKay Co., 1965.
184 p. illus. S3878

Mansfield, Harold
Space Needle, U.S.A. Seattle, Craftsman Press, 1962.
72 p. illus. S3879

Mansfield, Harold
Vision: the story of Boeing: a saga of the sky and the new horizons of space. New York, Duell, Sloan and Pearce, 1966.
383 p. S3880

Marple, Elliot and Bruce H. Olson
The National Bank of Commerce of Seattle, 1889-1969: territorial to worldwide banking in eighty years. Including the story of Marine Bancorporation. Palo Alto, Ca., Pacific Books, 1972.
277 p. illus. S3881

Marshall, James Leslie
Eldbridge A. Stuart, founder of Carnation Company. Los Angeles, Carnation Co., 1949.
238 p. illus. S3882

Marshall, John R. and others.
A history of the Vancouver public schools. Dallas, Tex., Taylor, 1975.
296 p. illus. S3883

Marshall, Louise B
High trails: guide to the Pacific Crest Trail in Washington. 4th ed. Lynnwood, Signpost, 1973.
112 p. illus. S3884

Marshall, Louise B
100 hikes in western Washington. Photographs by Bob and Ira Spring. sketch maps by Marge Mueller. Seattle, The Mountaineers, 1966.
111 p. illus. S3885

Marston, Elizabeth
Rain forest: from palms to evergreens. Boston, Branden Press, 1969.
275 p. S3886

Martin, George Warren and Robert W. Scott.
Food in the wilderness: natural foods from the Northwest forests and meadows. 2nd ed. Bremerton, Wash., Dickson Fletcher, 1963.
68 p. illus. S3887

Martin, George Warren
The Olympic peaks as seen from Puget Sound: with historical notes. Bremerton, Wash., The author, 1962.
unpaged. illus. S3888

Maxey, Chester Collins
The world I lived in: a personal story. Philadelphia, Dorrance and Co., 1966.
496 p. illus. S3889

May, Allan
The sea people of Ozette. Everett, B & E Enterprises, 1975.
111 p. illus. S3890

May, Allan
Up and down the North Cascades National Park. Longmire, Mount Rainier Natural History Association, 1973.
96 p. illus. S3891

May, Pete, ed.
100 golden years: a 1972 look at the history of Goldendale, Washington, at the end of its first century, 1872-1972. Goldendale, Goldendale Centennial Corp., 1972.
87 p. illus. S3892

Meany, Edmond Stephen
Origin of Washington geographic names. Detroit, Mich., Gale Research Co., 1968. (Reprint of 1923 ed.)
357 p. S3893

Meinig, Donald W
The great Columbia plain: a historical geography, 1805-1910. Seattle, University of Washington Press, 1968.
632 p. S3894

Melton, William Ray
The Markey story: log of the Markey Machinery Company's first 50 years. Seattle, Markey Machinery Co., 1957.
unpaged. S3895

Mercer, Asa Shinn, 1839-1917
Washington territory: the great Northwest, her material resources and claims to emigration. Fairfield, Wash., Ye Galleon Press, 1971.
38 p. illus. S3896

Metcalfe, James Vernon
The life of Chief Seattle. Seattle, Catholic Northwest Progress, 1970.
15 p. illus. S3897

Milam, Lorenzo W
The Myrkin papers. Bellevue, The Duck Press, 1969.
273 p. S3898

Miller, Thelma Kay
Grass is gold: a biographical history. North Qunicy, Mass., Christopher Publishing House, 1969.
171 p. illus. S3899

Mitchell, Bruce
By river, trail and rail: a brief history of the first century of transportation in north central Washington, 1811 to 1911. Wenatchee, Wash., The Wenatchee Daily World, 1968.
31 p. illus. S3900

Moen, Wayne S. and Marshall T. Hunting.
Handbook for gold prospectors in Washington. Olympia, Washington State Dept. of Natural Resources Division of Geology and Earth Resources, 1975.
90 p. illus. S3901

Mohler, S.R.
The first 75 years. Ellensburg, Central Washington State College, 1967.
374 p. S3902

Molenaar, Dee
The challenge of Mt. Rainier. A record of the explorations and ascents, triumphs and tragedies of the Northwest's greatest mountain. Seattle, The Mountaineers, 1971.
332 p. illus. S3903

Molohon, Bernard W
Sons of Marcus Whitman. Seattle, Sterling Publications, 1957.
150 p. S3904

Moltke, Alfred William
Memoirs of a logger. College Place, Wash., College Press, 1965.
415 p. illus. S3905

Montgomery, James W
Liberated woman: a life of May Arkwright Hutton. Spokane, Ginkgo House Publishers, 1974.
134 p. illus. S3906

Moon, Mary
Washington calling. Photographs by Willie C. Clarke. Vancouver, B.C., Tad Publishing, 1974.
96 p. illus. S3907

Moore, F. Stanley
An historical geography of the settlement around Lake Whatcom prior to 1920. Bellingham, Western Washington State College, Institute for Freshwater Studies, 1973.
78 p. illus. S3908

Morgan, Murray
Skid road: an informal portrait of Seattle. Rev. ed. New York, Viking Press, 1960.
282 p. S3911

Moser, Don
The peninsula: a story of the Olympic country in words and photographs. San Francisco, The Sierra Club, 1962.
170 p. illus. S3912

The Mountaineers.
Mountaineering: the freedom of the hills. Seattle, The Mountaineers, 1960.
430 p. illus. S3913

Mower, Lois
Government in Spokane County. Spokane, League of Women Voters of the Greater Spokane Area, 1969.
78 p. illus. S3914

Mozino, Jose Mariano
Noticias de Nutka: an account of Nootka Sound in 1792. Seattle, University of Washington Press, 1970. (Translated and edited by Iris Higbie Wilson).
142 p. illus. S3915

Munk, Ivan D., comp
Then & now: a photographic history of the Spokane area. Spokane, Richard's Printing Co., 1974.
96 p. illus. S3916

Munson, Kenneth and Gordon Swanborough
Boeing: an aircraft album. New York, Arco Publishing Co., 1972.
144 p. illus. S3917

Munyan, May G.
Du Pont--the story of a company town. Puyallup, The Valley Press, 1972.
240 p. illus. S3918

Murray, Keith A
The story of banking in Whatcom County, with a short history of the Bellingham National Bank. Bellingham? 1954.
49 p. illus. S3920

Nance, Ellwood Cecil, 1900-
The Daniel V. McEachern story: saga of a Seattle Scot. College Place, Wash., College Press, 1958.
246 p. illus. S3921

Neese, Harvey C
The Palouse washout: a 20th century tragedy. Troy, Id., Wildlife Resources, 1973.
23 p. illus. S3922

Neil, Dorothy
My Whidbey Island, as seen and reported in the Whidbey News-Times, 1946 to 1975. Oak Harbor, Whidbey News-Times, 1975.
60 p. illus. S3923

Neils, Selma M
So this is Klickitat. Portland, Metropolitan Press for the Klickitat Woman's Club, 1967.
176 p. illus. S3924

Nelson, Amanda Wimpy
My sister and I. Fairfield, Ye Galleon Press, 1974.
38 p. illus. S3925

Nelson, John Henry
We never got away. Yakima, Wash., Franklin Press, 1965.
204 p. illus. S3926

Nesbit, Robert Carrington
"He built Seattle:" a biography of Judge Thomas Burke. Seattle, University of Washington Press, 1961.
455 p. illus. S3927

Newell, Gordon R
The green years: the development of transportation, trade and finance in the Puget Sound region from 1886 to 1969 as recalled by Joshua Green. Seattle, Superior Publishing Co., 1969.
200 p. illus. S3928

Newell, Gordon R
Ships of the inland sea: the story of the Puget Sound steamboats. Portland, Binfords & Mort, 1951.
241 p. illus.
Also: 2nd ed., 1960. S3930

Newell, Gordon R
So fair a dwelling place: a history of Olympia and Thurston County, Washington. Olympia, Olympia News Publishing Co., 1950.
62 p. illus. S3931

Newell, Gordon R
Totem tales of old Seattle: legends and anecdotes. By Gordon Newell and totemizer Don Sherwood. Seattle, Superior Publishing Co., 1956.
176 p. illus. S3932

Newell, Robert and Laurienne Newell
17 Spokane bike trips. Spokane, C.W. Hill Printers, 1973.
89 p. illus. S3933

Nordstrom, John W
The immigrant in 1887. Seattle, Frank McCaffrey at the Dogwood Press, 1950.
55 p. illus. S3934

Northwood, L.K. and Ernest A.T. Barth
Urban desegregation: negro pioneers and their white neighbors. Seattle, University of Washington Press, 1965.
131 p. map. S3935

O'Connor, Bill and Irene O'Connor
A glance at the mushrooms of the Olympic Rain Forest for the occasional visitor. Amanda Park, O'Connor Enterprises, 1973.
29 p. illus. S3936

O'Connor, Harvey
Revolution in Seattle: a memoir. New York, Monthly Review Press, 1964.
300 p. S3937

O'Connor, Irene
An introduction to the Quinault Valley Rain Forest. Text and illustration by Irene O'Connor. Hoquiam? Wash., c1962.
unpaged. illus. S3938

Odegaard, Charles Edwin
The University of Washington: pioneering in its first and second century. New York, Newcomen Society in North America, 1964, c1963.
24 p. illus. S3939

Ogden, Daniel M. and Hugh A. Bone.
Washington politics. N.Y., New York University Press, 1960.
77 p. charts. S3940

Old days in Camas Valley: including the "Pioneer history of Camas Valley", first published by the students of Camas Valley High School in 1923: the reminiscences of Bill Murray, pioneer of Camas Valley ... North Hollywood, Ca., Camas Press, 1951.
60 p. illus. S3941

Olin, Laurie
Breath on the mirror: Seattle's Skid Road community. Seattle, 1972.
55 p. illus. S3942

Olsen, Virginia E., ed.
The Willapa country history report. A recital of the historical background of the Raymond and Willapa Valley areas as it was compiled by the members of the History Committee of the Community Betterment Study Committee. Raymond, Wash., Raymond Herald & Advertiser, 1965.
176 p. illus. S3943

Olsen, Winnifred L
Tacoma beginning: the first 100 years. Tacoma, Tacoma School District, 1969.
160 p. illus. S3944

Olympic Mountain Rescue (Society)
Climber's guide to the Olympic Mountains. Seattle, The Mountaineers, 1972.
222 p. illus. maps. S3945

Overland, Larry
Early settlement of Lake Cushman. Belfair, Mason County Historical Society, 1974.
46 p. illus. S3946

Pabst, Marie
The flora of the Chuckanut formation of northwestern Washington. Berkeley, Ca., University of California Press, 1965. S3947

Patterson, Samuel
Narrative of the adventures and sufferings of Samuel Patterson ... Fairfield, Ye Galleon Press, 1967. (Facsimile reprint of 1817 ed.) S3948

Patterson, Vernon Dysart
Washington boasts: here's a wealth of wit and wisdon, fact and fancy. regarding the great state named for our first president. Tacoma, Patterson and Howe, 1950, c1951.
61 p. illus. S3949

Paul, Charlotte
Minding our own business. New York, Random House, 1955.
300 p. illus. S3950

Peltier, Jerome, comp.
Warbonnets and epaulets: with pre- and post factors documented of the Steptoe-Wright Indian campaigns of 1858 in Washington Territory. Montreal, Canada, Payette Radio Ltd., 1971.
385 p. illus. S3951

Penhalurick, Darline
Beach guide: serving Washington's Olympic North Beach. Ocean Shores North Beach Printing Co., 1975.
34 p. illus. S3952

Peninsula Arts Association
An informal guide to Long Beach Peninsula and nearby area. Nahcotta, The author, 1973.
36 p. illus. S3953

Peterson, Lorin Westcott
Living in Seattle. By Lorin Peterson and Noah C. Davenport. Seattle, Seattle Public Schools, 1950.
273 p. illus. S3954

Pettitt, George Albert
The Quileute of La Push, 1775-1945. Berkeley, University of California Press, 1950.
120 p. illus. S3955

Phillippay, Minola C
As I remember. Steamboat Springs, Colo., Steamboat Pilot, 1971.
61 p. illus. S3956

Phillippay, Minola C
Kahlotus is home. Steamboat Springs, Colo., Steamboat Pilot, 1973.
82 p. illus. S3957

Phillips, James W
Washington state place names. Seattle, University of Washington Press, 1971.
167 p. maps. S3958

Pierce, Danny
Little no name. Kent, Wash., The author, 1959.
1 vol. S3959

Pierre, George
Autumn's bounty. San Antonio, Tex., The Naylor Co., 1972.
155 p. S3960

Poelker, Richard J. and Harry D. Hartwell
Black bear of Washington: its biology, natural history and relationship to forest regeneration. Olympia, Washington State Game Dept., 1973.
180 p. illus. S3961

Pollard, Lancaster
A history of the state of Washington. Portland, Binfords & Mort, 1951.
228 p. illus. S3962

Potts, Merlin K.
Mammals of Mount Rainier National Park. Longmire, Mount Rainier Natural History Association, 1949.
87 p. illus. S3964

Potts, Ralph Bushnell
Come now the lawyers. Menasha, Wisc., George Banta Co., 1972.
187 p. S3965

Potts, Ralph Bushnell
Seattle heritage. Seattle, Superior Publishing Co., 1955.
192 p. illus. S3966

Powe, L.A.
Water pollution control in Washington. Seattle, University of Washington, Center for Urban and Regional Studies, 1968.
1 vol. S3967

Prater, Gene
Snow trails: ski and snowshoe routes in the Cascades. Seattle, The Mountaineers, 1975.
127 p. illus. S3968

Preston, Howard Hall
Trust banking in Washington. Seattle, University of Washington Press, 1958.
145 p. illus. S3969

Price, Lester K
McNiel (History of a federal prison). McNeil Island, 1970.
96 p. illus. S3970

Prochnau, William W. and R.W. Larsen
A certain democrat: Senator Henry M. Jackson. Englewood Cliffs, N.J., Prentice-Hall, 1972.
360 p. illus. S3971

Pruter, A.T. and .L. Alverson, eds.
The Columbia River estuary and adjacent ocean waters: bioenvironmental studies. Seattle, University of Washington Press, 1972.
868 p. illus. S3972

Puget Sound League of Women Voters.
Nisqually in conflict. Seattle, League of Women Voters, 1970.
29 p. illus. S3973

Puget Sound Pulp and Timber Company, Bellingham.
Making Puget pulp: history of wood pulp making, pictorial tour of the Puget Sound plant. Bellingham, 1949.
26 p. illus. S3974

Pugnetti, Frances Taylor
Tiger by the tail: twenty-five years with the stormy Tri-City Herald. Pasco, Tri-City Herald, 1975.
352 p. illus. S3975

Ramsey, Guy Reed
Grant County postmarks, Washington. Ephrata, Wash., Grant County Historical Society, 1964.
40 p. illus. S3976

Ramsey, Guy Reed
Postmarked Washington: Chelan, Douglas and Kittitas counties. Wenatchee, Wenatchee World, 1973.
112 p. illus. S3977

Ramsey, Guy Reed
Postmarked Washington: Klickitat, Benton and Franklin counties. Goldendale, Klickitat County Historical Society, 1967.
80 p. illus. S3978

Ramsey, Guy Reed
Postmarked Washington: Okanogan County. Omak, Okanogan Historical Society, 1966.
60 p. illus. S3979

Rasmussen, Margaret L
Ocean shores, Washington: the exciting growth years. Ocean Shores, 1974.
104 p. illus. S3980

Rayburn, Barbara, ed.
Let's go! Daytripping in and around the Palouse. Pullman, American Association of University Women, Pullman Branch, 1974.
87 p. illus. S3981

Reese, Gary Fuller
Did it really happen in Tacoma: a collection of vignettes of local history. Tacoma, Tacoma Public Library, 1975.
74 l. S3982

Reese, Gary Fuller
Origin of geographic names of Tacoma/Pierce County, Washington. Tacoma, Tacoma Public Library, 1974.
99 p. S3983

Reid, John H.
Adopted by the United States (as told to Ray V. Cloud). Seattle, The author, 1960.
166 p. S3984

Relander, Click and George M. Martin
Yakima, Washington jubilee, 1885-1960. Yakima, Wash., Franklin Press, 1960.
52 p. illus. S3989

Reppeto, Paul
Way of the logger. Chehalis, Logger's World Inc. 1970.
40 p. illus. S3990

Richardson, David Blair, 1926-
And for eternity: a souvenir history of the Orcas Island Community Church, Eastsound, Washington, 1887-1972. Eastsound, The author, 1972.
50 l. illus. S3992

Richardson, David Blair
Magic islands: a treasure-trove of San Juan Islands lore. Orcas, Wash., Friday Harbor Journal, 1964.
95 p. illus. S3993

Richardson, David Blair
Pig War Islands: Eastsound, Orcas Publishing Co., 1971.
362 p. illus. S3994

Richert, Emma B
Long, long ago in Skokomish Valley of Mason County, Washington. Shelton, Wash., Shelton-Mason County Journal, 1965.
84 p. ports. S3995

Riley, Carroll L. and others.
Investigation and analysis of the Puget Sound Indians: influences of white contact on the Indians of northern Puget Sound, by June M. Collins; the Quileute Indians of Puget Sound presented before Indian Claims Commission, the Medicine Creek tribes, by Herbert C. Taylor, Jr.; the Snohomish Indian people, by Colin E. Tweddell. New York, Garland, 1974.
694 p. S3996

Robbins, Tom
Guy Anderson (artist) Photographs by Bob Peterson. Seattle, Gear Works Press, 1965.
40 p. illus. S3998

Roberts, Colette
Mark Tobey. N.Y., Grove Press, Inc., 1960.
63 p. illus. S3999

Rosenow, Beverly Paulik, ed.
The journal of the Washington State Constitutional Convention, 1889, with an analytical index by Quentin Shipley Smith. Book Publishing Company, 1962.
931 p. S4000

Roslyn Community Study.
Spawn of coal dust; history of Roslyn, 1886-1955. Roslyn, Roslyn Museum, 1971.
350 p. illus. S4001

Ross, Fred K
50 years of newspapering. Edmonds, The author, 1975.
98 p. illus. S4002

Ruby, Robert H. and John A. Brown
The Spokane Indians: children of the sun. Norman, University of Oklahoma Press, 1970.
346 p. illus. S4006

Rundell, Hugh A
Washington names: a pronunciation guide of Washington place names. 2nd ed. Pullman, Wash., Washington Radio Station KWSC and Extension Services, Washington State University, 1959.
106 p. S4007

Russell, Elizabeth C., and others.
Harrah's yesterdays: historical portrait of a Yakima Valley town. Spokane, I.D. Ltd., 1971.
24 p. illus. S4008

Sainsbury, George and Nanci Hertzog
The dam book: recreation on Washington reservoirs: campsites, boat ramps, picnic spots, museums and points of interest. Mercer Island, Klatawa Enterprises, 1970.
222 p. illus. S4009

St. John, Harold
Flora of southeastern Washington and adjacent Idaho. 3rd ed. Escondido, Ca., Outdoor Pictures, 1963.
583 p. illus. S4010

Salo, Leo J
A baseline survey of significant marine birds in Washington state. Olympia, Washington State Dept. of Game, 1975.
417 p. maps. S4011

Sampson, Martin Jacob
Indians of Skagit County. Mount Vernon, Skagit County Historical Society, 1972.
72 p. illus. S4012

San Juan Islands almanac. Friday Harbor, Long House Printcrafters, 1974.
120 p. illus. S4013

Satterfield, Archie and Merle E. Dowd.
The Seattle guidebook. Mercer Island, Writing Works, 1975.
198 p. illus. S4014

Satterlee, Brandon
The dub of South Burlap: the story of a newspaper that made a holler in the wilderness. New York, Exposition Press, 1952.
240 p. illus. S4015

Scates, Shelby.
Firstbank: the story of Seattle-First National Bank. Seattle, Seattle First National Bank, 1970.
130 p. illus. S4016

Scaylea, Josef
Moods of the mountain. Seattle, Superior Publishing Co., 1967.
48 p. illus. S4017

Scheuerman, Richard D
Pilgrims on the earth: a German Russian Chronical (sic). Fairfield, Ye Galleon Press, 1974.
89 p. illus. S4019

Schmitz, Henry
The long road travelled: an account of forestry of the University of Wahsington. Seattle, University of Washington Arboretum Foundation, 1973.
268 p. illus. S4020

Schmoe, Floyd Wilfred
For love of some islands: memoirs of some years spent in the San Juan Islands of Puget Sound. New York, Harper and Row, 1964.
226 p. illus. S4021

Schmore, Floyd Wilfred
A year in paradise. New York, Harper and Row, 1959.
235 p. illus. S4022

Schnackenberg, Walter C
The lamp and the cross. Sagas of Pacific Lutheran College from 1890 to 1965. Tacoma, Pacific Lutheran University Press, 1965.
182 p. illus. S4023

Schoenberg, Jacob A
Castles to cabins. Spokane, Gonzaga University Press, 1966.
S4024

Schoenberg, Wilfred P
Gonzaga University: seventy-five years, 1887-1962. Spokane, Gonzaga University, 1963.
612 p. illus. S4025

Scholz, Albert J
My cup runneth over: memoirs of A.J. Scholz. Spokane, Jack Deno and Associates, 1973.
96 p. illus. S4026

Scofield, Winifred M
Washington's historical markers. Portland, Touchstone Press, 1967.
79 p. illus. S4027

Scoggin, Martha L
Pioneer days on Scoggin Ridge and Pataha Prairie. Spokane, A.I.S. Trade Service, 1973.
138 p. illus. S4028

Scott, Lillian
Lilly, early years on Puget Sound: autobiography. Seattle, Trick & Murray, 1975.
36 p. illus. S4029

Seabury, Lloyd
A pioneer family: reminiscences of the past. The author, 1975.
91 p. illus. S4030

Seattle Art Museum
J.F. Koenig. Seattle, 1970.
147 p. illus. S4031

Seattle Art Museum
Skagit Valley artists: Seattle Art Museum Pavilion, Seattle Center, March 1 - April 14, 1974. Seattle, 1974.
50 p. illus. ports. S4032

Seattle Art Museum
Tobey's 80: a retrospective. Seattle, University of Washington Press, 1970. (80 reproductions of Mark Tobey).
unpaged. S4033

Seattle Historical Society.
Seattle century. Seattle, Superior Publishing Co., 1952.
104 p. illus. S4034

Sharpe, Grant William
101 wildflowers of Mt. Rainier National Park. Seattle, University of Washington Press, 1957.
40 p. S4035

Sheller, Roscoe
Bandit to lawman. Yakima, Wash., Franklin Press, 1966. (Biography of Matt Warner.)
176 p. illus. S4036

Sheller, Roscoe
Courage and water, a story of Yakima Valley's Sunnyside: a factual story of the founding, development and growth ... Edited by Joseph P. Lassoie. Portland, Binfords & Mort, 1952.
263 p. illus. S4038

Sheller, Roscoe
The fabulous Roza: a proud history of the Roza Irrigation District ... Sunnyside, Wash., 1962?
31 p. illus. S4039

Sheller, Roscoe
Me and the model T. Yakima, Wash., Franklin Press, 1965.
217 p. illus. S4040

Sheller, Roscoe
The name was Olney. Yakima, Wash., Franklin Press, 1965.
171 p. illus. S4041

Sheller, Roscoe
Sunnyside at sixty. Sunnyside, Wash., The author, 1962.
30 p. S4042

Sherwood, Kenneth K
Fiftieth General Hospital in World War II. Seattle, The author, 1970.
41 p. ports. S4044

Simpson, Jerry
Victorian Port Townsend. Port Townsend, Wash., The author, 1961.
unpaged. illus. S4046

Slauson, Morda C
One hundred years on the Cedar. Renton, Wash., 1967.
30 p. S4047

Smeltzer, Jean Allyn, comp.
Index to names of persons and subjects in Early Klickitat Valley days by Robert Ballou. Portland, The author, 1972.
16 p. illus. S4048

Smith, Fred
Rufus Woods of Wenatchee. Whitestone, N.Y., Graphics Group, 1948.
30 p. illus. S4049

Smith, Goldwin
The treaty of Wasinngton (1871): a study in imperial history. N.Y., Russell & Russell, 1971. (Reprint of 1941 ed.)
134 p. S4050

Smith, Stanley Hugh
Freedom to work. New York, Vantage Press, 1955.
217 p. illus. S4051

Snohomish, Washington, Historical Society.
River reflections, 1859 to 1910: a popular narrative history of Snohomish City. Snohomish, 1975.
144 p. illus. S4052

Speidel, William C
Seattle underground. a pictorial study with historical footnotes and interesting anecdotes about the forgotten city beneath modern Seattle. Seattle, Seattle Guide Inc., 1967.
16 p. illus. S4053

Speidel, William C
Sons of the profits, or there's no business like grow business: the Seattle story, 1851-1901. Seattle, Nettle Creek Publishing Co., 1967.
345 p. illus. S4054

Speidel, William C
The wet side of the mountains: or, prowling western Washington. Seattle, Nettle Creek Publishing Co., 1974.
450 p. illus. S4055

Sprague, Roderick, 1933-
An archaeological survey of the proposed Blue Creek dam reservoir, Walla Walla County, Washington. By Roderick Sprague and John D. Combes. Pullman, Washington State University, 1965.
26 p. illus. S4056

Sprague, Roderick
Archaeloloy in the Sun Lake area of central Washington. Pullman, Washington State University, 1962, c1960.
iv, 48 p. illus. S4057

Sprague, Roderick
Excavations in the Little Goose and lower Granit Dam reservoirs, 1965, by Roderick Sprague and John D. Combes. Pullman, Washington State University, 1966.
49 p. illus. S4058

Sprague, Roderick
Excavations in the Little Goose dam reservoir, 1966. By Roderick Sprague, Frank Leonhardy and Gerald Schroedl. Pullman, Washington State University, 1968.
40 (4) p. illus. tables. S4059

Spring, Bob and others.
Cool, clear water: the key to our environment. Seattle, Superior Publishing Co., 1970.
174 p. illus. S4060

Spring, Bob and Ira Spring
The Mount Rainier National Park. Text by Harvey Manning. Seattle, Superior Publishing Co., 1974.
1 vol. illus. S4061

Spring, Bob and Ira Spring
The Olympic National Park. Text by Harvey Manning, Seattle, Superior Publishing Co., 1974
1 vol. illus. S4062

Spring, Ira
50 hikes in Mount Rainier National Park. Seattle, Mount Rainier Natural History Association and The Mountaineers, 1969.
120 p. illus. S4064

Spring, Ira and Harvey Manning.
101 hikes in the north Cascades. Seattle, The Mountaineers, 1970.
231 p. illus. S4065

Spring, Ira and Harvey Manning.
102 hikes in the Alpine Lakes, south Cascades, and Olympics. Seattle, The Mountaineers, 1971.
240 p. illus. S4066

Spring, Norma J
Mount Rainier, a Washington camera adventure by Bob and Ira Spring. Text by Norma and Patricia Spring. Seattle, Superior Publishing, 1955.
unpaged. photos. S4067

Stagner, Howard Ralph
Behind the scenery of Mount Rainier National Park. Longmire, Wash., Mount Rainier National Park Natural History Association, 1947.
64 p. illus. S4068

Stave, Thomas
Spokane sketchbook. Drawings and architectural observations by Roland Colliander and others. Seattle, University of Washington Press, 1974.
96 p. illus. S4069

Steele, E.N.
The immigrant oyster (ostrea gigae): now known as the Pacific oyster. Olympia, Warren's Quick Print, 1964.
179 p. illus. S4070

Steele, E.N.
The rise and decline of the Olympic oyster. Elma, Wash., Fulco Publications, c1957.
126 p. S4071

Steen, Herman
The O.W. Fisher heritage. Seattle, Frank McCaffrey publishers, 1961.
224 p. illus. S4072

Steinbrueck, Victor
Market sketchbook. Seattle, University of Washington, 1968.
128 p. S4073

Steinbrueck, Victor
Seattle architecture, 1850-1953. New York, Reinhold, 1953.
56 p. illus. S4074

Steinbrueck, Victor
Seattle cityscape, sketches, commentary. Seattle, University of Washington Press, 1962.
192 p. illus. S4075

Steinbrueck, Victor
Seattle cityscape #2. Seattle, University of Washington Press, 1973.
111 p. illus. S4076

Sterling, E.M.
The south Cascades, the Gifford Pinchot National Forest. Photos by Bob and Ira Spring. Seattle, The Mountaineers, 1975.
96 p. illus. S4077

Sterling, E.M.
Trips and trails: camps, short hikes and viewpoints in the north Cascades and Olympics. Seattle, The Mountaineers, 1967.
211 p. illus. S4078

Stevenson, Jim
Seattle firehouses of the horse drawn and early motor era. Seattle, The author, 1972.
99 p. illus. S4079

Steward, Chuck. Bicycling around Seattle. Rev. ed. Seattle, Recreation Consultants, 1975.
40 p. maps. S4080

Stewart, Edgar Irving
Washington, northwest frontier. New York, Lewis Historical Publishing Co., 1957.
4 vols. S4081

Stolpe, John
A look at the Lummis: articles on the Lummi Indians of Whatcom County. Bellingham, Goliards Press, 1972.
27 p. illus. S4082

Styner, Stan
A water tour of Seattle. Mercer Island, Child Tourist Publications Inc., 1961.
31 p. illus. S4083

Sucher, David, ed.
The Asahel Curtis sampler: photographs of Puget Sound past. Seattle, Puget Sound Access, 1973.
71 p. illus. S4084

Sucher, David
Puget Sound Access: a part-of-the-Earth catalog. Seattle, Puget Sound Access, 1971.
61 p. illus. S4085

Sundberg, Trudy James
Portrait of an island. Oak Harbor, Wash., Whidby Press, 1961.
44 p. illus. S4086

Sundborg, George
Hail Columbia: the thirty year struggle for Grand Coulee Dam. New York, Macmillan, 1954.
467 p. S4087

Sunset Travel Guide to Washington. 3rd ed. Menlo Park, Ca., Lane Books, 1973. (First ed. published in 1956 with title: Discovery trips in Washington.)
160 p. illus. maps. S4088

Suttles, Wayne
The economic life of the coast Salish of Haro and Rosario Straits. New York, Garland, 1974.
570 p. illus. S4089

Swan, James G
Almost out of this world: glimpses of life in Washington Territory. Tacoma, Washington State Historical Society, 1971.
126 p. illus. S4090

Swett, Ira L., ed.
The Puget Sound electric railway. Los Angeles, Interurbans Electric Railway Publications, 1960.
163 p. illus. S4092

Swift, Joan
Brackett's Landing: a history of early Edmonds. Edmonds, Wash., The author, 1975.
50 p. illus. S4093

Symons, Thomas William
The Symons report on the upper Columbia River and the great plain of of the Columbia. Fairfield, Wash., Ye Galleon Press, 1967. (Reprint of 1882 ed.)
133 p. illus. S4094

Tabor, Rowland W
Guide to the geology of Olympic National Park. Seattle, University of Washington Press, 1975.
144 p. illus. S4095

Taylor, Eva Cook
The lure of Tubal-Cain. Port Townsend, Wash., Jefferson County Historical Society, 1972.
54 p. illus. S4096

Teagle, Ernest C
Out of the woods: the story of McCleary. Montesano, Wash., Vidette Press, 1956.
47 p. S4097

Thomas, Christy
Bylines and bygones. New York, Exposition Press, 1964.
269 p. S4098

Thomas, Robert B
Chuckanut chronicles. 2nd ed. Bellingham, Chuckanut Fire District Auxiliary, 1971.
64 p. illus. S4100

Thompson, Margaret (Hollinshead)
Benton County, Washington. 2nd ed. Prosser, Wash., 1958.
20 p. map. S4102

Thompson, Raymond
Big bend country heritage. Lynnwood, Raymond Thompson Co., 1974.
2 vols. illus. S4103

Thompson, Wilbur and Allen Beach.
Steamer to Tacoma. Bainbridge Island, Wash., Driftwood Press, 1963.
76 p. illus. S4104

Thurston, Claude
Sixty years of progress. The anniversary history of Walla Walla College. College Place, Wash., Walla Walla College Press, 1952.
400 p. illus. S4105

Tobey, Mark
Mark Tobey: the world of a market. Seattle, University of Washington Press, 1964.
80 p. illus. S4106

Travis, Helga Anderson
Blalock, island of dreams. Prosser, Prosser Record-Bulletin, 1975.
30 p. illus. S4108

Travis, Helga Anderson
Mool Mool, the story of Fort Simcoe. Kennewick, Wash., Meverden Press, 1953.
29 p. illus. S4109

Travis, Helga Anderson
The Umatilla Trail: pioneer days in Washington Territory. New York, Exposition Press, 1951.
243 p. illus. S4110

Treacy, William and Raphael Levine.
Wild brand on the olive tree. In collaboration with Patricia Jacobsen. Portland, Binfords & Mort, 1974.
137 p. illus. S4111

Trunk, Carl H
History of the city of Spokane. Illustrations by Pete Long. Spokane, Wash., 1969, c1968.
114 p. illus. S4112

Underhill, Ruth Murray
Beaverbird: a story of Indians on the coast of Washington before the coming of the whites. New York, Coward-McCann, 1959.
224 p. S4113

Vagners, Juris
Oil on Puget Sound: an interdisciplinary study in systems engineering. Seattle, University of Washington Press, 1972.
629 p. illus. S4114

Van Cleve, Fred H
Friday Harbor then and now. Friday, Harbor, Long House Printcrafters, 1972.
89 p. illus. S4115

Vaughn, Wade
Puget Sound invasion. Seattle, The author, 1975.
84 p. illus. S4116

Wagner, Henry Raup
Spanish explorations in the Straits of Juan de Fuca. New York, A.S. Press, 1971. (Reprint of 1933 ed.)
323 p. maps. S4117

Wahl, Terence R. and Dennis R. Paulson
A guide to bird finding in Washington. Bellingham, Whatcom Museum of History and Art, 1972.
95 p. illus. S4118

Walkinshaw, Robert
On Puget Sound. Drawings by Jeanie Walter Walkinshaw. New York, Putnam, 1951.
294 p. illus. S4119

Wallace, Robert F.
An evaluation of wildlife resources in the state of Washington. Pullman, State College of Washington, Bureau of Economic and Business Research, 1956.
63 p. illus. S4120

Warren, James Ronald
Pictorial history of Seattle, from frontier town to modern metropolis. Bellevue, Wash., The author, 1962.
36 p. illus. S4121

Washington state constitution: stumbling block or stepping stone? Proceedings of the thirty-first annual Summer Institute of Government, 1966. Seattle, Distributed by University of Washington Press, 1966.
79 p. S4122

Washington State Association of County Commissioners.
The book of the counties, 1953. Pullman, 1953?
155 p. illus. S4123

Washington State Historical Society
Early Washington communities in art. With introduction and notes by Bruce Le Roy. Tacoma, 1965.
1 vol. unpaged. illus. S4124

Washington State Historical Society
Exploration Northwest. Tacoma, 1969.
17 p. illus. S4125

Washington State Historical Society.
Historic ports of Puget Sound. Introduction and notes by Bruce Le Roy. Tacoma, Wash., 1967.
32 p. illus. S4126

Washington State Historical Society.
Northwest history in art, 1778-1963. Tacoma, The Society, 1963.
(38) p. illus. S4127

Washington (State) State Library, Olympia.
The negro in the state of Washington, 1788-1967: a bibliography of published works and of unpublished source materials on the life and achievements of the negro in the evergreen state. Olympia, 1968.
ii, 14 p. S4128

Washington (State) University. Board of Regents.
Communism and academic freedom. The record of the tenure cases at the University of Washington including the findings of the Committee on Tenure and Academic Freedom and the president's recommendations. Seattle, University of Washington Press, 1949.
125 p. S4129

Washington (State) University. Institute of Labor Economics.
Job opportunities for racial minorities in the Seattle area. Seattle, University of Washington Press, 1948.
30 p. tabs. S4130

Washington Water Power Company, Spokane.
The PUDs of Washington state: promises compared with performance. Prepared for the employees of the Washington Water Power Co. Spokane, 1952.
167 p. S4131

The Washington Water Power Company
The Washington Water Power Company, 1889-1964. 75 years of service to Spokane and the inland empire. Spokane, Spokesman-Review, 1964.
(13) p. illus. S4132

The way it was: Anaku Iwacha: Yakima legends. Yakima, Franklin Press, 1974.
225 p. illus. S4133

Weldon, Robert K
A guide to the trails of Mount Rainier National Park. By Robert K. Weldon and Merlin K. Potts. Rev. ed. Longmire, Wash., Mount Rainier Natural History Association, 1960, c1950.
48 p. illus. S4134

Welsh, William D
A brief historical sketch of Port Townsend, Washington. Rev. ed. Port Townsend, Press of the Port Townsend Leader, 1956.
24 p. illus. S4135

Weyerhaeuser Company.
Weyerhaeuser Compamy history. Tacoma, 1974.
51 p. illus. S4136

Whatcom Museum of History and Art.
Arts of a vanished era, an exhibition (catalog), text by Susan H.L. Barrow and G.F. Grabert. Bellingham, Wash., 1968. S4137

Whatcom Museum of History and Art.
A report: master carvers of the Lummi and their apprentices. Bellingham, Whatcom Museum of History and Art, 1971.
31 p. illus. S4139

Whipple, Carolyn R
Victory at eighty. New York, Carlton Press, 1975.
126 p. S4140

Whitebrook, Robert Ballard.
Coastal exploration of Washington. Palo Alto, Ca., Pacific Books, 1959.
146 p. S4141

Whiting, Joseph Samuel
Forts of the state of Washington. a record of military and semimilitary establishments designated as forts. From May 29,1792 to November 15, 1951. 2nd ed. Seattle, 1951.
139 p. illus. S4142

Whitmore, Ada Ruth and Chloe E. Walling, eds.
Glancing back through the years. Alder Creek Pioneer Association, 1969.
64 p. illus. S4143

Widel, Glen and Elizabeth Widel
Okanogan County ... a profile. Wenatchee, Wenatchee Bindery and Printing Co., 1973.
124 p. photos. S4144

Willis, Margaret, ed.
Chechacos all: the pioneering of Skagit. Mount Vernon, Skagit County Historical Society, 1973.
212 p. illus. S4145

Willis, Margaret, ed.
Skagit settlers: trials and triumphs, 1890-1920. Mount Vernon, Skagit County Historical Society, 1975.
228 p. illus. S4146

Wills, Robert H
High trails: a guide to the Cascade Crest trail. Seattle, University of Washington Press, 1962.
157 p. illus. S4147

Wolcott, Ernest E
Lakes of Washington. Vol 1: western Washington. Vol. 2: eastern Washington. 3rd ed. Olympia, Washington State Dept. of Ecology, 1973.
2 vols. S4148

Wollam, Dan, comp.
The Anacortes story. Anacortes, Wash., The Anacortes American, 1965.
38 p. illus. S4149

Wood, Charles R. and Dorothy M. Wood
Milwaukee road west. Seattle, Superior Publishing Co., 1972.
192 p. illus. S4151

Wood, Robert L
Across the Olympic mountains: the Press expedition, 1889-1890. Seattle, University of Washington Press, 1967.
220 p. illus. S4153

Wood, Robert L
Trail country: Olympic National Park. Seattle, The Mountaineers, 1968? S4154

Wood, Robert L
Wilderness trails of Olympic National Park. Seattle, The Mountaineers, 1970.
219 p. illus. S4155

Woods, Erin and Bill Woods
Bicycling the backroads around Puget Sound. Seattle, The Mountaineers, 1972.
200 p. illus. S4156

Worthylake, Mary M
Nika Illahee (my homeland). Chicago, Melmont Publishers, 1962.
32 p. illus. S4157

Wright, Donald DeLano
To die is not enough: a true account of murder and retribution. Boston, Houghton Mifflin, 1974.
238 p. illus. S4158

Writers' Program. Washington (State).
The new Washington, a guide to the evergreen state, compiled by workers of the Writers' Program of the Work Projects Administration. Rev. ed. with added material by Howard McKinley Corning. Portland, Binfords & Mort, 1950, c1941.
687 p. illus. S4159

Wynecoop, David C
Children of the sun: a history of the Spokane Indians. Wellpinit, 1969.
80 p. illus. S4160

Yanan, Eileen
Coyote and the Colville. Omak, St. Mary's Mission, 1971.
76 p. illus. S4161

Yates, Keith L
The life of Willie Willey: nature boy, traveler, ambassador of good will. New York, Exposition Press, 1966.
76 p. ports. S4162

Yocum, Charles Frederick
Waterfowl and their food plants in Washington. Seattle, University of Washington Press, 1951.
272 p. illus. S4163

Yoshida, Jim
The two worlds of Jim Yoshida. New York, Morrow, 1972.
256 p. S4164

INDEX

To Charles W. Smith's

Pacific Northwest Americana, Third Edition 1950
(Basic Volume)

and

The Supplement 1949-1974

By

Michael K. Moore

Index to Basic Volume and the Supplement

(Note: "S" preceding the numerical listing indicates that the reference is to the Supplement, not the Basic Volume. For example, S692 appears on page 50 of the Supplement, and 10184 appears on page 342 of the Basic Volume.)

- E -

- F -

- H -

-K-

-M-

-N-

-S-

-W-

-Y-

-Z-